Themis
Bar Review

Multistate Essay Exam
Outlines

Agency
Conflict of Laws
Corporations
Family Law
Partnerships
Secured Transactions
Trusts
Wills and Decedents' Estates

Final Review Outlines

All other trademarks are the property of their respective companies.

The material herein is intended to be used in conjunction with the myThemis Portal™ in order to provide basic review of legal subjects and is in no way meant to be a source of or replacement for professional legal advice.

ISBN 978-1-946020-98-7

Themis
BarReview

AGENCY

I. THE AGENCY RELATIONSHIP

A. INTRODUCTION

The law of agency addresses the legal consequences of one person (the **agent**) acting on behalf of, and subject to the control of, another person (the **principal**).

Agency relationships are anchored in contract and tort law. Under contract law, agents perform acts of negotiating and making contracts with third persons. A contract made by an agent on behalf of a principal with a third person establishes certain rights and duties, depending on the agent's level of authority and how the contract is executed. On the other hand, tort law focuses on the vicarious liability that attaches to a principal for torts or crimes committed by an agent.

1. Background

Agency relationships are consensual, requiring assent by both parties. For this reason, whenever two parties with the necessary legal capacity mutually consent to a relationship in which one will act on behalf of the other and subject to the other's control, they have formed an agency relationship.

The most recognized principals are employers who control the actions of their employees (agents). A corporation or other business organization can be a principal, and the officers and other employees of the corporation are agents (just as partners are agents of a partnership).

Although agency relationships are generally based on consent, agency may be imposed by operation of law (e.g., estoppel or a state motorist statute).

2. Creation of an Agency Relationship

The most common method of creating an agency relationship is **by appointment** (oral or written). Generally, a principal's appointment of an agent need not comply with specific formalities (for example, a writing) to be effective. However, many states require an agent's appointment to be in writing when the agency relates to interests in property (e.g., a power of attorney).

The principal will generally be bound by any contract created on the principal's behalf, by an agent with the power to bind the principal, whether the power to bind is:

i) Expressed orally or in a writing;

ii) Implied by a principal's conduct; or

iii) Misinterpreted by a third party.

EXAM NOTE: Partnership and corporations questions often require application of agency law. Be prepared to (i) identify the existence of agency relationships, (ii) discuss whether the principal is subject to liability for the agent's actions, (iii) articulate an agent's fiduciary duty to the principal and whether the agent has breached that duty, and (iv) determine if or when an agency relationship has terminated.

3. Determining the Existence of an Agency Relationship

An agency relationship is created when:

i) A **principal manifests assent** to an agent;

ii) The agent acts on the **principal's behalf**;

iii) The agent's actions are subject to the **principal's control**; and

iv) The **agent manifests assent** or otherwise consents.

> **EXAM NOTE:** Points are obtained for agency questions by listing the elements that create an agency relationship and demonstrating how they are or are not present.

B. THE PRINCIPAL

1. Background

Any individual or entity (e.g., a government, an organization, an association) that has the legal capacity to possess rights and incur obligations can be a principal.

Principals may delegate tasks, give instructions, direct employee tasks, and monitor employee activities.

2. The Principal's Control

An agent agrees to be subject to the principal's control, and a principal agrees to be bound by the acts of its agent within the scope of the agent's authority. The fact that a principal lacks the right to control the full range of an agent's actions (professional judgment), or fails to exercise the right to control the agent, does not eliminate the principal's rights or affect the existence of an agency relationship.

It is sufficient that the principal has the right to control the result or the ultimate objectives of the agent's work.

> **EXAM NOTE:** Do you need to identify a principal quickly? Look for (i) the types of principals listed below when reading fact patterns and (ii) examples of any person, individual, or entity that exerts control over another party. The key word is "**control**."

3. Types of Principals

Agency questions may arise in connection with several types of principals.

> **EXAM NOTE:** The current Restatement (Third) of Agency reflects a change in terminology from master-servant relationship to employer-employee relationship.

a. Individual

Any individual who has contractual capacity and is not a minor has the legal capacity to enter into an agency relationship as a principal and to appoint an agent. Status as a principal is established by the individual's intent to delegate an act and control the way in which the act is performed by another.

b. Master or employer

A master (often referred to as an employer) is a principal who employs an agent to perform services and who controls—or has a right to control—the physical conduct of the employee's performance. Restatement (Second) of Agency § 2(1) (1958). An agent who is subject to this level of control is referred to as a servant or employee.

The more control a principal exerts over an agent's actions, the more likely it is that a master-servant (or employer-employee) relationship exists.

Courts usually determine a principal's status as a master/employer based upon the control that the principal asserts over the servant/employee.

Several factors contribute to this analysis, such as whether:

i) The principal exercises significant control over the details of the worker's day-to-day activities;

ii) The principal supplies the tools at the place of employment;

iii) The principal pays the worker on a structured pay period;

iv) The worker's skill level is specialized; and

v) The principal directs the work to completion.

c. Entrepreneur

Any business owner who has the legal capacity to contract with a person to represent him and conduct business on his behalf can be a principal.

> **EXAM NOTE:** Look for business owners (e.g., sole proprietors without partners) to be frequently highlighted as principals in agency and partnership fact patterns.

d. Corporation

A corporation is a legal entity created for the purpose of conducting business. A corporation must have legal existence to be considered a principal in an agency relationship. Corporations that are yet to be formed (i.e., future incorporation pending) cannot be principals.

Corporate officers, employees of the corporation, and other persons can serve as agents of the corporation.

e. Partnership

A partnership is an association of two or more persons for the purpose of carrying on as co-owners of a business for profit. The partnership can be considered the principal in an agency relationship. Partners, employees of the partnership, and other persons, such as attorneys, can all serve as agents of the partnership.

C. THE AGENT

1. Background

Generally, any person with minimal capacity can serve as an agent. An agent is not required to have the capacity to form contracts. Therefore, minors or incompetents can serve as agents. Entities may also serve as agents. Agents may perform a variety of general or specialized tasks.

Depending on the level of the agent's authority, or the manner in which the agent conducts business with a third party, the agent may incur personal liability for acts that are unauthorized by the principal or that are illegal, negligent, or outside the scope of the agent's employment.

The consensual nature of the agency relationship requires an agent to:

i) Have minimal capacity;

ii) Manifest assent and consent to act on the principal's behalf; and

iii) Manifest assent to be subject to the principal's control.

2. Formalities of an Agency

Creating an agency relationship is relatively easy because:

i) An agent need not receive consideration (a gratuitous agent); and

ii) A principal's appointment of an agent generally need not be in writing or comply with other formalities.

> **EXAM NOTE:** Do you need to identify an agent quickly? Look for (i) the types of agents listed below in fact patterns and (ii) persons who work on behalf of, and are subject to the control of, another person/principal.

3. Types of Agents

a. Individual

Any individual with minimal capacity (some understanding that a contract is being initiated and the general nature of its subject matter) has the requisite capacity to be an agent. Status as an agent is established by the agreement to act on behalf of, and subject to the control of, the principal.

b. Servant or employee

A servant (often referred to as an employee) is an agent who is subject to the principal's control with respect to the physical conduct of the employee's performance. Generally, employees are paid hourly or by time periods (e.g., weekly, biweekly, monthly). Their work is an integral part of the work of the employer, tasks are generally completed under the employer's direction, and employees are employed for long periods of time with the same employer. The more control an employer exerts over an agent's day-to-day activities, the more likely the agent qualifies as an employee.

c. Independent contractor

An agent who is not a servant/employee is referred to as an independent contractor. Courts examine several factors to determine whether an agent is an employee or an independent contractor. The most important factor is that an independent contractor is not subject to the principal's control regarding the physical conduct (i.e., the means and method) of the agent's performance.

An independent contractor can be identified as a person who:

i) Bears the risk and benefits from good management;

ii) Maintains a high level of independence;

iii) Is free to work for others;

iv) Agrees to be paid a fixed fee;

v) Receives payment based on results;

vi) Is liable for work performed; and

vii) Accepts responsibility to remedy defects at her own expense.

> **EXAM NOTE:** Questions may refer to an independent contractor as a "nonemployee agent."

d. Gratuitous agent

A gratuitous agent is an agent who does not receive compensation. This does not prevent the creation of an agency relationship, but it generally does prevent the formation of an enforceable contract between an agent and a principal due to the lack of consideration.

e. General and special agents

A general agent is an agent with broad authority over a wide variety of tasks, involving a continuity of service in a particular kind of business, without renewed authorization for each transaction or decision. General agents include store managers and purchasing agents.

Special agents generally have limited authority regarding a specific transaction or a string of repetitious acts. Common types of special agents include real-estate agents, subagents, insurance agents, commission merchants, and bailees.

f. A trustee as an agent

A trustee is an agent and is subject to the control of the settlor of the trust or one or more of its beneficiaries. A trustee maintains a fiduciary relationship with and holds property for the benefit of the settlor. Restatement (Third) of Agency § 1.04(10) (2006).

g. Subagents

A subagent is a person appointed by an agent to perform functions that the agent has agreed to perform on behalf of a principal. The agent is liable to the principal for the conduct of the subagent. When an appointing agent hires employees, those employees are presumed to be subagents of the appointing agent, acting on behalf of the appointing agent's principal.

Example: Employees of an advertising firm working on the account of a customer of the firm are presumed to be subagents of the firm.

A real-estate broker who successfully markets property to a prospective buyer (i.e., a "showing broker") is treated as a subagent of the broker with whom a prospective seller has listed the property (i.e., a "listing broker").

1) Power to appoint a subagent

An agent may appoint a subagent only if the agent has actual or apparent authority to do so.

2) Duties of a subagent

A subagent owes a duty of loyalty to the principal as well as to the appointing agent.

3) Contractual liability

a) Agent

The agent is responsible to the principal for the subagent's conduct. Thus, the agent may be liable for a loss incurred by the principal as a consequence of the subagent's misconduct.

b) Principal

A principal is bound by the subagent's acts to the same extent as if the agent had undertaken the acts. Notice received by a subagent is treated as notice to the principal; knowledge possessed by the subagent is imputed to the principal. The principal is not obligated to compensate the subagent when the subagent and the agent create an agreement between them concerning compensation or other duties.

c) An agent serving co-principals

An agent has a duty of loyalty to the principal. In a situation in which an agent is serving more than one principal, and there is no substantial conflict among the principals' interests or their instructions to the agent, the agent may fulfill duties owed to all principals.

If a conflict exists between the principals, then the agent may not work for the conflicting principals.

4) Tort consequences

An agent who appoints a subagent may be vicariously liable for torts committed by the subagent.

D. FORMATION OF AGENCY RELATIONSHIPS

1. Capacity

To become a principal and be bound by an agent's actions, a person must have capacity both to consent to the agency relationship and to enter into the transaction to which the agent purports to bind the principal.

In contrast, virtually any person can serve as an agent. A person can serve as an agent as long as he has the physical and mental capability to do whatever he has been appointed to do.

a. Minors

A person under the age of majority does not have the legal capacity to form contracts. Therefore, a minor generally may not be bound to a contract by an agent. However, a minor can serve as an agent.

b. Incompetents

A person who has a factual incapacity, such as incompetence, due to a mental condition related to medication, drugs, alcohol, or illness, does not have the legal capacity to be a principal, but she may be an agent.

c. Unincorporated associations

An unincorporated association is a non-legal entity in which two or more persons voluntarily associate with mutual consent or purpose. Examples of unincorporated associations include religious, literary, professional, charitable, or social associations; they each lack the capacity to form agency relationships.

2. Consent

Both the principal and the agent must consent to the agency relationship. The agent does not have to verbally consent, but she may manifest assent by performing acts on behalf of the principal. Restatement (Third) of Agency § 1.01, cmts. c, d; § 103 (2006).

Note that termination of an agency relationship may be unilateral. The principal or agent may terminate the agency without the other's consent.

3. Consideration

The parties may create an agency relationship without consideration.

Example: A and B are good friends. B has a new job starting in one week, but she does not want to drive her new sports car from Ohio to California. A offers to drive B's car to California, and B offers to pay A's expenses while she is on the road. A declines the offer of payment. A (the agent) is entitled to compensation for her act of driving B's (the individual-principal's) car to California, just as B has the obligation to compensate A. However, their prior oral agreement negates the need for compensation, and the principal-agent relationship remains intact.

4. Writing Requirement

A writing is generally not necessary to create an agency relationship. In some jurisdictions, statutes require that the principal's authorization of the agent be in writing and comply with specific requirements. The most common example is when the agent contracts to sell or buy real property.

When a statute requires the principal's authorization to be in writing, the requirement is often referred to as the "**equal-dignities rule**," i.e., the authorization must be of equal dignity to the underlying transaction. The equal-dignities rule operates to protect the principal against third-party actions. Therefore, a principal can raise the lack of written authorization as a defense. It does not apply in a contract action brought by a principal against a third party or in an action brought by an agent against the principal. Restatement (Third) of Agency § 3.02, cmt. b (2006).

II. LIABILITY OF THE PRINCIPAL AND THE AGENT TO THIRD PARTIES

A. BACKGROUND

Once an agency relationship has been created, the principal potentially can be bound to contracts by the agent and subject to vicarious liability for the agent's tortious conduct.

B. CONTRACTUAL LIABILITY OF THE PRINCIPAL

A principal is subject to liability on a contract that the agent enters into on the principal's behalf if the agent has the power to bind the principal to the contract.

An agent has the power to bind the principal to a contract when:

i) The agent has **actual authority** (express or implied);

ii) The agent has **apparent authority**; or

iii) The principal is **estopped** from denying the agent's authority.

In addition, even if an agent acts with no power to bind the principal, the principal can become subject to liability on the contract if the principal ratifies the contract.

1. Actual Authority

Actual authority may be either express or implied.

a. Express actual authority

Express actual authority can be created via:

i) Oral or written words;

ii) Clear, direct, and definite language; or

iii) Specific detailed terms and instructions.

Example: Specific, detailed instructions such as, "Hire Nikki Jones today."

1) Objective and subjective standard of intent

For express (actual) authority to exist, the principal's manifestation must cause the agent to believe that the agent is doing what the **principal wants** (subjective standard), and the agent's belief must be **reasonable** (objective standard).

A principal's unexpressed subjective intent regarding an agent's authority is ineffective. Remember, it is the *manifestation of a principal's intent* (spoken/written words, instructions, statements, or any conduct by the principal) that forms the basis for actual authority. Restatement (Third) of Agency § 2.01, cmt. c (2006).

2) The principal's manifestations (assent/intent)

For actual authority to exist, a principal must make a manifestation that causes the agent reasonably to believe that the agent is authorized. Silence or the failure to dissent by a principal to the actions or words of an agent when a reasonable person would do so can constitute a manifestation of assent for an agent to act on the principal's behalf. A principal must give the agent **clear notice** if the principal disagrees with the agent's actions.

3) Manifestation must reach the agent

A principal's manifestation must reach the agent to create actual authority. The principal might communicate with the agent directly, or the manifestation might reach the agent by some other means, such as through another agent of the principal.

4) Express authority granted in error

A principal's manifestation intended for one agent and given to another agent in error can create express authority to the agent who received the manifestation by mistake. The same result occurs when a principal's manifestation concerning the subject matter is incorrect.

Example: A business owner asks A (an employee) to sign an invoice that just came over the fax machine for $400. B (also an employee), who is standing next to A says "Okay," picks up the invoice from the fax machine, and signs it.

5) A third person's knowledge of actual authority is irrelevant

For express actual authority to exist, the agent must believe that the agent is doing what the principal wants (subjective standard), and the agent's belief must be reasonable (objective standard). Awareness of the agent's authority by a third party does not determine the nature or extent of the authority.

b. Implied actual authority

Implied actual authority allows an agent to take whatever actions (designated or implied in the principal's manifestations) are properly necessary to achieve the principal's objectives, based on the agent's reasonable understanding of the manifestations and objectives of the principal. Restatement (Third) of Agency § 2.01, cmt. b (2006).

Example: The authority to interview is implied in the agent's authority to hire.

The authority to make purchases on behalf of the principal may create implied authority in an agent to:

i) Make payments for goods and services purchased;

ii) Accept deliveries; and

iii) Collect funds.

1) Customary implied authority

In the absence of instructions to the contrary, an agent has implied authority to act within accepted business customs or general trade usage within an industry. The agent must be aware of the normal business customs or usage before she acts.

2) Implied authority by position

A principal may manifest assent to the actions of his agent by placing the agent in a position that customarily has certain authority, such as vice president or treasurer.

3) Implied by acquiescence

Implied authority based upon acquiescence commonly results from:

i) A principal's acceptance of the agent's acts as they occur; or

ii) The principal's failure to object to the unauthorized actions of the agent that:

    a) Affirm the agent's belief that those actions further the principal's objectives; and

    b) Support the agent's perceived authority to act in the future.

Thus, it is imperative that a principal stop, correct, and clarify any unacceptable act performed by an agent when the act takes place, so as not to grant implied authority as to the future actions of the agent.

> **Example:** A, the manager of a restaurant, has been signing the invoices for wine (without authorization) delivered to the restaurant for the last four months, since the owner of the restaurant, B, has been working on opening the outside café. B has never expressly authorized A to sign for the wine orders, but when he saw A sign for an order on two occasions, B failed to object to A's unauthorized action. A currently has implied authority by acquiescence to sign for future wine orders, and B will be liable for A's acts on his behalf.

4) Implied authority due to emergency

Agents have implied authority to take all reasonably necessary measures in cases of emergency, in the absence of the principal and/or specific instructions to act.

5) Implied authority to delegate

In general, agents are prohibited from delegating either express or implied authority to a third person without the principal's express authorization. The rationale for the rule is that the agency relationship is consensual, and the principal has not agreed to a third party acting in the place of the known agent. Yet, in certain cases, a principal may be shown to have granted implied authority to the agent to delegate his duties to a third person or subagent.

a) Mechanical or ministerial acts

An agent generally has the implied authority to hire a subagent to perform mechanical acts (such as clearing debris from a work site).

b) Specific to situation or circumstance

An agent has the authority to employ a subagent for a specific situation when it is required by law that an individual have a professional perform a specific task.

> **Example:** A surgeon hires the anesthesiologist and surgical nurses. The surgeon is the agent of the patient, hiring professional staff to assist as needed.

c) Custom or usage

An agent may delegate duties to a subagent to facilitate a transaction because of business or industry customs or trade usage.

> **Example:** Lawyers hire notaries, paralegals, and legal secretaries to help administer client cases.

d) Impossibility

The agent may delegate acts that she could not perform for a variety of reasons.

> **Example:** A wedding planner may contract with a minister to officiate at a wedding because the wedding planner (as an agent of the bride) cannot legally perform the ceremony.

2. Apparent Authority

Apparent authority, also known as the doctrine of "ostensible agency," derives from the **reasonable reliance of a third party** on that party's perception of the level of authority granted to the agent by the principal. The perception is based on the principal's behavior over a period of time.

> **EXAM NOTE:** The bar exam frequently tests your ability to differentiate between implied actual authority and apparent authority.
>
> **Implied authority** results when the principal's words or actions cause an *agent* to reasonably believe in the agent's authority to act.
>
> **Apparent authority** results when the principal causes a *third party* to reasonably believe that the agent has authority to act.
>
> To determine if a third party has a reasonable belief of apparent authority, look for a principal's manifestation that reaches the third party and could reasonably cause the third party to believe that the agent is authorized. The key is the **principal's behavior**, not the agent's, and the third party's perception that results from it.

Apparent authority, unlike estoppel, does not require the third party to establish that she acted in reliance on the principal's manifestations or that she suffered a detriment as a consequence of such reliance.

> A change in position by the third party may be evidence of the third party's belief in the agent's possession of actual authority.

a. Actor/imposter agent

It is not uncommon for an individual purporting to be an agent at the time of his acts to have no agency relationship or authority delegated by a principal. This person is called an "actor" or "imposter," and a principal may be held liable for the imposter's acts when the principal negligently allows an imposter to have the appearance of actual authority to act on the principal's behalf.

b. Third party's reasonable belief

Unlike implied actual authority, which is based on the agent's reasonable belief as to the agent's authority, apparent authority focuses on the **reasonable belief of the third party**.

1) Reasonable belief factors

To determine whether a third party's belief is reasonable, look to:

i) Past dealings between the principal and the agent of which the third party is aware;

ii) Trade customs regarding how a similar transaction is normally accomplished;

iii) Relevant industry standards;

iv) The principal's written statements of authority;

v) Transactions that do not benefit the principal; or

vi) Extraordinary or novel transactions for the principal or similar types of principals.

2) The agent's position

Information, known by a third party, that a person is an agent for an organization without knowledge of the person's position in the organization (e.g., president) is an insufficient basis to support a belief in the agent's authority to act for the organization.

However, by appointing an agent to a specific position (e.g., vice president, treasurer, general manager), the principal makes a manifestation to the public that the agent has the customary level of authority possessed by a person in the agent's position.

3. Termination of Authority

An agent's actual authority may be terminated by:

i) The principal's revocation;

ii) The principal's agreement with the agent;

iii) A change of circumstances;

iv) The passage of time;

v) The principal's death or suspension of powers;

vi) The agent's death or suspension of powers;

vii) The principal's loss of capacity; or

viii) A statutorily mandated termination.

a. The principal's power to revoke/the agent's power to renounce

1) In general

Either party to the agency relationship may revoke or renounce consent that was previously given. A revocation or renunciation is effective as soon as the other party has notice of it.

Either party has the power to terminate the agency relationship, even if they contracted not to do so. In that case, either party may be liable for breach of contract. The remedy for breach is limited to damages.

2) Power coupled with an interest

A principal cannot revoke the authority of an agent if the agent's power is coupled with an interest in the subject matter of the power. For example, if a borrower conveys an interest in real property to a lender under a deed of trust, and also confers on the lender the power to sell the property in the event of default, then the lender's interest is coupled with an interest in the property. Therefore, the borrower cannot revoke the lender's authority to sell.

Termination of an agency relationship is unilateral; either party may assert the right to terminate the agreement.

b. Termination of an agency agreement

The principal and agent can mutually agree to terminate the agreement that formed their agency relationship.

When an existing agreement between the agent and the principal specifies the circumstances under which the agent's actual authority terminates, the occurrence of that circumstance terminates the agency, and the agent should reasonably conclude that the principal no longer would assent to the agent acting on the principal's behalf.

c. Changed circumstances

Agency relationships may end as a result of:

i) A change in a statute relating to the subject matter;

ii) Insolvency of either party;

iii) A dramatic change in business conditions;

iv) The destruction of the subject matter of the agency relationship; or

v) A disaster (natural or unnatural).

The agency relationship terminates when the changed circumstance should cause the agent to reasonably believe that the principal no longer consents to the agent acting on the principal's behalf.

d. Passage of time

When the principal and agent do not specify the duration of an agent's authority, such authority terminates after a reasonable period of time.

e. Death of the principal

1) In general

The traditional common-law rule is that the principal's death terminates all power of the agent to act, including actual authority, regardless of whether the agent or third party has notice of the principal's death.

There is a modern judicial trend to hold that the principal's death does not terminate an agent's authority until the agent has notice of the principal's death.

2) Durable power of attorney

If a principal grants an agent authority in a durable power of attorney (*discussed below*), then the principal's death may not necessarily terminate the agent's authority, depending on the circumstances under which the durable power of attorney is granted. For example, in certain cases, an agent under a durable power of attorney may order an autopsy and demand and receive medical records for the deceased principal.

3) Power coupled with an interest

The principal's death does not terminate the authority of an agent if the agent's power is coupled with an interest in the subject matter of the power.

f. Death of the agent

The death of the agent *automatically* terminates the agent's actual authority. Authority does not pass to the agent's estate or heirs.

g. The principal's loss of capacity

1) In general

The common-law rule is that an individual principal's loss of capacity terminates the agent's actual authority. There is a modern trend holding that actual authority does not terminate *until the agent has notice* that the principal has been adjudicated to lack capacity or that the principal's loss of capacity is permanent.

2) Durable power of attorney

A principal may override the loss-of-capacity rule by giving an agent a durable power of attorney in advance of the incapacity. An agent's authority under a durable power of attorney continues despite the principal's lack of capacity. A durable power of attorney must be in writing, evidence the agent's appointment, and express the principal's intention that the power will not be affected by the principal's future disability or incapacity or, alternatively, will take effect upon such an event.

As long as the principal has capacity, he may revoke a durable power of attorney.

h. Statutorily mandated termination

The occurrence of circumstances specified by statute may affect the agency relationship and modify or terminate actual authority. For example, under the Uniform Commercial Code (UCC), a bank may generally pay a customer's checks for 10 days after the customer's death, despite knowledge of the death. UCC § 4-405 (2007).

i. The agent's breach of fiduciary duty

The agent's authority terminates when he breaches his fiduciary duty to the principal.

4. Estoppel

A person who has not represented that an individual is authorized to act as an agent may be estopped from denying the existence of an agency relationship or an agent's authority with respect to a transaction entered into by the agent. Estoppel applies when a third party is justifiably induced to make a detrimental change in position because that third party believed the transaction was entered into for the principal and either the principal:

i) Intentionally or carelessly caused the belief; or

ii) Having notice of such belief and the possibility that the belief might induce others to change their positions in reliance on it, failed to take reasonable steps to notify them of the facts.

In short, a principal, or purported principal, is liable for the appearance of authority arising solely from the **principal's failure** to take reasonable steps and use ordinary care.

Example: P has two co-agents, A and B. P learns that B, acting without actual or apparent authority, is informing P's neighbors that A has the authority to sell P's ring, which P has specifically forbidden A from doing. P's next-door neighbor purchases P's ring from A, in justifiable reliance on B's representation as to A's authority. P, in her suit to rescind the sale, may be estopped (prevented) from denying B's authority to make the representation as to A's authority. Restatement (Third) of Agency, § 2.05, Illustration 1 (2006).

5. Ratification

A principal can ratify an act performed by another person, whether or not the person is an actual agent of the principal. Ratification occurs when a principal affirms a prior act that was done or purported to be done on the principal's behalf. The principal's affirmation may be either express or implied (such as through conduct), and consideration is not required. For ratification to occur, the following elements must exist:

i) The principal must ratify the **entire act**, contract, or transaction (either by express manifestation of assent or conduct that justifies a reasonable assumption of consent);

ii) The principal must have the **legal capacity** to ratify the transaction at the time it occurs; the third party must also have the legal capacity to engage in the transaction;

iii) The principal's ratification must be **timely** (before the third party withdraws from the transaction); and

iv) The principal must have knowledge of the material facts involved in the original act.

If the principal ratifies the agent's action, then the principal is bound just as if the action had been authorized at the time it occurred. This is true even if the agent acted without power to bind the principal (i.e., with no actual or apparent authority, and when estoppel does not apply). However, if the principal's ratification occurs after such a material change that it would be unfair to enforce the transaction against the third party, the third party can avoid the transaction. *Pape v. Home Insurance Co.*, 139 F.2d 231 (2d Cir. 1943).

C. **THE PRINCIPAL'S LIABILITY TO THIRD PARTIES IN TORT FOR THE AGENT'S CONDUCT**

A principal may be vicariously as well as directly liable to a third person who is tortiously harmed by an agent's conduct. The doctrine of vicarious liability asserts that a principal is liable for the acts of an agent, even though the principal is innocent of fault and not directly guilty of any tort or crime. Common torts include negligence, misrepresentation, false imprisonment, and battery.

1. **The Principal's Vicarious Liability for the Agent's Torts**

   a. **Respondeat superior**

   Under the doctrine of respondeat superior, a principal may be vicariously liable for a tort committed by an agent acting **within the scope of his employment**. The principal is liable despite the absence of tortious conduct by the principal. This is also known as "derivative liability."

   > If the agent is not liable, then the principal cannot be vicariously liable.

   1) **General rule**

      A principal is vicariously liable to a third party harmed by the agent's conduct when:

      i) The agent is a servant (often referred to as an "employee"); and

      ii) The agent commits a tort while acting within the scope of employment.

      Note that an agent who appoints a subagent may be vicariously liable for torts committed by the subagent.

      > **EXAM NOTE:** The bar exam frequently tests vicarious liability of an employer. Don't forget to use key terminology, such as acting **"within the scope of employment"** or **"scope of the employment relationship."**

   2) **"Servant/employee" defined**

      A servant or employee is an agent whose principal controls or has the right to control the manner and means of the agent's performance of work. Because of the level of control of their employers, bus drivers, food servers, and corporate officers would all be classified as employees.

      When a lent employee, also known as a "borrowed servant," commits a tort, the employee's initial employer or the employer for whom the employee is currently working, or both, may be liable to a third party harmed by the lent employee's conduct. Recent court decisions have assessed liability based upon a determination as to which of the employers controlled the agent's actions at the time the harm occurred.

      > **EXAM NOTE:** Remember that the key to determining liability is whether the *employer has the right to control the employee's conduct.*

   3) **Scope of employment**

      An employee acts within the scope of employment when either:

      i) Performing work assigned by the employer; or

ii) Engaging in a course of conduct subject to the employer's control.

When an employee acts independently of any intent to serve any purpose of the employer, the employer may escape liability.

> **EXAM NOTE:** To attach liability and hold the employer vicariously liable, you must establish that (i) there is an employer/employee relationship, and (ii) the employee's harmful conduct was committed while working within the scope of employment.

An employee does not act outside the scope of employment merely because he performs the work carelessly, makes a mistake in performing the work, or fails to perform assigned work. Moreover, an employee who disregards an employer's instructions or violates a generally applicable law, such as a speed limit, is not necessarily acting outside the scope of employment when the employee believes that compliance would jeopardize the employee's timely completion of his assigned task.

a) An employee's use of physical force against another

Although most jobs do not include the use of physical force against another person, an employee's assigned work may contemplate the necessity of using physical force to complete the assigned task, such as a "runner" for a bail bondsperson, who tracks down individuals who have jumped bail and returns them to custody.

b) Intentional torts

Intentional torts are not automatically excluded from the scope of employment. They may fall within the scope of employment when (i) the conduct is within the space and time limits of the employment; (ii) the agent was motivated in part to act for the employer's benefit; and (iii) the act was the kind of act that the employee was hired to perform.

> **Example:** A salesperson who intentionally misrepresents a product to a potential customer for the purpose of making a sale may be acting within the scope of employment. Restatement (Third) of Agency § 7.07, cmt. c (2006).

c) Work-related travel

i) Commuting

Generally, travel between work and home by an employee is not within the scope of employment. An exception exists when the employer provides the employee with a vehicle and asserts control over how the employee uses the vehicle. Restatement (Third) of Agency § 7.07, cmt. e (2006).

ii) Travel during the workday

Travel required to perform work, such as travel from an employer's office to a job site or between job sites, is generally within the scope of employment

d) Frolic and detour

i) Frolic

When an employee's personal errand involves a **significant deviation** from the path that otherwise would be taken for the purposes of performing work, the errand is a frolic. Once a frolic begins, an employee is outside the scope of his employment until he resumes performance of his assigned work.

ii) Detour

Travel by an employee during the workday that involves a personal errand may be within the scope of employment when the errand is merely a detour (i.e., a *de minimis* departure from an assigned route).

b. An agent's apparent authority

A principal is vicariously liable for a tort committed by an agent with apparent authority when the agent's appearance of authority enables him to commit a tort or conceal its commission. Such torts include fraudulent and negligent misrepresentation, defamation, tortious institution of legal proceedings, and conversion of property.

1) Apparent authority

For apparent authority to exist, a third person must believe that the agent acted with actual authority, and such belief must be *reasonable* and be *traceable to a manifestation* by the principal.

If the third party's belief in the agent's authority to make the statement is reasonable, then the misrepresentation will be attributed to the principal. The third party might be able to rescind the contract and sue for damages.

> **Example:** A principal retains a real-estate agent to sell the principal's personal residence and informs a prospective buyer that the agent will answer all questions concerning the property. The agent falsely informs the buyer that the house has been rewired to comply with new regulations. The agent's statements may be attributed to the principal because of the agent's apparent authority to make such statements on the principal's behalf.

2) Effect of an agent's motivation or lack of benefit to a principal

The fact that an agent's conduct is not beneficial to the principal does not protect the principal from liability for such conduct.

2. A Principal's Direct Liability to Third Parties

A principal is directly liable to a third person harmed by an agent's conduct if:

i) The principal authorizes or ratifies the agent's conduct;

ii) The principal is negligent in selecting, supervising, or otherwise controlling the agent; or

iii) The principal delegates to an agent performance of a non-delegable duty to use care to protect other persons or their property, and the agent breaches the duty.

a. An agent with actual authority or a principal's ratification

A principal is subject to liability for an agent's conduct if the principal authorizes the conduct or intends its consequences. For example, a principal who authorizes an agent to destroy a competitor's place of business is liable to the competitor.

If an agent uses means other than those the principal intended, then the principal is nevertheless vicariously liable if the agent's choice of means is within the agent's actual authority.

If the agent's conduct is not tortious, the principal may still be liable if the same conduct by the principal would have rendered the principal liable.

Example: A principal has information that the agent does not, such as the nature of an object being sold. A statement by the agent about the object to a third-party buyer may not support a finding of misrepresentation; however, the same statement made by the principal would constitute misrepresentation.

A principal is also liable if she ratifies an agent's conduct. Ratification requires that the principal affirm a prior act that was done or purportedly done on the principal's behalf.

b. Negligence in selecting or controlling an agent

A principal who is negligent in selecting, supervising, or otherwise controlling an agent runs the risk of liability attaching to that negligence. Basic tort requirements of duty, breach, causation, and damages must be satisfied for the principal to be liable.

As a general tort rule:

i) A person who conducts an activity through another person;

ii) Is liable for harm to a third party;

iii) Caused by the actor when the person fails to exercise reasonable care;

iv) With respect to the selection of the actor and the actor's performance of the activity.

A principal has a duty to a third party with respect to actions by an agent if there is a **special relationship** between a principal and the third party, such as that between a common carrier and a passenger.

c. Non-delegable duties

A principal who has a non-delegable duty cannot avoid liability by delegating the duty to another person. Generally, a duty is non-delegable when the responsibility is so important to the community that a person should not be permitted to transfer it to another person. Examples include the duty of a landlord to keep premises in a safe condition and the duty to use care in inherently dangerous activities such as the use of explosives.

D. AN AGENT'S LIABILITY

1. An Agent's Liability in Contractual Dealings

a. An agent's liability as a party to a contract

When an agent enters into a contract on the principal's behalf and binds the principal to the contract, the agent might also become a party to (and liable on) the contract. Whether the agent becomes a party depends on the terms of the contract and the degree to which the agent discloses to the third party the existence and identity of the principal.

1) Disclosed principal

A principal is a disclosed principal if the third party has notice of both the existence and identity of the principal. Unless the agent and third party agree otherwise, an agent who enters into a contract on behalf of a disclosed principal *does not* become a party to the contract. To avoid becoming a party to the contract, the agent must:

i) Enter into the contract on behalf of the disclosed principal;

ii) Affirmatively disclose to the third party both the existence and identity of the principal; and

iii) Not agree to become a party to the contract.

2) Partially disclosed principal

A principal is a partially disclosed principal if the third party has notice of the principal's existence but not the principal's identity. Unless the agent and the third party agree otherwise, an agent who enters into a contract on behalf of a partially disclosed principal becomes a party to the contract.

If the agent binds the principal to the contract, or if the principal ratifies the contract, then both the principal and agent are parties to the contract with the third party.

3) Undisclosed principal

A principal is an undisclosed principal if the third party has no notice of the principal's existence. An agent who enters into a contract on behalf of an undisclosed principal becomes a party to the contract. Thus, when the agent does not inform a third party of the identity or the existence of the principal, the agent becomes liable to the third party on the contract.

If the agent binds the principal to the contract, then both the principal and the agent are parties to the contract with the third person. Once the third party discovers the existence of the principal, however, the **election of remedies doctrine** requires the third party to choose to hold liable either the principal or the agent. If the third party obtains a judgment against one of them, then the judgment operates as an election, and the third party is precluded from seeking to hold the other party liable on the contract.

Generally, a third party is liable to an undisclosed principal on a contract made with an agent on behalf of the principal unless:

i) The principal or undisclosed principals are excluded by the form or terms of the contract; or

ii) The principal's existence is fraudulently concealed, i.e., the agent falsely represents to the third party that the agent does not act on behalf of the principal.

Generally, an undisclosed principal is liable to a third party if:

i) The third party is induced to make a detrimental change in position by an agent without actual authority;

ii) The principal knew of the agent's conduct and that it might induce others to change positions; and

e. Duty to indemnify

Subject to an agreement to the contrary, a principal has a duty to indemnify the agent against pecuniary loss suffered in connection with the agency relationship and within the scope of the agent's actual authority. The principal's duty to indemnify includes expenses and other losses incurred by an agent (such as attorney's fees) in defending an action brought by a third party.

> A principal is not obligated to indemnify losses that result from an agent's own negligence, illegal acts, or other wrongful conduct.

3. A Principal's Remedies for Breach by an Agent

A principal has the right to recover for a breach of the agent's fiduciary obligation, as well as for the agent's breach of contract and for actions of the agent that exceed the scope of employment, and for which tort law provides a remedy.

A principal may pursue one or more of the following remedies against an agent who breaches a duty:

i) An injunction;

ii) A breach-of-contract action for monetary damages;

iii) A tort action for harm suffered, including punitive damages;

iv) Avoidance or rescission of a contract or a transaction;

v) Restitution;

vi) An accounting to the principal for the value of the agent's use of the principal's property;

vii) Termination of the agency relationship;

viii) Forfeiture of commission or other compensation paid or payable; and

ix) Disgorgement of profits earned by the agent without the principal's consent.

B. RIGHTS AND DUTIES OF AN AGENT

In general, an agent has a right to be compensated, allowed to work without interference, reimbursed for losses, provided with a safe work environment, and indemnified for working on behalf of a principal.

1. Rights of an Agent

a. Right to receive compensation

An agent has a right to receive compensation for her services if the principal expressly or impliedly promises to compensate the agent. When no amount has been specified in the agency relationship, an agent has the right to be compensated in the customary manner of the business trade. However, a principal does not have a duty to pay compensation to subagents engaged by an agent, unless the principal agrees to do so.

b. Right to have the principal not interfere with the agent's work

The principal also has a duty to cooperate with the agent and assist the agent in performing the tasks associated with the objectives of the agency.

c. Right to indemnification and reimbursement

An agent has the right to indemnification for losses incurred when the agent transacted lawful business with actual authority.

Example: If the agent, having actual authority from the principal, purchases goods from a third party, and the principal refuses to pay, then the third party may be able to sue the agent for damages. The principal would be responsible for compensating the agent for costs associated with the principal's breach, such as damages and attorney's fees paid by the agent.

An agent also has the right to be reimbursed by the principal for expenses incurred by the agent in connection with the agency relationship. Generally, this right is limited to payments made or necessary expenses incurred by an agent within the scope of the agency.

An agent does not have the right to be indemnified for losses that result from an agent's own negligence, illegal acts, or other wrongful conduct.

d. Right to work in a safe environment

The principal must provide a safe working environment, including tools, equipment, and conditions for an agent or employee.

e. Remedies available to an agent

An agent might have a claim against the principal founded in contract or tort law. However, the agent is required to choose the remedy sought and to mitigate his damages prior to and during the period that the agent seeks relief.

To sue for breach of contract, the agent must establish that a right to compensation exists. This normally means that the agent must be a compensated agent, i.e., there must have been consideration to support the agency relationship.

The agent may file a claim for compensation owed to him under the terms of the contract with the principal. Such a claim could take the form of a suit in damages to recover compensation or a lien against the principal.

2. Duties of an Agent

An agent has two basic types of duties to a principal—a duty of loyalty, which includes a fiduciary duty, and a performance-based duty, which includes the duty of care.

a. Duty of loyalty

Agency is a special relationship that gives rise to fiduciary duties on the part of the agent. As a fiduciary, the agent owes the principal a duty of loyalty, which generally requires the agent to act solely for the benefit of the principal (and not for the benefit of the agent or third parties) in matters connected with the agency. This duty applies to all agents, whether they are gratuitous or compensated and can vary depending on the parties' agreement. The agent's general duty of loyalty requires the agent to do, or not do, many specific things, which are discussed below.

1) Duty not to deal with the principal as an adverse party

Unless the principal and agent have agreed otherwise, the agent has a duty not to deal with the principal as an adverse party in any transaction connected with the agency without the principal's knowledge. For example, an agent cannot, without the principal's knowledge, purchase goods from the principal if the principal has retained the agent to sell those goods.

2) Duty to refrain from acquiring a material benefit

The agent's duty of loyalty requires her to refrain from acquiring a material benefit in connection with transactions or other actions undertaken on the principal's behalf, unless the principal consents to the agent acquiring the benefit.

3) Duty not to usurp a business opportunity

The agent's duty not to usurp a business opportunity is a component of the duty of loyalty. It arises when either the nature of an opportunity or the circumstances under which the agent learned of it require the agent to offer the opportunity to the principal.

Thus, the agent may not seek or accept monetary or beneficial gain from a third party during the course of the agency without the principal's consent. The prohibition on the agent benefitting monetarily from transactions conducted for the principal is often referred to as the "agent's duty to account for profits."

4) Duty not to compete

An agent has a duty to refrain from competing with the principal concerning the subject matter of the agency and from assisting the principal's competitors.

5) Duty to disclose—multiple principals

An agent who acts for more than one principal in a transaction between or among them owes duties of disclosure, good faith, and fair dealing to each.

6) Duty not to use the principal's confidential information

An agent has a duty to refrain from using the principal's confidential information for the benefit of anyone other than the principal, including the agent. This duty survives termination of the agency relationship.

b. Performance-based duties

An agent owes performance-based duties to the principal, including a duty of obedience and a duty to perform with reasonable care.

1) Contractual duties

Although an agency relationship does not require a contract between the agent and the principal, an agent has an implied duty to act in accordance with the terms of any contract between the parties.

2) Duty of care

An agent has a duty to act with the care, competence, and diligence normally exercised by agents in similar circumstances, as reflected by local community standards. The agent's special skills and knowledge are taken into account in determining whether the agent employed due care and diligence.

3) Duty of obedience

An agent must act within the scope of her actual authority and comply with a principal's lawful and reasonable instructions.

4) Duty to provide information

An agent has a duty to provide relevant information to the principal pertaining to the subject matter of the agency and that the agent knows (or should know) the principal would wish to have.

5) Duty to keep and render accounts

An agent has the duty to keep the principal's property separate from the agent's property. Also, an agent has a duty to keep and render an accounting of the principal's money and other property.

> **EXAM NOTE:** When answering questions that require you to address the duties of an agent to the principal, make sure you state the "must have" duties:
>
> i) **Duty of care** to perform with *reasonable diligence and skill*;
>
> ii) **Duty to provide information** to the principal regarding all matters relating to the agency relationship;
>
> iii) **Duty of loyalty** to the principal and to *work only for his benefit*;
>
> iv) **Duty of obedience** to the principal; and
>
> v) **Duties** not to usurp a business opportunity from the principal; not to take financial gain from the principal; to provide an accounting; and not to commingle the principal's property with that of a third party.

Conflict of Laws

CONFLICT OF LAWS

Table of Contents

CONFLICT OF LAWS

Editor's Note
Transactions or events that give rise to legal disputes can have connections to two or more legal jurisdictions. The laws of such jurisdictions may differ with regard to the resolution of such disputes. Courts have developed legal doctrines and rules to determine what effect may be given to the fact that a case may have a significant relationship to more than one legal jurisdiction. This outline covers the basic doctrines that are used in different jurisdictions to address these conflicts of law.

I. DOMICILE

Domicile is a legal concept that can be significant for both choice-of-law determinations and jurisdictional purposes. If a person is domiciled in a particular state, then the person will be subject to personal jurisdiction in that state's courts whether or not the person can be found and personally served process. *Milliken v. Meyer*, 311 U.S. 457 (1940). In the conflict-of-laws context, domicile will be considered an important contact in jurisdictions that apply a "contacts" approach to choice of law. *See* § II.B.2 Most-Significant-Relationship Approach, *infra*. Ordinarily, the determination of a person's domicile is a question of fact.

A. DOMICILE OF INDIVIDUALS

Individuals can have more than one residence at a time, but they can have only one domicile at a time, which can be acquired either by choice or by operation of law.

1. Domicile by Choice

If a person has legal capacity, then the person's domicile is the location where he has chosen to establish domicile. In general, domicile will be where the person is present with the intent to remain for an unlimited time and when he abandons any prior domicile. Thus, courts will look at the person's physical presence and intent to determine a person's domicile.

a. Physical presence

Actual physical presence in the location is required to establish the location as the person's domicile. The person, though, need not be present for any specific amount of time to establish domicile, so long as the amount of time is coupled with the intent to establish domicile.

b. Intent

To establish a location as the domicile, a person must demonstrate, in addition to physical presence in a location, the intent to make the location his home for the time being, or the absence of an intent to go elsewhere. Presence under compulsion, such as a person in prison, will not establish domicile by choice.

Permanency is not required, but the intent to remain must be bona fide. In general, the person's actions and statements are used to establish intent. Ownership of real estate, voting, payment of taxes, having a bank account, or registration of an automobile are all factors that could be used to establish intent; however, none of these factors is conclusive.

c. Potential problem of multiple states claiming domicile

A forum state will apply its own law in determining questions of domicile. Although a person may have only one domicile, two states could theoretically conclude that the person is domiciled within their jurisdictions.

2. Domicile by Operation of Law

Domicile by operation of law occurs when an individual does not have the legal capacity to choose her domicile, as in the case of infants and incompetents. Historically, a married woman's domicile was that of her husband, although today married women may choose their states of domicile.

a. Infants

Infants (i.e., minor children) are domiciled where their custodial parents are domiciled. If a child is emancipated, then the child may establish her own domicile.

b. Incompetents

A person lacking the mental legal capacity to choose a domicile will retain her parents' domicile. If the person once had legal capacity, chose a domicile, and then lost legal capacity, then her domicile remains the place where she was domiciled before losing capacity.

B. DOMICILE OF CORPORATIONS

A corporation's domicile is always the state where it is incorporated.

C. CONTINUITY OF DOMICILE

Once established, a domicile is presumed to continue until a new domicile is acquired. The burden of showing a change in domicile is on the party that asserts it. Temporary or even prolonged absences will not, by themselves, result in a change of domicile. Thus, a domiciliary of one state can live in another state for years and retain his domicile in the original state, so long as he intends to return to that state. An old domicile by choice continues even though a new residence is established until there is the intention to create a new domicile.

D. CHANGE OF DOMICILE

A change of domicile takes place when a person with capacity to change his domicile is physically present in a place and intends to make that place home, at least for the time being. The physical presence and the intent must concur.

> **EXAM NOTE:** Before addressing choice of law, a court must have proper jurisdiction over a matter. This subject is discussed fully in the Civil Procedure outline. Keep in mind that once you have determined that a particular court has jurisdiction over a case, that court still may refuse to hear the case if it believes that venue should be somewhere else. Once you have determined jurisdiction, if the transactions or events giving rise to the dispute involve more than one state, you generally need to determine which state's law governs the different issues in the case.

II. CHOICE OF LAW

When a cause of action involves contacts with more than one state, the forum court must determine which state's law is to be applied to decide the issues in the case. State choice-of-law rules generally have three sources: (i) specific choice-of-law statutes, (ii) contractual choice-of-law agreements, and (iii) general choice-of-law rules governed by forum state common law. Choice-of-law issues are possible whenever a lawsuit involves a foreign element, such as a nonresident party or an event outside the forum state.

A. LIMITATIONS ON CHOICE OF LAW

Both the U.S. Constitution and state and federal statutes can limit a court's power to apply a particular choice-of-law rule. In certain circumstances, an agreement between the parties can also require the application of a particular choice of law in court.

1. **Constitutional Limitations**

   The U.S. Constitution can limit a state court's ability to apply its own substantive law to litigation having multistate issues.

   a. **Due process**

      Under the Due Process Clause of the Fourteenth Amendment, the U.S. Supreme Court has held that a forum state may apply its own law to a particular case only if it has a significant contact or significant aggregation of contacts with the state such that a choice of its law is neither arbitrary nor fundamentally unfair. *Allstate Ins. Co. v. Hague*, 449 U.S. 302 (1981). If the forum state's only contact is the fact that the cause of action was brought in its courts or the fact that the plaintiff once lived there, then application of the substantive law of the forum state will violate due process. *Home Ins. Co. v. Dick*, 281 U.S. 397 (1930).

   b. **Full faith and credit**

      Under Article IV, § 1 of the U.S. Constitution, "[f]ull faith and credit shall be given in each State to the public acts, records and judicial proceedings of every other State." The Supreme Court has held that the term "public acts" includes both a state's statutes and its substantive case law. *Carroll v. Lanza*, 349 U.S. 408 (1955). The Full Faith and Credit Clause requires a forum state to apply the law of another state when the forum state has no contacts with or interest in the controversy, but it does not prevent the forum state from applying its own law when the forum has such contacts or interest in the controversy. *Allstate Ins. Co. v. Hague*, 449 U.S. 302 (1981). In addition, the Full Faith and Credit Clause does not require a state to apply another state's law in violation of its own legitimate public policy. *Franchise Tax Bd. of California v. Hyatt*, 538 U.S. 488 (2003).

2. **Statutory Limitations**

   a. **State statutes**

      Some states have statutes requiring certain choice-of-law rules to be applied in particular cases. For example, the Uniform Commercial Code (UCC) contains choice-of-law provisions that require a forum state to apply the UCC if the state has a reasonable relationship to the transaction.

   b. **Federal statutes**

      Certain federal statutes may preempt a state from claiming jurisdiction over certain cases. For example, federal courts are given exclusive jurisdiction in patent, antitrust, and bankruptcy matters.

3. **Party-Controlled Choice of Law**

   Most courts will enforce a contractual choice-of-law provision if it is:

   i)   A valid agreement with an effective choice-of-law clause;

   ii) Applicable to the lawsuit under the terms of the contract;

   iii) Reasonably related to the lawsuit (i.e., the law to be applied is from a state with connections to the parties or the contract); and

   iv) Not in violation of the public policy of the forum state or another interested state.

   Note that a state's legislature may restrict the power of contracting parties to choose a governing law.

B. APPROACHES TO CHOICE OF LAW—IN GENERAL

So long as there is no constitutional mandate or statutory directive dictating which law applies, courts generally approach choice-of-law questions using one of three different approaches. These approaches are: (i) the vested-rights approach of the Restatement (First) of Conflict of Laws, (ii) the most-significant-relationship approach of the Restatement (Second) of Conflict of Laws, and (iii) the governmental-interest approach.

> Note that a state may use different choice-of-law approaches for different substantive areas of the law. Thus, a state might use the vested-rights approach for contract cases, while applying the most-significant-relationship approach for tort matters.

1. Vested-Rights Approach

This approach, used in the Restatement (First) of Conflict of Laws, is a territorial approach. It looks to the jurisdiction where the parties' rights are vested, meaning where the act or relationship that gives rise to the cause of action occurred or was created. Generally, this approach looks for the location where the last liable event took place.

a. Characterization

In determining where vesting occurred, the forum court will first characterize the issues in the cause of action. Initially, this involves a determination of whether the issue is substantive or procedural. If the issue is procedural, then the forum court will apply its own procedural rules. If the issue is substantive, then the court must identify the substantive area of the law involved. In general, the forum court will apply its own state law to determine whether an issue is one of tort, contract, property, domestic relations, etc. Note that in characterizing an issue in a particular way (e.g., as contract rather than tort or as substantive rather than procedural), a court may be able to avoid the application of a particular foreign law in favor of its own state's law, or vice versa.

b. Determination of the choice-of-law rule to be applied

After characterizing the issue in the cause of action, the forum court will then determine what the forum state's choice-of-law rules require with regard to the characterized issue. For example, if the issue has been characterized as a tort, then the law of the forum state may require that the law of the place of the injury apply.

2. Most-Significant-Relationship Approach

While the vested-rights approach of the Restatement (First) of Conflict of Laws offered certainty, ease of application, and predictability of results, many courts and commentators criticized it for often resulting in the application of a jurisdiction's law that was applied only because the jurisdiction had a fortuitous or attenuated connection to the events giving rise to the case.

Attempting to fix these problems, the Restatement (Second) of Conflict of Laws applies the law of the state with the **most significant relationship** to the issue in question. This approach is also sometimes referred to as the center-of-gravity approach or the grouping-of-contacts approach. It focuses on the policy objectives behind competing laws of different states.

When determining which state has the most significant relationship, the forum court generally considers the "connecting facts" or contacts that link each jurisdiction to the case, as well as the seven policy principles that are set forth in the Restatement (Second) of Conflict of Laws.

The seven principles are:

i) **The needs of the interstate or international system:** This principle is designed to achieve judicial efficiency and facilitate agreement between the two competing jurisdictions involved in the case.

ii) **The relevant policies of the forum:** The forum state must determine how its policies relate to the issues at hand for a particular case in a specific area of the law.

iii) **Policies of interested states:** The forum state evaluates its own laws as well as those of interested states to determine which laws should apply.

iv) **Party expectations:** The court will look to see if the parties have any justified expectations that should be protected. This principle applies *only* to planned transactions, such as contracts.

v) **Policies underlying the substantive areas of law:** The court must consider how the application of a particular law in a particular substantive area will affect basic policies relating to that area of the law.

vi) **Certainty, predictability, and uniformity:** The court will strive to achieve these goals and ultimately discourage forum shopping.

vii) **Ease of future application:** In the interest of making the final application of law easy, the court evaluates how difficult the application of the second jurisdiction's law would be to the case at hand. The court then decides if it should be used.

The list is not exclusive, and the particular factors will vary in importance according to the type of case at issue.

The forum court will: (i) isolate the precise legal issue that results in a conflict between the competing states, (ii) identify the policy objectives that each state's law seeks to achieve with respect to such issue, and (iii) determine each state's interest in view of its policy objectives to determine which state has a superior connection with the dispute. The contacts with each interested state are analyzed and their relative importance is considered, recognizing that different choices of law may be made with regard to different issues in a single case.

> **EXAM NOTE:** Note that the Restatement (Second) of Conflict of Laws includes specific presumptive rules for several different substantive areas of the law. *See* § II.C Rules for Specific Areas of Substantive Law, *infra*. Nonetheless, the forum court must still examine the seven principles listed above to determine if the presumptive rule should not be applied because another state has a more significant relationship under the seven principles.

3. **Governmental-Interest Approach**

Under the governmental-interest approach, it is presumed that the forum state will apply its own law, but the parties may request that another state's law be applied. If a party makes such a request, then that party must identify the policies of competing laws.

If there is a false conflict (i.e., the forum has no interest in the litigation), then the court applies the law of the state that does have an interest in the case. If there is a true conflict (i.e., the forum state and another state both have an interest in the litigation), then the forum state will review its own policies to determine which law should apply. If the conflict cannot be resolved, then the law of the forum state is applied.

However, if the forum state has no interest in applying its own laws (i.e., is a disinterested forum), and the doctrine of forum non conveniens is available, then the forum court should dismiss the case. The doctrine of forum non conveniens allows a court to dismiss an action, even if personal jurisdiction and venue are otherwise proper, if it finds that the forum would be too inconvenient for parties and witnesses and that a more convenient venue is available.   Some of the factors that are generally considered include: (i) the availability of an alternative forum, (ii) the law that will apply, and (iii) the location of the parties, witnesses, and evidence. If forum non conveniens is not available, then the forum state may either make its own determination as to which law is better to use or apply the law that most closely matches its own state law. If no state has an interest, then the forum law generally prevails.

States have an interest in applying their conduct-regulating laws (i.e., laws designed to regulate conduct) when the wrongful conduct occurs within their territory or when a state domiciliary is injured. States have an interest in applying their loss-shifting laws (i.e., immunize people from liability) when doing so would benefit a state domiciliary.

4. Conflict-of-Laws Rules in Federal Diversity Cases

Under *Klaxon Co. v. Stentor Electric Mfg. Co.*, 313 U.S. 487 (1941), in federal diversity cases, the federal district court is generally required to apply the conflict-of-laws rules of the state in which it sits. However, such application of a state's conflict-of-interest rules is required only to the extent that the state's rules are valid under the Full Faith and Credit and Due Process Clauses of the U.S. Constitution. *Allstate Ins. Co. v. Hague*, 449 U.S. 302 (1981). If a diversity case was transferred from a federal court in another state under federal venue law, 28 United States Code ("U.S.C.") § 1404(a), then the first state's choice-of-law rules will be applied. *Van Dusen v. Barrack*, 376 U.S. 612 (1946).

5. *Dépeçage*

Under the traditional approach to choice of law, the forum court is required to analyze a case in its entirety, applying only one state's law to all of the issues in the case. Modern approaches to choice of law require the forum court to consider separately which state's law should govern for each substantive issue if the issue would be resolved differently under the law of two or more potentially interested jurisdictions. This approach, which can allow the law of one state to govern one or more particular issues while still other issues are controlled by the law of one or more other states, is known as *dépeçage*.

6. Renvoi

a. Doctrine

The doctrine of renvoi requires that a forum court that is applying the law of another state to decide a matter also apply that foreign state's conflict-of-laws rules. Such rules might require the forum state to refer to its own law (this is known as remission) or to the laws of another state (this is known as transmission). Theoretically, this could result in a vicious circle with no state's internal laws being able to be applied.

b. Rejection

Most states generally reject the application of renvoi either by choosing not to apply the whole law of the foreign state or by accepting the reference back to its own law and applying only that law to the case. The governmental-interest approach wholly rejects the application of renvoi. The Restatement (Second) of Conflict of Laws generally rejects the application of renvoi, but it does require that a state look to the whole law of the foreign state in determining title or succession to land.

c. Federal Tort Claims Act

The Federal Tort Claims Act, 28 U.S.C. § 1346(b), requires application of the whole law, including the conflict rules, of the place where the act or omission occurred. *See Richards v. United States*, 369 U.S. 1 (1962). Thus, the forum will refer to the place where the act or omission occurred and then apply the conflict-of-laws rules of that state.

C. RULES FOR SPECIFIC AREAS OF SUBSTANTIVE LAW

1. Torts

a. Vested-rights approach

Under the vested-rights approach of the Restatement (First) of Conflict of Laws, a tort case will be governed by the law of the place where the wrong was committed (i.e., *lex loci delicti*). This means the place where the last event necessary to make the actor liable for the tort took place (generally the place where the person or thing that is injured is situated at the time of the wrong). The place of injury will generally govern whether the plaintiff has sustained a legal injury, what conduct creates liability, the standard of care to be applied, defenses, and damages.

b. Most-significant-relationship approach

Under the most-significant-relationship approach of the Restatement (Second) of Conflict of Laws, the seven policy principles discussed at § II.B.2 Most-Significant-Relationship Approach, *supra*, are applied to determine the applicable substantive rules of law. Within the context of those principles, the court considers four important contacts: (i) the place of the injury, (ii) the place where conduct causing injury occurred, (iii) the domicile, residence, place of incorporation, or place of business of the parties, and (iv) the place where the relationship is centered. Restatement (Second) of Conflict of Laws § 145. In tort matters, the default rule under the Restatement (Second) of Conflict of Laws approach is that the place of injury controls, unless another state has a more significant relationship to the parties or to the occurrence of the tort.

c. Governmental-interest approach

Under the governmental-interest approach, the forum state generally looks to its own law, so long as that state has a legitimate interest in applying its own law. Another state's law would be applied if a party makes a request for such application and the forum court determines that the other state's law should apply in accordance with the forum state's policies. *See* § II.B.3 Governmental-Interest Approach, *supra*.

2. **Contracts**

a. **Express choice of law of the parties**

If there is an express choice-of-law provision in the contract, then that law will govern unless:

i) It is contrary to public policy;

ii) There is no reasonable basis for the parties' choice; or

iii) There was fraud or mistake and true consent was not given.

If there is no express choice-of-law provision in the contract, then the forum court will apply the vested-rights approach, the most-significant-relationship approach, or the governmental-interest approach, depending on the choice-of-law rules applicable in the forum state.

b. **Vested-rights approach**

Under the vested-rights approach of the Restatement (First) of Conflict of Laws, certain contractual issues are deemed to vest in the location where the contract was executed, while others are deemed to vest in the location where the contract was to be performed.

1) **Location where the contract is executed**

a) **Validity of the contract**

In general, the place of execution governs issues regarding the validity of the contract, including the capacity to contract, the formalities of the contract (e.g., whether there must be a writing and whether it must be signed), and the consideration for the contract.

b) **Defenses to formation of the contract**

Generally, issues regarding whether there are defenses to the formation of the contract are governed by the law of the place of the execution of the contract. This can include defenses such as misrepresentation, fraud, and illegality.

c) **Interpretation of the contract**

The interpretation of a contract is governed by the law of the place of execution.

2) **Location where the contract was to be performed**

a) **Details of performance**

The details of performance are governed by the law of the place of performance. Such details can include:

i) The time and manner of performance;

ii) The person who is obligated to perform and the person to whom performance is to be made;

iii) The sufficiency of performance; and

iv) Any excuse for nonperformance.

c. Most-significant-relationship approach

1) In general

Under the most-significant-relationship approach of the Restatement (Second) of Conflict of Laws, the seven policy factors (discussed at § II.B.2 Most-Significant-Relationship Approach, *supra*) are considered, as are the following:

i) The location of the contracting, negotiation, and performance;

ii) The place where the contract's subject matter is located; and

iii) The location of the parties' domiciles, residences, nationalities, places of incorporation, and places of business.

Generally, when the location of negotiation and performance are the same, the forum court will apply the law of that state.

2) Default rules

Under the Restatement (Second) of Conflict of Laws approach, there are also default rules that apply to certain kinds of contracts. These default rules will generally apply **unless** another state is found to have a more significant relationship with regard to the issue.

i) **Land contracts** are controlled by the law of the state of the situs of the land;

ii) **Personalty contracts** are controlled by the law of the state where the place of delivery is located;

iii) **Life-insurance contracts** are controlled by the law of the state where the insured is domiciled (*see* § I Domicile, *supra*, for a discussion of the rules regarding domicile);

iv) **Casualty insurance contracts** are controlled by the law of the state where the insured risk is located;

v) **Loans** are controlled by the law of the state where repayment is required;

vi) **Suretyship contracts** are controlled by the law of the state governing the principal obligation; and

vii) **Transportation contracts** (covering both persons and goods) are controlled by the law of the state where the place of departure is located.

> **EXAM NOTE:** Remember, the most significant relationship still prevails, and the default rules relating to these specific kinds of contracts are subject to exception if there are other factors showing a more significant relationship to another state.

d. Governmental-interest approach

The governmental-interest approach does not change based on substantive areas of law. *See* § II.B.3 Governmental-Interest Approach, *supra*, for the rules governing the governmental-interest approach.

3. Property

Property can be classified as real or personal. The law of the place where the property is situated generally determines whether it is real or personal. Note that the law can change when property is removed from one state to another. Thus, the character of the same property, whether personal or real, may vary according to its location.

a. Tangible personal property

1) UCC

The UCC generally governs most issues involving the sale of (or security interests in) tangible personal property. Under the UCC, the parties may stipulate to the applicable law that will govern the transaction or, in the absence of such stipulation, the forum state will apply its version of the UCC "to transactions bearing an appropriate relation to" the forum state. UCC § 1-301. If a particular code provision specifies the applicable law, a contrary agreement is effective only to the extent permitted by the law (including the conflict-of-laws rules) so specified. UCC § 1-301(c).

Under the UCC, the law governing the perfection, the effect of perfection or nonperfection, and the priority of security interests in tangible collateral is generally the law of the state in which the debtor is located. UCC § 9-301(1). In general, this means the principal residence of an individual, the place of business of an organization, and the chief executive office of an organization with more than one place of business. UCC § 9-307(b). Registered organizations (i.e., corporations, limited partnerships, and other entities requiring registration under state law), however, are located in their state of registration rather than the state of their principal place of business. UCC § 9-307(e). If the debtor or the collateral moves to another state, then the secured party generally has a fixed period of time to perfect his security interest there or it will become unperfected and will be deemed never to have been perfected as against a previous or subsequent purchaser of the collateral for value. The period of time is generally four months in the case of the debtor and one year in the case of collateral. UCC § 9-316.

When the debtor and the collateral are located in different states, there are special rules. If the security interest is a possessory security interest, then the law of the state where the collateral is located determines perfection, the effect of perfection or nonperfection, and the priority of that security interest. UCC § 9-301(2). In addition, with regard to tangible negotiable documents, goods, instruments, money, or tangible chattel paper, the law of the state where the collateral is located determines the effect of perfection or nonperfection and the priority of a nonpossessory security interest in the collateral, while the law of the place of the debtor continues to determine the issue of perfection itself unless the collateral is a fixture or timber to be cut, in which case the law of the location of the collateral also controls the issue of perfection itself. UCC § 9-301(3).

2) Transactions not covered by the UCC

For transactions not covered by the UCC, one of the following approaches will generally be followed by the forum court.

a) Vested-rights approach

Under the vested-rights approach of the Restatement (First) of Conflict of Laws, the creation and transfer of interests in tangible personal property are governed by the law of the state in which the property was located at the time of the transaction at issue. This rule controls even when the property at issue may have been taken to another state without the permission of the owner.

b) Most-significant-relationship approach

Under the most-significant-relationship approach of the Restatement (Second) of Conflict of Laws, the law of the situs of the tangible personal property at the time that the relevant transaction took place generally determines the choice of law. However, if it is determined that another state has a more significant relationship to the transaction, then that state's law will apply.

c) Governmental-interest approach

The governmental-interest approach does not change based on substantive areas of law. *See* § II.B.3 Governmental-Interest Approach, *supra*, for the rules governing the governmental-interest approach.

b. Intangible property

1) UCC

As noted above (*see* § II.C.2 Contracts, *supra*), under the UCC, the law governing the perfection, the effect of perfection or nonperfection, and priority of security interests in intangible collateral is generally the law of the state in which the debtor is located. UCC § 9-301.

For issues involving corporate securities, the law of the issuer's state of incorporation generally controls. UCC § 8-110.

2) Transactions not covered by the UCC

a) Vested-rights approach

An intangible (e.g., a claim, a share of stock, a promissory note) has no physical situs. Under the vested-rights approach of the Restatement (First) of Conflict of Laws, such intangibles are governed by the law of the state in which the intangible was created.

b) Most-significant-relationship approach

Under the most-significant-relationship approach of the Restatement (Second) of Conflict of Laws, the transfer of intangible property is governed by the law of the state to which the transaction is most significantly related. *See* § II.B.2 Most-Significant-Relationship Approach, *supra*, for the seven factors that are generally used to determine the most significant relationship.

c) Governmental-interest approach

The governmental-interest approach does not change based on substantive areas of law. *See* § II.B.3 Governmental-Interest Approach, *supra*, for the rules governing the governmental-interest approach.

c. Real property

1) Vested-rights approach

Under the vested-rights approach of the Restatement (First) of Conflict of Laws, the law of the situs of the real property governs legal issues concerning the title and disposition of real property and whether any interests in the property can be gained or lost. Such issues can include the formalities required for instruments affecting the title to real property and the validity of transfers and mortgages of the property. The forum state will refer to the law of the situs state even with regard to the choice-of-law rules.

2) Most-significant-relationship approach

Under the most-significant-relationship approach of the Restatement (Second) of Conflict of Laws, the law of the situs of the real property is generally presumed to be most significant. *See* § II.B.2 Most-Significant-Relationship Approach, *supra*, for the seven factors that are generally used to determine the most significant relationship.

3) Governmental-interest approach

The governmental-interest approach does not change based on substantive areas of law. *See* § II.B.3 Governmental-Interest Approach, *supra*, for the rules governing the governmental-interest approach. Note, though, that under the governmental-interest approach, less importance is placed on the situs than under the other two major choice-of-law approaches. If another state has a more significant relationship to the case, then its law will prevail.

4) Equitable conversion

Some states apply the doctrine of equitable conversion, under which as soon as a valid contract is made for the sale of real property, the buyer is deemed the owner of the land, and the seller is deemed a trustee for the buyer. At the same time, the seller is deemed the owner of the money, while the buyer is deemed a trustee for the seller. Whether the doctrine of equitable conversion will apply to a transaction is governed by the law of the state in which the land at issue is located.

> **Example:** Alice is domiciled in state 1 and contracts with Bill to sell him land in state 2. Under state 1's law, a purchaser has equitable title to land under a contract of sale. Under state 2's law, Bill has no equitable interest in the land. Because the land is located in state 2, the doctrine of equitable conversion is inapplicable, and Bill has no equitable interest in the land.

d. Trust property and trust administration

Transfers of trust property are governed by the appropriate rules indicated above for the particular type of property. A property question that involves the administration of a trust, however, is usually governed by the law of the place where the trust is administered.

4. Inheritance

There are many questions that may arise when determining the law that governs inheritance. These questions include the validity of the will, the rights of nonmarital or adopted children to inherit property, and the marital rights of the surviving spouse. Which state's laws will govern these issues will depend upon the type of property at issue.

a. Personal property

Questions regarding the transfer of personal property from someone who dies intestate or who has a will are governed by **the law of the deceased's domicile** at the time of death.

b. Real property

Questions regarding the transfer of real property from someone who dies intestate or who has a will are governed by **the law of the situs**.

> **EXAM NOTE:** Note that for the decedent's personal property, the question of whether a person has died testate or intestate is determined by the law of the decedent's domicile, but for the decedent's real estate, this question is decided by the law of the place where the real estate is situated.

c. Equitable conversion

As noted above (*see* § II.C.3.c.4 Equitable conversion, *supra*), the application of the doctrine of equitable conversion is governed by the law of the state in which the land at issue is located. The doctrine of equitable conversion can also apply to testamentary directions to sell real property and distribute the proceeds. If the directions are absolute and leave the executor with no discretion, then the real estate is turned into personalty under the doctrine of equitable conversion as soon as the will takes effect. Thus, if a will instructs an executor to sell real property, then the doctrine of equitable conversion may be applicable, and the interest in real property may be treated as an interest in personalty if the will is valid under the law of the state where the real property is located.

5. Corporations

Under the vested-rights approach of the Restatement (First) of Conflict of Laws, the law of the state of incorporation governs questions regarding the existence of the corporation (creation and dissolution) and issues about its structure, the rights of shareholders, and other internal corporate affairs. The Restatement (Second) of Conflict of Laws concurs in concluding that the law of the state of incorporation decides such questions. *See* § II.B.3 Governmental-Interest Approach, *supra*, for the rules governing the governmental-interest approach.

6. Family Law

a. Marriage

1) In general

In general, marriages are valid where they took place and are recognized in all other states. This also holds true for voided marriages. If a marriage violates a particularly strong public policy of the domicile of either party, however, it will be invalid. Such policies can include bigamy and incest.

2) Violation of a prohibitory rule

A marriage that is valid in the state where it took place but that violates a prohibitory rule of the domicile of one of the parties will be void in the state where the marriage would have been prohibited if the parties immediately return to that state and become domiciled there. A prohibitory rule is a rule that expresses the strong public policy of a state, such as rules against bigamy, incest, or marriage below a minimum age. Even though one state may refuse to recognize such a marriage, other states are not required to respect such policy and may choose to recognize the marriage.

3) Annulment

In cases of annulment, the court will generally look to the jurisdiction where the ceremony took place to determine whether the law permits the annulment.

b. Divorce and marital property

Questions of law relating to the grounds for divorce are controlled by the law of the plaintiff's domicile in a divorce matter.

For issues regarding marital property already owned by either spouse at the time of the marriage, the law of the situs will control with regard to real property, while the law of the domicile will control with respect to personal property. For personal property acquired during the marriage, the law that controls is the law of the domicile of the parties at the time of the acquisition. For real property acquired during the marriage, the law that controls is the law of the situs of the real property. Note, though, that if marital funds or property are used by one spouse to acquire land in another state, then the land that is acquired has the same character as the funds or property used to acquire it. Thus, if a wife in a community-property state purchases a house in a separate-property state using community funds, the house will be community property and not separate property.

In determining the enforceability of a premarital agreement, most states apply the law of the state with the most significant relationship to the matter at hand. *See* Restatement (Second) of Conflict of Laws § 188.

c. Legitimacy

Legitimacy is the legal kinship between a child and her parent(s). The status of a child's legitimacy at birth is governed by the law of the domicile of the parent whose relationship to the child is in question.

d. Legitimation

A child who was born illegitimate may, by force of law, become legitimate through the marriage of her parents or if the child's parent acknowledges the child as his own. A child will usually be legitimate if this would be the child's status under the local law of the state where either (i) the parent was domiciled when the child's status of legitimacy is claimed to have been created, or (ii) where the child was domiciled when the parent acknowledged the child as his own.

e. Adoption

The forum court will apply its own state law to determine whether to grant an adoption.

7. Workers' Compensation

Workers' compensation is governed by state statutes and administered by state agencies. Conflicts between state laws can develop, though, particularly with regard to which state can award benefits.

a. Jurisdiction

1) In general

Any state with a legitimate interest in an injury and its consequences may apply its workers'-compensation act. *Alaska Packers Ass'n. v. Indus. Accident Comm'n*, 294 U.S. 532 (1935). In general (and this can vary depending on the state's statute), a state will have a legitimate interest if it is the state where (i) the employment relationship was entered into by the worker and the employer, (ii) the injury to the employee occurred, (iii) the employment relationship principally occurred (even if the injury did not occur there), or (iv) the employee or the employee's dependents reside. *See Pac. Employers Ins. Co. v. Indus. Accident Comm'n*, 306 U.S. 493 (1939); Restatement (Second) of Conflict of Laws § 181 (1971).

Note that issues that arise with regard to workers' compensation are not always a choice of law between one state and another. Rather, the forum court decides whether its state's interests are sufficient to permit a recovery under its own workers'-compensation statute. If the forum court determines that it does not have sufficient interest to apply its statute, then the case will likely be dismissed without prejudice. The forum court will not choose to apply another jurisdiction's workers'-compensation act.

2) Contractual choice-of-law provision

An employer and employee may agree as part of the employment contract that a certain state's workers'-compensation laws will govern. Such agreement will generally be upheld so long as it is reasonable and does not violate the public policy of another state that has a legitimate interest.

b. Recovery in more than one state

If more than one state is involved and has a legitimate interest, then each state's workers'-compensation statutes should be compared before determining which law governs. For example, if one state bars an independent tort action or limits such an action under its workers'-compensation statute (see discussion below) while another does not, then that can significantly affect the decision of in which state the worker will want to file a compensation claim.

A subsequent workers'-compensation award in another state is barred only if there is "unmistakable language by a state legislature or judiciary" barring such recovery. *Industrial Commission of Wis. v. McCartin*, 330 U.S. 622 (1947). Amounts paid under a prior award must be credited against any subsequent recovery in another state to avoid a double recovery.

c. Immunity

The law is currently unclear as to whether an employee is permitted to bring a tort or wrongful-death action against an employer from whom the employee has already been awarded damages in a workers'-compensation action in another state if the workers'-compensation statute of the other state grants the employer immunity from tort liability. A plurality of the U.S. Supreme Court has held that a state may grant supplemental workers'-compensation benefits to an employee who previously received such benefits against the same person under another state's workers'-compensation statute. *See Thomas v. Washington Gas Light*, 448 U.S. 261 (1980). As noted above, the second state is required to credit the amount awarded by the first state in order to avoid a double recovery.

Immunity is generally given only to the employer under a state's workers'-compensation act. Thus, other parties, such as manufacturers of defective equipment, could be liable in tort despite the workers'-compensation award. *See Carroll v. Lanza*, 349 U.S. 408 (1955). A third party that is held liable in tort will generally not be permitted to seek indemnification from the injured employee's employer who has complied with the state's workers'-compensation statute.

D. DEFENSES AGAINST APPLICATION OF FOREIGN LAW

There are generally three arguments against the application of foreign law, that the law to be applied is:

i) Procedural, rather than substantive;

ii) Against public policy; or

iii) A penal law.

1. **Substance/Procedure Distinction**

   If the foreign law sought to be applied is procedural, then the forum state's law will always govern. The forum state's law is applied to determine whether a law is substantive or procedural, so long as the result is not arbitrary or so unreasonable as to constitute a denial of due process or full faith and credit.

   a. **Procedural**

      Questions about the following matters are generally considered procedural and are controlled by the law of the forum state:

      i) The proper court in which to bring an action;

      ii) The form of the action to be brought;

      iii) The sufficiency of the pleadings;

      iv) The effect of splitting a cause of action;

      v) The proper or necessary parties to an action;

      vi) Whether a counterclaim may be brought;

      vii) Venue;

      viii) The rules of discovery;

      ix) The right to a jury trial;

      x) Service of process;

      xi) The burden of proof;

      xii) Trial procedure; and

      xiii) The methods of enforcing a judgment.

   b. **Evidence and privileges**

      1) **Admissibility of evidence**

         Questions regarding the admissibility of evidence are usually considered procedural and are controlled by the law of the forum state.

      2) **Existence or validity of privilege**

         Issues relating to the existence of a privilege are treated differently from other evidentiary issues depending on the choice-of-law approach applicable in the forum. Under the vested-rights approach of the Restatement (First) of Conflict of Laws, the existence and validity of a privilege is considered procedural and is governed by the law of the forum state. Under the most-significant-relationship approach of the Restatement (Second) of Conflict of Laws, the law of the state with the most significant relationship to the privileged communication will control. Under the governmental-interest approach, the underlying interests of the competing states are weighed to determine whether a particular privilege should apply.

      3) **Parol evidence rule**

         Questions regarding the application of the parol evidence rule are considered substantive and are controlled by the law of the state that governs the validity of the contract. *See* § II.C.2 Contracts, *supra*.

c. Statute of limitations

Statutes of limitations are usually considered procedural, with the law of the forum state controlling. The theory for such treatment is that the statute of limitations bars the remedy but does not extinguish the underlying substantive right. However, there are several exceptions to this general rule.

1) Right versus remedy

If the statute of limitations limits a statutory right, as opposed to simply limiting a remedy, it will be substantive rather than procedural. Generally, a limitation period in a statute that creates a right, such as a wrongful-death act, will be treated as substantive.

2) Prescription or adverse possession

If the statute of limitations vests as a result of prescription or adverse possession, it will be treated as substantive.

3) Borrowing statutes

Most states have adopted "borrowing statutes," which bar suits on foreign causes of action that are precluded under the shorter of the forum state's statute of limitations or the statute of limitations of the place where the cause of action arose (for tort cases, the place of the wrong; for contract cases, generally the place where the contract was to be performed).

4) Restatement (Second) of Conflict of Laws approach

The most-significant-relationship approach of the Restatement (Second) of Conflict of Laws applies to statute of limitations issues. *See* § II.B.2 Most-Significant-Relationship Approach, *supra*. Under this approach, the forum will apply its own state's statute of limitations barring the claim, unless (i) maintenance of the claim would serve no substantial interest of the forum, and (ii) the claim would be barred under the statute of limitations of a state having a more significant relationship to the parties and the occurrence. Restatement (Second) of Conflict of Laws § 142 (1988 Revision).

d. Statute of repose

Statutes of repose limit the time within which an action may be brought, regardless of whether an injury has occurred or been discovered. It cuts off the right to a cause of action before it accrues. It is considered substantive rather than procedural, and it is controlled by the law of the state that governs the action under its choice-of-law rules.

e. Statute of Frauds

A Statute of Frauds is considered substantive rather than procedural. Questions regarding the Statute of Frauds are controlled by the law of the state that governs the validity of the contract. *See* § II.C.2 Contracts, *supra*.

f. Survival of actions

The issue of whether a tort action survives the death of the plaintiff is treated as substantive and is controlled by the law of the state that governs the action under its choice-of-law rules.

g. Damages

States are split as to whether the measure of damages is procedural or substantive. The majority rule is that damages are substantive and measured by the law that governs the subject matter from which the damages arise.

h. Federal diversity cases

Under the *Erie* doctrine, in diversity jurisdiction cases, federal district courts must apply the substantive law of the state where the court sits. *Erie R. Co. v. Tompkins*, 304 U.S. 64 (1938). The *Erie* doctrine does not require that the state's procedural laws be applied, however, and if a Federal Rule of Civil Procedure addresses the procedural issue at hand, then that rule will be applied. If no federal rule applies, then the district court must follow state law with regard to substance, but it can choose to ignore state law with regard to procedure, under certain circumstances. To determine whether a given law is substantive or procedural, the court considers whether the failure to apply state law would lead to different outcomes in state and federal courts. If the answer is yes, then the court will generally apply state law.

2. Laws Against Public Policy

Both the Restatement (First) of Conflict of Laws and the Restatement (Second) of Conflict of Laws provide that if a foreign law violates the public policy of the forum state, then the forum court may refuse to apply that law. If the public-policy exception is applicable, then the court dismisses the action without prejudice. Public-policy concerns must be fundamental and strongly held, and the mere variance between the foreign law and the forum law is not enough to deny the application of the foreign law. The forum court must closely scrutinize the foreign law and the forum state's public policy. Under the governmental-interest approach, this defense is not incorporated. Instead, the forum state will apply its public policy affirmatively in reaching a decision to apply its own law.

3. Penal Laws

Both the Restatement (First) of Conflict of Laws and the Restatement (Second) of Conflict of Laws provide that a forum state will not enforce another state's penal laws. For penal laws, only an actual criminal prosecution is prohibited, not a civil action involving monetary sanctions, which might otherwise be considered a penalty. The Restatement (Second) of Conflict of Laws specifically excludes wrongful-death actions and cases based on the statutory liability of officers, directors, and shareholders of corporations for debts from being considered penal in nature.

E. PROOF OF FOREIGN LAW

Historically, the laws of another state were not considered law at all but were treated as facts to be proven in court. If the law that controlled was not forum law, then the parties were required to carefully comply with the forum's rules for pleading and proving foreign law. Such rules were procedural and governed by forum law. If neither party raised the applicability of foreign law in its pleadings, then forum law would generally be applied.

Most states today allow their courts to take judicial notice of other states' laws and federal laws and treat them as law rather than fact. Some states allow judicial notice of the laws of a foreign country. Others require that they be proved as fact. By federal common law, federal courts must take judicial notice of the laws of all states. *Lamar v. Micou*, 114 U.S. 218 (1885). Federal law requires pleading and proof of foreign country law. *See* Federal Rules of Civil Procedure 44.1.

III. RECOGNITION OF FOREIGN JUDGMENTS

A. FULL FAITH AND CREDIT JUDGMENTS

Article IV, § 1 of the U.S. Constitution, the Full Faith and Credit Clause, provides that "Full Faith and Credit shall be given in each State to the public Acts, Records, and judicial Proceedings of every other State." The clause is invoked primarily to enforce the judgment of one state court in another state. If a valid judgment is rendered by a court that has jurisdiction over the parties, and the parties receive proper notice of the action and a reasonable opportunity to be heard, then the Full Faith and Credit Clause requires that the judgment receive the same effect in other states as it receives in the state where it was rendered. Thus, a party who obtains a judgment in one state may petition the court in another state to enforce the judgment. The issues are not relitigated, and the court in the state where enforcement is sought must honor the judgment of the other state's court.

Almost all of the states have adopted the Uniform Enforcement of Foreign Judgments Act (UEFJA) which provides uniform procedures for filing an out-of-state judgment with the clerk of court. Filing the judgment under UEFJA gives it the same effect as a judgment of the court in the state in which it is filed.

Note, though, that the party against whom enforcement is sought may collaterally challenge the original state judgment based on lack of personal jurisdiction, or subject-matter jurisdiction, if the jurisdictional issues were not litigated or waived in the original action. *Durfee v. Duke*, 375 U.S. 106 (1963).

The requirement of full faith and credit extends to the res judicata effect of the original state court judgment. Thus, if the original state court judgment would bar a subsequent action in the original state, then it acts to bar a subsequent action in any other state. This is the case even if the subsequent action would otherwise be permitted in that state.

1. Requirements

For a judgment to meet the full faith and credit requirements, it must:

i)   Have been brought in the proper jurisdiction;

> Note that if the question of jurisdiction was fully and fairly litigated in the original case, such determination will itself be entitled to full faith and credit, even if it was wrong.

ii) Be finalized, with no appeals outstanding; and

iii) Be on the merits, meaning the substantive issues were decided by a court, rather than the matter being resolved by procedural issues such as improper jurisdiction, venue, or the statute of limitations.

> A judgment on the merits would include a judgment entered after full trial, a summary judgment, a judgment as a matter of law, and a default judgment.

A determination of whether the full faith and credit requirements have been met is made by looking to the law of the state that rendered the judgment. If a valid, final judgment is inconsistent with another valid, final judgment, then the most recent judgment is entitled to full faith and credit.

2. Defenses to Full Faith and Credit of Judgments

a. Penal judgments

Penal judgments (cases in which the judgment is punishment for an offense against the public) do not have to be enforced.

b. Equitable defenses

Equitable defenses such as extrinsic fraud do not have to be enforced. Note that only extrinsic fraud cases, such as a misrepresentation of facts by a party or a party's attorney that does not allow the case to be tried fully with all of the evidence, fall under this defense. Intrinsic fraud, such as perjured testimony, would not constitute a valid defense.

c. Inconsistent judgments

If there are inconsistent judgments between the same parties with regard to the same cause of action, then courts resolve this problem by recognizing the last judgment that was rendered.

d. Erroneous proceedings—no defense

A state may not refuse to recognize the judgment of another state because the other state made a mistake of fact or law. Such mistakes must generally be attacked on direct appeal of the original judgment.

3. Res Judicata Effects

If all of the Full Faith and Credit requirements are met, then the judgment is entitled to res judicata in other states as well as in the original state that decided the judgment. These effects include merger and bar.

a. Merger

If the judgment is final and the plaintiff won, then a merger of the plaintiff's cause of action into the plaintiff's judgment occurs. As a result, the defendant is prohibited from relitigating on the merits of the case.

b. Bar

If a judgment has been rendered and the final judgment is in favor of the defendant, then the plaintiff may not file another suit for that same cause of action in another state.

4. Collateral Estoppel

Collateral estoppel eliminates the opportunity for parties to litigate an issue again in a subsequent suit. Collateral estoppel applies when:

i) The substantive issue of the case at hand was previously litigated;

ii) The issue was necessary to supporting the judgment in the initial proceeding; and

iii) The party against whom collateral estoppel will be applied was either a party in the original suit or had access to information from the original proceeding and had a full and fair opportunity to litigate the issue in the original suit.

5. Enforcement

Judgments determined to be entitled to full faith and credit must be enforced. This is true even if the judgment was granted erroneously, as long as it is not barred by one of the defenses discussed above (merger and bar). The law of the state that is recognizing the judgment governs the method of enforcement.

6. **Federal Court Judgments**

   a. **Federal-to-state recognition**

   Under 28 U.S.C. § 1738, federal courts must also give full faith and credit to state court judgments. The same rules as discussed above for states apply with respect to a federal court. A federal court will not give greater effect to a state court judgment than the state itself would give.

   b. **State-to-federal recognition for diversity cases**

   If a federal court with diversity jurisdiction over an action issues a judgment, then a state court must give such judgment the same res judicata effect that the judgment would have been given by the courts of the state where the federal court was located. *Semtek Int'l Inc. v. Lockheed Martin Corp.*, 531 U.S. 497 (2001).

B. **RECOGNITION OF JUDGMENTS FROM FOREIGN COUNTRIES**

1. **Comity**

   Comity is the voluntary agreement to recognize a foreign judgment. In most cases, full faith and credit is not extended to cases decided in foreign countries, except in cases in which there are treaties agreeing to recognize certain judgments. U.S. courts have discretion to decide whether to recognize foreign country judgments. In deciding whether to recognize such judgments, the forum court will consider whether the foreign court had jurisdiction over the matter and whether the foreign court used fair procedures in deciding the case. If recognition of a foreign country judgment is granted, then the law of the state that is recognizing the judgment governs the method of enforcement.

2. **Uniform Foreign Money-Judgments Recognition Act**

   Many states have adopted the Uniform Foreign Money-Judgments Recognition Act. The act covers foreign judgments that grant or deny specific lump sums of money, but it excludes judgments for taxes, judgments for alimony or child support, and penal judgments.

C. **RECOGNITION OF DIVORCE JUDGMENTS**

Divorce decrees from other states are entitled to full faith and credit as long as the original state had jurisdiction to issue the decree and the decree is valid in the original state. Decrees have proper jurisdiction if at least one person resides where the decree was issued.

1. **Bilateral Divorce**

   If the court has personal jurisdiction over both spouses and at least one spouse is domiciled in the state, then the divorce judgment will be a valid bilateral divorce and will be entitled to full faith and credit.

2. **Ex Parte Divorce**

   An ex parte divorce is a divorce based on the domicile of only one of the spouses. For an ex parte divorce to be afforded full faith and credit, it must adhere to the subject-matter jurisdiction rules, namely that at least one person must reside in the state. Personal jurisdiction must exist over one spouse. The difference between a bilateral divorce and an ex parte divorce is that in an ex parte divorce, full faith and credit is **not** given to other marital agreements such as property rights, alimony, and child custody. However, a divorce order dealing with property rights, alimony, or custody will be binding if the nondomiciled spouse agrees. A bilateral divorce decree will generally receive full faith and credit with regard to such matters.

3. Estoppel Against Collateral Attack

Anyone who has an interest in a case may collaterally attack the validity of another state's decrees. However, when the third party is in privity with one of the parties to the divorce, the third party may be estopped from making an attack based on that party's relationship to the initial proceedings. The spouse who brought the proceeding in the original court is estopped from challenging its validity.

4. Child Custody

There is a reciprocal statute in all 50 states that governs child custody: the Uniform Child Custody Jurisdiction and Enforcement Act (UCCJEA). Under the UCCJEA, a court can make initial custody decisions if it is in the child's home state, and all other states must give full faith and credit to such decisions. Other states cannot modify these custody decrees unless the original court has no significant connection to the child or parents anymore (i.e., neither the child nor the parents reside in that state anymore).

5. Property and Alimony

Bilateral divorces usually include all issues related to property and alimony. Full faith and credit is given to these provisions in a divorce. In ex parte divorces, however, the parties must settle issues related to property and alimony in a court that has personal jurisdiction over both parties.

6. Divorce Judgments From Foreign Countries

Courts will generally extend comity to foreign divorce judgments, as long as the requirements of domicile are met. With respect to other divorce-related agreements such as alimony, property, and child custody, the rules are usually followed the same as if the judgment came from another state.

Corporations

CORPORATIONS

Table of Contents

CORPORATIONS

I. FORMATION

A. PRE-INCORPORATION TRANSACTIONS

1. Promoters

Prior to the formation of a corporation, a promoter engages in activities, such as procuring capital and entering into contracts, to bring the corporation into existence as a business entity.

a. Liability for pre-incorporation agreements

A promoter is personally liable for **knowingly acting** on behalf of a corporation before incorporation and is jointly and severally liable for all liabilities created while so acting, even after the corporation comes into existence, unless a subsequent novation releases the promoter from liability. Revised Model Business Corporation Act (RMBCA) § 2.04. To establish liability, it is insufficient that a person should have known that the corporation was not formed; actual knowledge of the entity's pre-incorporation status is required. *See Sivers v. R & F Capital Corp.*, 858 P.2d 895, 898 (Or. Ct. App. 1993). In addition, if a party who contracts with a promoter knows that the corporation has not yet been formed and agrees to look only to the corporation for performance, then the promoter is not liable.

> **EXAM NOTE:** Promoter liability is often tested in the context of pre-incorporation agreements. Remember that promoters are liable to third parties for pre-incorporation agreements even after incorporation, unless a novation occurs, the promoter has no actual knowledge that the corporation's charter has not yet been issued, or the contracting party knows that a corporation has not yet been formed and agrees to look only to the corporation for performance.

b. Fiduciary duty to the corporation

A promoter stands in a fiduciary relationship with the pre-incorporated corporation. The promoter can be liable to the corporation for violating a fiduciary duty, such as by making a secret profit (e.g., failing to disclose a commission on a pre-incorporation transaction).

c. Right to reimbursement

Although a promoter can seek compensation for pre-incorporation activities undertaken on the corporation's behalf and reimbursement for related expenses, the promoter cannot compel the corporation to make such payments, because the promoter's acts, although done to benefit the corporation, are not undertaken at the corporation's direction.

2. Corporation's Liability for Pre-incorporation Transactions

a. General rule—no liability

A corporation is not liable for pre-incorporation transactions entered into by a promoter. The fact that the promoter entered into a transaction to benefit a future corporation is not sufficient to hold the corporation liable.

Because a corporation is not necessarily in existence during a pre-incorporation transaction, a principal-agent relationship does not exist between the corporation and the promoter.

b. Exception—liability upon contract adoption

The corporation can be liable when the corporation adopts the contract. Adoption of a contract can be express or implied. Adoption takes place when the corporation accepts the benefits of the transaction or gives an express acceptance of liability for the debt, such as through board resolution after incorporation.

3. Incorporator Liability

An incorporator is a person who signs and files the articles of incorporation with the state. By performing such acts, an incorporator does not engender liability for a contract entered into by a promoter of the corporation.

B. INCORPORATION

1. Procedures

To form a corporation, a document, referred to as the "articles of incorporation" or "charter," must be filed with the state.

a. Articles of incorporation

The articles of incorporation must include certain basic information about the corporation, such as its name, the number of shares it is authorized to issue, the name and address of its registered agent, and the name and address of each incorporator. RMBCA § 2.02(a).

1) Corporate name

The corporation's name must contain the word "corporation," "company," "incorporated," "limited," or an abbreviation thereof.

2) Corporate purpose

The articles of incorporation may include a statement of the corporation's purposes. A broad statement of such purpose, such as "to engage in any lawful activity," is acceptable. The RMBCA presumes that each corporation has the broadest lawful purpose unless a more limited purpose is defined in the articles of incorporation. RMBCA § 3.01.

3) Corporate powers

In addition to specifying purposes, the articles of incorporation may enumerate powers that the corporation possesses. Most states automatically grant all corporations broad powers, such as the powers to buy and sell property and to sue and be sued. RMBCA § 3.02. Some states place restrictions on various corporate actions, including corporate loans to officers and directors. For a corporation with stock listed on a national securities exchange, federal law prohibits the corporation from making personal loans to a director or an executive officer of the corporation. 15 U.S.C. § 78m.

4) Corporate duration

A corporation has perpetual existence unless the articles of incorporation provide otherwise. RMBCA § 3.02.

b. Filing requirements

The articles of incorporation must be filed with a state official, usually with the secretary of state, and a filing fee paid. Unless a delayed date is specified in the articles, the corporate existence begins when the articles of incorporation are filed. The articles may not set an earlier date than the date of filing. RMBCA § 2.03(a).

Once the requirements are met, some states treat the corporation as having been formed as of the date of the filing, while other states consider the corporation a legal entity only when the state has accepted the articles of incorporation. RMBCA §§ 1.23, 2.03.

2. Ultra Vires Actions

When a corporation that has stated a narrow business purpose in its articles of incorporation subsequently engages in activities outside that stated purpose, the corporation has engaged in an ultra vires act. When a third party enters into a transaction with the corporation that constitutes an ultra vires act for the corporation, the third party generally cannot assert that the corporation has acted outside those powers in order to escape liability.

a. Challenges to ultra vires acts

An ultra vires act can be challenged in only the following three situations:

i) A shareholder can file suit to enjoin the corporation's ultra vires action;

ii) The corporation can take action against a director, an officer, or an employee of the corporation who engages in such action; or

iii) The state can initiate a proceeding against the corporation to enjoin its ultra vires action.

RMBCA § 3.04(b).

b. Enjoining an ultra vires act

An ultra vires act will be enjoined only if it is equitable to do so.

3. Effect of Incorporation—"De Jure" Corporation

When all of the statutory requirements for incorporation have been satisfied, a de jure corporation is created. Consequently, the corporation, rather than persons associated with the corporation (i.e., shareholders, directors, officers, and other employees), is liable for activities undertaken by the corporation.

4. Defective Incorporation

a. Lack of good-faith effort to incorporate

When a person conducts business as a corporation without attempting to comply with the statutory incorporation requirements, that person is liable for any obligations incurred in the name of the nonexistent corporation. RMBCA § 2.04.

b. Good-faith effort to incorporate

When a person makes an unsuccessful effort to comply with the incorporation requirements, that person may be able to escape personal liability under either the de facto corporation doctrine or the corporation by estoppel doctrine.

1) De facto corporation

The owner must make a good-faith effort to comply with the incorporation requirements and must operate the business as a corporation without knowing that these requirements have not been met. If the owner has done so, then the business entity is treated as a de facto corporation, and the owner, as a de facto shareholder, is not personally liable for obligations incurred in the purported corporation's name. Note, however, that the RMBCA has abolished this doctrine, as have many of the jurisdictions that have adopted the RMBCA. *See, e.g., In re Estate of Woodroffe*, 742 N.W.2d 94 (Iowa 2007).

2) Corporation by estoppel

A person who deals with an entity as if it were a corporation is estopped from denying its existence and is thereby prevented from seeking the personal liability of the business owner. This doctrine is limited to contractual agreements. In addition, the business owner must have made a good-faith effort to comply with incorporation requirements and must lack knowledge that the requirements were not met.

II. STOCK AND OTHER CORPORATE SECURITIES

A. TYPES

Traditionally, there are two broad types of securities by which a corporation secures financing for its endeavors: stocks, which carry ownership and control interests in the corporation, and debt securities, which do not. Over time, many securities have been created that blur this distinction. However, every corporation is required to have stock that is entitled to vote on matters of corporate governance (e.g., the election of directors to the board) and stock that represents the basic ownership interest in a corporation. RMBCA § 6.01(b). Stocks that possess these two characteristics are referred to as "common stock." Stocks having preference over other stock to such items as distributions are referred to as "preferred stock."

In general, upon liquidation, a secured creditor of the corporation will generally take precedence over a preferred shareholder with regard to the corporation's funds, and a preferred shareholder will take precedence over a common shareholder. Preferred shareholders generally take precedence over common shareholders with regard to distributions by the corporation.

B. ISSUANCE OF STOCK

When a corporation sells or trades its stock to an investor, the transaction from the corporation's perspective requires the issuance of stock. The corporation may issue such stock, provided the articles of incorporation authorize the issuance. RMBCA § 6.03(a).

1. Authorization

In general, the issuance of stock must be authorized by the board of directors. RMBCA § 6.21(b). Many states also permit the shareholders to authorize the issuance of stock if the articles of incorporation so provide. RMBCA § 6.21(a).

2. Consideration

a. Types of consideration

The RMBCA removed restrictions on the types of consideration that can be accepted by a corporation in payment for its stock. Acceptable consideration includes money, tangible or intangible property, and services rendered to the corporation. RMBCA § 6.21(b).

b. Payment of consideration

When the corporation receives consideration for stock, the stock is deemed fully paid and nonassessable. RMBCA § 6.21(d). A shareholder who fails to pay the consideration is liable to the corporation, and any issued stock may be canceled. If stock has not been fully paid, then the corporation or a creditor of the corporation may be able to recover the unpaid amount from the shareholder. RMBCA § 6.22(a).

c. Valuation of consideration

Under the RMBCA, the board of directors must merely determine that the consideration received for the stock is adequate. Moreover, once the board makes such a determination, the adequacy of the consideration is not subject to challenge. RMBCA § 6.21(c).

1) Par-value stock

A corporation may, but is not required to, issue par value stock. For such stock, the corporation is required to receive at least the value assigned to that stock (i.e., par value), which need not be its market value and which can even be a nominal amount.

2) Watered stock

Because stock is deemed validly issued, paid in full, and nonassessable once the corporation receives adequate consideration (as determined by the board of directors), the RMBCA does not recognize or address the issue of "watered stock," i.e., stock that is issued for consideration less than par value.

3. Stock Subscriptions

Prior to incorporation, persons may subscribe to purchase stock from the corporation when it comes into existence.

a. Revocability

Unless the subscription agreement provides otherwise, a pre-incorporation subscription is irrevocable for six months from the date of the subscription, but a revocation can happen if all subscribers agree to it. RMBCA § 6.20(a).

b. Nonpayment by subscriber

A corporation can pursue normal collection methods when a subscriber fails to pay the subscription amount. In addition, the corporation can sell the stock to someone else, provided the corporation has made a written demand for payment and given the subscriber at least 20 days to comply with the demand. RMBCA § 6.20(d).

4. Stock Rights, Options, and Warrants

In addition to stock, a corporation may issue rights, options, or warrants to buy its stock. Generally, the board of directors has the authority to issue these instruments and to dictate their terms. RMBCA § 6.24.

5. Shareholder's Preemptive Rights

When the board of directors decides to issue new shares, the rights of shareholders to purchase those shares in order to maintain their proportional ownership share in the corporation are known as "preemptive rights." Shareholders automatically had such rights at common law, but the RMBCA explicitly precludes preemptive rights unless the articles of incorporation provide otherwise. RMBCA § 6.30(a).

Example: A and B, the only shareholders of Corporation X, each own 50 shares of stock. The board of directors of Corporation X authorizes the issuance of another 20 shares. With preemptive rights, A and B would each be entitled to purchase 10 additional shares of stock and would retain a 50 percent ownership interest in the corporation. Without such rights, A or B could become the controlling owner of Corporation X by purchasing at least 11 additional shares of the new stock offering.

a. Waiver

If the corporation elects to have preemptive rights, then a shareholder may waive that right. A waiver evidenced by a writing is **irrevocable**, regardless of whether it is supported by consideration. RMBCA § 6.30(b)(2).

b. Exceptions

Preemptive rights do not apply to shares that are:

i) Issued as compensation to directors, officers, agents, or employees of the corporation;

ii) Authorized in the articles of incorporation and issued within six months from the effective date of incorporation; or

iii) Sold for payment other than money (e.g., property).

RMBCA § 6.30(b)(3).

6. Federal Restrictions—Registration of Securities

Under the federal Securities Act of 1933, a corporation that issues stock or other securities may be required to register the security with the U.S. Securities and Exchange Commission (SEC). In addition to filing the required registration statement with the SEC, which involves significant disclosures about the company offering the security, the issuer is also required to provide the buyer of the security with a prospectus. The prospectus represents the main part of the registration statement, and it includes information about the company, its business, and its financial performance.

a. Public offerings

In general, registration is required only for public offerings of stocks or other securities that are considered public offerings. Offerings that are considered private, called "private placements," are exempt from the registration requirements. Private placements include stock sold by a corporation to institutional investors, sophisticated investors, and companies with annual sales of less than $1 million.

b. Civil liabilities

The purchaser of a security from a corporation that has not complied with the registration requirements may sue the corporation to rescind the transaction. In addition, the purchaser can sue for compensatory damages caused by a material misrepresentation or omission in the registration statement. The purchaser need not have relied on the error or omission, but she cannot have purchased with knowledge of the error or omission. Any of the following individuals may be liable:

i) The issuer;

ii) Any other signer of the registration statement (generally senior executives of the issuer);

iii) A director of the issuer at the time the statement is filed;

iv) An expert whose opinion is used in the registration statement; or

v) The underwriter of the issue.

The issuer is strictly liable, but the other defendants may defend on the basis of the reasonableness of their actions. This is referred to as a "due diligence" defense.

C. DISTRIBUTIONS

A distribution is the transfer of cash or other property from a corporation to one or more of its shareholders. The most common form of distribution is a dividend, which is normally a cash payment made to shareholders. Other forms of distribution include a distribution of indebtedness or a corporation's purchase of its own stock. RMBCA § 1.40(6).

1. Authorization by Board of Directors

The power to authorize a distribution rests with the board of directors. RMBCA § 6.40. Having authorized a distribution and set sufficient parameters, the board may delegate to a board committee or corporate officer the power to fix the amount and other terms of the distribution.

In general, a shareholder cannot compel the board of directors to authorize a distribution, because that decision is usually discretionary. When a board acts in bad faith and abuses its discretion by refusing to declare a distribution, however, a court may order the board to authorize a distribution. *Dodge v. Ford Motor Co.*, 170 N.W. 668 (Mich. 1919).

2. Limitations on Distributions

A corporation may not make a distribution if it is insolvent or if the distribution would cause the corporation to be insolvent. RMBCA § 6.40(c).

a. Insolvency determination

A corporation must pass two tests to be deemed solvent and, as such, capable of making a distribution: an equity test and a balance-sheet test.

1) Equity test

Under the equity test, a corporation must be able to pay off its debts as they come due in the usual course of business. RMBCA § 6.40(c)(1).

2) Balance-sheet test

Under the balance-sheet test, a corporation's total assets must exceed its total liabilities plus liquidation preferences of senior securities. RMBCA § 6.40(c)(1).

b. Time of measurement

In the case of a dividend, a corporation's solvency is measured on the date the dividend is declared; in the case of a stock purchase, it is measured on the date the purchase price is paid. RMBCA § 6.40(e).

3. Director's Liability for Unlawful Distributions

A director who votes for or assents to an unlawful distribution, in violation of the director's duties of care and loyalty, is personally liable to the corporation for the amount of the distribution in excess of the lawful amount.

a. Contribution from directors

A director is entitled to contribution from any other director who also is liable for the unlawful distribution. RMBCA § 8.33(b)(1).

b. Recoupment from shareholders

If a shareholder knowingly accepts an unlawful distribution, then a director is entitled to recoupment from that shareholder's pro rata portion of the unlawful distribution. RMBCA § 8.33(b)(2).

4. Dividend Distributions

Dividends are distributed to persons who are shareholders on the record date set by the board of directors. If the board does not set a date, then the dividend is payable to persons who are shareholders on the date that the board authorized the dividend. RMBCA § 6.40(b).

5. Suit to Compel a Dividend Distribution

A shareholder can sue to enforce her individual right; this is not the same as a derivative lawsuit that the shareholders bring on behalf of the corporation. *See, generally, Doherty v. Mutual Warehouse Co.*, 245 F.2d 609 (5th Cir. 1957); *Knapp v. Bankers Securities Corp.*, 230 F.2d 717 (3d Cir. 1956) (the right to compel a dividend is a primary and a personal right of the shareholder).

To prevail in a suit to compel a dividend distribution, a shareholder must prove the existence of (i) funds legally available for the payment of a dividend and (ii) bad faith on the part of the directors in their refusal to pay. *See Gay v. Gay's Super Markets, Inc.*, 343 A.2d 577 (Me. 1975).

6. Shares Reacquired by Corporation

Stock authorized and issued by the corporation is known as "outstanding stock." Such stock may be reacquired by the corporation through purchase or redemption (i.e., stock acquired by a forced sale). Upon repurchase or redemption, that stock constitutes authorized but unissued shares. If the articles of incorporation prohibit the reissuance of stock, then the number of authorized shares is automatically reduced by the number of shares purchased. RMBCA § 6.31.

7. Debt Distribution

Distribution of a corporation's indebtedness, such as bonds or promissory notes, is subject to the same requirements as other distributions. When indebtedness is to be repaid over time (i.e., on an installment basis), the lawfulness of the distribution is tested as of the date of distribution. RMBCA § 6.40(e). Corporate indebtedness received as a lawful distribution is on par with a corporation's general unsecured creditors. RMBCA § 6.40(f).

8. Stock Dividends—Not a Distribution

A corporation may issue its own stock to current shareholders without charge in lieu of making a distribution of cash or other property. Commonly referred to as "stock dividends" or "stock splits," these transactions do not alter the corporation's assets or liabilities, nor do they constitute a distribution. RMBCA § 6.23.

D. SALE OF SECURITIES

Generally, a shareholder is free to sell his stock to anyone at any time or price. Such freedom is subject to two significant restrictions: limitations imposed on shareholders of closely held corporations and penalties imposed on transactions that violate federal securities law.

1. Private Restrictions on Sale

Restrictions on the transfer of stock are generally found in closely held corporations. This is because owners of a closely held corporation often seek to maintain control over the corporation's business and profits by limiting the number of shareholders in a corporation. This limitation can be accomplished through restrictions on the transferability of shares.

a. Conspicuously noted

If the corporation issuing the shares imposes a restriction on transferability, the stock certificate must contain either a full and conspicuous statement of the restriction or a statement that the corporation will provide a shareholder with information about the restriction upon request and without charge. RMBCA § 6.27(b).

b. Enforceability

A restriction on the transfer of a security, even if otherwise lawful, may be ineffective against a person who has no knowledge of the restriction. Unless the security is certified and the restriction is conspicuously noted on the security certificate, that restriction is not enforceable against a person who has no knowledge of it. RMBCA § 6.27(b).

c. Forms of restriction

Restrictions on the transfer of stocks can take various forms, including:

    i)   An outright prohibition on transfers;

    ii)   Transfers requiring consent from the corporation or its shareholders;

    iii) Options to buy the stock held by the corporation or its shareholders;

    iv)   A right of first refusal (i.e., stock must be offered to the corporation or its shareholders before selling it to another person);

    v)   The corporation requires or has the right to buy back the stock; or

    vi)   A buy-sell agreement with either the corporation or its shareholders being obligated to buy the stock.

When a restricted transfer is permitted, the transfer itself may be required upon the occurrence of a specific event, such as the retirement, death, or divorce of the shareholder. RMBCA § 6.27(d).

d. Challenge to restrictions

Stock-transfer restrictions have been subject to challenge as unreasonable restraints on alienation. Of the various forms noted above, the outright prohibition on transfer and the need for prior consent are the most susceptible to attack. However, because the test is one of reasonableness, even these two forms may be justified in particular circumstances, such as when a corporation seeks to preserve its status because it is dependent on the number or identity of its shareholders. RMBCA § 6.27(c).

Because many of these restrictions are created through contractual arrangements, they may be subject to contractual defenses. In addition, the restrictions may be narrowly interpreted and subject to equitable challenges such as abandonment, waiver, or estoppel.

e. Persons bound by restrictions

Parties to an agreement that restricts stock transfers are bound by the terms of the contract. Other parties are not subject to a transfer restriction unless they are aware of it. If the restriction is noted on the face of the stock certificate, then the buyer may be treated as having had constructive notice of the restriction.

A transfer restriction imposed through an amendment of the articles of incorporation or corporate bylaws raises the question of whether persons who were shareholders before the restriction was imposed are subject to it. The RMBCA does not subject such shareholders to a restriction unless the shareholders voted in favor of the restriction or were parties to the restriction agreement. RMBCA § 6.27(a).

2. Sale of Control in a Closely Held Corporation

A shareholder with a controlling interest in a corporation that sells to an outsider may have a fiduciary obligation to the other shareholders. *See* § IV.E.2. Controlling Shareholder, *infra*.

3. Federal Causes of Action

Violations of 17 C.F.R. § 240.10b-5 ("**Rule 10b-5**") and Section 16(b) of the Securities Exchange Act of 1934, 15 U.S.C. § 78p, ("**Section 16(b)**"), which are based on the purchase and sale of stock and other securities, are federal causes of action and must be pursued in federal court. Because each involves a federal claim, diversity of citizenship is not needed.

The SEC also may enforce these provisions through civil penalties and criminal prosecution.

a. Rule 10b-5 action

The fraudulent purchase or sale of any stock or other security (e.g., bonds, stock options, and warrants) can give rise to a Rule 10b-5 action. For a private person to pursue a Rule 10b-5 action, **each** of the following requirements must be met:

i)   The plaintiff purchased or sold a security;

ii) The transaction involved the use of interstate commerce;

iii) The defendant engaged in fraudulent or deceptive conduct;

iv) The conduct related to material information;

v)   The defendant acted with scienter, i.e., with intent or recklessness;

vi) The plaintiff relied on the defendant's conduct; and

vii) The plaintiff suffered harm because of the defendant's conduct.

1) Plaintiff's purchase or sale of security

To maintain a Rule 10b-5 action, the plaintiff must have either bought or sold a security. A person who refrains from buying or selling a security because of the defendant's conduct cannot bring a Rule 10b-5 action for damages. *Blue Chip Stamps v. Manor Drug Stores*, 421 U.S. 723 (1975). (Note: Courts are split as to whether a private action for injunctive relief is possible by someone who did not buy or sell stock. However, the SEC can bring such an action.)

The defendant is not required to be a participant in the transaction. Only the plaintiff must be a buyer or seller.

a) Forced-sale doctrine

Under the forced-sale doctrine, the forced exchange of shares in a merger or similar transaction constitutes a sale.

2) Use of interstate commerce

Interstate commerce must be used in connection with the transaction. Use of a telephone, mail, or e-mail to make the transaction satisfies this requirement, as does the use of a national securities exchange.

An in-person transaction may not necessarily satisfy the interstate commerce requirement.

3) Fraudulent or deceptive conduct

A Rule 10b-5 action requires fraudulent or deceptive conduct by the defendant in connection with the sale or purchase of a security. The defendant can engage in such conduct by (i) making an untrue statement of a material fact or (ii) failing to state a material fact that is necessary to prevent statements already made from being misleading.

a) Opinions and predictions

Generally, an opinion or a prediction is not false merely because it does not purport to be factual. However, such a statement may be fraudulent if the defendant made the statement without a reasonable basis or did not make the statement in good faith. *See* Securities Exchange Act Rule 3b-6.

i) Bespeaks-caution doctrine

Under the bespeaks-caution doctrine, a statement of opinion or prediction accompanied by adequate cautionary language does not constitute a false or misleading statement. Securities Exchange Act Rule 21E.

b) Nondisclosure and insider trading

The mere possession of material information that is not public knowledge does not give rise to Rule 10b-5 liability; a person who has such insider knowledge does not incur liability **unless he also trades stock or other securities on the basis of such knowledge**. This is often referred to as the "disclose or abstain" rule.

i) Possession as use of information

In establishing that a person has traded on the basis of nonpublic information, a person is presumed to have traded on the basis of the information that he possessed at the time of the trade. An exception exists for trades made in accordance with a preexisting written plan. Securities Exchange Act Rule 10b-5-1.

ii) Affected traders

There are four types of traders who may be liable for failure to disclose information: (i) insiders, (ii) constructive insiders, (iii) tippees, and (iv) misappropriators.

(a) Insiders

An insider is a director, an officer, or other employee of the corporation who uses nonpublic information for personal gain.

(b) Constructive insiders

A constructive insider is a person who has a relationship with the corporation that gives that person access to corporate information not available to the general public. Such individuals include lawyers, accountants, consultants, and other independent contractors.

(c) Tippees

A tippee is a person who is given information by an insider or a constructive insider (the "tipper") with the expectation that the information will be used to trade the stock or other securities. The tipper must receive a personal benefit from the disclosure or intend to make a gift to the tippee.

To be liable, the tippee must have known (or should have known) that the information was provided to him in violation of the insider's duty to the corporation. *Dirks v. SEC*, 463 U.S. 646 (1983).

(d) Misappropriators

A misappropriator is a person who uses confidential information in order to trade stock or other securities in violation of the duty of confidentiality owed to the corporation. *United States v. O'Hagan*, 521 U.S. 642 (1997).

4) Materiality

A defendant's conduct must involve the misuse of material information. A fact is material if a reasonable investor would find the fact important in deciding whether to purchase or sell a security. *Basic, Inc. v. Levinson*, 485 U.S. 224 (1988).

5) Scienter

A defendant is not strictly liable for making a false or misleading statement or for negligently making such a statement. Instead, the defendant must make the statement intentionally or recklessly. This fault requirement is also known as "scienter." *Ernst & Ernst v. Hochfelder*, 425 U.S. 185 (1976).

6) Plaintiff's reliance

To maintain a Rule 10b-5 action, a plaintiff must establish that he relied on the defendant's fraudulent conduct. However, when the defendant's fraudulent conduct is not aimed directly at the plaintiff, such as if the defendant issues a press release, then courts have permitted the plaintiff to establish reliance by finding that the defendant's conduct constituted a fraud on the market. *Basic, Inc. v. Levinson*, 485 U.S. 224 (1988).

a) Justifiable reliance

Not only must a plaintiff rely on the defendant's fraudulent conduct, but such reliance also must be justifiable. In ascertaining whether the plaintiff's reliance is justifiable, mere negligence by the plaintiff is not sufficient to prevent the plaintiff's recovery.

7) Harm to the plaintiff

The plaintiff must establish that he suffered harm caused by the defendant's fraudulent conduct.

a) Damages

Generally, a plaintiff is entitled to recoup his "out-of-pocket" loss, which is the difference between the stock's value at the time of the fraud and the price that the plaintiff paid or received for the stock. In determining the stock's value at the time of the fraud, the value cannot exceed the mean average market price of the stock during the 90-day period after disclosure of such fraud. Securities Exchange Act Rule 21D(e). Punitive damages are not allowed.

b) Rescission

Rescission may be permitted if the defendant was involved in the transaction as a seller or buyer.

c) Defendant's liability

When a defendant has engaged in a knowing violation, she is jointly and severally liable for the damages. If a defendant's violation results from reckless behavior, then her liability is proportionally limited to the damages for which she is responsible. Securities Exchange Act Rule 21D(f).

b. Section 16(b) action

A corporate insider can be forced to return short-swing profits to the corporation through a Section 16(b) action. An insider's reasons for trading are immaterial. Even an insider who does not possess nonpublic material information must return short-swing profits.

The following four elements are necessary for a Section 16(b) cause of action:

1) Applicable corporations

Only the following publicly traded corporations are protected by Section 16(b): (i) corporations that have securities traded on a national securities exchange or (ii) corporations that have assets of more than $10 million and more than 500 shareholders of any class of stock or other equity security.

2) Corporate insiders

Only corporate directors, officers (e.g., president, vice president, secretary, treasurer, or comptroller), and shareholders who hold more than 10 percent of any class of stock are subject to a Section 16(b) action. Generally, transactions made before becoming a corporate insider are not considered in determining short-swing profits. However, transactions made after ceasing to be a corporate insider are considered in determining short-swing profits.

3) Short-swing profits

During any six-month period, a corporate insider who both buys and sells his corporation's stock is liable to the corporation for any profits made. Profits are computed by matching the highest sale price with the lowest purchase price, then the next highest sale price with the next lowest purchase price, and so on, during the six-month period. Any loss is not taken into account, and all shares are matched with other shares only once.

> **Example:** On January 1, President sells 200 shares of ABC Corporation's stock for $500 each that she had purchased several years before for $100 each. On May 1, President purchases 200 shares of stock for $400 each. President has a short-swing profit of $20,000 (i.e., the sale of 200 shares at $500 each, less the purchase of 200 shares at $400 each).

4) Reporting

A corporate insider is required to report a change in his stock ownership to the SEC to encourage compliance with the short-swing profits rule.

4. State Cause of Action

The primary state cause of action available to persons who have traded stock is the tort of fraud.

5. Tender Offer

A tender offer is an offer to shareholders of a publicly traded corporation to purchase their stock for a fixed price, which is usually higher than the market price. It is frequently used to effect a hostile takeover of a corporation (i.e., a takeover that is opposed by the current management of the corporation).

a. For more than five percent

A person who acquires more than five percent of any class of stock must file a statement with the SEC that reveals his ownership interest, the source of his funding, and his purpose in acquiring the stock.

b. Persons subject to disclosure rules

A tender offer made by a person subject to the disclosure rules must also provide specific shareholder rights. Securities Exchange Act Rule 14(d)(g).

III. GOVERNANCE

A. INSTRUMENTS

1. Articles of Incorporation

The articles of incorporation must be filed to incorporate, but they need not spell out the manner in which the corporation is to be governed. RMBCA § 2.02(b).

a. Articles of correction

If the articles of incorporation contain an inaccuracy or were defectively executed, then articles of correction may be filed with the state to correct the inaccuracy or defect. RMBCA § 1.24.

b. Amendment of articles

The corporation can amend its articles with any lawful provision. The procedure for securing approval to amend the articles of incorporation varies depending on whether the corporation has issued stock. Once the necessary approval is obtained, articles of amendment must be filed with the state.

1) No stock issued

If the corporation has not issued stock, the board of directors—or, if the board does not exist, the incorporators—may amend the articles of incorporation. RMBCA § 10.02.

2) Stock issued

If stock has been issued, then corporations generally must follow a two-step approval process:

i) The board of directors must adopt the amendment to the articles of incorporation; and

ii) The board must submit the amendment to the shareholders for their approval by majority vote.

RMBCA § 10.03(a)–(b).

2. Bylaws

The bylaws contain any lawful provision for the management of the corporation's business or the regulation of its affairs that is not inconsistent with the articles of incorporation. When there is a conflict between the articles of incorporation and the bylaws, the articles of incorporation control. RMBCA § 2.06(b).

Generally, the board of directors adopts the initial bylaws. RMBCA § 2.06(a). However, a majority vote by either the directors or the shareholders can adopt, amend, or repeal a bylaw, unless (i) the corporation's articles reserve that power exclusively to the shareholders, or (ii) the shareholders, in amending, repealing, or adopting a bylaw, expressly provide that the board of directors may not amend, repeal, or reinstate that bylaw. RMBCA § 10.20(b).

Generally, shareholders may amend the bylaws to limit the board of directors' ability to amend, repeal, or reinstate a shareholder-approved bylaw. However, a shareholder-approved bylaw dealing with director nominations may not limit the board's power to amend, add, or repeal to ensure an orderly process. Thus, if shareholders approve a bylaw amendment that limits further board changes, the board could only amend or add to the bylaw to safeguard the voting process; it could not repeal the shareholder-approved bylaw.

B. ORGANIZATIONAL MEETING

Once the articles of incorporation are filed, an organizational meeting is held at which the appointment of officers, adoption of bylaws, and approval of contracts may take place. When the incorporators hold the meeting, election of the board of directors also takes place. RMBCA § 2.05.

IV. SHAREHOLDERS

A. MEETING REQUIREMENTS

There are two basic types of shareholder meetings: annual and special. In addition, shareholders may express their collective will through written consent.

1. Annual Meeting

A corporation is required to hold a shareholders' meeting each year. Generally, the time and place of the meeting are specified in the corporate bylaws. The primary purpose of the annual meeting is to elect directors, but any business that is subject to shareholder control may be addressed. RMBCA § 7.01.

2. Special Meeting

A corporation may also hold a special meeting, the purpose of which must be specified in the notice of the meeting. Generally, a special meeting may be called by the board of directors or shareholders who own at least 10 percent of the shares entitled to vote at the meeting. RMBCA §§ 7.02, 7.05(c).

3. Notice of Meeting

Shareholders must be given notice of either type of meeting. To properly call a meeting, the corporation must notify all shareholders entitled to a vote at the special meeting in a timely manner. A shareholder may waive notice either in writing or by attending the meeting. Usually, notice must be given no less than 10 days and no more than 60 days before the meeting date. The notice must include the time, date, and place of the meeting. RMBCA §§ 7.05, 7.06.

4. Failure to Hold

The failure to hold the annual meeting does not affect the existence of the corporation or invalidate any business conducted by the corporation. RMBCA § 7.01(c). A shareholder may seek a court order compelling the corporation to hold an annual or a special meeting. RMBCA § 7.03.

5. Action by Unanimous Written Consent

Instead of voting at a meeting, all shareholders may take any action that could have been undertaken at a meeting by unanimous written consent.

B. VOTING REQUIREMENTS

1. Voting Eligibility

Typically, ownership of stock entitles the shareholder to vote. There are two basic issues regarding shareholder voting: who the owner of the stock is and when such ownership is measured.

a. Ownership issues

Generally, a corporation maintains a list of shareholders who are entitled to vote (i.e., record owners). RMBCA § 7.20(a). A beneficial owner is not entitled to vote at a meeting of shareholders. A person who is not a record owner may nevertheless be entitled to vote. For example, a beneficial owner of the stock may compel the record owner to recognize the beneficial owner's right to vote. See RMBCA § 7.23. Similarly, a guardian for an incompetent or a personal representative of a decedent's estate may compel the corporation to allow her to vote in lieu of the record owner. Voting rights issues may also arise when stock is jointly held.

1) Unpaid stock

When stock has been subscribed to but not fully paid for, the subscriber's right to vote such stock may be limited or denied.

2) Corporation's stock

A corporation is generally not entitled to vote its stock. Stock that has been authorized but not issued by a corporation cannot be voted by the corporation. Similarly, stock that has been authorized and issued by a corporation and then reacquired by the corporation (i.e., treasury stock) cannot be voted.

3) Stock in another corporation

A corporation that owns stock in another corporation generally can vote such stock as any other shareholder can.

b. Transfer issue—record date

When stock is sold or otherwise transferred, an issue may arise as to whether the transferor or the transferee of the stock is entitled to vote at a subsequent shareholders' meeting. Typically, the record date is fixed by the board of directors, although the date can be set by reference to the articles of incorporation or the corporate bylaws and, failing corporate guidance, by statute. The record date can be no more than 70 days prior to the meeting. Only the owner of the stock at the close of business on the record date has the right to vote the stock at the upcoming meeting. A transferee of shares after the record date who wants to vote at a scheduled shareholder meeting should obtain a proxy to vote the shares from his transferor. RMBCA § 7.07.

2. Voting Power

Typically, each share of stock is entitled to one vote. However, a corporation, through its articles of incorporation, can create classes of stock that have greater voting power (e.g., each share is entitled to five votes) or that cannot vote (i.e., nonvoting stock). RMBCA § 7.21(a).

3. Quorum Requirements

For a decision made at a shareholders' meeting to be valid, there must be a quorum of the shares eligible to vote present at the meeting. Usually, the required quorum is a majority of votes entitled to be cast on a matter. A share that is present for any purpose at a meeting is deemed present for quorum purposes. RMBCA § 7.25.

4. Approval Requirements

Although approval of the shares entitled to vote on an issue is the generally accepted standard, when there are classes of shares, each class of stock may be required to approve the issue separately. RMBCA § 7.26.

a. Level of approval

The requisite level of shareholder approval is a majority, but approval by a plurality may be permissible, especially if the issue is the election of directors. RMBCA §§ 7.25(c), 7.28(a). A plurality vote requirement for directors means that the individuals with the largest number of votes are elected as directors up to the maximum number of directors to be chosen at the election.

b. Basis for determining level

Usually, the level of shareholder approval is based on the number of votes cast. For some issues, such as fundamental changes, the level of shareholder approval is based on the number of votes eligible to be cast.

5. Special Voting for Directors

Corporations may choose directors by cumulative voting if so provided in the articles of incorporation.

a. Cumulative voting

When more than one director is to be elected, corporations can allow shareholders to cumulate their votes and cast all those votes for only one (or more than one) of the candidates. The effect of cumulative voting is to allow minority shareholders to elect representatives to the board.

Example: A owns 30 shares of X, Inc. stock. B owns the remaining 70 shares. X, Inc. has three directors. Without cumulative voting, A is unable to elect any of the three directors because B owns a majority of the shares. With cumulative voting, A can elect at least one director by casting all of her 90 votes (i.e., 30 votes per director times three directors) for one director.

b. Staggered terms

Typically, all directors of the corporation are elected annually. However, some corporations provide for the election of fewer than all of the directors, thereby staggering the terms of the directors, which provides for some continuity on the board from election to election. The main purpose for staggered terms is to limit the impact of cumulative voting.

6. Proxy Voting

A shareholder may vote in person or by proxy. A proxy vote must be executed in writing and delivered to the corporation or its agent. A proxy is valid for 11 months unless otherwise specified. A proxy is revocable unless it expressly provides that it is irrevocable and the appointment of the proxy is coupled with an interest. Any act by the shareholder that is inconsistent with a proxy, such as attending a shareholder meeting and voting the shares, revokes the proxy. RMBCA § 7.22. In the case of multiple proxies given, the last given revokes all previous proxies.

Whether a proxy is coupled with an interest depends on whether the proxy holder has (i) a property right in the shares or (ii) a security interest given to him to protect him regarding any obligations he incurred or money he advanced. Typically, proxy holders who have a property interest in the shares or a security interest are those who have purchased the shares or otherwise have a business arrangement with the corporation (such as a creditor or an employee of the corporation).

7. Voting Together With Other Shareholders

a. Voting pool—retention of legal ownership

Shareholders may enter into a binding voting agreement, also known as a "voting pool," which provides for the manner in which they will vote their shares. Under such an agreement, shareholders retain ownership of their stock. Such an agreement is a contract that may be specifically enforced. It does not need to be filed with the corporation, and there is no time limit. RMBCA § 7.31.

b. Voting trust—transfer of legal ownership

A voting trust constitutes a separate legal entity to which the shareholders' stock is transferred. Although the shareholders retain beneficial ownership of their shares, legal ownership is transferred to the trustee, who votes the shares and distributes the dividends in accordance with the terms of the trust. The trustee owes a fiduciary duty to the trust and the beneficial owners of the stock. A voting trust must be in writing, it is limited to 10 years, and the trust instrument must be filed with the corporation. RMBCA § 7.30.

c. Management agreements

Generally, shareholders may agree to alter the way in which a corporation is managed even though the agreement is inconsistent with statutory provisions. Among the matters on which shareholders may agree are:

i)   Elimination of the board of directors or restrictions on the discretion or powers of the board of directors;

ii) Authorization or making of distributions;

iii) Determination of who is a member of the board of directors, the manner of selection or removal of directors, and the terms of office of directors;

iv) The exercise or division of voting power by or between the shareholders and directors or by or among any of them, including director proxies;

v) A transfer to one or more shareholders or other persons all or part of the authority to exercise corporate powers or to manage the business and affairs of the corporation; and

vi) The manner or means by which the exercise of corporate powers or the management of the business and affairs of the corporation is affected.

RMBCA § 7.32(a).

1) Form of agreement

The agreement must be set forth either (i) in the articles of incorporation or the corporate bylaws and approved by all persons who are shareholders at the time of the agreement or (ii) in a written agreement that is signed by all persons who are shareholders at the time of the agreement and is made known to the corporation. The agreement may be amended only by persons who are shareholders at the time of amendment. RMBCA § 7.32(b).

2) Length of agreement

Unless otherwise fixed in the agreement, the agreement is valid for 10 years. RMBCA § 7.32(b).

3) Rescission of agreement

A person who purchases stock in a corporation with a management agreement without knowledge of the agreement can rescind the purchase agreement. RMBCA § 7.32(c).

4) Limitation on type of corporation

Such an agreement cannot be entered into with respect to a corporation that has shares listed on a national securities exchange, and such an agreement ceases to be effective for a corporation when its shares are listed on such an exchange. RMBCA § 7.32(d).

5) Effect on liability

If the agreement limits the discretion or powers of the board of directors, then the directors are relieved of liability for acts or omissions to the extent of the limitation, and the persons in whom such discretion or powers are vested are subject to liability. The existence of the agreement is not a ground for imposing personal liability on shareholders for corporate acts or debts, even though the shareholders, by virtue of the agreement, fail to observe the corporate formalities. RMBCA § 7.32(e)–(f).

C. INSPECTION OF CORPORATE RECORDS RIGHTS

A shareholder has a right to inspect and copy corporate records, books, papers, etc. upon five days' written notice stating a **proper purpose**.

NOTE: As a litigant against the corporation, the shareholder also has a right to discovery. However, courts encourage shareholders to seek inspection of corporate documents before bringing suits alleging improper corporate transactions and breaches of fiduciary duty. *See Brehm v. Eisner*, 746 A.2d 244 (Del. 2000). That said, the right to inspection does continue to exist even while a lawsuit is proceeding. *See King v. VeriFone Holdings, Inc.*, 12 A.3d 1140, 1145–46 (Del. 2011).

1. Shareholders With Inspection Rights

Generally, not only a shareholder of record but also a beneficial owner of the shares enjoys inspection rights. RMBCA § 16.02. Some states restrict access to corporate records to shareholders who have owned stock for at least a limited amount of time and/or own a minimum amount of stock.

2. Records Subject to Inspection

Generally, a shareholder can inspect any corporate records, but the inspection may be limited to specified records, such as excerpts from the minutes of a board meeting. RMBCA § 16.02(b). Note that a proper purpose is not required for a shareholder to inspect minutes of a *shareholder's* meeting.

3. Time and Place Limits on Inspection

The inspection right is usually restricted to normal business hours at the corporation's principal place of business. Five days' advance written notice is required. RMBCA § 16.02.

4. Purpose Limitation on Inspection

A shareholder's inspection right is conditional on having a **proper purpose**. RMBCA § 16.02(c). Once a proper purpose is stated, all other purposes are considered irrelevant. A proper purpose is one that relates to the shareholder's interest in the corporation, such as determining the value of one's shares in a closely held corporation even though the shareholder does not plan to sell the shares. Improper purposes may include harassment of corporate officials, acquiring corporate secrets, or idle curiosity. *Sec. First Corp. v. U.S. Die Casting & Dev. Co.*, 687 A.2d 563 (Del. 1997). Whether a particular document is essential to a stated inspection purpose depends on the context in which the shareholder's inspection demand arises. The shareholder has the burden of showing credible evidence of improper conduct, and must show the documents or records are essential to the stated proper purpose. *Espinoza v. Hewlett-Packard Co.*, 32 A.3d 365 (Del. 2011).

5. Enforcement of Right

Some states enforce a shareholder's inspection right indirectly by imposing fines on the corporate official who improperly refuses a shareholder access to the corporate records. Under the RMBCA, direct enforcement of a shareholder's inspection right is recognized in an expedited court proceeding, under which the shareholder can secure access to the corporate records and reimbursement for litigation costs. RMBCA § 16.04.

6. Disclosure of Financial Statement

Under the SEC, publicly held corporations that have issued securities are required to supply shareholders with an annual audited financial statement. Securities Exchange Act of 1934 Rule 14(a); Securities Acts Amendments of 1964 Rule 14(c). Likewise, the RMBCA requires all corporations to furnish shareholders with an annual financial statement. RMBCA § 16.20.

D. SUITS BY SHAREHOLDERS

A shareholder may bring a direct or a derivative action against the corporation in which the shareholder owns stock. How the action is characterized will affect the requirements for bringing suit and to whom any recovery is paid.

1. Direct Actions

A shareholder may pursue two basic types of direct actions: (i) an action to enforce shareholder rights or (ii) a non-shareholder action, the recovery from which is to the benefit of the indirect shareholder.

a. Action to enforce shareholder rights

A shareholder may sue the corporation for breach of a fiduciary duty owed to the shareholder by a director or an officer. Typical actions are based on the denial or interference with a shareholder's voting rights, the board's failure to declare a dividend, or the board's approval or failure to approve a merger.

b. Non-shareholder actions

A shareholder may sue the corporation on grounds that do not arise from the shareholder's status as a shareholder.

> **Example:** A shareholder who is struck by a vehicle owned by the corporation and driven by a corporate employee may pursue a negligence claim, against the corporation, as the injured party of the corporation's tortious conduct.

2. Derivative Actions

In a derivative action, a shareholder is suing on behalf of the corporation for a harm suffered by the corporation. Although the shareholder also may have suffered harm, recovery generally goes to the corporation. For example, a shareholder may bring a derivative action to force a director to disgorge a secret profit earned by the director on a transaction with the corporation.

a. Who may bring suit—standing

In addition to being a shareholder at the time the action is filed and continuing to be a shareholder during the litigation, a plaintiff must also have been a shareholder at the time of the act or omission (or one who receives the shares through a transfer by operation of law from such a shareholder) to bring a derivative action. This is known as the "**contemporaneous ownership**" rule. In addition, the shareholder must fairly and adequately represent the interests of the corporation. RMBCA § 7.41.

> **Excluded as a plaintiff:** A creditor of a corporation cannot bring a derivative action.

b. Demand upon board

The plaintiff in a derivative action must make a written demand upon the board of directors in order to take action. A derivative action may not commence until **90 days** have passed from the date of demand.

1) Futility exception

In some states, a demand upon the board is not required if the demand would be futile. Factors for determining futility include whether the directors are disinterested and independent and whether the transaction was the product of a valid exercise of business judgment. *Marx v. Akers*, 666 N.E.2d 1034 (1996). Under the RMBCA, however, there is a universal demand requirement for all derivative actions. Therefore, the futility exception is not recognized in states that have adopted the RMBCA. RMBCA § 7.42.

2) Irreparable injury excuse

The plaintiff may be excused from waiting a reasonable time for the board to respond to the demand if the delay would result in irreparable injury to the corporation. RMBCA § 7.42(2).

3) Effect of board rejection of demand

If the board specifically rejects the demand, then the rejection is tested against the business judgment rule. If there is a business justification for the rejection, then the plaintiff must establish that the board's rejection was due to a lack of care, loyalty, or good faith to persuade the court to override the board's refusal. *Findley v. Garrett*, 240 P.2d 421 (Cal. 1952).

c. Litigation expenses

Although the plaintiff-shareholder is usually not entitled to share in a recovery, she can seek reimbursement from the corporation for reasonable litigation expenses, including attorney's fees, if the lawsuit has resulted in a substantial benefit to the corporation. If the court finds that the proceeding was commenced or maintained without a reasonable cause or for an improper purpose, then it may order the plaintiff-shareholder to pay the defendant's litigation expenses. RMBCA § 7.46.

d. Dismissal of derivative proceeding

The board can seek dismissal of the shareholder's derivative action if a majority of the board's qualified directors (i.e., directors without a material interest in the action) determine in good faith, after conducting a reasonable inquiry upon which its conclusions are based, that maintaining the action is not in corporation's best interests. RMBCA § 7.44. The board's failure to investigate credible allegations of corporate illegality constitutes lack of good faith. *Stone v. Ritter*, 911 A.2d 362, 364–65 (Del. 2006).

E. LIABILITY

One reason the corporate form is favorable is that the investors in a corporation are subject to limited liability for corporate acts, and they are only at risk to the extent of their investment. This principle of limited liability is subject to challenge, primarily with respect to shareholders of closely held corporations.

1. Piercing the Corporate Veil

If a plaintiff can "pierce the corporate veil," then a corporation's existence is ignored, and the shareholders of the corporation are held personally liable.

Although courts are reluctant to hold a director or an active shareholder liable for actions that are legally the responsibility of the corporation (even if the corporation has a single shareholder), they will sometimes do so if the corporation was markedly noncompliant or if holding only the corporation liable would be singularly unfair to the plaintiff.

a. Totality of circumstances

In most jurisdictions, no bright-line rule exists for piercing the corporate veil, and courts look at the "totality of circumstances." Courts generally look to whether the corporation is being used as a "façade" for a dominant shareholder's personal dealings (i.e., whether the corporation is an "alter ego" of the shareholder). Additionally, courts look to whether there is "unity of interest and ownership" between the entity and the members to ensure that the corporation in fact did not have an existence independent of the members.

In general, a plaintiff must prove that the incorporation was merely a formality and that the corporation neglected corporate formalities and protocols, such as voting to approve major corporate actions in the context of a duly authorized corporate meeting. This is often the case when a corporation facing legal liability transfers its assets to another corporation with the same management and shareholders. It also happens most often with single-person or small, closely held corporations that are managed in a haphazard manner.

b. Factors to consider

Factors considered by the courts when piercing the corporate veil include:

i) Undercapitalization of the corporation at the time of its formation;

ii) Disregard of corporate formalities;

iii) Use of corporate assets as a shareholder's own assets;

iv) Self-dealing with the corporation;

v) Siphoning of corporate funds or stripping of corporate assets;

vi) Use of the corporate form to avoid existing statutory requirements or other legal obligations;

vii) A shareholder's impermissible control or domination over the corporation; and

viii) Wrongful, misleading, or fraudulent dealings with a corporate creditor.

Not all of the above factors need to be met for the court to pierce the corporate veil. Some courts might find that one factor is so compelling in a particular case that it will find the shareholders personally liable.

The failure of a shareholder to respect the corporate entity is insufficient by itself to justify piercing the corporate veil; such failure must also adversely affect the third party's ability to recover from the corporation.

2. Controlling Shareholder

a. Fifty percent plus one

When one shareholder—or a group of shareholders acting in concert—holds a high enough percentage of ownership in a company to enact changes at the highest level, the shareholder or group is a "controlling shareholder." Anyone controlling **50 percent of a corporation's shares, plus one**, is automatically a controlling shareholder.

A much smaller interest can be controlling if the remaining shares are widely dispersed (as in a large, publicly traded corporation) and not actively voted. Additionally, a corporation that requires a two-thirds supermajority of shares to vote in favor of a motion can effectively grant control to a minority shareholder or block of shareholders that owns just more than one-third of the shares of the corporation. Thus, in some cases, a shareholder can essentially maintain control of a corporation with only 33.4 percent of the outstanding shares.

b. Fiduciary duties

Although shareholders do not owe fiduciary duties to the corporation or to each other, a fiduciary duty to the minority shareholders may arise if the controlling shareholder is (i) selling that interest to an outsider, (ii) seeking to eliminate other shareholders from the corporation, or (iii) receiving a distribution denied to the other shareholders.

A controlling shareholder has a duty to disclose to the minority shareholder any information that it knew or should have known if it is information that a reasonable person would consider important in deciding how to vote on a transaction.

A controlling shareholder breaches her fiduciary duty to the minority shareholders if nondisclosure causes a loss to the minority shareholders. A loss includes being deprived of a state remedy that would otherwise have been available. Furthermore, when a majority shareholder purchases the interest of the minority, it has a fiduciary duty of fair dealing. The controlling shareholder bears the burden of demonstrating that the process she employed was fair and that the price she selected was fair. *Weinberger v. UOP, Inc.*, 457 A.2d 701 (Del. 1983).

V. BOARD OF DIRECTORS

The board of directors manages and directs the management of the corporation's business and affairs. The board also authorizes the officers and other corporate employees to exercise the powers possessed by the corporation. RMBCA § 8.01.

A. COMPOSITION REQUIREMENTS

1. Number of Directors

Traditionally, a board needed three or more directors, but today a board can have as few as one director, regardless of the number of shareholders. In its articles of incorporation or bylaws, a corporation may permit the board to vary the number of directors. RMBCA § 8.03.

2. Qualifications of Directors

A corporation cannot serve as the director of another corporation; a director must be a natural person. Unless required by the articles of incorporation or the bylaws, a director need not be a shareholder of the corporation or resident of a particular state. RMBCA §§ 8.02, 8.03.

B. SELECTION OF DIRECTORS

Directors are selected by the shareholders at the annual shareholders' meeting and may be elected by straight or cumulative voting and by one or more classes of stock. RMBCA §§ 7.28, 8.03.

C. TERM OF DIRECTORS

1. Annual Terms

Typically, a director serves for a one-year term that expires at the first annual meeting after the director's election. RMBCA § 8.05.

2. Staggered Terms

A director may serve for longer than one year if the terms are staggered. With staggered terms, each year some directors are elected for multiyear terms. The main purpose of staggered terms is to limit the impact of cumulative voting. RMBCA §§ 8.05, 8.06.

3. Holdover Director

A director whose term has expired may continue to serve until a replacement is selected. RMBCA § 8.05(e).

4. Resignation of Director

A director may resign at any time by delivering a written notice to the board, its chair, or the corporation. RMBCA § 8.07.

5. Removal of Director

At common law, shareholders had the inherent power to remove a director. However, because directors were deemed to have an entitlement to their offices, they could be removed only for cause based on substantial grounds (such as breach of fiduciary duty, fraud, criminal conduct, etc.).

The current trend in most states and the RMBCA is to allow shareholders to remove a director with or without cause, unless the articles of incorporation provide otherwise.

a. Meeting requirements

A director may be removed only at a meeting called for the purpose of removing the director, and the meeting notice must state that removal is at least one of the purposes of the meeting. RMBCA § 8.08(d).

b. Voting requirements

A director who was elected by a particular voting class of stock can be removed only by that same class (or by court proceeding). RMBCA § 8.08(b).

If cumulative voting is not authorized, then a shareholder vote removes a director if the number of votes for removal exceeds the number of votes against removal. RMBCA § 8.08(c).

If cumulative voting is authorized, then a director may not be removed if the votes sufficient to elect the director are cast against the director's removal. RMBCA § 8.08.

Notwithstanding the foregoing, a director can be removed by court proceeding.

6. Replacement or New Director

When there is a vacancy on the board or an increase in the number of directors, either the shareholders or the directors may fill the vacancy. When the vacancy leaves the board without a quorum, the directors remaining can elect a replacement director by a majority vote. RMBCA § 8.10(a).

D. COMPENSATION OF DIRECTORS

Directors of a corporation may receive compensation for serving as directors. RMBCA § 8.11.

E. MEETING REQUIREMENTS

1. Types of Meetings

The board of directors may hold regular or special meetings. Unless the articles of incorporation or bylaws provide otherwise, a director is entitled to two days' notice of the date, time, and place of a **special meeting**, although the purpose is not required. A **regular meeting** may be held without notice of the date, time, place, or purpose of the meeting. A director may waive notice of a meeting at any time by a signed written waiver. In addition, a director's attendance waives notice of that meeting unless the director promptly objects to lack of notice. RMBCA §§ 8.20–.23.

2. Presence at Meetings

A director is not required to be physically present at a meeting. A meeting may be conducted through conference call or any other means that allow each director to hear the other directors during the meeting. RMBCA § 8.20(b).

3. Action Without a Meeting

The board of directors may act without holding a meeting by unanimous written consent to the action. RMBCA § 8.21.

F. VOTING REQUIREMENTS

1. Quorum Rules

For the board of directors' acts at a meeting to be valid, a quorum of directors must be present at the meeting. RMBCA § 8.24(a).

a. Number of directors

A majority of all directors in office constitutes a quorum, unless a higher or lower number is required by the articles of incorporation or bylaws. RMBCA § 8.24.

b. Presence of directors

Unlike a shareholder, a director must be present at the time that the vote is taken in order to be counted for quorum purposes. RMBCA § 8.24. Presence includes appearances made using communications equipment that allows all persons participating in the meeting to hear and speak to one another.

2. Passage Level

Typically, the assent of a majority of the directors present at the time the vote takes place is necessary for board approval. However, the articles of incorporation or bylaws may specify a higher level of approval. RMBCA § 8.24(c).

3. Director Dissent

A director may incur liability for illegal or improper action taken by the board at a meeting at which the director is present, even though the director does not vote in favor of the action.

To forestall such liability, the director must:

i)   Promptly object to the holding of the meeting;

ii) Ensure that his dissent or abstention from the specific action is noted in the minutes of the meeting; or

iii) Not vote in favor of the action and deliver written notice of his dissent to the presiding officer of the meeting before its adjournment or to the corporation immediately afterward.

RMBCA § 8.24(d).

4. Voting Agreements

Generally, an agreement between directors as to how to vote (i.e., a pooling agreement) is unenforceable. Each director is expected to exercise independent judgment. A director also may not vote by proxy.

G. COMMITTEES

The board of directors may take action through one or more committees. RMBCA § 8.25.

1. **Composition of a Committee**

   A committee may consist of two or more directors. RMBCA § 8.25.

2. **Selection of Committee Members**

   Generally, a majority of the directors must vote for the creation of a committee and the appointment of a director to a committee. RMBCA § 8.25(b).

3. **Committee's Powers**

   A committee may generally exercise whatever powers are granted to it by the board, the articles of incorporation, or the bylaws. RMBCA § 8.25(d)–(e).

   A committee may not:

   i) Declare distributions, except within limits set by the board;

   ii) Recommend actions that require shareholder approval;

   iii) Fill vacancies on the board or its committees; or

   iv) Adopt, amend, or repeal bylaws.

4. **Type of Committees—Sarbanes-Oxley Act**

   Typically, the board of a publicly held corporation has an audit committee, a compensation committee, and a nominating committee. A corporation with stock listed on a national securities exchange or a national securities association must have an audit committee that has direct responsibility for selecting, compensating, and overseeing the corporation's outside auditors. The members of the audit committee must be independent directors (i.e., not otherwise employed or compensated by the corporation).

   > Outside auditors cannot otherwise be employed by the corporation. Sarbanes-Oxley Act 301.

H. DUTIES

A director owes two basic duties to the corporation: (i) a duty of care and (ii) a duty of loyalty. In discharging these duties, a director is required to act in good faith and in a manner that the director reasonably believes to be in the best interests of the corporation. RMBCA § 8.30.

1. **Duty of Care**

   a. **Prudent person**

      Directors have a duty to act with the care that a **person in a like position would reasonably believe appropriate under similar circumstances**. As an objective standard, the director is presumed to have the knowledge and skills of an ordinarily prudent person. In deciding how to act, the director is also required to use any additional knowledge or special skills that he possesses.

   b. **Reliance protection**

      A director is entitled to rely on the performance of—as well as on information, reports, and opinions supplied by—the following persons if the director reasonably believes them to be reliable and competent:

      i) Officers and other employees of the corporation;

      ii) Outside attorneys, accountants, or other skilled or expert individuals retained by the corporation; and

iii) A committee of the board of which the director is not a member.

RMBCA § 8.30(e).

c. Business judgment rule

The business judgment rule is a rebuttable presumption that a director reasonably believed that his actions were in the best interests of the corporation. The exercise of managerial powers by a director is generally subject to the business judgment rule. A typical decision protected by the business judgment rule includes whether to declare a dividend and the amount of any dividend.

1) Overcoming the rule

To overcome the business judgment rule, it must be shown that:

i) The director did not act in good faith (e.g., consciously allowing conduct that violates the law or legal norms; intense hostility of the controlling faction against the minority; exclusion of the minority from employment by the corporation; high salaries or bonuses given, or corporate loans made to, the officers in control; and the existence of a desire by the controlling directors to acquire the minority stock interests as cheaply as possible);

ii) The director was not informed to the extent that the director reasonably believed was necessary before making a decision;

iii) The director did not show objectivity or independence from the director's relation to or control by another having material interest in the challenged conduct;

iv) There was a sustained failure by the director to devote attention to an ongoing oversight of the business and affairs of the corporation;

v) The director failed to timely investigate a matter of significant material concern after being alerted in a manner that would have caused a reasonably attentive director to do so; or

vi) The director received a financial benefit to which he was not entitled, or any other breach of his duties to the corporation.

RMBCA § 8.31(a).

2) Good faith

The presumption of good faith afforded by the business judgment rule is overcome if the challenger shows fraud, dereliction of duty, condoning illegal conduct, or a conflict of interest.

(a) Fraud

A director who knowingly disseminates false information that results in corporate injury or injury to a stockholder violates her fiduciary duty. *Malone v. Brincat*, 722 A.2d 5 (Del. 1998).

(b) Dereliction of duty

A director who consciously disregards his duties is not acting in good faith. When willful ignorance is the basis for a claim of director liability, the challenger must show a **consistent or systemic failure** of the directors to exercise oversight. *In re Caremark Int'l*, 698 A.2d 959 (Del. Ch. 1996). The necessary conditions for director oversight liability are that (i) the directors failed to implement any reporting or information system or controls, or (ii) notwithstanding these controls, the directors failed to monitor or oversee its operations, thereby making themselves uninformed of risks. In either case, imposition of liability requires a showing that the directors knew that they were not discharging their fiduciary obligations. *Id.*

(c) Condoning illegal conduct

A director breaches her fiduciary duty when she fails to act on "red flags" of corporate illegality. *See Graham v. Allis-Chalmers Mfg. Co.*, 188 A.2d 125, 130 (Del. 1963). Examples of conduct that deemed to show lack of good faith include bribing state officials or foreign governments even when doing so is common practice, violating labor laws, and business policies that incentivized employees to commit fraud.

(d) Conflict of interest

A director is not protected by the business judgment rule if he has a personal interest in the outcome of a corporate action.

d. Exculpatory provisions in the articles of incorporation

A corporation's articles of incorporation may include an exculpatory provision shielding directors from liability for money damages for failure to exercise adequate care in the performance of their duties as directors. Typically, exculpatory provisions do not protect directors from liability for any breach of the duty of loyalty, for acts or omissions that are not in good faith, or for any transactions from which the director received an improper personal benefit. *See* Del. Gen. Corp. Law § 102(b)(7); Model Bus. Corp. Act § 2.02(b)(4).

2. Duty of Loyalty

The duty of loyalty requires a director to act in a manner that the director reasonably believes is in the best interests of the corporation. RMBCA § 8.60. Typically, a director breaches this duty by placing his own interests before those of the corporation.

a. Director's conflicting interest transaction—self-dealing

A director who engages in a conflict-of-interest transaction with his own corporation, also known as "self-dealing," has violated his duty of loyalty unless the transaction is protected under the safe-harbor rule. The business judgment rule does not apply when a director engages in a conflict-of-interest transaction with his corporation. In addition, a director must not profit at the corporation's expense.

1) Types of transactions

A conflict-of-interest transaction is any transaction between a director and his corporation that would normally require approval of the board of directors and that is of such financial significance to the director that it would reasonably be expected to influence the director's vote on the transaction. RMBCA § 8.60(1)–(2). The interest involved can be direct or indirect, but it must be financial and material. The standard of determining whether the interest is material is objective and calls upon the trier of fact to determine whether a reasonable director in similar circumstances would have been influenced by the financial interest when voting on the matter. MBCA § 8.60 cmt. 4.

2) Related persons

Corporate dealings with persons who are related to the director are also subject to conflict-of-interest rules. Related individuals include the director's immediate family, parents, siblings, and grandchildren, including the spouses of these individuals, as well as a trust or an estate of which any of those individuals is a substantial beneficiary or the director is a fiduciary.

In addition, the conflict-of-interest rules can apply to transactions between the corporation and another entity with which the director is associated, such as another corporation of which the director is a director, an employee, or an agent or a partnership of which the director is a general partner, an employee, or an agent. RMBCA § 8.60(1), (3).

3) Safe-harbor rules

a) Standards for upholding transactions

There are three safe harbors by which a conflict-of-interest transaction may enjoy protection:

i) Disclosure of all material facts to, and approval by a majority of, the board of directors without a conflicting interest;

ii) Disclosure of all material facts to, and approval by a majority of, the votes entitled to be cast by the shareholders without a conflicting interest; and

iii) Fairness of the transaction to the corporation at the time of commencement.

RMBCA § 8.61.

b) Fairness of transaction

The fairness test looks at the substance and procedure of the transaction. Substantively, the court determines whether the corporation received something of comparable value in exchange for what it gave to the director. Procedurally, the court determines whether the process followed by the directors in reaching their decision was appropriate. RMBCA §§ 8.60(5), 8.61(b)(3). Interested directors who were on both sides of the transactions in question have the burden of establishing the substantive and procedural fairness of the transactions. *HMG/Courtland Properties, Inc. v. Gray*, 749 A.2d 94, 115 (Del. Ch. 1999).

c) Effect of safe-harbor provisions

Satisfaction of the safe-harbor defenses is not necessarily a complete defense, and some states instead hold that the burden of proof shifts to the party challenging the transaction to establish that the transaction was unfair to the corporation. *Kahn v. Lynch Communication System*, 638 A.2d 1110 (Del. 1994).

4) Remedies

A conflict-of-interest transaction that is not protected by a safe-harbor provision may be enjoined or rescinded. In addition, the corporation may seek damages from the director. RMBCA § 8.61.

5) Business judgment rule

Approval of a conflict-of-interest transaction by fully informed disinterested directors triggers the business judgment rule and limits judicial review to issues of gift or waste, with the burden of proof on the party attacking the transaction. *See* Del. Gen. Corp. Law § 144(a)(1); *Marciano v. Nakash*, 535 A.2d 400, 405 n.3 (Del. 1987).

b. Usurpation of corporate opportunity

In addition to a conflict-of-interest transaction, a director may violate his duty of loyalty by usurping a corporate opportunity rather than first offering the opportunity to the corporation. RMBCA § 8.70.

1) Corporate opportunity

In determining whether the opportunity is one that must first be offered to the corporation, courts have applied the "interest or expectancy" test or the "line of business" test.

a) "Interest or expectancy" test

Under the "interest or expectancy" test, the key is whether the corporation has an existing interest (e.g., an option to buy) or an expectancy arising from an existing right (e.g., purchase of property currently leased) in the opportunity. An expectancy can also exist when the corporation is actively seeking a similar opportunity.

b) "Line of business" test

Under the broader "line of business" test, the key is whether the opportunity is within the corporation's current or prospective line of business. Whether an opportunity satisfies this test frequently turns on how expansively the corporation's line of business is characterized.

c) Other factors

Courts look at additional factors in determining whether an opportunity belongs to the corporation. These factors include: (i) the relationship between the person offering the opportunity and the director and corporation, (ii) how and when the director acquired knowledge of the opportunity, and (iii) the relationship of the director to the corporation.

c. Competition with corporation

A director who engages in a business venture that competes with the corporation has breached his duty of loyalty to the corporation. However, a director may engage in unrelated business that does not compete with the corporation. Note that corporate officers and other employees more frequently engage in this kind of breach than directors do.

3. Indemnification and Insurance

When a director is involved in a legal action as a consequence of her role as director, she may seek indemnification for expenses incurred as well as for any judgment or award declared against her. Indemnification may be (i) mandatory, (ii) prohibited, or (iii) permissive. RMBCA §§ 8.50–8.59.

a. Mandatory indemnification

A corporation is **required** to indemnify a director for any reasonable expense, including court costs and attorney's fees, incurred in the **successful** defense of a proceeding against the director in his role as a director. In addition, a corporation must indemnify a director when ordered by the court. RMBCA §§ 8.52, 8.56.

b. Prohibited indemnification

A corporation is prohibited from indemnifying a director against liability because of the receipt of an improper personal benefit. RMBCA § 8.51(d)(2).

c. Permissive indemnification

A corporation **may** indemnify a director in the unsuccessful defense of a suit when:

i) The director acted in good faith with the reasonable belief that his conduct was in the best interests of the corporation, or that his conduct was at least not opposed to the best interests of the corporation; and

ii) In the case of a criminal proceeding, the director did not have reasonable cause to believe that his conduct was unlawful.

Indemnification can extend to liability as well as expenses when the action is brought by a third party, but only to expenses if the action is brought by or on behalf of the corporation. RMBCA § 8.51(a)(1), (d)(1).

The authorization for permissive indemnification requires the approval of a disinterested majority of directors or shareholders or an independent attorney chosen by disinterested directors. RMBCA § 8.55.

d. Advance of expenses

A corporation may, upon a petition by the director, advance litigation expenses to the director. Upon termination of the action, the director must repay such expenses if he is not entitled to indemnification for them. RMBCA § 8.53.

e. Liability insurance

A corporation may acquire insurance to indemnify directors for actions arising from service as a director. The insurance can cover all awards against a director as well as expenses incurred by him, even though the corporation could not otherwise indemnify the director for such amounts. RMBCA § 8.55.

f. Applicability to officers

An officer of a corporation is entitled to indemnification on the same basis and subject to the same restrictions as a director. RMBCA § 8.56.

I. INSPECTION RIGHTS OF DIRECTORS

A director is entitled to inspect and copy corporate books, records, and other documents for any purpose related to the performance of his duty as a director. When the corporation refuses to grant the director access to these items, the director can seek a court order to enforce this right. RMBCA § 16.05.

VI. OFFICERS AND OTHER EMPLOYEES

A. TYPES

Typically, a corporation's officers are composed of a president, secretary, and treasurer. An individual may hold more than one office, but some states prohibit a person from serving dual roles when such officers serve as a check on each other. The RMBCA does not specify which officers a corporation must have, but it simply indicates that the corporate bylaws are responsible for delineating the officers of the corporation. RMBCA § 8.40.

B. SELECTION

The primary officers of a corporation are elected by the board of directors. These officers may in turn be empowered by the board of directors or the bylaws to select other corporate officers and employees. RMBCA § 8.40(b).

C. AUTHORITY

An officer's authority can be actual, implied, or apparent. Actual authority wielded by an officer is defined by the corporate bylaws or set by the board of directors. An officer has implied authority to perform those tasks that are necessary to carry out the officer's duties by virtue of her status or position, so long as the matter is within the scope of ordinary business. However, the officer does not have the authority to bind the corporation by extraordinary acts. In determining whether a transaction is extraordinary, the court might consider the economic magnitude of the action in relation to corporate earnings and assets, the extent of the risk involved, the time span of the action's effect, and the cost of reversing the action. Finally, an officer has apparent authority if the corporation holds the officer out as having authority to bind the corporation to third parties.

D. DUTIES—CARE AND LOYALTY

The specific duties of an officer are defined by the corporate bylaws or set by the board of directors. RMBCA § 8.41. The duties of care and loyalty that are imposed on the directors of a corporation are also owed by the officers of a corporation. Moreover, all employees, as agents of the corporation, owe the corporation these duties of care and loyalty. RMBCA § 8.42.

1. Financial Reports—Sarbanes-Oxley Requirements

The chief executive officer (CEO) and chief financial officer (CFO) of a publicly traded corporation must certify the accuracy of the corporation's financial reports that are filed with the SEC. Sarbanes-Oxley Act 302. In addition to facing criminal penalties for filing a false report, when financial reports must be restated because of such misconduct, a CEO and CFO must forfeit incentive-based pay and must return profits from stock sales for one year. Sarbanes-Oxley Act 304.

E. LIABILITY

As an agent of the corporation, an officer does not incur liability to third parties merely for the performance of duties for the corporation. Of course, an officer can be liable to a third party if the officer has acted in his personal capacity (e.g., guaranteed a corporate loan) or has engaged in purposeful tortious behavior.

F. INDEMNIFICATION AND INSURANCE

An officer is entitled to indemnification to the same extent and subject to the same restrictions as a corporate director. Similar insurance rules apply as well.

G. REMOVAL

An officer may be removed at any time, with or without cause. RMBCA § 8.43. The existence of an employment contract between an officer and the corporation does not prevent the removal of the officer, but it may give rise to contractual remedies such as damages if removal constitutes a breach of contract.

H. OTHER EMPLOYEES

An employee who is not an officer is an agent of the corporation and is subject to the responsibilities of an agent. In turn, the employee is owed duties by the corporate principal. As an agent, the employee has the ability to act on behalf of the corporation to the extent of the employee's authority and is usually protected as an agent from liability for actions undertaken in accordance with that authority.

VII. MERGERS AND ACQUISITIONS

A. MERGERS

1. Definition

A **merger** is the combination of two or more corporations such that only one corporation survives. The surviving corporation may be created as a result of the merger, rather than existing before the merger, in which case the process is referred to as a "**consolidation**." RMBCA §§ 1.40, 11.01, 11.02.

2. Procedure

Although the business aspects of effecting a merger can be complex, the statutory procedure is simple. To merge:

i) The board of directors for each corporation must approve of the merger;

ii) The shareholders of each corporation must usually approve of the merger; and

iii) The required documents (e.g., plan of merger, amended articles of incorporation) must be filed with the state.

RMBCA § 11.04.

a. Shareholder approval

1) Voting requirements

Shareholder approval requires a majority vote, meaning a majority of the votes cast, but the shareholders' meeting at which the vote is taken is subject to a quorum requirement, which is usually a majority of shares entitled to vote. RMBCA § 11.04.

2) Voting by class

If the corporation has more than one class of stock, and the amendment would affect the rights of a particular class of stock, then the holders of that class of stock must also approve of the amendment. RMBCA § 11.04.

3) Mergers without shareholder approval

####### a) Parent-subsidiary merger

A merger between a parent corporation and a subsidiary corporation when the parent owns at least 90 percent of the voting power of each class of outstanding stock of the subsidiary may occur without the approval of the shareholders of the subsidiary. A parent corporation may also effect a merger between two 90 percent or more owned subsidiary corporations without the need for approval by the shareholders of either corporation. In all these mergers, approval by a subsidiary's board of directors is also not required. RMBCA § 11.05.

####### b) Minnow-whale merger

A merger of a small corporation (i.e., a "minnow") into a large corporation (i.e., a "whale") may not require approval of the shareholders of the surviving large corporation. Approval is not required if the merger cannot result in an increase of more than 20 percent in the voting power of the outstanding stock of the surviving corporation, if the articles of incorporation of the surviving corporation will not differ from the articles before the merger, and if the premerger shareholders of the surviving corporation are otherwise unaffected by the merger. RMBCA §§ 6.21(f), 11.04.

3. Corporate Assets and Liabilities

All assets and liabilities owned by a corporation that are merged into another corporation are then owned by the surviving corporation after the merger. RMBCA § 11.07.

B. ASSET ACQUISITION

The sale or other transfer of a corporation's assets does not require approval by the shareholders or board of a transferor corporation. However, asset transfers that resemble a merger may require approval by both the board of directors and the shareholders of the transferor corporation.

1. Applicable Transfers

A transfer involving all, or substantially all, of the corporation's assets outside the usual and regular course of business is a fundamental corporate change for the transferor corporation. Thus, the corporation must follow the fundamental change procedures.

2. Approval Procedure

The approval procedure for an asset transfer follows the approval procedure for a merger, except that only the transferor corporation's board of directors and shareholders are entitled to vote on the transaction. RMBCA § 12.02.

3. Transferor's Liabilities

a. Transferor's continued responsibility

Apart from an agreement with a creditor that releases the transferor corporation from liability, the transferor corporation remains liable for its debts, including those associated with the transferred assets. The transferor may be able to obtain indemnification from the transferee for such liability.

b. Transferee's escape from liability

Unlike in a merger, in a sale or other transfer, the transferee corporation is generally not responsible to the transferor's creditors for the liabilities of the transferor corporation, unless the transferee corporation assumes such liabilities.

C. STOCK ACQUISITION

A corporation may acquire stock in another corporation and thereby secure control of that corporation without going through the process of effecting a statutory merger. The two primary means by which a corporation can acquire stock in another corporation is by exchanging its own stock for that stock or by paying cash or other property for the stock.

1. Stock-for-Stock Exchange

A corporation may offer its own stock to shareholders in another corporation in exchange for their stock in that corporation (i.e., a stock swap). Generally, a shareholder in the other corporation may retain his stock and not participate in the stock swap. However, the RMBCA sets out a procedure, labeled a "share exchange," which parallels the procedure for a merger. If followed, this procedure requires all shareholders to participate in the stock swap. As with a merger, with such an exchange, dissenting shareholders are given the right of appraisal. RMBCA § 11.03.

2. **Stock Purchase**

A corporation may purchase stock in another corporation on the open market or make an offer to buy the stock from the current shareholders (i.e., a tender offer).

D. **DISSENTING SHAREHOLDER'S RIGHT OF APPRAISAL**

A shareholder who objects to a merger or an acquisition may be able to force the corporation to buy his stock at a fair value as determined by an appraisal. This right is also available for shareholders whose rights are materially and adversely affected by an amendment of the corporation's articles of incorporation. RMBCA §§ 13.01–.31.

1. **Qualifying Shareholders**

A shareholder who is entitled to vote on a merger, an acquisition, or an amendment of the corporation's articles of incorporation has appraisal rights. In addition, a minority shareholder in a short-form merger can exercise appraisal rights, even though such a shareholder cannot vote on the merger. RMBCA § 13.02(a).

If a shareholder can sell his stock in a market that is both liquid and reliable, such as the New York Stock Exchange or the American Stock Exchange, the shareholder does not have a right of appraisal, because the market is providing him with the opportunity to sell his stock at its fair value. RMBCA § 13.02(b).

2. **Procedure**

a. **Notice to corporation**

To exercise the right of appraisal, a shareholder must send a written notice to the corporation of her intent to do so. This notice must be delivered to the corporation **before** the shareholders vote on the proposed action. RMBCA § 13.21(a).

b. **No favorable vote**

When the proposed corporate action is submitted to the shareholders for their approval, the shareholder must not vote in favor of the action (i.e., she must abstain or vote "no"). RMBCA § 13.21(a).

c. **Demand for payment**

After the proposed corporate action has been approved, the shareholder must make a written demand upon the corporation for payment. RMBCA § 13.21.

d. **Fair market value**

The corporation must pay shareholders what it estimates as fair market value. If the corporation and the shareholder do not agree on a price for the shareholder's stock, then the fair value of the stock is determined through a court action.

3. **Exclusivity of Remedy**

A shareholder who has an appraisal right cannot challenge the corporate action except on the grounds of fraud or illegality. RMBCA § 13.02(d).

VIII. TERMINATION OF CORPORATE STATUS

A corporation may terminate its status as a corporation either voluntarily by agreement or involuntarily by court order or state action.

A. VOLUNTARY DISSOLUTION

1. Procedure Prior to the Issuance of Stock

Prior to the issuance of stock, a corporation may voluntarily dissolve by a majority vote of the incorporators or initial directors. RMBCA § 14.01.

2. Procedure After the Issuance of Stock

A corporation that has issued stock may voluntarily dissolve if (i) the board of directors adopts a proposal for the dissolution of the corporation and (ii) the majority of shareholders approve. RMBCA § 14.02.

3. Effect of Dissolution—Winding Up

A dissolved corporation may continue to exist as a corporation for the limited purpose of winding up its affairs and liquidating its business. This includes (i) collecting assets, (ii) disposing of property that will not be distributed to shareholders, (iii) discharging liabilities, and (iv) distributing property among shareholders according to their interests.

It does not include (i) transferring title to the corporation's property, (ii) preventing transfer of shares or securities, (iii) changing quorum or voting requirements, (iv) terminating the authority of the registered corporate agent, or (v) preventing commencement of a proceeding by or against the corporation. RMBCA § 14.05.

4. Dissolution Distribution

The directors of a corporation are responsible for distribution of the corporate assets and may be liable for improper distributions. Such assets must be distributed in the following order:

i) To creditors of the corporation to pay the debts and other obligations of the corporation, including bona fide obligations owed to shareholders;

ii) To shareholders of stock with preferences in liquidation; and

iii) To shareholders of other stock.

RMBCA § 14.09.

B. INVOLUNTARY DISSOLUTION

Modern corporate statutes allow minority shareholders to ask the court to dissolve the corporation. A court may order involuntary dissolution if the shareholder shows one of the statutory grounds.

1. Petitioner

Either a shareholder or a creditor of a corporation may bring an action for involuntary dissolution of a corporation.

a. Creditor

A creditor may pursue the involuntary dissolution of a corporation only if the corporation is insolvent. RMBCA § 14.30(c).

b. Shareholder

A shareholder may pursue the involuntary dissolution of a corporation if:

    i) The corporate assets are being **misapplied** or wasted;

    ii) The directors or those in control of the corporation are acting illegally, **oppressively**, or fraudulently;

    iii) The **directors are deadlocked** in the management of the corporation's affairs, the shareholders are unable to break the deadlock, and irreparable injury to the corporation is threatened or being suffered; or

    iv) The **shareholders are deadlocked** in voting power and have failed to elect successors to the directors whose terms have expired.

RMBCA § 14.30(b). In a minority of states, deadlock is the exclusive ground for involuntary dissolutions. In some states, other grounds are available only to close corporations.

c. Oppression doctrine

The doctrine of shareholder oppression protects the minority from the improper exercise of majority control. Recent cases have made involuntary dissolution easier by interpreting statutory provisions regarding involuntary dissolution to refer to protecting the **reasonable expectations** of the shareholders in the corporation. *Matter of Kemp & Beatley, Inc.*, 473 N.E.2d 1173 (N.Y. 1984). Other courts have indicated that dissolution should be considered in light of the feasibility of protecting the expectations the parties originally had with regard to agreements about various forms of compensation. *Meiselman v. Meiselman*, 307 S.E.2d 551 (N.C. 1983).

2. Court's Power

Upon the petitioner's establishment of the necessary grounds, the court may dissolve the corporation. RMBCA § 14.30(a). The court has equitable powers to issue injunctions, appoint a receiver, and take other steps necessary to preserve the corporation's assets. RMBCA § 14.31. If the court orders the dissolution of the corporation, then the distribution of the corporation's assets generally adheres to that of a voluntary distribution unless equity requires otherwise.

C. FORFEITURE/ADMINISTRATIVE DISSOLUTION

The state may force a corporation to forfeit its right to exist or administratively dissolve the corporation if the corporation has (i) failed to pay fees or taxes, (ii) failed to file required reports or notices, or (iii) abused its powers. RMBCA §§ 14.20–14.21, 14.30(a). Continuing to operate as a corporation after forfeiture can result in the personal liability of the operators.

IX. SPECIAL TYPES OF CORPORATIONS

A. CLOSELY HELD AND CLOSE CORPORATIONS

The terms "closely held corporation" and "close corporation" are frequently used interchangeably to refer to a corporation with only a few shareholders and a more relaxed style of governance. Shareholders often serve as both directors and officers of the corporation. Stock of such a corporation is not publicly traded, and many states allow shareholders to do away with many of the corporate formalities.

B. FOREIGN CORPORATION

A foreign corporation is a corporation that is incorporated in another state. To do business in a state other than its state of incorporation, a corporation is required to register with that state and receive a "certificate of authority." Failure to do so prevents the foreign corporation from suing, but not from being sued, in state courts until registered. However, it does not impair the validity of corporate acts or contracts or prevent the corporation from defending any proceeding within the state. Many actions, such as holding board meetings, maintaining bank accounts, and selling through independent contractors, do not constitute doing business within a state. RMBCA §§ 15.01–15.32.

C. PROFESSIONAL CORPORATION

A professional corporation is a corporation with a purpose that is statutorily limited to the rendering of a professional service. A shareholder in a professional corporation must be a member of the applicable profession. In addition, a professional corporation does not shield an employee from liability arising from her own malpractice. However, it may provide protection against vicarious liability arising from malpractice by other professionals in the corporation.

D. S CORPORATION

A corporation is usually subject to tax as a "C corporation," which is a separate taxable entity from its shareholders, causing the corporation to face double taxation. The corporation pays taxes first on profits and again as shareholders on distributions received from the corporation. However, a corporation may elect to avoid double taxation as an "S corporation," in which the income and expenses of the corporation are passed through to shareholders (who are then taxed on such items directly). 26 U.S.C. § 1361, et seq.

To become an S corporation for federal tax purposes, a corporation must file Internal Revenue Service (IRS) Form 2553, and the IRS must approve the application. Companies that file as S corporations can have no more than 100 shareholders. Only individuals, estates, certain exempt organizations, or certain trusts may be shareholders, and the shareholders must all be either U.S. citizens or resident aliens (nonresident aliens are not permitted). The S corporation may not have more than one class of stock. Each shareholder must consent to the S corporation election for a corporation to become an S corporation.

E. BENEFIT CORPORATION

Many states have enacted benefit corporation acts. A benefit corporation is a for-profit entity with the corporate purpose of creating a general public benefit. Such benefits may include providing services to low-income or underserved individuals or communities, improving human health, preserving the environment, and promoting the arts, sciences, or advancement of knowledge.

X. LIMITED LIABILITY COMPANY

A limited liability company (LLC) is a legally recognized business entity distinct from its members that enjoys the pass-through tax advantage of a partnership but also the limited liability of a corporation. An LLC also provides flexibility in managing the entity.

All states have an LLC statute. The Uniform Limited Liability Company Act (ULLCA) was approved in 1996 and revised in 2006 and 2011; states have been slowly enacting the ULLCA. Many of the rules applicable to corporations and corporate governance have counterparts applicable to LLCs. Some of these rules are detailed below.

A. CREATION

1. Articles of Organization

An LLC is created by filing articles (certificate) of organization with the state, which merely reflects the existence of an LLC. Note that this document is different from articles of incorporation, a document that has a substantially greater power to affect the rules for the corporate entity and its owners. The articles of organization must include the LLC's name, mailing address, and, if there are no members upon filing, a statement to that effect.

2. Operating Agreement

An LLC may adopt an operating agreement that governs any or all aspects of its business. The operating agreement generally takes precedence over contrary statutory provisions, and statutory default provisions apply when the operating agreement is silent on an issue. An operating agreement is considered a contract that is governed by contract principles of law.

a. Form of agreement

The agreement can be oral, in a record, or implied by conduct, or any combination thereof, which is why the ULLCA refers to the agreement as a "record" rather than a writing.

b. Modification

Unless the operating agreement provides otherwise, the assent of all the persons then members is required for something to be considered part of the operating agreement. An agreement among fewer members might be enforceable among those members, but it would not be part of the operating agreement.

3. Membership

Many LLC statutes require that there be at least two members; however, one-member LLCs are possible. However, a person cannot become a member of an LLC without the consent of all other members of an LLC.

a. Transferability of membership

Unless the members otherwise agree, most LLC statutes provide that a member cannot transfer her LLC interest unless all members consent. The transfer of a membership interest to another person does not automatically give that person the right to participate in the management of the LLC. Instead, the transferee merely acquires the transferor's right to share in the LLC's profits and losses. ULLCA § 503. Some LLC statutes permit the articles of organization to provide standing consent for new members.

1) Charging order

Many statutes also permit transfer of financial rights to creditors, who can obtain a charging order against the member's interest. ULLCA § 503. A charging order constitutes a lien on a judgment debtor's transferable interest and requires the LLC to pay to the judgment debtor any distribution that otherwise would be paid to the member. A charging order is the sole method by which a judgment creditor of a member or transferee can extract any value from a member's ownership interest in an LLC. ULLCA §503(h). The operating agreement generally has no power to alter the provisions of this section to the prejudice of third parties.

b. Termination of membership

Withdrawal of a member from an LLC does not automatically trigger dissolution of the LLC. The LLC may elect to liquidate the fair value of that person's interests, as of the date the person ceased to be a member, based upon the person's right to share in distributions from the LLC. The continuing members of the LLC following the withdrawal of a member will be deemed to have entered into an operating agreement in effect immediately prior to the withdrawal, and the members bound by the operating agreement shall be only those members who have not withdrawn.

c. Allocation of profits and losses

Typically, the operating agreement of the LLC determines the manner in which profits and losses will be allocated among the members of the LLC. In the absence of such an agreement, profits and losses are allocated and distributions are made according to each member's contributions to the LLC.

d. Inspection rights

Most LLC statutes provide LLC members with inspection rights similar to shareholders (i.e., for a proper purpose and upon reasonable request). Whether a request is reasonable depends on the scope, reasons, importance of the information to the member, etc.

B. MANAGEMENT

An LLC can be member-managed (direct management of the LLC by its members) or manager-managed (centralized management of the LLC by one or more managers who need not be members). Unless the operating agreement or certificate of incorporation provide otherwise, the default management arrangement is a member-management. Nonetheless, a manager-managed LLC that does not designate a manager is still manager-managed with the manager position vacant. ULLCA § 407(c).

1. Liabilities

A member of an LLC is generally **not** liable as a member for an LLC's obligations. If a member renders professional services in an LLC, the member, as well as the LLC, may be liable for torts committed while rendering such services.

A manager or a managing member of an LLC is not personally liable for obligations incurred on behalf of the LLC. Members of a manager-managed LLC do not have the right to maintain a direct action against the manager of the LLC when the alleged misconduct caused harm only to the LLC.

a. Piercing the veil

Although LLC members are not liable for LLC obligations, most states recognize the possibility of piercing the veil of limited liability of an LLC in certain circumstances.

Although state courts have recognized piercing the veil in the LLC context, there must exist some circumstances that would justify piercing the veil on equitable grounds, such as undercapitalization of the business, commingling of assets, confusion of business affairs, or deception of creditors. Although less relevant in the LLC context, some courts will cite a failure to follow formalities in the LLC context as part of the rationale for piercing the LLC veil as well. *See Bonner v. Brunson*, 585 S.E.2d 917 (Ga. Ct. App. 2003).

Courts that pierce the veil rely on various theories to do so, including the "mere instrumentality" and "unity of interest and ownership" theories. *See Litchfield Asset Mgmt. Corp. v. Howell*, 799 A.2d 298 (Conn. App. Ct. 2002).

1) Mere instrumentality

Under the "mere instrumentality" test, a member would have to show that (i) the members dominated the entity in such a way that the LLC had no will of its own, (ii) the members used that domination to commit a fraud or wrong, and (iii) the control and wrongful action proximately caused the injury.

2) Unity of interest and ownership

Under the "unity of interest and ownership" test, a petitioner must demonstrate that there was such a unity of interest and ownership between the entity and the members that, in fact, the LLC did not have an existence independent of the members and that failure to pierce the veil through to the members would be unjust or inequitable.

2. Duties

Generally, members owe each other and managers (if any) a duty of loyalty and a duty of care. The operating agreement may amend those duties so long as the amendment is not "manifestly unreasonable."

a. Duty of loyalty

The duty of loyalty of a member in a member-managed LLC includes the duties to account to the company for any benefit derived by the member related to the company's activities or property, to refrain from dealing with the company on behalf of one having an adverse interest in the company, and to refrain from competing with the company. *See* ULLCA § 409 (b).

b. Duty of care

A member's duty of care is subject to the business judgment rule; it requires the member to act with the care that a person in a like position would reasonably exercise under similar circumstances and in a manner the member reasonably believes to be in the best interests of the company. *See* ULLCA § 409 (c).

Though managers (or members in a member-managed LLC) owe a duty of care to the LLC, they are not liable for simple negligence. The duty of care consists of refraining from engaging in grossly negligent conduct or reckless conduct, intentional misconduct, or a knowing violation of law. However, some state statutes reject the "gross negligence" standard and impose an ordinary negligence standard when determining breaches of a duty of care. In these states, the business judgment rule may apply to protect LLC managers from liability when decisions are made in good faith. ULLCA § 409(c).

c. Fiduciary waiver

Although courts generally frown upon corporate agreements that attempt to waive the duty of loyalty in self-dealing transactions, because LLCs are seen as more contractual in nature than corporations, fiduciary waivers are recognized in LLCs. Many LLC statutes even allow members to agree to specific types or categories of activities that do not violate the duty of loyalty, as long as the agreement is not **manifestly unreasonable**. ULLCA § 1103(b)(2).

3. Authority to Bind the LLC

The ULLC does not provide statutory apparent authority and instead relies on agency law principles. ULLCA § 110(a)(1), (3).

a. Member-managed LLC

Members of a member-managed LLC have broad authority to bind the LLC similar to that of a partner in a general partnership. ULLCA § 301(a). Each member has equal rights with respect to the management of the LLC. Unless the operating agreement otherwise provides, an act outside the ordinary course of the activities of the company may be undertaken only with the consent of all members. ULLCA § 407(b)(4).

b. Manager-managed LLC

Members of a manager-managed LLC do not have authority to bind the LLC. Matters relating to the activities of the company are decided exclusively by the managers. ULLCA § 407(c)(1).

4. Dissociation

A member can withdraw or dissociate at any time and without reason, even if doing so violates the operating agreement, by providing notice to the LLC. Written notice is not required under the ULLCA. Dissociation does not discharge the member's interest or liability, and does not necessarily trigger dissolution and winding up. Rather, by dissociating the member relinquishes his right to participate in the LLC and is entitled to distributions by the LLC only if the continuing members receive payment.

C. DIRECT AND DERIVATIVE SUITS

The direct/derivative distinction as an important safeguard to the members' agreed-upon arrangements in the operating agreement.

1. Direct Suits

Members may bring direct actions against the LLC and other members to enforce their rights as members under the operating agreement and the state LLC statute. To do so, a member must plead and prove an actual or threatened injury, which is not solely the result of an injury suffered by the LLC. ULLCA § 901. Although a member may sue the LLC or another member to enforce the member's rights under the operating agreement, members of a manager-managed LLC do not have the right to maintain a direct action against the manager of the LLC when the alleged misconduct caused harm only to the LLC. *See also Wright v. Herman*, 230 F.R.D. 1, 10 (2005).

2. Derivative Suits

Members may bring a derivative action on behalf of the LLC to enforce rights of the LLC. To do so, demand must be made on the other members or manager to bring an action if the member fails to do so, unless such demand would be futile. ULLCA § 902. The members must further allege in their complaint the efforts that they made to secure the manager's initiation or the reasons for not doing so. ULLCA § 904.

D. DISSOLUTION

Many of the more recent LLC statutes do not limit the duration of LLCs; duration is perpetual unless the operating agreement provides otherwise. ULLCA § 203. As is the case for other business entities, an LLC may merge with another LLC or another business entity (e.g., partnership, corporation).

1. Events Causing Dissolution

An LLC may dissolve upon the occurrence of various events, such as upon:

   i) Consent of all the members;

   ii) Passage of 90 consecutive days without members;

   iii) Court order; or

   iv) An event causing dissolution per the terms of the operating agreement.

ULLCA § 701.

2. Involuntary Dissolution

Some LLC statutes allow a member to seek a court order for involuntary dissolution if a controlling member acts in a way that is **oppressive and directly harmful** to the member seeking the order. ULLCA § 701(a)(5). Whether the member is successful depends on whether the action violated the member's **reasonable expectations**. Unless the operating agreement provides otherwise, the court may also order a remedy other than dissolution. ULLCA § 701(b). Finally, some states allow LLC members to contractually waive their right to petition for judicial dissolution.

3. Winding Up

In winding up its activities, the LLC must (i) discharge the company's debts, obligations, or other liabilities and (ii) settle and close the company's activities, and marshal and distribute the company's assets.

In addition, the LLC may perform acts necessary or appropriate to the winding up, including:

i) **File** a statement of dissolution or statement of termination;

ii) **Preserve** the company activities and property as a going concern for a reasonable time;

iii) **Prosecute** and defend actions and proceedings, whether civil, criminal, or administrative;

iv) **Transfer** the company's property; or

v) **Settle** disputes by mediation or arbitration.

ULLCA § 701.

Family Law

FAMILY LAW

Table of Contents

FAMILY LAW

I. GETTING MARRIED

Marriage is a civil contract. Similar to most contracts, marriage involves parties who are legally capable of consent, the exchange of consideration in the form of mutual promises, and the imposition of rights and obligations. Conversely, unlike most contracts, a marriage contract cannot be modified or terminated without state intervention. *Maynard v. Hill*, 125 U.S. 190 (1888). A marriage is valid if there is a license and a solemnization of the marriage (i.e., a ceremony).

There are typically two types of marriage recognized by law: ceremonial (or statutory) marriage and common-law marriage.

A. CEREMONIAL MARRIAGE

A ceremonial or statutory marriage requires that the parties obtain a license to get married. The couple must meet several requirements to obtain this license.

1. Licenses

a. Requirements

1) Age restrictions

All U.S. jurisdictions impose **minimum age restrictions** on individuals who wish to marry. Almost all U.S. jurisdictions require an individual, in the absence of parental consent, to be at least **18 years old**. Most U.S. jurisdictions permit individuals less than 18 years old to marry, generally requiring parental consent to, and/or judicial approval of the marriage. Statutory age requirements for marriage have withstood constitutional scrutiny. *See, e.g., Moe v. Dinkins*, 669 F.2d 67 (2d Cir. 1982) (the rational-basis test applies to the minimum age requirement to marry, and the state's important interest in promoting the welfare of children by preventing unstable marriages among those who lack capacity is a legitimate state interest).

2) Waiting period

Additionally, most U.S. jurisdictions impose a **waiting period** between the date of the marriage and the date of the marriage ceremony. The waiting period may typically be waived by the court in cases of an emergency.

3) Premarital medical testing

Some states also require a form of **premarital medical testing**. The requirements range from filing a health certificate or certifying the absence of a venereal disease to the testing of blood for certain diseases, including measles, tuberculosis, and sickle cell anemia. While a state can mandate the testing, it cannot condition the issuance of the license on the results of the test. *See T.E.P. v. Leavitt*, 840 F. Supp. 110 (D. Utah 1993) (invalidating a Utah statute prohibiting the marriage of an HIV afflicted individual as unconstitutional under the Americans With Disabilities Act).

4) Expiration date

By statute, most U.S. jurisdictions impose an expiration date on a marriage license.

b. When not issued

A marriage license will *not* be issued when:

    i) One of the parties is **married to someone else**;

    ii) The parties are **too closely related** as defined by statute;

    iii) The parties entered into the marriage as a **sham**; or

    iv) The parties are **incapable of understanding** the nature of the act.

Uniform Marriage and Divorce Act (UMDA) § 207.

> Most jurisdictions further provide that marriage licenses will not be issued when, at the time that the license was sought, one or both parties were **under the influence** of alcohol, drugs, or another substance that rendered the person(s) incapable, or when a party lacked consent due to duress or fraud.

c. Same-sex marriage

Same-sex couples may now marry in all states. In addition, all states and the federal government must recognize a same-sex marriage legally entered into in another state. *Obergefell v. Hodges*, 576 U.S. ___, 135 S. Ct. 2584 (2015); *U.S. v. Windsor*, 570 U.S. ___, 133 S. Ct. 2675 (2013).

2. Solemnization

Most states do not prescribe a particular form of the marriage ceremony, but many require that any ceremony solemnizing the marriage be performed in front of at least two witnesses. Some states even allow for a proxy to stand in for one of the parties who cannot attend the ceremony as long as the party provides written authorization for the third person to act as a proxy. Additionally, in most jurisdictions, a judge, political official, or member of the clergy of a recognized religious organization must solemnize a marriage. The marriage license must be completed and filed with the appropriate government office.

B. COMMON-LAW MARRIAGE

Common-law marriages are defined as marriages when the parties:

    i) **Agree** they are married;

    ii) **Cohabit** as married; and

    iii) **Hold themselves out** in public as married.

UMDA § 209.

Unlike with a ceremonial marriage, no ceremony takes place and no license is issued for a common-law marriage. A common-law marriage is not valid if either party was married to someone else at the time that the common-law marriage was entered into. UMDA § 209.

1. Recognition of Common-Law Marriages

Most states have abolished common-law marriages. Common-law marriages are recognized only in Colorado, the District of Columbia, Iowa, Kansas, Montana, Rhode Island, South Carolina, Texas, and Utah. Some states (Georgia, Idaho, Ohio, Oklahoma, and Pennsylvania) recognize common-law marriages that occurred within the state before a certain date.

Even though most states do not permit common-law marriages, almost all states recognize common-law marriages entered into in a jurisdiction that does recognize such relationships. Despite the Full Faith and Credit Clause of the U.S. Constitution, which requires each state to give full faith and credit to the "public acts, records, and judicial proceedings of every other state," the U.S. Supreme Court has recognized that states have greater freedom in applying the laws of another state in a particular circumstance than in enforcing a judgment by a court in another state. *Baker v. General Motors Corp.*, 522 U.S. 222 (1998). Under conflict-of-law principles, a state need not recognize a marriage valid under the law of the place in which it was contracted if it violates a strong public policy of the state asked to recognize the marriage. Some jurisdictions recognize a common-law marriage when the parties had only a short, transitory visit to the permitting state, while other jurisdictions require that the parties be domiciled in the permitting state. Some jurisdictions consider the inquiry on an individual basis, weighing the harm to the claimant seeking recognition and the state's policy against such marriage.

> **EXAM NOTE:** On the bar exam, assume that the jurisdiction has abolished common-law marriage unless the question states otherwise.

2. Legal and Mental Capacity

For a couple to enter into a common-law marriage, they both must have the legal and mental capacity to do so. To satisfy the legal capacity requirement, they must be old enough and not too closely related. The determination of mental capacity is the same used to determine eligibility to obtain a license in a ceremonial marriage (e.g., they must understand the nature of the act).

3. Intent

Jurisdictions vary on the proof necessary to establish the requisite elements for a common-law marriage. *See, e.g., Buford v. Buford*, 874 So.2d 562 (Ala. 2004) (clear and convincing evidence); *Callen v. Callen*, 620 S.E.2d 59 (S.C. 2005) (preponderance of the evidence). The parties must produce evidence that they intended to enter into the marriage, and this must be evidenced by **words in the present tense** made for the purpose of establishing a valid legal marital relationship.

Words in the future tense that indicate the parties agree to get married at a later date are **not** valid to show intent.

In the event that the parties are unable to show evidence of their intent to marry in present-tense words, the court may look to cohabitation or reputation to determine if the couple holds or held themselves out as married. The courts, however, have consistently held that cohabitation alone does not support a common-law marriage. *In re Thomas' Estate*, 367 N.Y.S.2d 182 (N.Y. Sur. 1975).

C. HEARTBALM ACTIONS

Traditionally, if a marriage failed to take place, the jilted party was permitted to file a heartbalm action, which is a civil suit for money damages based on the damage to the jilted party's reputation when the engagement was broken. Abolished by the majority of states, only nine jurisdictions (Hawaii, Illinois, Mississippi, Missouri, New Hampshire, New Mexico, North Carolina, South Dakota, and Utah) currently recognize heartbalm actions, which include actions for breach of promise to marry, seduction, alienation of affection, criminal conversation, and jactitation of marriage (falsely holding oneself out as married).

> **EXAM NOTE:** On the bar exam, assume that the jurisdiction has abolished heartbalm actions, unless the question states otherwise.

D. THE MARRIAGE RELATIONSHIP

The relationship between spouses brings with it myriad rights and responsibilities, as well as constitutional privacy issues that are germane to married couples. As the marriage relationship and individual rights continue to evolve, new law will more than likely continue to develop.

When it comes to disputes of intact families, courts treat such matters as private ones that should be resolved within the home. Unless and until the parties separate, courts will refuse to decide such disputes. *See Kilgrow v. Kilgrow*, 107 So. 2d 885, 888-89 (Ala. 1958).

II. ENDING A MARRIAGE

A valid marriage, including a common-law marriage, can be terminated only by **annulment**, **divorce**, or **death**.

A. ANNULMENT

An annulment voids a marriage and declares it as having never been valid (as opposed to divorce, which terminates a valid marriage). An annulment action involves two types of relationships: void and voidable.

1. Void Marriage

A void marriage is treated as if it never happened. It does not need to be judicially dissolved and will not be legally recognized for any purpose. UMDA § 208.

a. Prior existing marriage

If either party has a valid prior existing marriage at the time that the subsequent marriage is entered into, then the latter marriage is void. However, if one of the parties had a good-faith belief that the marriage was valid, then some states allow the marriage to become valid once the impediment is removed. Other states require that once the impediment is removed, the parties must continue to cohabit, and one party must still continue to believe in good faith that it is a valid marriage.

1) Good-faith belief in the death of a spouse

Most states have adopted what is known as an "Enoch Arden" statute in bigamy cases. In those jurisdictions, there is a defense to bigamy if the parties had a good-faith belief that the previous spouse was dead. The courts differ in the treatment of such marriages. Some jurisdictions require a divorce proceeding from the original spouse once the existence of the spouse is determined as a prerequisite to validating the later marriage.

2) Presumption of validity

There is a presumption that the latest marriage is valid. This presumption is rebuttable by cogent evidence of the existence of a prior valid marriage at the time that the latest marriage was entered into.

b. Incest

Incest is marriage or sexual relations between people related within the prohibited degree of kinship. All states restrict marriages by consanguinity (blood relationships), and nearly half bar marriages between first cousins. Typically, most consanguinity statutes also prohibit marriages between relatives of half blood, and many prohibit it when the relationship is by adoption. *But see Bagnardi v. Harnett*, 366 N.Y.S.2d 89 (N.Y. 1975) (marriage between adoptive father and daughter permissible); *Israel v. Allen*, 577 P.2d 762 (Colo. 1978) (unconstitutional to prohibit adoptive siblings from marrying).

c. Mental incapacity

A person must be able to understand the nature of the marriage contract, and its duties and responsibilities, to enter into a marriage. Note that a marriage contract entered into during a lucid moment is valid, as long as the person understood the nature of the contract at the moment the contract was executed.

2. Voidable Marriage

A voidable marriage is valid until one spouse seeks to legally void the marriage. There must be a **judicial decree** to dissolve the marriage. Grounds for a voidable marriage include age, impotence, intoxication, and fraud or duress. UMDA § 208.

a. Age

A party who is under the age of consent to marry and who did not seek the consent of his parents or the court may apply to have the marriage annulled. If the partner, however, is of legal age to marry, then the partner may not attack the validity of her marriage to an underage person. In many states, the declaration of validity may also be brought by the underage party's parents or legal guardian. Many courts, however, will prohibit the filing of an annulment based on age once the party who was not of legal age has attained such age and continued to freely cohabit with the other party as a married couple.

> **Example:** A, who is 16, marries B, who is 21, in a state that requires parental consent or court approval when a party is under the age of 18. Neither consent nor approval is obtained. Until A reaches the age of 18, only A, her parents, or her legal guardian may seek an annulment. If A turns 18 before seeking the annulment, then the court will most likely deny the request.

b. Impotence

A marriage is voidable if one party is "naturally and incurably" impotent, unless the other party knew about the condition before the marriage.

c. Intoxication

If either party was under the influence of drugs or alcohol at the time of marriage, which made that party incapable of contracting into a marriage, then that marriage may be annulled. In most jurisdictions, however, the parties must be able to demonstrate that they did not ratify the marriage by continuing to voluntarily live with each other after the ceremony.

d. Fraud, misrepresentation, duress, coercion, or force

Most states permit an annulment when the marriage was the result of a fraud that goes to the essence of a marriage. To annul a marriage based on fraud, it must be based on present—not future—facts. Most courts require that the parties immediately cease living together once the fraud is discovered. Concealment of defective morals, character, habits, fortune, and temper are typically insufficient grounds for an annulment. Jurisdictions have differed, however, on claims of misrepresentation when a woman has falsely claimed to be pregnant by a man, or on claims relating to a party's religious beliefs.

e. Lack of intent

Most jurisdictions permit annulment when the parties participated in the marriage ceremony as an act of jest or hilarity and do not have the requisite intention to be bound by the act. Most courts annulling marriages in such circumstances have determined that the interest of the public would not be served by requiring the parties to remain married. This also includes cases in which the parties, in advance, agree to only some, but not all, of the conventional aspects of marriage, including sexual and emotional fidelity, economic interdependence, and commitment to the relationship. Often seen in cases with immigration issues, this type of marriage is commonly referred to as a "limited purpose" marriage.

3. Equitable Distribution of Property in an Annulment

Just because a marriage is terminated by annulment rather than divorce does not mean that parties to annulled marriages have no rights. The party seeking the annulment still has a right to request an equitable distribution of property and, in some cases, spousal support. That party may also seek child support, custody, attorney's fees, and other costs related to the dissolution of the marriage. Many jurisdictions have statutorily provided courts with the ability to award spousal support. In states without this statute, courts will not award spousal support. However, many of these states allow temporary spousal support during the pendency of the suit. Also, most courts will not reinstate spousal support from a previous marriage.

4. Children

Children of an annulled marriage are nevertheless considered marital children.

5. Defenses

When a marriage is void, the only way to defend against the annulment is to deny the existence of the impediment that voided the marriage. Removing the impediment merely makes the marriage voidable, but it will not necessarily prevent the annulment.

In annulling voidable marriages, courts recognize the equitable defenses of unclean hands, laches, and estoppel.

6. Putative Marriage Doctrine

Most jurisdictions, either by statute or common law, have adopted a version of the putative marriage doctrine (also known as "putative spouse doctrine"). *See, e.g., Williams v. Williams*, 97 P.3d 1124 (Nev. 2004); *In re Marriage of Himes*, 136 Wash. 2d 707 (1998); Colo., Rev. Stat. Ann. § 14-2-111 (West 2003). The purpose of the doctrine is to protect a party who is unaware of an impediment to the marriage that makes it either void or voidable. Under the doctrine, a party who participated in a ceremonial marriage and believes in good faith that the marriage is valid may use a state's divorce provisions even if the marriage is later found void due to an impediment. UMDA § 209.

Because a putative marriage is not technically a marriage, divorce is not needed to terminate a relationship. The doctrine, however, is normally invoked to provide equitable relief, including maintenance and property distribution.

B. DIVORCE AND SEPARATION

Divorce is a legal dissolution of a marriage.

1. Residency Requirement

Most states have a residency requirement that requires at least one of the parties to be a resident of the state. The required length of residency in a state before a party can file for divorce can turn on several factors, such as whether the couple was married in the state or the grounds for divorce happened in the state.

2. **Grounds for Divorce**

Most jurisdictions recognize both fault and no-fault grounds for divorce, although a substantial minority recognize no-fault grounds as the only basis for a divorce. The no-fault statutes eliminate fault and wrong as grounds for dissolution.

a. **No-fault**

Every jurisdiction recognizes a no-fault ground for divorce. The majority of the jurisdictions require a party to allege that the marriage is **irretrievably broken** and there is no prospect of reconciliation (e.g., irreconcilable differences). Despite the terminology, the fact that the discord stems from a curable condition will not prevent divorce on a no-fault ground.

About half the states require that the couple be separated for a specific time (e.g., one year) prior to the filing of the divorce action. The fact that one spouse wishes to reconcile may lengthen the time period for obtaining a divorce, but it is not an absolute bar to a no-fault divorce.

Most jurisdictions have abolished the traditional defenses to divorce. The only defense would be to deny the ground for the divorce. However, unless both parties agree, this is generally insufficient to prevent the divorce.

b. **Fault**

Fault grounds for divorce include adultery, cruelty, desertion, habitual drunkenness, bigamy, imprisonment, indignity, and mental disorder. Most jurisdictions retain some level of fault-based grounds, although some have removed it from the law since the adoption of no-fault grounds. The use of fault-based divorce grounds has decreased dramatically since the adoption of no-fault-based grounds in most jurisdictions, although fault is often considered when awarding maintenance.

1) **Adultery**

Adultery is voluntary sexual intercourse with someone other than one's spouse. Because the details of adultery are rarely known to both parties, it is usually proven by circumstantial evidence. It must be shown that a party had the **opportunity and the inclination** to commit adultery. The facts of the case must provide enough evidence to conclude that the person was guilty of the adulterous act.

2) **Cruelty**

To prevail on the grounds of cruelty or inhumane treatment, most jurisdictions require that the plaintiff demonstrate a course of conduct by the other party that is harmful to the plaintiff's physical or mental health and that makes the continued cohabitation between the parties unsafe or improper. The conduct of the defendant must be serious and typically cannot be based on one isolated incident. The majority of jurisdictions permit divorces on the basis of cruelty in cases of physical abuse, while only some permit it in cases of only emotional abuse or mental cruelty.

3) **Desertion**

Desertion (also called "abandonment") results when one spouse, without cause or the consent of the other spouse, voluntarily leaves the marital home with the intent to remain apart on a permanent basis. Most jurisdictions require that the abandonment be for a statutorily designated period of time. Some jurisdictions also find desertion when one spouse forces another out of the marital home, and there is a fear of harm if that spouse returns. If the parties separate by mutual consent, the ground of desertion will not apply.

4) Habitual drunkenness

Some states permit habitual drunkenness as a ground for divorce if it is the frequent habit of getting drunk that causes impairment in the marital relationship. There is no requirement that the defendant be an alcoholic or that she be constantly under the influence of alcohol, but **more than an occasional level** of intoxication is required. A possible defense to the grounds of habitual drunkenness may be assumption of the risk.

5) Bigamy

Bigamy, which in most jurisdictions is also grounds for annulment, occurs when one of the parties in the marriage **knowingly** entered into a prior legal and existing marriage before entering into the current marriage.

6) Imprisonment

Imprisonment of one spouse for a specified period of time may be grounds for divorce.

7) Indignity

Indignity grounds arise when one spouse exhibits negative behavior toward the other that renders that spouse's condition intolerable and life burdensome. Indignity can include: vulgarity, unmerited reproach, habitual laziness, neglect, intentional incivility, manifest disdain, abusive language, malignant ridicule, habitual humiliating treatment, repeated accusations of infidelity, sexually deviant behavior, serious temper tantrums, or violence. Although it is still available in some states, indignity is no longer recognized in the majority of states.

8) Institutionalization

Institutionalization is grounds for divorce if a spouse's insanity or serious mental condition results in her being confined to a mental institution for a specified period of time prior to the commencement of the divorce, and there is **no reasonable prospect of discharge** or rehabilitation.

3. Defenses

Defenses apply only to a fault-based divorce and must be affirmatively pleaded when asserted.

a. Recrimination and unclean hands

Recrimination occurs when both spouses have committed a marital wrongdoing of like conduct. In other words, because both parties were guilty of the same offense (e.g., adultery) that would justify a divorce, a court could not grant the request. A similar defense is "unclean hands," when the plaintiff's own behavior or acts are questionable. Both of these defenses are most commonly seen in desertion, adultery, or cruelty cases.

b. Connivance

Connivance is consent to or participation in the marital wrong, usually adultery (e.g., allowing or benefitting from a spouse's prostitution).

c. Condonation

Forgiveness of a spouse is a defense to a fault-based divorce. There must be knowledge of the misconduct and forgiveness of the misconduct, and the party must resume marital relations with the guilty party. It is typically based on a promise not to engage in the misconduct again. At common law, once an act was forgiven, it could not become future grounds for divorce.

d. Collusion

Collusion occurs when both spouses "conspired to fabricate" grounds for divorce. Collusion defenses are not as common since the adoption of no-fault grounds in many jurisdictions.

e. Provocation

If misconduct is provoked by the moving party, then it is not grounds for divorce.

f. Insanity

Insanity is a valid defense when one spouse does not know the difference between right and wrong or lacks the ability to understand that an act is wrongful.

g. Consent

Consent is a defense to desertion or adultery.

h. Justification

Justification grounds may be established if one party left the home because of the other's misconduct. This is a defense to desertion.

i. Religion

A litigant that challenges a divorce on religious grounds will fail in all jurisdictions.

4. Limited Divorce and Separate Maintenance

Limited divorce, known in some states as a "divorce from bed and board," is recognized in most jurisdictions, but rarely used. When used, it is often for religious or medical reasons, as the parties do not sever the marital tie and are still considered legally married. They are, however, permitted to live apart. As with an absolute divorce, the court will determine support and property division.

A separate maintenance action provides for a decree of support for a party, typically the wife and any minor children. It does not, however, authorize the parties to live apart. As with a limited divorce, the parties are still considered married and cannot remarry.

5. Finalizing Divorce

When a divorce is initially granted, many states do not permit a divorce to be finalized until a specified period of time has elapsed. This is known as an "interlocutory" decree. During this interlocutory period, neither spouse can remarry.

C. MEDIATION

Mediation is a frequently used, less expensive, and often more effective manner to resolve separation disputes. A neutral, court-approved mediator assists both parties with spousal- and child-support issues, as well as custody and visitation rights. Discussions during the mediation process and the written agreement derived from the discussions remain confidential, unless both parties agree to their disclosure. The court may approve the agreement and make it part of the final judgment. A mediator must conduct the mediation process in an impartial manner and disclose all and potential grounds of bias and conflicts of interest. A mediator must facilitate the participants' understanding of what mediation is. A mediator should recognize a family situation involving domestic abuse and take appropriate steps to shape the mediation process accordingly. Additionally, a mediator shall structure the mediation process so that the participants make decisions based on sufficient information and knowledge.

D. DIVISION OF PROPERTY

There are two methods relating to the distribution of assets in the United States: **community property** and **equitable distribution**.

1. Community Property

Community property is a method for the distribution of marital assets that is used in nine states: Arizona, California, Idaho, Louisiana, Nevada, New Mexico, Texas, Washington, and Wisconsin. The guiding principle behind community property is that **marriage is a partnership**. Most community-property states require an equal division of the marital property.

2. Equitable Distribution

Most states follow a system of equitable distribution. The objective of the equitable-distribution system is to order a **fair distribution** of all marital property, taking into consideration all of the circumstances between the parties. Unlike a community-property division, an equitable distribution is not necessarily an equal division of marital assets. There are, however, a few states that presume that an equitable division is an equal division, but permit deviation when necessary to achieve a more equitable result.

3. Marital Property

In most states, all property acquired during the marriage is marital property and subject to equitable distribution. Some states subject all property owned by either spouse to equitable distribution (i.e., the "hotchpot" approach). The definition of marital property is typically broadly applied and includes retirement benefits and, under some circumstances, equity in nonmarital property. Classification of the appreciation in nonmarital property will typically depend on whether it remains separate property and if the appreciation can be attributable to spousal labor. Title to the property is immaterial. If a party claims that an asset is nonmarital and not subject to equitable distribution, then the burden is placed on that party to prove the assertion.

a. Exceptions to marital property

Most states treat certain property as separate, rather than marital, property. Among the types of property treated as separate property are the following:

i) Property **acquired before the marriage** or property acquired in exchange for property acquired before the marriage;

ii) Property **excluded by the parties' valid agreement** entered into before, during, or after the marriage;

iii) Property **acquired by gift or inheritance**, or property acquired in exchange for such property, except when it is between spouses;

iv) Property a party has **sold, granted, conveyed,** or otherwise disposed of in good faith and for value before the date of final separation;

v) Property to the extent that it has been **mortgaged or otherwise encumbered in good faith** for value before the date of final separation; and

vi) Any **award or settlement payment received** for any cause of action or claim that accrued before the marriage, regardless of when the payment was received.

> **Example:** One spouse was in a car accident two years before the marriage. That spouse was granted a settlement of $200,000 for her pain and suffering and invested it in the stock market before the marriage. The $200,000 would not be marital property.

b. Factors in the distribution of marital property

Courts consider the following factors in the distribution of property:

i) Length of the marriage;

ii) Prior marriages;

iii) Age, health, earnings, earning potential, liabilities, and needs of both spouses;

iv) Contributions to education;

v) Needs for future acquisitions;

vi) Income, medical needs, retirement of both spouses;

vii) Contributions to increases in marital property, including homemaking and child-rearing services;

viii) Value of separate property;

ix) Reduction in valuation in marital property by one spouse;

x) Standard of living;

xi) Economic circumstances of each spouse at the time of divorce; and

xii) Custodianship of any minor children.

In most states, the fact that a divorce is granted on a fault ground, such as adultery, is not a factor in the distribution of property. However, dissipation of marital property may be a factor. Dissipation occurs when one spouse uses marital property for his sole benefit after the marriage has irreconcilably broken down, such as the purchase of expensive gifts for a paramour.

4. Treatment of Specific Types of Marital Property

a. Professional licenses or degrees

The majority of jurisdictions do not treat a professional license or degree as a distributable property interest. *Simmons v. Simmons*, 708 A.2d 949 (Conn. 1998); *but cf. Elkus v. Elkus*, 572 N.Y.S.2d 901 (1 Dep't 1991) (a professional degree is an asset subject to equitable distribution). Most courts look at advanced degrees or licenses as an acquisition of knowledge as opposed to a property interest. A court may, however, view an advanced degree or license as increased earning capacity, which may have an effect on the determination of alimony. A court may also use its equity power to award a spouse reimbursement for his actual contribution toward the other spouse's educational and related living expenses. This is often referred to as the "cost-value" approach.

b. Retirement or pension benefits

Retirement or pension benefits acquired during the marriage are considered marital property and are subject to equitable distribution. This includes military pensions.

c. Personal-injury claim proceeds

Jurisdictions differ on the treatment of proceeds from personal-injury claims and worker's compensation claims. There are two basic approaches:

1) Marital property

In some jurisdictions, if the cause of action accrues between the date of the marriage and the final separation, the proceeds from the settlement or award are marital property. As long as the cause of action accrued during the marriage, the proceeds are marital property—even if the claim is paid after the final separation.

2) Separate and marital allocation

Other jurisdictions view the nature of the award to determine whether it is separate or marital property and allocate the award between nonmarital and marital property. Compensatory damages for pain, suffering, disability, and loss are considered the separate property of the injured spouse. Consortium losses are considered separate property of the non-injured spouse. Awards for lost wages, loss of earning capacity, and medical expenses are typically split. The court calculates the portion of the award attributable from the time of the accident until the termination of the marriage, and it treats that portion as marital property. Any part of the award attributable to loss of wages or medical expenses after the termination of the marriage is separate property.

d. Goodwill

The reputation and clientele of a professional practice (such as that of a doctor or lawyer) is considered marital property in some jurisdictions.

e. Accumulated sick and vacation days

Jurisdictions are split on the issue of whether vacation and sick days are marital property. Courts have held the following: (1) accrued vacation and sick days are marital property subject to division at the time of dissolution; (2) accrued vacation and sick days are marital property but are subject to distribution when received, as opposed to the time of dissolution; and (3) accrued vacation and sick days are not marital property. *Presby v. Presby*, 2004 Ohio 3050 (Ohio Ct. App. 2004) (accumulated days that can be cashed out are considered marital property to be distributed at the time of dissolution); *Ryan v. Ryan*, 261 N.J. Super 689 (1992) (when payment for the unused accumulated days was received at separation, it constituted marital property if the majority of the days were accrued during the marriage).

f. Future interest

A possible future interest in property (e.g., inheritance) is not distributable.

g. Social Security

Social Security benefits are not subject to equitable distribution. *Fleming v. Nestor*, 363 U.S. 603 (1960) (applying accrued property rights to the Social Security system would deprive it of the flexibility in adjustment that it demands).

h. Post-separation property

In most states, property acquired by one spouse until a divorce is granted can be marital property. Some states treat property acquired by a spouse after permanently separating from the other spouse as separate property. Still other states draw the line between marital and separate property on the date that the divorce action is filed.

i. Stock options

Stock options acquired during the marriage are marital property even if they will not be exercised until after the marriage.

5. Tax Consequences of Equitable Distribution

Equitable distribution payments are not taxed in the same manner as regular income. Property that is transferred between divorcing spouses is tax-free at that time. The transferee's tax basis is the same as the transferor's, and the property becomes taxable when it is sold.

6. Modification of a Property Division Award

A property division under either approach is not modifiable because it is based on the parties' assets at the time of divorce. Changes in the parties' circumstances after divorce are not considered once the award has been entered.

III. FINANCIAL SUPPORT OF SPOUSES AND CHILDREN

A. SPOUSAL MAINTENANCE

Spousal support (also called **maintenance** or **alimony**) is the obligation of one party to provide the other with support in the form of income. It is awarded in a divorce if one spouse cannot provide for his own needs with employment. Alimony payments can be made for a definite or indefinite period of time. Unlike property settlements, alimony obligations cannot be discharged in bankruptcy.

1. Factors

Each jurisdiction provides by statute the criteria to be applied by the court in determining the eligibility and amount of a maintenance award. The majority of jurisdictions consider some or all of the following factors when determining the support award.

a. Financial resources

Courts consider the financial resources of the spouse seeking support, including property to be awarded in the divorce and any child support. They also take each spouse's earning potential into account, as well as the ability of the spouse from whom support is sought to pay.

b. Standard of living

The couple's standard of living during the marriage is considered.

c. Time

Courts also consider the time it will take for a spouse to find employment or to complete any education or training necessary for a job.

d. Length of the marriage

The length of the marriage is considered in determining spousal support.

e. Contributions to the marriage

Contributions by one spouse to the marriage, particularly those that enhanced the earning potential of the other spouse (e.g., education, training), may be considered.

f. Age and health

The parties' age and health, both physical and mental, is considered in determining support.

g. Marital misconduct

Fault or marital misconduct may be taken into account in many states in determining spousal support. The weight that the marital misconduct is given in determining alimony is dependent on the jurisdiction, with some considering it as a factor and others giving it a preclusive effect. *See Stevens v. Stevens*, 484 N.Y.S.2d 708 (3d Dep't 1985) (marital fault may only be considered when the conduct of the recipient is egregious); 23 Pa. Cons. Stat. § 3701(b) (marital misconduct is one of 17 factors to be considered when determining alimony).

2. Types of Support

Spousal support may be any of the following types:

a. Lump sum

A lump-sum spousal support award is a fixed amount and may not be modified in the absence of fraud.

b. Permanent

Permanent alimony is an award for the remainder of the dependent spouse's life, unless certain circumstances occur. The purpose behind permanent alimony is to compensate the dependent spouse for either the lost earning capacity or benefit conferred to the other spouse during the marriage. It is primarily used in cases in which one spouse remained out of the workforce for homemaking or child-rearing purposes. Permanent alimony is typically awarded only when the marriage was one of long duration. Although jurisdictions differ on the definition of "long-term," it typically refers to a marriage of 15 years or more.

c. Limited duration

Limited-duration alimony is established for a limited period of time. Unlike rehabilitative or reimbursement alimony (discussed below), its purpose is not to facilitate an increased earning capacity of the dependent spouse or to compensate a spouse who has sacrificed. Limited-duration alimony is typically awarded when the marriage was of short duration (making permanent alimony inappropriate), but there is still an economic need for support.

d. Rehabilitative

Rehabilitative support is for a limited period of time, such as until the spouse receives education or employment. The purpose of rehabilitative alimony is to enhance and improve the earning capacity of the economically dependent spouse. For example, a spouse may be required to pay rehabilitative alimony for a period of four years while a dependent spouse attends college. The payments would automatically terminate at the end of the four-year period.

e. Reimbursement

The purpose of reimbursement alimony is to compensate a spouse for financial sacrifices made during the marriage that resulted in a reduced standard of living to secure an enhanced standard of living in the future. Often, this type of alimony is awarded only in cases in which one spouse did not work in order to secure an advanced degree or professional license. It is rarely used, and unlike the other forms of alimony, it is based on past contributions rather than present or future needs. Instead of reimbursement alimony, some jurisdictions treat this type of payment as property division.

f. Palimony

Available in only a few states, palimony is support provided by one unmarried cohabitant to another after the dissolution of their relationship. First recognized in 1976 by the *Marvin* decision, palimony is available only when the cohabitants have lived together in a stable, long-term relationship. *Marvin v. Marvin*, 557 P.2d 106 (Cal. 1976). The treatment of such cohabitation agreements and the resulting support of palimony vary among jurisdictions. A majority of jurisdictions distinguish between contracts that are based on sexual services and those in which the agreement is independent of the illicit relationship. Some courts also permit remedies to unmarried couples based on an implied-in-fact contract, resulting trust, constructive trust, or quantum meruit theories. In most states, the Statute of Frauds does not require that an express contract between cohabitants be in writing.

3. Modification of Support

In general, spousal support may be modified, even when it has been deemed permanent. The party seeking modification typically has the burden of establishing a significant change in circumstances in the needs of the dependent spouse or financial abilities of the obligor that warrant the modification. As with child support, a party who willfully or voluntarily reduces her income will not receive a reduction in her support payments.

a. Death

Spousal support generally continues until the death of a spouse. Support is usually not included as a liability of the deceased spouse's estate, unless specified by the court.

b. Remarriage

In most jurisdictions, if the receiving spouse remarries, then spousal support may be terminated. A subsequent annulment of this marriage generally does not revive a spousal-support obligation from a former marriage, even though an annulment usually results in a marriage being treated as invalid as of the date of its inception. The marriage of the obligor spouse can constitute a change in circumstances that justifies the reduction in spousal support to the receiving spouse.

c. Cohabitation

If the receiving spouse cohabits with someone who is not family, then spousal support may be modified if the recipient spouse's need for the support decreases as a result of the cohabitation. Support, however, typically is not automatically terminated, as the new cohabitant does not have a legal duty to support the alimony recipient. Cohabitation can also forestall the award of spousal support. The courts, however, will also consider the nature of the cohabitation, such as whether the cohabitation involves a sexual relationship.

Cohabitation does not terminate alimony pendente lite, which is paid during the pendency of the divorce litigation.

d. Retirement

Jurisdictions differ on whether an obligor can seek a reduction in spousal-support payments upon retirement. Some jurisdictions hold that the parties should have addressed the issue during the divorce proceedings and deny modification, while other jurisdictions find that the dependent spouse cannot expect to receive the same level of support after the supporting spouse retires.

4. Support During Marriage

At common law, a husband was obligated to support his wife, and the duty was enforceable under the necessaries doctrine. A necessary item was something suitable to the parties' station in life, including medically necessary care. Most jurisdictions have modified the necessaries doctrine to apply equally to both spouses, and often refer to them as "family expense" statutes. A minority of jurisdictions have abolished the doctrine as a violation of equal protection rights.

In those jurisdictions retaining the doctrine, a creditor may sue either spouse for payment of necessaries, but it may be required to seek payment first from the incurring spouse.

B. JURISDICTION

As with a court hearing other matters, a court hearing a family-related dispute must generally have both subject-matter jurisdiction and personal jurisdiction. Most states have statutory residency requirements, typically ranging from six weeks to two years, for a court to have subject-matter jurisdiction. The Full Faith and Credit Clause applies to divorce decrees as long as one of the spouses was a resident of the state that granted the decree.

Matrimonial courts have full equity powers in matrimonial actions, which include:

i) Division of property;

ii) Divorce or annulment;

iii) Custody;

iv) Support and alimony;

v) Award of attorney's fees;

vi) Enforcement of separation agreements; and

vii) All other matters related to matrimonial actions.

1. Divisible Divorce Doctrine

Under the doctrine of divisible divorce, also known as ex parte divorce, a court may have sufficient jurisdiction to grant a divorce but lack such jurisdiction with respect to other divorce-related matters, such as property division, alimony, and child support. A court with subject-matter jurisdiction over the divorce action as well as personal jurisdiction over one spouse can grant a divorce, but it cannot determine property division, alimony, or child-support issues without personal jurisdiction over the other spouse. If a court makes such a determination, the defendant can challenge the court's orders due to the court's lack of in personam jurisdiction over the defendant. *Estin v. Estin*, 334 U.S. 541 (1948); *Vanderbilt v. Vanderbilt*, 354 U.S. 416 (1957).

2. Collateral Attack on Jurisdiction

The only way for the nonresident defendant to attack the issuance of an ex parte divorce is to demonstrate that the plaintiff either was not domiciled in the divorcing state at the time that the judgment was granted or left the state's domicile immediately after the entry of the divorce. If the court had both personal and subject-matter jurisdiction over the parties, and the attacking party litigated or had the opportunity to litigate, then that person will be precluded from collaterally attacking the judgment in any jurisdiction. *Sherrer v. Sherrer*, 334 U.S. 343 (1948). This is often seen in cases in which the parties colluded to obtain an out-of-state divorce. Although persons other than the party may collaterally attack a divorce if standing exists (i.e., a child), they will be precluded from attacking it if the third person is in privity with any party who would have been estopped from attacking the judgment themselves.

3. Issues Relating to Indigent Parties

Courts cannot require that an indigent party pay costs and fees to access the court system. Such requirements are unconstitutional. *Boddie v. Connecticut*, 401 U.S. 371 (1971). Although there is no legal right to counsel for indigent parties in divorce proceedings, the court has the discretion to award attorney's fees and costs if the party is unable to afford the services of legal counsel.

C. CHILD SUPPORT

1. Child's Right to Support

Child support is the payment by one parent to the other for the support of a common child. The duration of child support varies with each jurisdiction. In all jurisdictions, both parents (custodial and noncustodial), regardless of marital status, are legally required to support their minor children (i.e., unemancipated and 18 years of age or younger). *Gomez v. Perez*, 409 U.S. 535 (1973) (a state law that bases the existence of a support obligation on marital status violates Equal Protection). Some jurisdictions, however, continue that obligation through college. Additionally, child support can be continued, even indefinitely, for a child incapable of self-support, provided that the inability to support is linked to a physical or mental disability.

The payment of child support is entirely separate from visitation rights. Such rights cannot be denied for nonpayment of support.

Parents cannot bargain away child-support payments, regardless of whether they intended to have a child. Parents can enter into private agreements regarding the payments, but they cannot agree to any release or compromise that would negatively affect the child's welfare.

2. Nonmarital Children

Nonmarital children historically were not entitled to child support or to inherit from their father's estate. Courts now use an intermediate scrutiny standard to analyze the constitutionality of government action, focusing on the purpose behind the distinction between marital and nonmarital children. As a result, child support, government benefits, and wrongful-death claims may no longer be denied to nonmarital children, and nonmarital children may inherit from their father's estate so long as paternity was proved prior to the father's death.

Nonmarital children may change their status and become marital children under certain circumstances, including when:

i) The parents marry after the birth of the child;

ii) The father consents to being named on the birth certificate;

iii) The father holds himself out or in some way acknowledges that he is the child's father; or

iv) A judicial decree establishes paternity.

3. Paternity

The obligation of child support falls on the child's parents. Questions may arise, however, as to the identity of the child's father. Once his identity is established, the child's father has rights to custody and visitation, but he is also under a duty to support the child. Paternity actions are confidential and not available to the public.

a. Blood test

When there is a question as to who is the father of a child, a court may order blood tests of the child and the possible fathers to determine paternity. If a defendant involved in a paternity matter is indigent, he is entitled to blood testing at the state's expense to establish or disprove paternity. *Little v. Streater*, 452 U.S. 1 (1981). If the test disproves paternity, then the case seeking child support must be dismissed.

b. Other evidence

In addition to the blood test, evidence such as (i) prior statements regarding paternity by deceased family members, (ii) medical testimony on the probability or improbability of conception, (iii) the defendant's acknowledgment of paternity, and, in some states, (iv) the resemblance of the child to the defendant is admissible to prove paternity.

c. Unconstitutional time limit on a paternity petition

A time limit on the filing of a paternity petition in order to secure support from the purported father is invalid unless there is a reasonable opportunity to pursue such an action and the limit is substantially related to the government's interest in restricting such an action (e.g., prevention of fraudulent claims). Otherwise, the time limit is a violation of the Equal Protection Clause of the U.S. Constitution because it subjects illegitimate children to restrictions not imposed on legitimate children. *Pickett v. Brown*, 462 U.S. 1 (1982). The suit may be brought by the child or the child's mother. The standard of proof varies by jurisdiction, but it could be as low as preponderance of the evidence or as high as clear and convincing proof.

d. Marital presumption

There is a marital presumption that a child born to a married woman is the child of that woman and her husband. Most states apply the presumption even when the wife is artificially inseminated, provided that the husband gave his consent to the procedure, and the procedure is performed by a physician. In some states, a wife is estopped from denying her husband's paternity of her child, but approximately half of the states permit rebuttal of the marital presumption if the husband is impotent, sterile, or lacked access to his wife. When rebuttal is permitted, some states permit a court to exclude evidence rebutting the presumption if rebuttal is contrary to the child's best interests.

e. Estoppel

A husband who is not the biological father of his wife's child may be estopped from denying his obligation to pay child support. Under the doctrine of equitable estoppel, the husband may be required to pay child support when:

i) There is a representation by the husband that he would provide for the child;

ii) The wife relied on his representation; and

iii) The wife suffered an economic detriment as a result of the reliance (e.g., loss of opportunity to obtain child support from the child's biological father).

Although many jurisdictions recognize the doctrine of paternity by estoppel, some jurisdictions will permit it to be used only as a basis to prevent a party from denying his obligation to support as opposed to preventing a biological father from asserting his rights. *See R.W.E. v. A.B.K.*, 961 A.2d 161 (Pa. Super. 2008). However, some states have recently begun placing greater emphasis on the interests of men who have been erroneously identified as fathers. In these jurisdictions, a husband's child support may be terminated, and paternity may be disestablished, without regard to a child's financial interests. *See, e.g., Williams v. Williams*, 843 So. 2d 720,723 (Miss. 2003); Ga. Code Ann. § 19-7-54 (2009).

4. Personal Jurisdiction Over an Out-of-State Parent

With respect to proceedings to establish or enforce child support or to determine parentage, a court obtains personal jurisdiction over an out-of-state parent pursuant to a long-arm provision in the Uniform Interstate Family Support Act (UIFSA), which has been adopted by every state. The ways in which a court can obtain personal jurisdiction are:

i) Personal service on the defendant parent;

ii) Consent of the defendant parent, such as by entering an appearance in the action;

iii) Past residency with the child in the state;

iv) Past residency in the state and the provision of prenatal expenses or support for the child;

v) Residency of the child in the state as a result of acts or directives of the parent defendant;

vi) The parent defendant engaged in sexual intercourse in the state, and the child may have been conceived by that act;

vii) The parent defendant asserted parentage in the putative father registry maintained by the state; or

viii) Any other basis consistent with federal and state constitutions for the exercise of personal jurisdiction.

It is important to note that the U.S. Supreme Court has not yet spoken on the constitutionality of the UIFSA's long-arm provisions. Several states, however, have upheld the provision as meeting the requisite due-process requirements. *See, e.g., Poindexter v. Poindexter*, 594 N.W.2d 76 (Mich. Ct. App. 1999); *County of Humboldt v. Harris*, 254 Cal. Rptr. 49 (Cal. Ct. App. 1988). In so holding, state courts have relied on the voluntary nature of the sexual act or conduct; that conception is a logical result of that conduct; and the state's strong interest in protecting its minor children in all regards, including financially. As the obligation to support a child extends to at least the age of majority, there is no time limit on the assertion of jurisdiction under this statute. UIFSA § 201, cmt.

For the jurisdictional requirements for the modification of a child-support order, *see* § III.E.3., Jurisdiction for Modification of Support, *infra*.

D. AMOUNT OF CHILD SUPPORT

All jurisdictions have adopted child-support guidelines to streamline the process by using objective bases for determining child-support awards. Child-support awards are typically based on income from any source and include wages, interest and dividends, rental income, and other income received, including retirement benefits, capital gains, and Social Security income. The guidelines are applied in all cases regardless of marital status.

1. Calculating Support

a. Income-shares model

Most jurisdictions have adopted an income-shares model, which operates on the theory that a child should receive the same proportion of parental income as if the parties continued to live together.

b. Percentage-of-income model

Other jurisdictions have adopted a percentage-of-income model, which determines the minimum amount of child support by using a percentage of the supporting (i.e., noncustodial) parent's net income, determined by the number of children supported. Certain expenditures, such as taxes or necessary medical expenditures, may be excluded when calculating net income. *See, e.g.,* 750 Ill. Comp. Stat. 5/505.

c. Melson formula

The Melson formula is similar to the income-shares model, but it takes into account six specific considerations, such as the minimum amount that each supporting parent must retain, the number of the supporting parent's dependents, and a Standard of Living Adjustment (SOLA). *See, e.g.,* Del. Fam. Ct. Civ. R. 52(c).

d. Deviations from child-support guidelines

In all jurisdictions, there is a rebuttable presumption that the amount calculated pursuant to the child-support guidelines is correct. 42 U.S.C. § 667. Deviations, however, are permitted as the circumstances warrant. If the court determines that the amount set forth under the guidelines should be deviated from, it must set forth specific findings explaining and supporting the deviation, including the amount that would have been awarded under the application of the guidelines. If a parent is unemployed or underemployed, the court may impute an income to calculate the child-support award. Conversely, if the parent(s) earn a significant income far exceeding the needs of the child, the court may modify the award to provide solely for the child's needs, but generously define the amount. Once a child-support award has been paid, the obligor is not permitted to monitor how the money is expended.

2. Other Considerations

Additional factors that the courts consider in determining the amount of support include:

i) Ages of the children;

ii) Unusual needs and unusual obligations (e.g., special education);

iii) Support obligations of the parties;

iv) Assets of the parties;

v) Medical expenses outside of insurance coverage;

vi) Standard of living;

vii) Duration of marriage, for spousal support or alimony pendente lite; and

viii) Best interests of the child.

3. Medical Insurance

In most jurisdictions, the cost of providing medical insurance for the child is included in the child-support award, if either of the parents has access to insurance. If there is no insurance available, then the court may include provisions for the procurement and payment of insurance after consideration of the medical needs of the child, the cost of the coverage, and the availability of a plan to meet the child's needs. Any premiums associated with the medical coverage shall be subtracted from the net income of the parent who is responsible for the payment.

E. MODIFICATION OF CHILD SUPPORT

1. Modification of Support

Most jurisdictions permit an award of child support to be modified. Although the statutory language varies, in general, modifications are permissible when there is a substantial change in circumstances regarding the child's needs or the parents' financial situation. Examples include a parent's change in occupation, remarriage of a parent who now has additional family obligations, increase in income, or a decrease in health. The burden to substantiate the change in circumstances is on the parent requesting the modification. Some jurisdictions, however, permit a modification to a support order after a certain passage of time, such as for a cost-of-living increase. Typically, a modification award is made retroactive to the date of service of the motion on the opposing party, but support obligations that have accrued prior to that date generally may not be modified. 42 U.S.C. § 666(a)(9) (prohibiting retroactive modification of child support).

a. Voluntary reduction in income

The amount of child support generally may not be reduced simply because of a voluntary reduction in the obligor's pay. In these circumstances, the court will usually set child support obligations based on the obligor's earning capacity, which is the amount that the person could realistically earn under the circumstances in consideration of the person's age, mental health, and physical condition.

However, in some jurisdictions, a voluntary reduction of the obligor parent's income may justify a reduction of child support obligations if certain conditions are met. All jurisdictions allowing a modification due to voluntary reductions in the obligor's income require the obligor parent to show that the reduction was made in good faith and not for the purpose of depriving the child or punishing the custodial parent. Some courts require an additional finding that the child will not suffer a significant hardship from the modification.

2. Termination of Support

A parent's obligation to pay support usually ends when the child reaches the age of majority (typically 18 years of age). Some jurisdictions, however, have the authority to order support beyond the age of majority when the child is in college. An additional exception applies when an adult child is unable to support himself due to circumstances such as a mental or physical disability. In most jurisdictions, termination may also take place if the child marries, the parental rights are terminated, the child commences active duty in the military, or the parent or child dies. A court, however, does have the right to order that a parent obtain insurance on his life for the benefit of the children to provide future support after his death.

Additionally, support may be terminated if a child is **emancipated** before the age of majority. To be emancipated, a minor child must be established as a self-supporting individual beyond the sphere of influence of his parents or independent of parental control. The mere employment of the child does not, by itself, establish emancipation. Also, the birth of a child by an unemancipated child does not result in an automatic emancipation and termination of support. However, the support rights of an employable child are contingent on the compliance by the child with reasonable parental demands; an employable child who fails to comply risks loss of parental support.

> **EXAM NOTE:** If there is a question as to whether a minor child has been emancipated, discuss the totality of the circumstances. Emancipation of a minor is *fact-specific*.

3. Jurisdiction for Modification of Support

Similar to the jurisdictional issues with child-custody orders, a state court may not modify an order of child support rendered by a court of continuing jurisdiction in another state unless the parties, including the child, no longer reside in that state or the parties expressly agree to permit another state to exercise jurisdiction. A court order that fails to adhere to this jurisdiction rule does not qualify for enforcement under the Full Faith and Credit Clause of the U.S. Constitution. 28 U.S.C. § 1738B(a) (Full Faith and Credit for Child-Support Orders Act); UIFSA § 205.

As with enforcement, a child-support order may be registered in another tribunal (e.g., order entered in Mississippi, but all parties moved to Minnesota and the order is then registered in Minnesota). It is important to note, however, that if an aspect of a child-support obligation may not be modified under the law of the state that first imposed the obligation, that aspect of the obligation may not be modified under the laws of any other state. UIFSA § 611, cmt. *See also, C.K. v. J.M.S.*, 931 So. 2d 724 (Ala. Civ. App. 2005) (although the amount of child support may be modified, the length of the obligation may not be changed, as it is a nonmodifiable aspect of the original order); *Wills v. Wills*, 745 N.W.2d 924, 926–29 (Neb. Ct. App. 2008).

4. Tax Consequences of Child Support

Neither the payor nor the recipient of the support may deduct the support from or include it in their income.

F. ENFORCEMENT OF AWARDS

Both child- and spousal-support orders are enforced through civil contempt orders, income withholding, or withholding of tax refunds.

1. Civil Contempt

Civil contempt requires compliance with a court order. An obligor with the ability to pay may be found in civil contempt and can be sent to jail and held until the amount owed is fully paid. Jurisdictions are currently split regarding whether the appointment of counsel is constitutionally required in civil contempt cases when the defendant is indigent. *Cf. Rodriquez v. Eighth Judicial Dist. Court*, 102 P.3d 41 (Nev. 2004) (Sixth Amendment right to counsel inapplicable); *Pasqua v. Council*, 892 A.2d 663 (N.J. 2006) (counsel for civil contempt obligors is required under the Due Process Clause and state constitution).

2. Criminal Contempt

Criminal contempt is a specific jail sentence imposed upon an obligor who willingly fails to pay the amount owed. When criminal contempt is sought by the court, the defendant is entitled to additional constitutional protections. *Hicks v. Feiock*, 485 U.S. 624 (1988) (violative of the Fourteenth Amendment Due Process Clause to place the burden of proving an inability to make support payments on the defendant).

3. Other Sanctions

Courts may impose other sanctions, such as issuing judgments, intercepting tax refunds, credit bureau reporting, suspending the obligor's driver's license or occupational license, seizing property or assets, garnishing the noncomplying party's wages, and ordering the payment of attorney's fees. Additionally, the Personal Responsibility and Work Opportunity Reconciliation Act of 1996 (PRWORA) permits the denial of a passport application when the noncustodial parent is more than $5,000 in arrears on his child-support obligation. PRWORA § 312.

4. Enforcement in Other Jurisdictions

Every jurisdiction has adopted the **Uniform Interstate Family Support Act** (UIFSA) to simplify collection of support payments when the obligor or child resides in a jurisdiction different from the one in which the original order was issued. Once an order is registered in another state, it is enforceable in the same manner and to the same extent as a child-support order issued by the original state. UIFSA § 603(b). If the order is properly registered, the Full Faith and Credit Clause of the U.S. Constitution applies to it. UIFSA § 603(b).

Only the issuing state may modify the original support order; the other state's responsibility is simply to enforce the order. If there is no personal jurisdiction over the obligor, then there is a two-state procedure that can be employed. Under this approach, an enforcement order can be obtained in the issuing state by filing an enforcement petition in the initiating state that will be forwarded to the issuing state's court. UIFSA § 203.

> **EXAM NOTE:** The modification and enforcement of interstate child support is always governed by the UIFSA, which has been adopted in every jurisdiction. If more than one state is involved in a fact pattern, always discuss the UIFSA, as the failure to follow its requirements does not result in its enforcement under the Full Faith and Credit Clause of the U.S. Constitution.

G. TAX CONSEQUENCES OF SUPPORT

A parent cannot deduct child-support payments or include them as income. The custodial parent automatically gets the child dependency exemption, unless the parties agree otherwise. Often the parties agree to alternate the exemption. The parent who pays medical expenses may deduct those expenses.

IV. CHILD CUSTODY

A. DEFINITION OF CUSTODY

Having custody (i.e., control) of a child can mean having **legal custody** or **physical custody**, or **both**. Either or both of these types of custody can be shared under a **joint custody** arrangement.

1. Legal Custody

Legal custody is the right of a parent to make major decisions, as contrasted with everyday decisions, regarding the minor child. Typically, areas of health, education, and religion are encompassed.

2. Physical Custody

Physical custody is the right to have the child reside with a parent or guardian and the obligation to provide for routine daily care and control of the child. As with legal custody, physical custody may be shared by both parents under a joint custody arrangement.

3. Joint Custody

Joint custody generally requires that the parents are both willing and able to cooperate with respect to the well-being of the child. Usually, joint custody is not imposed over the objections of one parent, but, even when it is, the arrangement must meet the best-interests-of-the-child standard.

Under a typical joint legal custody arrangement, neither parent has a superior right to make major decisions; instead, joint custody arrangements typically spell out a procedure for resolving conflicts. Joint legal custody is the outcome in the majority of cases. In fact, many jurisdictions have a statutory presumption in its favor.

Joint physical custody does not necessarily require a 50-50 time-sharing arrangement. It encompasses any situation in which the child maintains a residence at the home of each parent and spends a significant amount of time with each parent.

B. UNIFORM CHILD CUSTODY JURISDICTION AND ENFORCEMENT ACT (UCCJEA)

The purpose of the UCCJEA is to prevent jurisdictional disputes with courts in other states on matters of child custody and visitation. Almost all states have enacted the UCCJEA. Adjudication under the UCCJEA requires that the court possess subject-matter jurisdiction.

1. Initial Custody Determination (Home-State Jurisdiction)

A court has subject-matter jurisdiction to preside over custody hearings and either enter or modify custody or visitation orders if the state:

i)   Is the child's **home state** (the state in which the child has lived with a parent or guardian for at least **six consecutive months** prior to the custody proceeding, or since birth, if the child is less than six months old); or

ii) Was the child's home state in the **past six months**, and the child is absent from the state, but one of the parents (or guardians) continues to live in the state.

2. Significant-Connection Jurisdiction

A court can enter or modify an order if (i) **no other state** has or accepts home-state jurisdiction, (ii) the child and at least one parent have a **significant connection** with the state, **and** (iii) there is **substantial evidence** in the state concerning the child's care, protection, training, and personal relationships.

3. Default Jurisdiction

If no state has jurisdiction through home-state jurisdiction or substantial-connection jurisdiction, then a court in a state that has appropriate connections to the child has jurisdiction.

4. Exclusive-Continuing Jurisdiction

Courts that make the initial ruling in a custody case have exclusive jurisdiction over the matter until the court determines that:

i) The **parties no longer reside** in the state; or

ii) The **child no longer has a significant connection to the state**, and any substantial evidence connected to the child's condition is no longer available in the state.

5. When Courts Can Decline Jurisdiction

If a court has either initial or exclusive-continuing jurisdiction, the court may decline to exercise such jurisdiction if it finds the forum to be inconvenient after considering the following factors:

i) Whether **domestic violence** has occurred and is likely to continue in the future, and which state could best protect the parties and the child;

ii) The **length of time** the child has resided outside of the jurisdiction;

iii) The **distance** between the competing jurisdictions;

iv) The parties' relative **financial circumstances**;

v) Any **agreement of the parties** regarding which state should assume jurisdiction;

vi) The **nature and location of the evidence** required to resolve the pending litigation, including the child's testimony;

vii) The ability of each state's court to decide the issue expeditiously and the **procedures necessary** to present the evidence; and

viii) The **familiarity of each state's court** with the facts and issues in the pending litigation.

A court may also decline to exercise its jurisdiction if a party has "engaged in unjustifiable conduct," such as wrongfully removing a child from another state.

6. Temporary Emergency Jurisdiction

A jurisdiction that does not otherwise have jurisdiction may obtain temporary emergency jurisdiction and enter an order if the child is in danger and requires immediate protection. If a prior custody order is in existence, then the court rendering the emergency order must allow a reasonable time period for the parties to return to the state of original jurisdiction and argue the issues at hand before that court. If there is no prior custody order, then the emergency order remains in effect until a decision is rendered by the child's home state. If no future determination is made, then the emergency order continues in full force and effect.

7. Enforcement of Another State's Orders

a. Registration of order

A custody order from another state can be registered with or without a simultaneous request for enforcement. Typically, most jurisdictions require at least one certified copy of the order from the appropriate entity. The registering court can then grant any relief available for enforcement of the registered order.

b. Expedited enforcement of a child-custody determination

The UCCJEA uses a process similar to habeas corpus. After a petition is filed, the respondent must appear in person at a hearing held on the **first judicial day after service of the order** or, if that date is impossible, on the first judicial day possible. The petitioner will be awarded immediate physical possession of the child unless:

i) The custody or visitation order was not registered; and

a) The issuing court did not have jurisdiction;

b) The order had been stayed or vacated; or

c) The respondent was entitled to notice, but notice was not given before the court issued the order for which enforcement is sought; or

ii) The order was registered and confirmed, but the order was stayed, vacated, or modified.

c. Warrant for child custody

The court may issue a warrant, upon a petitioner's request, for the petitioner to take physical possession of a child if it finds that the child is likely to suffer serious physical injury or be removed from the state.

d. Law enforcement

The UCCJEA allows any law-enforcement official to take any lawful action to enforce a custody order or obtain the return of a child (i) if the official believes that the person holding the child has violated a criminal statute, or (ii) if requested to do so by a court of law.

8. Uniform Deployed Parents Custody and Visitation Act

The Uniform Deployed Parents Custody and Visitation Act (UDPCVA), enacted in 2012, integrates with the UCCJEA but applies specifically to parents who are also service members. Among other things, the UDPCVA provides that when imminent deployment is not an issue, courts cannot use a parent's deployment as a negative factor in determining the best interests of the child. The act also sets out a procedure for out-of-court custody agreements, sets guidelines for temporary custody, and prohibits entry of permanent custody orders before or during deployment without the service-member parent's consent.

C. UNIFORM CHILD CUSTODY JURISDICTION ACT (UCCJA)

Enacted prior to the UCCJEA, the UCCJA was established to create a uniform system to resolve interstate custody matters. Although the UCCJA was adopted by all 50 states, by the time of its adoption, Congress had enacted the Parental Kidnapping Prevention Act (PKPA), which conflicted in application with the UCCJA despite its common goal. In its original form, the UCCJA operated on principles that established jurisdiction over a child-custody case in one state and protected a custody order of that state from being modified in any other state as long as the original state retained jurisdiction. Unlike the UCCJEA and the PKPA, the UCCJA did not give first priority to the home state of the minor child. Similar to the PKPA, the UCCJA did not address enforcement of visitation rights. Almost all states have now replaced the UCCJA with the UCCJEA.

D. PARENTAL KIDNAPPING PREVENTION ACT (PKPA)

The PKPA, despite its name, applies not only to parental kidnapping cases, but also to civil interstate custody disputes, including visitation rights. Under the Supremacy Clause of the

U.S. Constitution, the PKPA takes precedence over any conflicting state law. *See, e.g., Murphy v. Woerner*, 748 P.2d 749 (Alaska 1988). The PKPA discourages forum shopping between states and allocates the powers and duties between states when a child-custody dispute arises. 28 U.S.C. § 1738A. If a jurisdiction fails to follow the PKPA's rules regarding jurisdiction, which are substantially similar to the UCCJEA rules (*see* § IV.B., Uniform Child Custody Jurisdiction and Enforcement Act (UCCJEA), *supra*), the order of the noncompliant jurisdiction is not entitled to full faith and credit.

The International Parental Kidnapping Crime Act (IPKCA) prohibits a parent from taking a child outside the United States and obstructing the other parent's physical custody of the child. The Hague Convention requires the return of a child wrongfully taken or retained in a foreign country, and it allows the custodial parent to file suit. The exception to this is if bringing the child back into the country would expose the child to grave physical or psychological harm.

E. BEST-INTERESTS-OF-THE-CHILD STANDARD

The standard for determining child custody is the **best interests and welfare of the child**. Generally, a parent is in the best position to care for a minor child, unless the parent is determined unfit.

There is no longer a presumption for custody in favor of the mother.

Many courts consider who the primary caretaker of the child was during the marriage and the separation, and prior to the divorce, as factors in determining who should have custody. *See, e.g., Garska v. McCoy*, 167 W.Va. 59 (W. Va. 1981); *but cf. Gianvito v. Gianvito*, 975 A.2d 1164 (Pa. Super. 2009) (the primary-caretaker doctrine not only encompasses the day-to-day care of the child, but also includes the quantity and quality of the time spent with the parent at the time of the hearing, rather than in the past). The primary-caretaker factor is based on a child's need for a stable and continuous relationship with the primary parent.

EXAM NOTE: For any fact pattern about a proceeding involving children, be sure to discuss the best-interests-of-the-child standard in determining custody.

1. Race or Religion

In most jurisdictions, the courts cannot use race as a factor in determining custody. Likewise, courts have typically refused to consider religion as a factor unless such religious practice would be detrimental to the child.

2. Parents' Sexual Conduct

In many, but not all, jurisdictions, courts may not consider the parents' prior sexual conduct, including gay or lesbian relationships, in making a custody decision, unless it can be determined that the conduct of the parent has or will have a negative effect on the child.

3. Third-Party Rights

Legal parents are presumptively entitled to custody of their children in cases against third parties, including grandparents or stepparents, unless it can be established that the legal parent is unfit or that awarding custody to the legal parent would be detrimental to the child.

If a natural parent has had little or no contact with a child, or if the child has lived with the third party for an extended period of time, then courts have employed the terms "parent by estoppel" and "de facto parent" to get around the presumption.

A minority of the jurisdictions apply the best-interests-of-the-child standard in all custody cases, even those between a parent and a third party. However, such a standard may run afoul of a parent's constitutional rights (*see* § IV.F., Visitation and Parenting Time, *infra*).

As with support obligations, custody rights may also turn on paternity issues (*see* § III.C.3, Paternity, *supra*).

4. Child's Preference

Most courts will consider the **wishes of the child** if the court can determine that the child has sufficient maturity to express a preference. Although age is not the sole factor in determining whether a child should be consulted, it is considered by the court. If children are consulted, then the court evaluates the reasons behind the preference.

5. Guardian *Ad Litem*

In a highly contested child-custody case, legal counsel may be appointed for the child. This attorney's duty is to advocate for the child's preferences and act on her behalf. The attorney's fees are usually paid by the parents.

6. Siblings

Courts traditionally avoid separating siblings from each other in order to maintain stability and promote sibling relationships.

7. Domestic Violence

Nearly every jurisdiction requires the court to consider the presence of domestic violence between the parties when awarding custody. Some jurisdictions have created rebuttable presumptions in favor of the nonabusive spouse.

F. VISITATION AND PARENTING TIME

Generally, the noncustodial parent is allowed reasonable visitation (or "parenting time") with a minor child. Because parents have a constitutional right to have contact with their children, the denial of visitation is unusual and typically only an issue when it would seriously endanger a child's physical, mental, or emotional health. The court will, however, place restrictions on the exercise of visitation, such as supervised parenting time or a denial of overnight visits. The parents, by agreement, usually determine the time, place, and circumstances of the visitation. If the parties cannot agree on the circumstances, then the court will determine the particular circumstances surrounding the parenting time.

1. Third Parties

In some situations, third parties, such as grandparents, stepparents, or gay or lesbian nonbiological co-parents, may seek parenting time. Visitation is sometimes granted to stepparents and same-sex nonbiological co-parents, but it is typically limited to those cases in which they have acted *in loco parentis* with the child prior to the divorce. Absent such a relationship, there are no protected rights of a stepparent or nonbiological co-parent to have ongoing contact with the child(ren) after divorce or death of the natural parent.

a. "Special weight" to a fit parent's decision

A fit parent has a fundamental right to the care, custody, and control of his children. *Troxel v. Granville*, 530 U.S. 57 (2000). *Troxel* requires that state courts must give "special weight" to a fit parent's decision to deny nonparent visitation; "special weight" has been held to mean a very significant difference.

b. Grandparent visitation

Although the majority of jurisdictions have statutes regarding grandparent visitation, they differ among states and often do not guarantee the right to visit.

In *Troxel*, the Supreme Court specifically implicated a fit parent's fundamental right to the care, custody, and control of the children in relation to grandparent visitation. Courts examining the request of grandparents for visitation will focus on the decision of the fit parents, statutory factors, and what is in the best interests of the child.

c. Unwed biological father

An unwed biological father has a substantive due process right under the U.S. Constitution to have contact with his child. However, this right exists only when the father demonstrates a commitment to the responsibilities of parenthood (e.g., participation in child-rearing or providing financial support). *Lehr v. Robertson*, 463 U.S. 248 (1983). In addition, many states have imposed a two-year limit on the establishment of paternity by an unwed biological father. Further, if the mother is married to another man and refuses to join in a paternity petition, then a state may preclude the purported biological father from pursuing the paternity petition. *Michael H. v. Gerald D.*, 491 U.S. 110 (1989).

2. Sexual Relationship or Cohabitation

Courts are unlikely to restrict visitation because of a parent's cohabitation with another or a parent's sexual relationship unless the cohabitation has an adverse impact on the children. Although jurisdictions differ in their handling of gay and lesbian relationships, the majority of jurisdictions do not prohibit overnight visitation unless the opposing parent can demonstrate a specific danger to the child's physical or emotional health.

3. HIV/AIDS

Courts cannot deny visitation merely because a parent has HIV/AIDS. *North v. North*, 648 A.2d 1025 (Md. App. 1994).

4. Interference

Interference or refusal to comply with a visitation order may be remedied by a change in custody or by contempt proceedings.

G. ENFORCEMENT

1. Sanctions

A party seeking enforcement of child-custody and visitation orders can request assistance through the court system. The court hearing the case may impose a variety of sanctions, including compensatory visitation, attorney's fees, court costs, fines, and jail time. Tort damages may also be awarded to a parent for the period of time that the child is wrongfully out of the parent's custody. In most states, a party cannot be denied parenting time for his failure to pay child support, or based merely on a child's wishes.

2. Habeas Corpus Proceedings

Although not available for child-custody disputes or visitation rights, a habeas corpus proceeding is a way in which a person who claims to have custody of a child, but who does not have physical custody of the child, can be heard by the court. In addition, during these proceedings, many jurisdictions will revisit the issue of which placement is in the best interests of the child.

Less limiting than habeas corpus is a suit in equity action, which enjoins conduct in violation of a custody order. The current trend has been to use suits in equity over habeas corpus proceedings.

3. Enforcement of Foreign Decrees

Custody and visitation orders between states are enforceable under the Full Faith and Credit Clause if the other state's decree has been registered in the state seeking enforcement (*see* § IV.B.7., Enforcement of Another State's Orders, *supra*). Generally, a local court cannot modify an out-of-state decree, unless (i) the foreign court declines jurisdiction and the local court has proper jurisdiction, and (ii) the out-of-state party is given sufficient notice of the hearing in the local court.

H. MODIFICATION

Once a custody order has been entered, absent relocation, a state retains subject-matter jurisdiction to modify the order while the child remains a minor. The majority of jurisdictions apply a change-in-circumstances standard, requiring some substantial and unforeseen change since the issuance of the prior order. Some jurisdictions have also applied time barriers before an application for modification can be filed absent consent or endangerment. The purpose behind requiring time barriers or a substantial change in circumstances is to promote stability in the child's life. The violation of a child visitation order does not automatically change who is designated as the custodial parent; it is a factor to consider in modification of an order. The failure to pay child support is not a basis on which to withhold visitation or modify an existing child-custody order.

If the custodial parent is proposing to relocate with the minor child, and the relocation will significantly impair the noncustodial parent's ability to see the child under the court-ordered visitation schedule, then it will almost always constitute a substantial change in circumstances warranting a modification. Note that prior to discussing the modification, if any, the court must provide the custodial parent with permission to relocate after applying the below factors.

1. Relocation

The law regarding whether a parent can modify a custody order and relocate with a minor child is diverse. Some jurisdictions consider the relevant facts, but they place the predominant weight on the best interests of the child. *See, e.g., Pollock v. Pollock,* 889 P.2d 633, 635 (Ariz. Ct. App. 1995). Other jurisdictions apply a presumptive right to relocate with the child, provided that the rights and welfare of the child are not prejudiced. More often, the custodial parent seeking relocation bears the burden of demonstrating that the relocation is for a legitimate and reasonable purpose, as opposed to restricting the noncustodial parent's visitation. *See, e.g.,* Conn. Gen. Stat. 46b–56d. Some states, however, will place the burden of proof on the parent objecting to the relocation, typically the noncustodial parent, to demonstrate that the move will not serve the child's best interests or that the move would also cause harm to the child. *See, e.g., Pennington v. Marcum,* 266 S.W.3d 759, 768–69 (Ky. 2008).

Provided that a legitimate purpose for the move can be ascertained, the trend of the courts is to permit the custodial parent and child to relocate. An application to relocate, however, should be made in advance of the relocation, and it must be based on anticipated present facts, not speculative ones. *See, e.g., Arthur v. Arthur,* 54 So. 3d 454 (Fla. 2010). Applications made after the relocation has taken place are often highly criticized by the court. Among the factors considered by the various jurisdictions are the following:

    i) The nature, quality, and involvement with the child of the parent who is not seeking relocation;

    ii) The age and needs of the child and the impact that the proposed relocation will have on that development, including any special needs of the child;

iii) The ability to preserve the relationship with the nonrelocating parent and the child through visitation arrangements;

iv) The child's preference, if the child is of sufficient maturity;

v) Whether the parent seeking relocation has any history of promoting or preventing parenting time with the nonrelocating parent;

vi) Whether the relocation will enhance the quality of life of the child and the parent seeking relocation;

vii) The reasons each parent has in requesting or opposing the relocation; and

viii) Any other factors that affect the best interests of the child.

It is important to note that the applicable standards may be even more restrictive when the parents share joint custody of the minor child. *See, e.g., O'Connor v. O'Connor,* 793 A.2d 810 (N.J. Super. Ct. App. Div. 2002); Tenn. Code Ann. § 36-6-108 (2005). In those jurisdictions, the standard is often more protective of the parent who is not seeking the relocation. Mediation can often be useful in assisting with resolving child-custody issues.

2. Cohabitation

Some states permit a hearing to consider a change in custody when the custodial parent is living with a nonmarital partner. However, a change in custody is generally not granted unless there is a showing that the cohabitation is having an adverse effect on the child.

I. TERMINATION

A child-custody order terminates upon the custodial parent's death or upon the child reaching the age of majority. In cases of death, the surviving parent generally receives custody of the child.

J. PARENTAL CONSENT

In certain circumstances, such as for medical procedures, parental consent must be obtained. This policy holds regardless of the parents' marital status. A doctor who performs surgery on a minor child without parental consent is liable in tort. There are some exceptions to this general rule, such as in the case of an emergency, when time is of the essence. Some states may permit an exception to the general rule of consent when the child is older or deemed mature, or when the medical concern is related to public health, such as the treatment of a venereal disease.

1. Religious Beliefs

At times, the parent's religious beliefs can conflict with what may be in the child's best interests. Often seen in cases in which medical treatment contradicts religious beliefs, the court can intervene, under the theory of *parens patriae*, to protect a child when necessary medical care is needed to prevent serious harm to the child's health. *Prince v. Massachusetts,* 321 U.S. 158, 170 (1994) ("Parents may be free to become martyrs themselves. But it does not follow they are free...to make martyrs of their children."). In those situations, a child can be declared neglected and the medical treatment ordered.

In some states, there are exemptions to the finding of abuse or neglect that permit the state to order the requisite medical care without finding the parent at fault. Such action by the court is typically taken only when the medical treatment is life-threatening and only after the court balances the risks and benefits of the medical treatment. The home state has jurisdiction if it has been the home state of the child within the six months prior to the beginning of the custody proceeding.

2. Upbringing

A parent has a right to raise her child as she sees fit. *Wisconsin v. Yoder*, 406 U.S. 205 (1972). This right of parents extends to decisions relating to the religious upbringing of a child.

V. MARITAL AGREEMENTS

> **EXAM NOTE:** Marital agreements are subject to the principles of contract law, just as other legal agreements are. When you see a bar exam question dealing with marital agreements and a violation of contract principles, be sure to raise the issue as you would in a contracts question.

A. TYPES OF MARITAL AGREEMENTS

1. Premarital Agreements

A premarital (also known as "prenuptial" or "antenuptial") agreement is a contract made before the marriage, typically containing terms that relate to division of property or spousal support in the case of a divorce and at death. As with any contract, consideration is required. A valid marriage is sufficient consideration for a premarital agreement.

Many jurisdictions have held that a premarital agreement must expressly state its applicability to divorce proceedings. Additionally, clauses relating to child custody and support are unenforceable. Adopted in 26 jurisdictions, the Uniform Premarital Agreement Act (UPAA) is a uniform law that relates specifically to these types of contracts and imposes the same standards that are discussed below at § V.B., Validity of Marital Agreements. Individual states have amended this act in various ways throughout the years, resulting in the 2012 enactment of the Uniform Premarital and Marital Agreements Act (UPMAA). The act applies the same standards and requirements for both marital agreements and premarital agreements. As of this printing, two states, Colorado and North Dakota, have enacted the UPMAA.

When there is an issue as to which state's law will govern whether a premarital agreement is enforceable, most states apply the law of the state with the most significant relationship to the agreement and the subsequent marriage. Some states apply the law of the state where the agreement was executed.

2. Separation Agreement

Separation agreements are made between spouses who are planning for divorce. These agreements can define property division, spousal support, child support, custody, and visitation. The court generally will enforce spousal maintenance and property division provisions so long as the agreement is not unconscionable or based on fraud. Provisions related to child support and custody, on the other hand, are modifiable by the court if the initial terms are not in the best interests of the child. These agreements are generally merged into the final judgment for divorce, as long as they are based on full and fair disclosure. When no merger occurs, enforcement is based on contract law rather than judgment enforcement.

3. Property-Settlement Agreement

The purpose of a property-settlement agreement is to settle the economic issues of the marital estate. It is entered into by the parties *before* a divorce decree is issued. As with a separation agreement, a court generally will enforce spousal maintenance and property division provisions so long as the agreement is not unconscionable or based on fraud.

B. VALIDITY OF MARITAL AGREEMENTS

A premarital agreement is enforceable if there has been **full disclosure**, the agreement is **fair and reasonable**, and it is **voluntary**. The agreement must be in **writing** and **signed** by the party to be charged. The agreement may be amended or revoked after the marriage, provided both parties sign a written agreement to that effect. The burden of proving its invalidity is by clear and convincing evidence. The UPAA requires that the party against whom enforcement is sought prove (1) involuntariness *or* (2) that the agreement was unconscionable when it was executed, that she did not receive or waive fair and reasonable disclosure, *__and__* she "did not have, or reasonably could not have had, an adequate knowledge" of the other's assets and obligations. UPAA § 6(a). Voluntariness, fairness, and asset disclosure are relevant to enforceability in all jurisdictions, even in states that have not adopted the UPAA. However, in non-UPAA jurisdictions, courts can refuse to enforce on any ground.

If the marriage is voided, a premarital contract is enforceable only if it will avoid an inequitable result.

1. Full Disclosure

Premarital agreements must provide full disclosure of financial status, including income, assets, and liabilities of all parties. Disclosure is an important consideration to the court, as it demonstrates that each party exercised a meaningful choice when they agreed to the terms of the contract. Absent full disclosure, a court will generally refuse to enforce the agreement.

2. Fair and Reasonable

To determine if a premarital contract's terms are reasonable, the courts consider the parties' wealth, age, and health. Courts will look at both whether the agreement is fair both procedurally and substantively. An agreement obtained by fraud, duress, or undue influence may be set aside as procedurally unfair. When a mediator participates in the creation of a settlement agreement, misconduct by the mediator (e.g., bias toward one spouse) can give rise to grounds for setting aside the agreement. If a confidential relationship between the spouses exists, then the burden of proving the fairness of the agreement or the absence of undue influence may be placed on the dominant spouse. Courts may also look at the terms of the agreement itself to see if they are so unfair as to be unconscionable.

Most courts evaluate fairness at the time of execution of the contract, and a minority of jurisdictions will evaluate it at both the time of execution and the time of enforcement.

The current trend is for courts to enforce contractual agreements that may not be fair as long as there has been fair disclosure.

3. Voluntary

The parties must enter into the contract voluntarily (i.e., free of fraud, duress, or misrepresentation). Courts consider factors such as time pressure, the parties' previous business experience, and the opportunity to be represented by independent counsel.

A party's insistence on the agreement as a condition to marriage is *not* considered duress.

> **EXAM NOTE:** Be sure to discuss whether procedural fairness exists if one party was not independently represented. Address the question of voluntariness by discussing whether the individual was both informed of her right to counsel and given the opportunity to consult counsel.

4. Impoverished Spouse

Even if a valid agreement has been voluntarily executed and it meets the test for reasonableness, fairness, and full disclosure, the agreement may be set aside if its result winds up leaving one spouse woefully impoverished to the extent that he becomes dependent on the state (i.e., welfare). It is irrelevant if abrogation of the exact terms of the agreement results.

5. Modification of Marital Agreements

Although a court may uphold a provision in a marital agreement that prevents modification of property rights, including spousal support, a court may always modify child-support provisions in a marital agreement even if the agreement states that no modifications may be made.

C. AGREEMENTS BETWEEN UNMARRIED COHABITANTS

1. Cohabitation Agreements

Contracts between unmarried persons are invalid if the only consideration is sexual relations. Agreements in which other consideration, such as full-time companionship or cooking, is exchanged for financial support will generally be enforced. These contracts may be express, regarding earnings or property rights, or implied. However, courts are less likely to enforce an implied contract.

2. Property Division Between Unmarried Cohabitants

When there is no express contract, courts will generally provide for equitable distribution of property based on a resulting trust, constructive trust, or quantum meruit theory to avoid unjust enrichment.

VI. RELATIONSHIP BETWEEN THE FAMILY AND THE STATE

A. ADOPTION

Adoption is a statutory legal action in which the previous parent-child relationship is terminated and a new parent-child relationship is established. Once the adoption has been completed, a new birth certificate with the adoptive parents' names is issued for the child. The records for most adoptions are sealed and kept confidential, but many states allow the adopted child to receive medical information on the birth parents. Additionally, most states have residency requirements for the county in which the adoption will take place and prohibit the payment of money to the natural parents other than costs related to medical care connected with the pregnancy.

1. Termination of a Natural Parent's Rights

For an adoption to be valid, the parental rights of the biological parents must be terminated. For those rights to be terminated, one of the following circumstances must occur.

a. Voluntary termination

The biological parents may **voluntarily** give up their rights as parents of the minor child and consent to the child's adoption by the adoptive parents.

1) Consent of unwed fathers

a) Consent by failure to register

Some jurisdictions have created adoption registries for the purpose of determining the identity and location of putative fathers and providing notice in the event of an adoption. A putative father's failure to register within a statutorily prescribed period of time constitutes a waiver of his right to notice of the adoption and irrevocably implies his consent to the adoption. *See, e.g., In Re J.D.C.*, 751 N.E.2d 747 (Ind. App. 2001); *Robert O. v. Russell K.*, 604 N.E.2d. 99 (N.Y. Ct. App. 1992). Termination in this fashion typically applies only to cases in which the father and child never developed a relationship. A situation in which the child is a newborn gives the unwed father a constitutional right to have an opportunity to develop a quality relationship with the child.

b) Limitations on the right to object

The right of an unwed father to object to an adoption may be denied if the father does not demonstrate a commitment to the responsibilities of parenthood, but it cannot be denied if such a commitment has been made. *Quilloin v. Walcott*, 434 U.S. 246 (1978); *Caban v. Mohammed*, 441 U.S. 380 (1979).

2) Consent of the prospective adoptee

In most jurisdictions, the prospective adoptee must consent to his adoption if he is over 14 years of age; some jurisdictions lower the age to 12 years.

3) Withdrawal of consent

Prior to a final decree of adoption, the parents' consent to adoption may be withdrawn with court approval. After the final decree is entered, however, no withdrawal of consent is allowed.

b. Involuntary termination

Unlike with consensual termination of parental rights, only a court can involuntarily terminate one's constitutional right to parent a child. The involuntary termination of parental rights typically occurs as part of an abuse, neglect, or dependency case after the state has intervened and made attempts to rectify the situation. Also, if consent is unreasonably withheld, then the court will waive such consent.

1) Requirements

Each jurisdiction provides the statutory grounds and requirements for termination of parental rights. They can include abandonment, incapacity, abuse of a sibling, termination of parental rights over a sibling, and abuse and neglect of the child over a period of time. Additionally, under the Adoption and Safe Families Act, a state can move for termination of parental rights when the child has been placed outside of the home and not with a relative for 15 of the past 22 months, provided certain reunification attempts have been made by the state.

Because the termination of parental rights has constitutional implications, it is considered an extreme remedy. The standard for determining whether termination is appropriate is clear and convincing evidence.

2) Adoption

Some jurisdictions also apply the traditional law of adoption, which permits an adoption upon the finding that a parent has abandoned the parent-child relationship. Jurisdictions vary on the use of a subjective versus objective test. When an objective standard is applied, the key is whether the parent has failed to act in a way that indicates a commitment to maintaining the parent-child relationship (e.g., visitation and support). When a subjective standard is applied, the key is whether the parent subjectively intended to abandon the parent-child relationship; objective evidence of a parental loss of interest in the relationship is insufficient.

c. Approval of adoption

After a thorough investigation regarding the fitness of the adoptive parents, the courts either approve or deny the adoption. The investigation may be waived if the adoptive parents are close family members of the child.

2. Legal Effects of Adoption

Once an adoption takes place, the adoptive parents have all of the rights and responsibilities that the biological parents would have had (e.g., support, custody, visitation, and inheritance), and the adopted child has all of the rights and responsibilities that a biological child would have had (e.g., intestate rights in the adoptive parents' estate). As the adoptive parents stand in the shoes of the adoptee's biological parents, the vast majority of jurisdictions will not permit visitation between the adoptee and her biological parents. A few states do authorize visitation between an adoptee and a nonparent, typically a stepparent, but only when there is a substantial relationship between the child and nonparent, and the visitation is in the child's best interests.

Generally, an adoption may not be dissolved, although some states have permitted dissolution in limited circumstances, such as the discovery of an undisclosed mental or physical illness. In evaluating dissolution claims, courts typically consider the length of the relationship, the child's needs, and the parent's motives.

B. ADOPTION ALTERNATIVES UNDER THE UNIFORM PARENTAGE ACT (UPA)

The UPA is a set of uniform rules for establishing parentage. As of this writing, the UPA has been adopted by nine state legislatures.

1. Assisted Reproduction

The UPA defines "assisted reproduction" as implanting an embryo or fertilizing a woman's egg with a man's sperm without sexual intercourse. UPA § 102. This may include in vitro fertilization, when fertilization occurs outside the woman's body, and the fertilized egg is then implanted into the woman's uterus. The donor is the man or woman who produces the sperm or egg used in assisted reproduction, but who is not considered the parent of the prospective child. Maternity is determined by the woman who gives birth to the child, unless a gestational agreement states otherwise. UPA § 201. Likewise, the husband of the woman who is determined to be the mother of the child is the child's father, unless the husband pursues an action to declare that he did not consent to the assisted reproduction. This action must commence within two years after the husband learns of the birth of the child. UPA § 705. If either the egg donor or sperm donor dies before implantation of the embryo, or before conception, that donor is not a parent of the resulting child, unless a writing by the deceased party states otherwise. UPA § 707.

2.   Gestational (Surrogacy) Agreement

Sometimes used interchangeably with the term "surrogacy," a gestational agreement is one in which a woman, known as the gestational mother or surrogate, agrees to carry a pregnancy, either through artificial insemination or by surgical implantation of a fertilized embryo, as a substitute for intended parents who cannot conceive. The intended parents are the individual or individuals who provide the egg or sperm of one or both of them used to implant into the surrogate. The intended parents agree to be the parents of the resulting child, with all the rights and obligations of parenthood. This agreement involves the gestational mother, and her husband if she is married, giving up all parental rights and obligations to the child being conceived.

All parties involved must petition the court for approval of the agreement. The court must have jurisdiction, which continues until the resulting child is six months old, and the appropriate government agency must perform a home study of the intended parents to determine their fitness. All parties must have entered the agreement voluntarily and made provisions for the proper medical care associated with the surrogate agreement. The agreement may not limit the right of the gestational mother to make healthcare decisions concerning herself or the embryo she is carrying. Consideration to the gestational mother, if any has been promised, must be reasonable. The agreement may be terminated for cause by any of the parties, including the court, prior to the gestational mother becoming pregnant. An agreement that is not approved by the court is not enforceable.

Once the court approves the agreement, a child born to the surrogate mother within 300 days after the assisted reproduction is presumed to be the product of the assisted reproduction. A subsequent marriage of the gestational mother has no effect on the validity of the agreement. The intended parents must file a notice of the child's birth for the court to declare them to be the legal parents.

It is important to note that in many of the states that have adopted legislation regarding assisted reproduction, gestational agreements are not given effect.

3.   "Frozen Embryo" Issues

A "frozen embryo" is the result of in vitro fertilization that is cryogenically preserved. Issues concerning ownership and parentage are complex and continue to be unresolved. Additional problems surface when one of the individuals who provided the egg or sperm dies, or the individuals get divorced. Absent an agreement, the decision as to whether or not transplantation will take place is made by weighing the interests of the parties. Ultimately, resolution of these issues may turn on whether the embryo is classified as a person or as property.

C.   DOMESTIC VIOLENCE

Every jurisdiction has some type of statute granting civil relief to victims of domestic violence. Although each jurisdiction has its own definition of what constitutes domestic violence, the definitions typically focus on physical abuse, as opposed to mental or emotional abuse.

1.   Scope of Statute

Virtually every jurisdiction requires that the perpetrator of the violence be in a relationship with the victim or be a household or family member. Jurisdictions differ, however, on the scope of coverage. Most states include spouses, former spouses, children, unmarried parents of a common child, and household or family members. Some jurisdictions also cover dating relationships. *See, e.g.,* N.J.S.A. 2C:25-19d. These statutes tend to focus on a continuum of behavior, but depending on the level of violence, a single episode may qualify for court protection.

2. Relief Granted

The major relief granted under most of the statutes is an injunctive order prohibiting the defendant's further abuse of and contact with the victim. It can, and typically does, include exclusive possession of the residence for the period of time, child-custody and parenting time, and support. In most jurisdictions, the application for a protective order is a two-step process. The applicant must obtain an ex parte order with limited injunctive relief, followed by a hearing, after notice has been given to the defendant, for a permanent order. The duration of the order depends on the jurisdictional statute and ranges for a period of one year to an indefinite length of time. The penalties for violating a protective order are criminal in nature and range from a fine to imprisonment.

> **EXAM NOTE:** In bar exam questions, a typical example of the relief obtained by a protective order is that the defendant not abuse the petitioner and have no contact with her.

D. RIGHTS AND OBLIGATIONS OF CHILDREN

Children are provided with special rights and limitations compared to adults. These distinctions are meant to protect children as well as provide them with expanded rights when necessary. In many cases, as with property and contracts, children may convey property or enter into contracts as minors, but upon the age of majority, they have the option of disaffirming the transaction. Conversely, a child does not have the capacity to make a valid will.

1. Right to Consent to Medical Care

A child's rights regarding medical care vary depending on the age of the child and the medical procedure. Children over a certain age may be able to provide the consent needed for treatment. Otherwise, parental consent is almost always necessary before a child can receive emergency medical treatment, even though the state may override the parent's failure to consent when the child's life is at risk. Nevertheless, in nonemergency situations, minors are allowed to consent to abortions, receive treatment for sexually transmitted diseases, and obtain birth control without the consent of their parents.

2. Liability for Torts and Criminal Acts

Generally, children are judged by a more moderate standard than adults when determining the liability for tortious behavior. Criminal acts, as well, generally are limited to adjudication in juvenile courts under juvenile laws. The purpose of this difference is to provide the child with supervision and rehabilitation. Usually, the decision regarding the extent of punishment is dependent on the age of the child; the younger the child, the more likely the court will show leniency.

3. Emancipation

In a few situations, a child no longer lives with his parents and is self-supporting. In such a case, the child may petition the court for a decree of emancipation. This means that the child is no longer considered a minor in the eyes of the law and therefore has all the duties and obligations of adulthood. Parents no longer have a duty to support him, and in fact, some jurisdictions require the child to support the parents in later years. Married minors are also considered to be emancipated in most states.

4. Limits on Parental Authority

A parent's authority over his child is not absolute. Laws are in place to protect children from harm, whether or not that harm is intentional. Child abuse and neglect laws, as well as compulsory school attendance statutes, are in place to ensure that a child is well taken care of and supervised appropriately. As has been discussed, the state may terminate parental rights despite parents' constitutional right to raise their children when it is in the best interests of the child. Grounds for termination include abandonment, neglect, failure to support, or inflicting serious harm, among others. The state must prove these allegations by clear and convincing evidence because of a parent's right to due process.

Partnerships

PARTNERSHIPS

Table of Contents

PARTNERSHIPS

EDITOR'S NOTE

This outline discusses the law of partnerships under the Revised Uniform Partnership Act of 1997 (RUPA), which governs partnerships (including limited liability partnerships) in most states.

I. PARTNERSHIP FORMATION AND RELATIONSHIPS

A. FORMATION OF A PARTNERSHIP

1. Partnership Requirements

A partnership is an association of two or more persons to carry on a for-profit business as co-owners. RUPA 101(6).

a. "Person" defined

For the purpose of a partnership, RUPA defines a "person" as an individual or legal entity, such as a corporation, limited liability company (LLC), trust, estate, governmental entity, or partnership. RUPA 101(10). The person must have the capacity to contract. The persons involved in the partnership are partners.

b. Required intent

To form a partnership, at least two persons must intend to carry on a business for profit as co-owners, but it is not necessary that such persons have the specific intent to form a partnership. In fact, co-owners' subjective intent not to form a partnership does not prevent the association from being a partnership. RUPA 202(a).

c. Necessary agreement

The only agreement necessary to create a partnership is the agreement to conduct a for-profit business as co-owners. Such an agreement may even be implied by the conduct of the parties when they have not entered into a written or oral agreement. RUPA 101(7).

d. Written versus oral agreement

Although a written agreement is not necessary to form a partnership, a partnership agreement is subject to the Statute of Frauds, which requires contracts that cannot be performed in one year to be in writing.

e. Extensive activity

Passive co-ownership of property by itself does not create a partnership. Courts will consider the amount of related activities directed toward achieving a business's end goal when determining whether a partnership exists. RUPA 202 cmt. 1.

> **Example:** A and B decide to sell flowers from A's garden at the local gardening fair. B secures the space at the fair and A cuts the flowers from the garden and prepares the bouquets for the fair. They verbally agree to split the profits 50-50. A and B have formed a partnership, even though there is no written partnership agreement.

f. Key test—sharing of profits

The key test applied to ascertain whether a business arrangement is a partnership is whether there is a sharing of the profits from the business; if so, such an arrangement generally is presumed to be a partnership, and persons who share in the profits are partners. RUPA 202(c)(3). [Note: The sharing of gross returns rather than profits does not create such a presumption. RUPA 202(c)(2).]

1) Exceptions

The sharing of profits from a business does not create a rebuttable presumption that the arrangement is a partnership and the recipients are partners in six statutorily enumerated circumstances:

i) Debt payments, including installment payments;

ii) Interest or other loan charges, even though the payment varies with the profits of the business;

iii) Rent;

iv) Wages or other compensation paid to an employee or independent contractor;

v) Goodwill payments stemming from the sale of a business, including installment payments; and

vi) Annuities or other retirement or health benefits paid to a beneficiary, representative, or designee of a deceased or retired partner.

RUPA 202(c)(3).

g. Effect of joint ownership of property

Joint ownership of property (e.g., tenancy in common) does not by itself establish a partnership, even when the joint owners share profits made from use of the property. RUPA 202(c)(1).

h. Subpartnership

A subpartnership, which is not a true partnership, refers to an agreement between a partner and a third party that the third party will share in the partner's profits from the partnership. The third party does not become a member of the partnership and has only a contractual claim against that partner for a share of the partnership's profits.

i. Joint venture

A joint venture is not a clearly defined legal entity. Frequently, courts use the term "joint venture" to describe a partnership for a specific, limited purpose. Courts usually apply partnership rules to a joint venture when the association has a business purpose rather than a personal purpose.

2. Purported Partner/Partner by Estoppel

Generally, if a partnership does not exist, a person cannot be liable to a third party as a partner. RUPA 308(e). However, even though a partnership does not exist, a person may, under circumstances enumerated below, be treated as a partner of a purported partnership. Similarly, there are situations when someone who is not a partner of an established partnership may still be treated as one. In either case, the person is characterized as a purported partner (or a partner by estoppel).

a. Liability of a purported partner

For liability as a purported partner to be imposed, the following elements must be established:

i) There must be a representation—orally, in writing, or implied by conduct—that a person is a partner in an actual or purported partnership;

ii) The purported partner must make or consent to the representation;

iii) A third party must have reasonably relied on the representation; and

iv) The third party must have suffered damages as a result of that reliance.

RUPA 308(a).

b. No duty to deny

A person who, without her consent, is held out by another as a partner is not under a duty to deny that representation. Merely being named by another in a statement of partnership authority is not enough to create liability as a partner. Furthermore, failing to file or amend a statement of dissociation does not create liability as a partner. RUPA 308(d), inc. cmt.

c. Public holding out

It is not a defense that the purported partner was unaware that he had been held out as a partner to the specific third party in question if the representation was made in a public manner. RUPA 308(a).

d. Person holding out another as a partner

When a person represents that another is a partner, who is not in fact a partner, the purported partner constitutes an agent of the person making the representation. The purported partner is also an agent of any partner of an existing partnership who consents to the representation. RUPA 308(b).

3. Nature of Partnership

a. Partnership as a separate entity

A partnership is a legal entity that is distinct from its partners. RUPA 201. A partnership may hold property and can also sue and be sued. RUPA 203, 307. Partners are not protected from personal liability for the partnership's obligations (unlike shareholders in a corporation, who are not personally liable for their corporation's obligations).

b. Partnership agreement

Although a formal agreement is not required to create a partnership, if the partners have entered into such an agreement, then the *agreement*, rather than RUPA, generally governs the relations among the partners and between the partners and the partnership when there is a conflict between the agreement and RUPA.

B. RELATIONSHIPS OF PARTNER WITH PARTNERSHIP AND BETWEEN PARTNERS

1. Partner as Agent

A partner is an agent of the partnership for its business purposes. RUPA 301(1). As an agent, the partner can commit the partnership to binding contracts with third parties.

2. Fiduciary Duties

A partner owes the partnership and the other partners two fiduciary duties—the duty of loyalty and the duty of care. RUPA 404(a).

a. Duty of loyalty

Under the duty of loyalty, a partner is required to refrain from the following activities:

i) Competing with the partnership business;

ii) Advancing an interest adverse to the partnership; and

iii) Usurping a partnership opportunity or otherwise using partnership property or business to derive a personal benefit, without notifying the partnership.

RUPA 404(b).

1) Loan by a partner

A partner, in addition to contributing to the partnership (which becomes part of the partnership's capital), may make a loan to the partnership. The lending partner is treated as any other creditor of the partnership, subject to other applicable laws. RUPA 404(f).

2) Limitation of duty

a) By written agreement

A partnership agreement may not eliminate the duty of loyalty. However, the agreement may identify specific types or categories of activities that do not violate this duty, if not manifestly unreasonable. For example, a real estate partnership agreement could permit a partner to retain commissions on partnership property bought and sold. RUPA 103(b)(3)(i), inc. cmt. 4.

b) Safe harbor

In addition, the agreement may provide a safe harbor with respect to a transaction between a partner and the partnership. Under a safe harbor, a certain number or percentage of the other partners—after full disclosure of the material facts—could authorize or ratify the transaction. RUPA 103(b)(3)(ii).

b. Duty of care

A partner is required to refrain from engaging in grossly negligent or reckless conduct, intentional misconduct, or a knowing violation of the law. RUPA 404(c). A partnership agreement may not reduce this duty unreasonably. RUPA 103(b)(4).

c. Timing of duties

The duties of loyalty and care generally apply only to partners. RUPA 404(b), (c), (g), inc. cmt. 2.

1) Prospective partners

Dealings between prospective partners in forming a partnership are not subject to these duties, but prospective partners may be subject to the general contractual obligations to deal honestly and without fraud. RUPA 404, cmt. 2.

2) Partnership dissociation or dissolution

Upon a partner's dissociation from a partnership or upon the partnership's dissolution, these duties do not apply unless the partner is engaged in winding up the partnership business. When a partner or the representative of the last surviving partner is engaged in winding up the partnership business, these duties are generally applicable, with the exception of the noncompete aspect of the duty of loyalty. RUPA 404(g).

d. Obligation of good faith and fair dealing

In observing the duties of loyalty and care and in exercising any rights, a partner has the obligation of good faith and fair dealing. RUPA 404(d). The partnership agreement cannot eliminate this obligation, but it can prescribe reasonable standards by which the performance of the obligation is measured. RUPA 103(b)(5).

3. Partnership Profits and Losses

a. Dictated by agreement

The partnership agreement controls a partner's rights to share in the partnership's profits and losses. The agreement may specify a percentage for sharing profits that differs from the percentage for sharing losses; neither profits nor losses are required to be shared on a per capita basis. RUPA 401(b).

b. No agreement or agreement silent

If there is no agreement or the agreement is silent as to the division of the profits and losses, each partner is entitled to an equal share of the partnership profits and losses. When the agreement addresses only the division of partnership profits, partnership losses are shared in the same manner. RUPA 401(b).

> **Example:** If Partner X gets 70% of the profits, then Partner X is liable for 70% of the losses.

4. Partner's Account

Each partner has a partnership account. That account consists of contributions to the partnership and the partner's share of the profits, reduced by any liabilities, distributions, or losses. RUPA 401(a).

5. Partnership Distributions

A partner cannot demand a distribution of partnership profits, but she is entitled to have her partnership account credited with a share of the profits. RUPA 401(a). Even when a distribution is made, a partner cannot demand that specific partnership property be distributed to her. Conversely, a partner cannot be forced to accept a distribution in kind. RUPA 402.

6. Partner's Partnership Interest

A partner has a partnership interest, which consists of the rights to share in the partnership's profits and losses and to receive distributions. This interest is personal property, regardless of the nature of the partnership's assets. RUPA 502.

a. Transfer to a third party

A partner has the right to transfer his partnership interest to a third party. The transfer (e.g., assignment) may include his entire interest or only part of it. RUPA 503(a)(1).

1) Effect on the partnership

The transfer of a partner's partnership interest to a third party does not trigger the dissolution of the partnership. RUPA 503(a)(2). In addition, the partnership is not required to give effect to the transfer until the partnership has notice of it. RUPA 503(e).

2) Effect on the transferor partner

The transfer of a partner's partnership interest to a third party does not trigger the partner's dissociation from the partnership. Instead, the transferor partner retains all rights and duties of a partner in the partnership apart from an interest in the distributions transferred. RUPA 503(a)(2), (d).

3) Rights of the transferee

The transferee has the right to receive distributions from the partnership to which the transferor partner would otherwise have been entitled, including both distributions made by the partnership as an ongoing concern and those made upon dissolution of the partnership and the winding up of its business. In addition, the transferee may seek a judicial order for dissolution of the partnership. In the event of dissolution, the transferee is entitled to an accounting, but only for the period beginning from the date of the last accounting agreed to by all of the partners. RUPA 503(b), (d).

a) Denied rights

The transferee is not entitled to participate in the management or conduct of the partnership business, to access partnership records, or to demand other information from the partnership. RUPA 503(a)(3).

4) Restriction on transfer

If the partnership agreement contains a restriction that prohibits the transfer of a partnership interest, then a transfer in violation of this restriction is ineffective as to a transferee who has notice of the restriction. RUPA 503(f).

b. Charging order

A creditor of a partner who has obtained a judgment against the partner may enforce that judgment against the partner's partnership interest only by obtaining a judicial charging order. The charging order constitutes a lien on the partner's partnership interest. Among the available remedies are a court-appointed receiver of the partner's distributions from the partnership and a court-ordered foreclosure of interest. The purchaser of the interest at a foreclosure sale is treated as a transferee. RUPA 504.

7. Property Ownership

All property acquired by a partnership, whether by contribution from a partner or by purchase or other transfer from a partner or a third party, is partnership property and belongs to the partnership, not to the individual partners. RUPA 101(11), 203. A partner cannot transfer an ownership interest in partnership property, voluntarily or involuntarily. RUPA 501.

Although the intent of the partners is determinative as to ownership, there are several statutory rules for titled property that are keyed to the title itself.

a. Titled property—designated as partnership property

When ownership of property is evidenced in a document (i.e., a title), property that is acquired in the name of the partnership is partnership property. Property may be acquired in the name of the partnership by a transfer to either (i) the partnership in its own name or (ii) one or more of the partners in their capacity as partners, provided the name of the partnership is indicated in the instrument transferring title to the property. Property is also partnership property when the property is titled in the name of one or more of the partners, provided such instrument indicates either the named person's capacity as a partner or the existence of the partnership. RUPA 204(a), (b).

b. Presumptions as to property—intent of the partners

When property is not regarded as partnership property, the intent of the partners controls in determining whether the property belongs to the partnership or to the individual partners. Two statutory presumptions are applicable in ascertaining that intent.

1) Presumed partnership property—purchased with partnership funds

Property is presumed to be partnership property if it was purchased with partnership assets or if partnership credit is used to obtain financing. RUPA 204(c).

2) Presumed partner's separate property

By contrast, property is rebuttably presumed to be a partner's separate property when (i) the property is acquired in the name of one or more partners, (ii) the instrument transferring title to the property does not indicate the person's capacity as a partner or the existence of a partnership, and (iii) partnership assets were not used to acquire the property. The use of property for partnership purposes is not enough to overcome this presumption. RUPA 204(d).

c. Other factors

When the statutory rules discussed above do not resolve the issue of ownership, such as when the property is titled in a partner's name and it is unclear whose funds purchased the property, then various factors may be considered to ascertain the partner's intent. Such factors include the property's use, treatment of the property for tax purposes, and the source of funds used to maintain or improve the property.

8. New Partner

To become a partner, a person must secure the consent of all of the existing partners. RUPA 401(i).

9. Management Rights

Each partner has equal rights in the management and conduct of the partnership. RUPA 401(f).

a. Ordinary partnership business

A **majority** of the partners can make a decision as to a matter in the ordinary course of the partnership's business, such as a distribution of partnership profits. RUPA 401(j).

b. Special partnership business

A decision as to a matter outside the ordinary course of the partnership's business requires the consent of **all partners**. An amendment of the partnership agreement also requires the consent of all partners. RUPA 401(j).

10. Remuneration for Services

A partner is not entitled to remuneration for services performed for the partnership. An exception exists when the partner renders services in winding up the business of the partnership, in which case the partner is entitled to reasonable compensation. RUPA 401(h).

11. Reimbursement and Indemnification

a. Reimbursement

A partner may make a loan in furtherance of the ordinary business of the partnership or to preserve the partnership's business or property. The partnership is required to repay the loan or reimburse the partner for the advances, including interest from the date of the loan or advance. RUPA 401(c)-(e).

b. Indemnification and a partner's personal liability

A partner may incur a personal liability in the ordinary course of conducting partnership business or in order to preserve the partnership's business or property. The partnership is required to indemnify the partner for such liabilities. RUPA 401(c).

12. Use of Partnership Property

A partner may use or possess partnership property only on behalf of the partnership. RUPA 401(g). A partner who derives a personal benefit from the use or possession of partnership property is required to compensate the partnership for such benefit. RUPA 404(b).

13. Access to Records

During business hours, a partnership must provide its partners and their agents (including attorneys) with access to all its records, including its financial records, and permit them not only to inspect but also to copy such records. RUPA 403(a). A partnership agreement may not restrict this access unreasonably. RUPA 103(b)(2). In addition, each partner and the partnership must furnish to a partner (or the partner's legal representative), without demand, any information concerning the partnership's business and affairs reasonably required for the proper exercise of the partner's rights and duties under the partnership agreement or RUPA and, on demand, any other information concerning the partnership's business and affairs unless the demand or the information demanded is unreasonable or improper. RUPA 403(c).

14. Lawsuits

a. Partnership as plaintiff

A partnership may pursue a legal action against a partner for breach of the partnership agreement or for violating a duty owed to the partnership that caused the partnership harm. RUPA 405(a).

b. Partner as plaintiff

A partner may pursue a legal action against the partnership or another partner to enforce the partner's rights under the partnership agreement or the RUPA. In addition, a partner may pursue a legal action to enforce the partner's rights and otherwise protect the partner's interests that arise independently of the partnership relationship. RUPA 405(b).

1) Accounting

A partner may seek an accounting as to the partnership business at any time.

2) Torts

A partner may sue another partner to recover for injuries caused by the tortfeasor partner. The tortfeasor's negligence cannot be imputed to a plaintiff-partner to prevent the injured partner from suing. RUPA 405, cmt 2.

15. Dissociation

A partner may cease to be associated with the carrying on of the partnership business through the process of dissociation. A partner's dissociation may be voluntary or involuntary.

a. Events causing a partner's dissociation

The following events trigger a partner's dissociation from the partnership:

i) The partner's notice to the partnership of the partner's express will to withdraw;

ii) An occurrence specified in the partnership agreement;

iii) The expulsion of the partner pursuant to the partnership agreement;

iv) The expulsion of the partner by the unanimous vote of the other partners, if it is unlawful to carry on the partnership business with that partner;

v) The expulsion of the partner by court order because the partner has either (i) engaged in misconduct that adversely and materially affected the partnership business, (ii) willfully and persistently caused a material breach of the partnership agreement, or (iii) breached a duty owed to the partnership or other partners;

vi) The partner's voluntary or involuntary bankruptcy, a general assignment of the partner's interest for the benefit of the partner's creditors, or appointment of a trustee, receiver, or liquidator of the partner's property;

vii) The partner's death;

viii) The appointment of a guardian or general conservator for the partner, or a specific judicial determination that the partner has become incapable of performing his duties under the partnership agreement; or

ix) The termination of an entity partner (such as a limited liability company), or the distribution by an estate or a trust of the partnership interest.

RUPA 601.

1) Limits on partnership agreement restrictions

A partnership agreement cannot prevent a partner from withdrawing from the partnership, but it can require that the partner's notice of withdrawal be in writing. RUPA 103(b)(6). Similarly, a partnership agreement cannot prevent the partnership or other partners from seeking judicial expulsion of a partner. RUPA 103(b)(7).

b. Partner's power to dissociate

A partner has the power to dissociate from the partnership at any time, even if the dissociation is wrongful. RUPA 602(a).

1) Circumstances under which a partner's dissociation is wrongful

For a partnership that is unlimited by time or undertaking, a partner's dissociation is wrongful only when it is in breach of an express provision of the partnership agreement.

For a partnership that is for a definite term or undertaking, the partner's dissociation is wrongful when, before the expiration of the term or completion of the undertaking, the partner:

i) Withdraws, unless withdrawal follows within 90 days of *another* partner's wrongful dissociation or dissociation due to death, bankruptcy, or other circumstances described below;

ii) Is expelled by court order;

iii) Is a debtor in bankruptcy; or

iv) Is not an individual, a trust, or an estate, and the partner willfully dissolved or terminated.

RUPA 602(b).

2) Effect of wrongful dissociation

Wrongful dissociation results in dissolution if a majority of the remaining partners express a will to wind up the partnership within 90 days of dissociation. RUPA 801(2). If the partnership does not dissolve and wind up, the wrongfully dissociated partner is not entitled to payment of any portion of the buyout price until the expiration of the term or completion of the undertaking, unless the partner proves to the court that earlier payment will not cause undue hardship to the business of the partnership. A deferred payment must be adequately secured and bear interest. RUPA 701(h). A partner who wrongfully dissociates is liable to the partnership and the other partners for damages caused by the dissociation. RUPA 602(c).

c. Effect of dissociation

A partner's dissociation does not necessarily cause the dissolution of the partnership and the winding up of its business (*see* II.C.1. "Events Causing Dissolution," *infra*). However, it does have a variety of other consequences for both the partner and the partnership.

1) Dissociated partner's management rights

A dissociated partner generally does not have the right to participate in the management or conduct of the partnership business. RUPA 603(b).

2) Dissociated partner's duties

A partner's duty not to compete terminates upon dissociation. The dissociated partner's other duties of loyalty and care terminate with respect to post-dissociation events, unless the partner participates in winding up the partnership's business if the partnership itself dissolves. RUPA 603(b).

3) Purchase of dissociated partner's interest

When a partner dissociates from the partnership but the partnership is not dissolved, the partnership must buy out the dissociated partner's partnership interest. RUPA 701(a).

a) Valuation of interest

The dissociated partner's interest is valued as if the partnership business was wound up on the date of the dissociation. For this purpose, the partnership is valued as the greater of either the liquidation value of its assets or the value of the partnership as a going concern. RUPA 701(b).

b) Payment to the partner

Absent an agreement to the contrary, within 120 days of the dissociated partner's demand for payment, the partnership generally is required to pay the partner the partnership's estimate of the partner's interest, less any offsets. RUPA 701(d), (h).

c) Judicial action

A dissociated partner may maintain an action against the partnership to determine the buyout price and to compel the partnership to pay that amount to the partner. RUPA 701(i).

4) Indemnification of a dissociated partner

When a partnership purchases a dissociated partner's interest, the partnership must generally indemnify the partner against all partnership liabilities, whether the liabilities were incurred before or after the dissociation. An exception exists for liabilities incurred by the partnership due to the dissociated partner's post-dissociation actions. RUPA 701(d).

5) Dissociated partner's pre-dissociation actions

A dissociated partner is generally liable for partnership obligations incurred before dissociation. RUPA 703(a). An exception exists when the partnership creditor, with notice of the partner's dissociation, agrees to a material change in the obligation's terms to which the dissociated partner did not consent. RUPA 703(d). In addition, a dissociated partner can obtain a release from a partnership obligation with the agreement of both the partnership creditor and the partners who continue the business. RUPA 703(c).

6) Dissociated partner's post-dissociation actions

If a partner dissociates from the partnership but the partnership is not dissolved, then the dissociated partner can enter into a transaction with a third party that binds not only the dissociated partner as a partner, but also the partnership. The partnership is bound when, at the time of the transaction, the other party to the transaction (i) reasonably believes that the dissociated partner is a partner, (ii) does not have notice of the partner's dissociation, and (iii) is not deemed to have knowledge of the dissociated partner's lack of authority. Liability is limited to transactions entered into within two years of the partner's dissociation. RUPA 702, 703.

a) Statement of dissociation

Either the partnership or the dissociated partner may file a statement of dissociation with the state. This statement, which constitutes a limit on the dissociated partner's authority, is treated as giving third parties notice of the dissociation as of 90 days after the statement is filed. Consequently, it can be used to reduce the window of partnership liability for a dissociated partner's actions from two years to 90 days. RUPA 704.

7) Partnership's post-dissociation actions

The continued use of a partnership name, including a name that includes the dissociated partner, does not automatically make the dissociated partner liable for the debts of the continuing business.

C. RELATIONSHIPS WITH THIRD PARTIES

1. Partner's Power to Bind the Partnership

a. Partner as agent of the partnership

A partner is an agent of the partnership for the purpose of its business and can contractually bind the partnership when the partner acts with either actual or apparent authority. RUPA 301(1).

1) Actual authority—binding on the partnership

A partner's act that was authorized by the partnership binds the partnership. RUPA 301(2). Actual authority includes both express authority and implied authority.

i) Express authority can arise from the partnership agreement itself, an authorization of the partners, or a statement of authority filed with the state.

ii) Implied authority is based on a partner's reasonable belief that an action is necessary to carry out his express authority.

2) Apparent authority—binding if in the ordinary course of business

A partner's act that was not authorized by the partnership may nevertheless bind the partnership under the principle of apparent authority. For apparent authority to apply, the partner must perform the unauthorized act in the ordinary course of apparently carrying on either the partnership business or business of a kind carried on by the partnership. In addition, the third party with whom the partner was dealing cannot hold the partnership liable when that party knew or had received notification that the partner lacked authority. RUPA 301(2).

a) Third party's knowledge or notification

For the partnership to escape liability, the third party generally must possess actual knowledge of the partner's lack of actual authority. An exception exists when the partnership has notified the third party in writing of the partner's lack of authority and the third party is aware of the notification or the notification is delivered to the third party's place of business or other place for receiving communications. RUPA 102(a), (d). In addition, with respect to the transfer of real estate, a third party is regarded as knowing a restriction on a partner's authority contained in a properly filed statement of authority.

3) Transfer of titled partnership property

A partner has authority to transfer titled partnership property in some circumstances.

a) Partnership property held in partnership name

A partner has the authority to transfer partnership property held in the partnership's name by executing an instrument of transfer (e.g., a deed) in the partnership's name. This authority is subject to limitation or elimination by a statement of partnership authority. RUPA 302(a)(1).

b) Partnership property held in partner's name

A partner has the authority to transfer partnership property held in one or more partners' names by executing an instrument of transfer (e.g., a deed) in the partners' names. This authority exists whether or not the instrument transferring the property to the partnership reflected the existence of the partnership or the status of the transferees as partners. RUPA 302(a)(2), (3).

c) Recovery of partnership property from transferee

A partnership may be able to recover partnership property transferred by a partner without authority. RUPA 302(b).

i) Partnership property in which partnership interest is indicated

If the partnership's interest in the property was indicated in the instrument through which the partnership acquired the property, the partnership may recover the property from any initial transferee if the property was transferred by a partner without authority.

ii) Partnership property in which partnership interest is not indicated—notification requirement

If the partnership interest in property was not indicated in the instrument through which the partnership acquired the property, the partnership may recover property transferred by a partner without authority, but only from a transferee who was aware that the property belonged to the partnership and that the partner executing the transfer did so without authority. RUPA 302(b)(2).

iii) Shelter rule for subsequent transferees

A partnership cannot recover partnership property transferred by a partner without authority from a subsequent transferee if the partnership could not recover the property from any earlier transferee. RUPA 302(c).

4) Partnership's knowledge and notice

A partner's knowledge or notice of a fact relating to the partnership is generally immediately imputed to the partnership. An exception exists when a fraud on the partnership is committed by or with the consent of the partner. RUPA 102(f).

5) Ownership of all partnership interests

A person who holds all of the partners' interests in a partnership, such as by purchase or by being the sole surviving partner, effectively has title to all of the partnership property and has the power to transfer that title to himself in the name of the nonexistent partnership. RUPA 302(d).

b. Statements of partnership authority and denial

To clarify the existence and scope of a partner's authority, statements of partnership authority and denial may be filed with the state. RUPA 105, 303, 304.

1) Statement of partnership authority

A partnership may file a statement of partnership authority. This statement may specify the extent of a partner's authority to enter into transactions on behalf of the partnership. RUPA 303.

a) Grant of authority

A purchaser of partnership property (or other person who gives value in a transaction with a partner) may point to a grant of authority contained in a filed statement as conclusive evidence of such authority. There is no requirement that the person relied upon or was aware of the statement at the time of the transaction. However, the person cannot have had actual knowledge that the partner did not in fact possess the necessary authority to enter into the transaction. RUPA 303(d).

b) Limitation of authority

A limitation on a partner's authority contained in a filed statement generally does not constitute constructive notice to a third party of that limitation. An exception exists with regard to a limitation contained in a statement on the authority of a partner to transfer real property held in the name of the partnership. To constitute constructive notice, a certified copy of the statement must be filed in the office for recording transfers of that real property. RUPA 303(e), (f).

2) Statement of denial

A partner may file a statement of denial, which may deny any fact asserted in a statement of partnership authority and may specifically deny any grant of authority. A person named as a partner may also file a statement that denies that status. RUPA 304.

2. Effect of Partner's Tortious Acts

A partnership is liable for a partner's tortious acts, including fraud, committed in the ordinary course of the partnership business or with partnership authority, whether actual or apparent. When the partner enjoys immunity from liability for such acts, the partnership is not entitled to assert that immunity. RUPA 305, inc. cmts.

3. Liability to Third Parties

a. Liability for partnership obligations

As a separate entity, a partnership is subject to suit for its obligations. RUPA 307(a), (b).

A partner is jointly and severally liable for all partnership obligations. RUPA 306(a).

1) Limitation on incoming partner's liability

A person admitted as a partner into an existing partnership is not personally liable for any prior partnership obligations. However, any capital contribution made by an incoming partner to the partnership is at risk for the satisfaction of such partnership obligations. RUPA 306(b).

2) Limitation on dissociated partner's liability

A partner who has dissociated from a partnership generally continues to be liable for any partnership obligation incurred before the dissociation. In addition, a dissociated partner may be liable for partnership obligations incurred after the dissociation. (See I.B.15.c. Effect of dissociation, *supra*, for details.)

b. Effect of judgment

Individual partners need not be named in a suit against the partnership in order to collect a judgment out of partnership assets. However, a judgment against a partnership is not a judgment against its partners. Unless there is also a judgment against the partner, a judgment against a partnership cannot be satisfied from a partner's assets, only from the partnership's assets. RUPA 307(a-c), inc. cmts. 2, 3.

Even though a partner is personally liable for a partnership obligation, a partnership creditor generally must exhaust the partnership's assets before levying on the partners' personal assets. Exceptions exist when the partnership is a debtor in bankruptcy, the partner has consented, or the partner is liable independent of the partnership, such as when the partner was the primary tortfeasor. In addition, a court may authorize execution against a partner's assets when the partnership's assets are clearly insufficient, exhaustion of the partnership's assets would be excessively burdensome, or it is otherwise equitable to do so. RUPA 307(d).

c. Criminal liability

A partnership may be convicted of a crime for which the penalty is a fine levied on partnership assets. However, mere membership in a partnership is not sufficient to make a partner criminally liable for the acts of another partner. *United States v. A & P Trucking Co.*, 358 U.S. 121 (1958).

II. PARTNERSHIP CHANGES AND TERMINATION

A partnership may be converted into one or more partnerships or limited partnerships. RUPA 905. Some states also specifically recognized the right of a limited partnership to merge into one or more partnerships or limited partnerships. *See* Revised Uniform Limited Partnership Act (RULPA) at § 1102 (2001). In addition, pursuant to the Model Business Corporation Act (MBCA), a corporation may merge with one or more partnerships or limited partnerships. MBCA § 11.02.

A. CONVERSION

1. Partnership to Limited Partnership

A partnership may be converted into a limited partnership. RUPA 902(a).

a. Conversion procedure

Unless the partnership agreement specifies otherwise, the conversion must be approved by all of the partners of the general partnership. Once the conversion is approved, the partnership must file the articles of conversion with the state. The conversion takes effect upon the filing of the articles of conversion unless the statement itself specifies a later date. RUPA 902(b)-(d).

b. Liability of a former general partner

A general partner who becomes a limited partner as a consequence of a conversion remains liable for any obligation incurred by the partnership before the conversion. In addition, such a partner, despite being a limited partner, may be liable for obligations incurred by the limited partnership within 90 days after the conversion becomes effective when the other party to the transaction reasonably believes at the time of the transaction that the limited partner is a general partner. RUPA 902(e).

2. Limited Partnership to Partnership

A limited partnership may be converted into a partnership. RUPA 903(a).

a. Conversion procedure

Notwithstanding a contrary provision in the limited partnership agreement, the conversion must be approved by all of the general and limited partners. Once the conversion is approved, the limited partnership must cancel its certificate of limited partnership. The conversion takes effect upon the cancellation of that certificate. RUPA 903(b)-(d).

b. Liability of a former limited partner

A limited partner who becomes a general partner as a consequence of a conversion remains liable only as a limited partner for any obligation incurred by the limited partnership before the conversion. As a general partner, such a partner is liable for any obligation of the partnership incurred after the conversion. RUPA 903(e).

3. Effect on the Partnership

A conversion of a partnership to a limited partnership, or a limited partnership to a partnership, does not affect the resulting partnership or limited partnership as an entity. Property owned by the partnership or limited partnership before the conversion remains vested in the resulting partnership. Legal proceedings by or against the preconversion partnership or limited partnership can continue as if the conversion had not occurred. RUPA 904.

B. MERGER

Different from a conversion, a partnership can **merge** into another business entity. For example, a partnership can merge into a limited partnership.

1. Plan of Merger

A plan of merger must set forth (i) the name of each partnership or limited partnership that is a party to the merger, (ii) the name of the surviving entity into which the other entities will merge, (iii) the type of entity the surviving entity will be, (iv) any terms and conditions of the merger, (v) the manner of converting interests and obligations of the merging entities into interest or obligations of the surviving entity, and (vi) the street address of the surviving entity's executive office. RUPA 905.

2. Approval Required

If a **partnership** is a party to the merger, then the merger must be approved by all of the partners, unless otherwise specified in the partnership agreement. If a **limited partnership** is a party to the merger, then the merger must be approved by either (i) the vote required by the law of the jurisdiction in which the limited partnership is organized or (ii) in the absence of a law, by all partners or by whatever number of partners is specified in the partnership agreement. RUPA 905.

3. Date Merger Is Effective

The merger takes effect upon approval of all necessary parties, the filing of all required documents, or any date specified in the plan of merger, whichever is later.

4.   Effect of Merger

When a merger becomes effective, all parties to the merger other than the surviving entity cease to exist. All property and obligations of the entities that are parties to the merger become the property and obligations of the surviving entity. All proceedings against a party to the merger either may continue as if the merger had not occurred or may substitute the surviving entity into the proceeding. Any partner of a party to a merger who does not become a partner of the surviving entity is dissociated from the entity as of the date the merger takes effect. RUPA 906.

A partner of the surviving entity is liable for (i) all obligations for which he was personally liable before the merger, (ii) all of the surviving entity's obligations that were incurred by a party to the merger before the merger (although those obligations must be satisfied by the entity's property), and (iii) all obligations incurred by the surviving entity after the merger takes effect, unless otherwise provided by law. RUPA 906(c).

C.   TERMINATION OF PARTNERSHIP

Termination of a partnership is a two-step process—dissolution and winding up. The happening of an event triggers **dissolution**, the first step in the termination of a partnership. Next, the partnership must **wind up** its business, which is a process that entails liquidating the assets, paying off creditors, and distributing any remaining funds to the partners. The partnership is not terminated until the partnership business is wound up.

1.   Events Causing Dissolution

The events that may trigger dissolution differ depending on whether the partnership is a partnership at will or one for a definite term or particular undertaking. RUPA 801.

a.   Dissolution of partnership at will

A partnership at will is an open-ended partnership that does not have a fixed termination based on a period of time or particular undertaking. RUPA 101(8). It is dissolved when a partner chooses to dissociate from the partnership by giving notice of her withdrawal. RUPA 801(1).

b.   Dissolution of partnership for a term or undertaking

A partnership for a definite term or particular undertaking is dissolved when:

  i)   The term expires or the undertaking is completed;

  ii)   All partners agree to dissolve the partnership; or

  iii) A partner is dissociated due to death, bankruptcy, or other circumstance, and within 90 days of such occurrence, at least half of the remaining partners agree to dissolve the partnership.

RUPA 801(2).

1)   Continuation after term expires or undertaking is completed

When the partners continue the business without any settlement or liquidation after the term expires or the undertaking is completed, there is a presumption that they have agreed to continue the business. The partnership is then transformed into a partnership at will; the rights and duties of the partners remain the same as they were. RUPA 406.

c.   Dissolution of any partnership

Any partnership is dissolved when any of the following events occurs:

i)   A dissolving event agreed to in the partnership agreement;

ii) An event that makes it unlawful for all or substantially all of the partnership business to be continued, provided that the illegality is not cured within 90 days after the partnership receives notice;

iii) A judicial determination is sought by a partner that the economic purpose of the partnership is likely to be unreasonably frustrated, another partner has engaged in conduct relating to the partnership business that makes it not reasonably practicable to carry on the business with that partner, or it is not otherwise reasonably practicable to carry on the partnership business in conformity with the partnership agreement; or

iv) A judicial determination is sought by a transferee of a partner's partnership interest that it is equitable to wind up the partnership business after expiration of the partnership term or completion of the undertaking or at any time, if the partnership was a partnership at will at the time of the transfer or when the charging order was issued.

RUPA 801(3)-(6). A partnership agreement cannot vary the requirements set forth in items ii) through iv) for the dissolution of the partnership.

2. Winding Up

A partnership that has dissolved continues only to wind up its business. RUPA 802(a).

a. Persons who may wind up

Any partner who has not wrongfully dissociated may participate in winding up the partnership's business, including the legal representative of the last surviving partner. RUPA 803(a)(b). (Note: The legal representative of a deceased partner who was not the last surviving partner only has the rights of a transferee of the deceased partner's partnership interest. RUPA 601, cmt. 8.)

b. Judicial supervision of winding up

Any partner, legal representative, or transferee may seek judicial supervision of the winding up. RUPA 803(a).

c. Power of person winding up the business

A person who is winding up the partnership business may dispose of and transfer partnership property and may discharge the partnership's liabilities. That person also may preserve the partnership business or property as a going concern for a reasonable time to maximize its value. In winding up the partnership's business, the person may distribute assets of the partnership to settle partners' accounts. RUPA 803(c).

d. Consequences of partner's post-dissolution acts for the partnership

After dissolution, the partnership is bound by a partner's act that is appropriate for winding up the partnership as well as any act undertaken by a partner that would have bound the partnership before dissolution, if the other party does not have notice of the dissolution. RUPA 804. Each partner is liable to the other partners for his share of partnership liability incurred by such post-dissolution acts. In addition, a partner who knowingly undertakes an act inappropriate for winding up the partnership business is liable to the partnership for any damage caused to the partnership for such an act. RUPA 806.

e. Statement of dissolution

After dissolution, a partner who has not wrongfully dissociated may file a statement of dissolution. A statement of dissolution, which constitutes a limitation on a partner's authority, is treated as giving third parties notice of the dissolution 90 days after the statement is filed. RUPA 805.

f. Distribution of partnership assets

In winding up a partnership's business, creditors have priority over partners to the partnership's assets. RUPA 807.

1) Discharge of partnership obligations

Partnership assets are first applied to discharge partnership obligations to creditors (including partners who are creditors of the partnership) before being distributed to the partners. RUPA 807(a).

> Unlike the UPA, the RUPA does not subordinate the obligations to partner creditors to those of third-party creditors. However, even partner creditors remain personally liable, as a partner, for any outside debt remaining unsatisfied. Accordingly, the obligation to contribute sufficient funds to satisfy the claims of outside creditors may result in the equitable subordination of inside debt when partnership assets are insufficient to satisfy all obligations to non-partners. RUPA 807, cmt. 2.

2) Settlement of partners' accounts

Each partner's account, which reflects not only that partner's contributions to the partnership but also the partner's share of the partnership's pre-dissolution profits and losses, must be adjusted to reflect the profits and losses that result from the liquidation of the partnership assets. After these adjustments, any partners with a negative account balance must contribute to the partnership the amount necessary to bring the account balance to zero. Then the partnership must make a final liquidating distribution to any partner with a positive account balance. RUPA 807(b).

3. Continuation of Partnership After Dissolution

Once a partnership has been dissolved, but before the winding up of its business is complete, the partnership may resume carrying on its business as if dissolution had never occurred. To do so, all partners (including any properly dissociated partners) must agree to waive the right to terminate the partnership. RUPA 802(b).

a. Effect on the partner and the partnership

Any liability incurred by the partnership or by a partner after the dissolution and before the waiver is determined as if dissolution had never occurred. RUPA 802(b)(1).

b. Effect on a third party

The waiver does not adversely affect the rights of a third party who dealt with the partnership before the party knew or was notified of the waiver. RUPA 802(b)(2), inc. cmt. 3.

> **Example:** A subsequent waiver does not reinstate a partnership loan that was callable upon dissolution and was called by the lender.

III. OTHER PARTNERSHIP ENTITIES

A. LIMITED LIABILITY PARTNERSHIPS

A limited liability partnership (LLP) is a partnership in which a partner's personal liability for obligations of the partnership is eliminated. To enjoy LLP status, the partnership must file a statement with the state. In other respects, an LLP is governed by the same rules as a partnership.

1. Formation

An LLP is formed by filing a statement of qualification with the state. LLP status is effective on the date that the statement is filed, unless a later date is specified in the statement. RUPA 1001(c), (e). The filing of a statement of qualification to transform a partnership into an LLP does not create a new partnership. RUPA 201(b).

a. Authorization

The transformation of a partnership into an LLP must be approved by the vote necessary to amend the partnership agreement. If the partnership agreement is silent on this voting requirement, the approval of the transformation requires the approval of all partners. RUPA 1001(b).

b. Name

The name of an LLP must end with "Registered Limited Liability Partnership," "Limited Liability Partnership, "R.L.L.P.," "L.L.P.," "RLLP," or "LLP." RUPA 1002.

c. Partnership agreement

A partnership agreement cannot vary the law applicable to LLPs. RUPA 103(b)(9).

2. Liabilities of Partners and the Partnership

A limited partner in an LLP is not personally liable for an obligation of an LLP, regardless of the type of obligation (e.g., tort, contract). A limited partner is personally liable for his own personal misconduct (e.g., negligence, negligent supervision). RUPA 306(c), inc. cmt. 3.

An obligation of an LLP is solely an obligation of the partnership, notwithstanding a contrary provision in the partnership agreement that existed before the vote to transform from a partnership to an LLP. RUPA 306(c). The LLP's assets may be reached to satisfy an LLP obligation.

3. Termination of LLP Status

The cancellation of a statement of qualification transforms the LLP into a simple partnership but does not trigger dissolution. RUPA 201(b). The state may revoke the statement of qualification of an LLP for the failure to file an annual report; this revocation has the same effect as cancellation. RUPA 1003(c), (d).

B. LIMITED PARTNERSHIPS

Limited partnerships are governed by the Revised Uniform Limited Partnership Act of 1976 with the 1985 amendments (RULPA), which is linked to the RUPA. A limited partnership is a partnership formed by two or more persons that has at least one general partner and at least one limited partner. RULPA 101(7). A limited partner's liability for partnership debts is limited to the amount of her capital contribution to the partnership. RULPA 303(a).

1. **Formation**

   a. **Certificate of limited partnership**

   To form a limited partnership, a certificate of limited partnership must be filed with the state. RULPA 201(a).

   1) **Contents and execution**

   The certificate must contain only the name of the limited partnership, its in-state address, the name and address of its in-state agent for service of process, the name and business address of each general partner, and a statement about the duration of the limited partnership. All of the general partners must sign the certificate. RULPA 201(a), 204(a)(1).

   2) **Effective date**

   The limited partnership comes into existence upon the filing of the certificate unless the certificate specifies a later date. RULPA 201(b).

   3) **Incomplete certificate**

   A certificate need only substantially comply with statutory requirements in order to have effect as to third parties. RULPA 201(b).

   4) **Effect of failure to file**

   If a certificate of limited partnership is not filed, then the limited partnership is not formed. If a person makes a contribution to a purported limited partnership and erroneously believes in good faith that he has become a limited partner, then he is liable to a third party who transacts business with the purported limited partnership, believing in good faith that the person was a general partner at the time of the transaction. A similar result occurs when a person is mistakenly listed as a general partner in the certificate. RULPA 304.

   b. **Type of business**

   A limited partnership generally may carry on any business that a partnership without limited partners may carry on. RULPA 106.

2. **Limited Partners**

   a. **Admission**

   A person may become a limited partner upon the creation of the limited partnership. Thereafter, that person may be admitted as a limited partner by acquiring her interest directly from the partnership only upon the written consent of all partners, unless the partnership agreement otherwise provides. An assignee of a partnership interest, including a general or a limited partner's interest, may become a limited partner if the partnership agreement permits or all partners consent. RULPA 301, 704(a).

   b. **Voting rights**

   A limited partner has the right to vote only to the extent allowed under the partnership agreement. RULPA 302. A limited partner does not have the right to vote on any partnership matter as a separate class. RULPA 405.

   c. **Record access right**

   A limited partner has the right to inspect and copy records of the limited partnership. In addition, a limited partner has the right to demand information regarding the business and financial condition of the partnership and other pertinent information about partnership affairs from the general partners. RULPA 305.

d. Limited partner's transaction of business with the partnership

A limited partner may lend money to and transact other business with the limited partnership. In such transactions, the limited partner has the same rights and obligations as a person who is not a partner. RULPA 107.

e. Liability to third parties

A limited partner is generally not personally liable for the obligations of a limited partnership unless the limited partner also serves as a general partner or participates in the control of the business. RULPA 303(a).

1) Safe harbor list of activities

Solely doing one or more of the following activities does not constitute participation in the control of the business:

i) Being a contractor for, or an agent of, the limited partnership or a general partner; or being an officer, director, or shareholder of a corporate general partner;

ii) Consulting with or advising a general partner with respect to the limited partnership's business;

iii) Acting as surety for the limited partnership or guaranteeing or assuming an obligation of the limited partnership;

iv) Requesting or attending a meeting of partners;

v) Winding up the limited partnership; or

vi) Proposing, approving, or disapproving limited partnership matters, such as the sale or transfer of substantially all of the assets of the limited partnership or the admission or removal of a general or limited partner.

RULPA 303(b).

2) Extent of liability

Even if a limited partner participates in the control of the business, she is personally liable only to persons who transact business with the limited partnership, reasonably believing, based on the limited partner's conduct, that the limited partner is a general partner. RULPA 303(a).

3) Use of name

A limited partner who allows his name to be used in the name of the limited partnership is liable to a creditor who extends credit to the limited partnership, unless the creditor has actual knowledge that the limited partner is not a general partner. RULPA 303(d).

f. Withdrawal

Unless the written partnership agreement provides otherwise, a limited partner must give six months' prior written notice to each general partner before withdrawing. RULPA 603.

3. **General Partners**

   a. **Admission**

   A person may become a general partner upon the creation of the limited partnership. Thereafter, a person may be admitted as a general partner only upon the written consent of all partners, unless the partnership agreement otherwise provides. (Note: An assignee of a general partner's partnership interest may become a *limited* partner but not a general partner, as long as the partnership agreement permits it or all other partners consent.) RULPA 401, 704(a).

   b. **Rights and powers**

   Except as provided in the partnership agreement, a general partner has the rights and powers of a partner in a partnership without limited partners and is subject to the same restrictions as such a partner. RULPA 403(a).

   > **Example:** A general partner may have the right to vote on limited partnership matters in any manner specified in the partnership agreement. RULPA 405.

   c. **Contributions and distributions**

   A general partner may contribute to the limited partnership, share in its losses and profits, and receive distributions from it. RULPA 404.

   d. **General partner's transaction of business with the partnership**

   A general partner may lend money to and transact other business with the limited partnership. In such transactions, the general partner has the same rights and obligations as a person who is not a partner. RULPA 107.

   e. **Liability to third parties**

   A general partner is personally liable to third parties for the obligations of the limited partnership. Except as provided in the partnership agreement, a general partner also has liabilities to the partnership and the other partners. RULPA 403(b).

   > **EXAM NOTE:** Although the general partner in a limited partnership has unlimited liability, the typical general partner is an entity such as a corporation that has its own liability shield.

   f. **Termination of general partner status**

   1) **Withdrawal**

      At any time, a general partner may withdraw from a limited partnership by giving written notice to the other partners. When the withdrawal violates the partnership agreement, the general partner may be liable to the limited partnership for any damages from his breach of the agreement. RULPA 602.

      The withdrawal of a sole general partner does not necessarily trigger the dissolution of a limited partnership, however; the limited partners have 90 days in which to consent to continue the business and appoint a new general partner (by a majority of rights to receive distributions). RULPA 801.

   2) **Additional events causing a general partner to cease being a partner**

      Additional events include:

      i) Assignment of her partnership interest, unless the partnership agreement provides otherwise (RULPA 702);

ii) Removal as a general partner in accordance with the partnership agreement;

iii) Financial difficulties, such as bankruptcy and insolvency;

iv) Death or adjudicated incompetency of a natural person; or

v) Termination of a partner as a business entity.

RULPA 402.

4. **Contributions**

a. **Form of contribution**

A general or limited partner may contribute cash, property or services. A partner may also contribute a promise to pay cash (e.g., a promissory note), to provide property, or to perform services. RULPA 501.

b. **Liability for contribution**

Except as provided in the partnership agreement, a partner is obligated to the limited partnership with respect to any written, enforceable promise of a future contribution. When a partner is unable to perform services due to death or disability, the partner or his estate must pay to the partnership the cash value of such services. RULPA 502(a), (b).

1) **Compromise of obligation**

A partner who is required to contribute or to return money or other property paid or distributed can compromise this obligation only with the consent of all partners. RULPA 502(c).

2) **Liability to creditor**

With respect to a partnership creditor, the partner is liable for this obligation when the creditor acts in reliance on it. RULPA 502(c).

5. **Profits and Losses**

The partners may choose to allocate profits and losses on any basis, provided such allocation is in writing. In the absence of such a written agreement, both profits and losses are allocated among the partners based on each partner's partnership contributions, provided such contributions have not been returned to the partner. RULPA 503, 504.

6. **Distributions**

a. **Allocation of distributions**

The partners may choose to make distributions on any basis, provided such basis is in writing. Without a written agreement, distributions are allocated among the partners in the same manner as profits and losses are shared. RULPA 503, 504.

b. **Right to distribution**

A partner's right to any type of distribution can be specified in the partnership agreement. If it is not, a partner does not have a right to receive a distribution from the limited partnership before withdrawal or dissolution of the partnership. RULPA 601. Upon withdrawal from the partnership, a partner has the right to receive a distribution of the fair value of his partnership interest, as measured on the date of withdrawal, within a reasonable time after withdrawal. RULPA 604.

c. Distribution as a return of contribution

A distribution constitutes a return of a partner's contribution to a limited partnership to the extent that it reduces her share of the net assets to less than her contribution. A partner is liable to the partnership for a return of a contribution to the extent necessary to discharge the limited partnership's liabilities to creditors. The partner's liability extends for one year after the return of the contribution, unless the return was wrongful, in which case the time period is lengthened to six years. RULPA 608.

7. Assignment of Partnership Interest

In general, a partnership interest in a limited partnership is personal property that can be assigned in whole or in part. Upon assignment of the interest, the partner ceases to be a partner in the limited partnership, but the assignee generally has rights only to receive the distribution to which the assignor partner would otherwise be entitled. RULPA 701-705.

a. Assignee as limited partner

An assignee of a limited partnership interest, including a general partnership interest, may become a limited partner if the partnership agreement permits it or if all partners agree. An assignee becomes liable for obligations of the assignor to make and return contributions known to the assignee at the time he became a limited partner, but the assignor is not released from those obligations or from obligations arising from false statements in the certificate of limited partnership. RULPA 704.

8. Termination

a. Dissolution

A partnership terminates after it is dissolved and its affairs are wound up. The following events cause a partnership to dissolve:

i) The occurrence of an event specified in the partnership agreement or reaching the termination date specified in the certificate of limited partnership;

ii) The written consent of all partners;

iii) The withdrawal of a general partner or other occurrence in which the general partner ceases to be a general partner, unless there is at least one other general partner to carry on the partnership business or, within 90 days, all partners agree in writing to carry on the business and appoint any necessary general partners; or

iv) A decree of judicial dissolution based on a determination that it is not reasonably practical to carry on the business in conformity with the partnership agreement.

RULPA 801, 802.

b. Winding up

Unless the partnership agreement provides otherwise, the task of winding up the limited partnership's affairs falls to the general partners who have not wrongfully dissolved the limited partnership. When there are not any such general partners, the limited partners may wind up the partnership's affairs. Alternatively, a partner, her legal representative, or an assignee may petition a court to wind up the limited partnership's affairs. RULPA 803.

c. Distribution of assets

Upon winding up, the partnership's assets are distributed to the following parties in order:

i) Partnership creditors, including partners who are creditors; then

ii) Partners and former partners who are entitled to distributions that have accrued but not been paid; then

iii) Partners for the return of their contributions; and finally

iv) Partners in the proportions in which they share distributions.

RULPA 804.

9. Limited Partner's Derivative Action

A limited partner has the right to bring a derivative action on behalf of the limited partnership. RULPA 1001-1004.

a. Demand on a general partner

A limited partner may bring an action if the general partners have refused to do so or if an attempt to cause the general partners to bring such an action is likely to fail. In the complaint, the limited partner is required to detail such effort or explain the reasons for not making the effort.

b. Proper plaintiff

To bring the action, the limited partner must be a partner at the time of bringing the action as well as at the time of the wrongful transaction, unless the status of partner devolved on him by operation of law or pursuant to the terms of the operating agreement.

c. Recovery

If the action is successful, the limited partner may receive an award for his reasonable expenses, including attorney's fees. The limited partnership is entitled to the remainder of the judgment proceeds.

Secured Transactions

SECURED TRANSACTIONS

Table of Contents

SECURED TRANSACTIONS

I. IN GENERAL

A secured transaction under Uniform Commercial Code (UCC) Article 9 typically involves a relationship between two parties, a **debtor** and a **creditor**, that arises when the debtor has given certain assurances in the form of a **security interest** in specific property (i.e., **collateral**) to assure that the obligation will be performed. These assurances involve special rights enjoyed by the creditor as a secured party in the collateral, such as the right to seize and sell the property to satisfy the outstanding debt. To enjoy this protection, the creditor must adhere to specific requirements (e.g., attachment, perfection) and is subject to special restrictions in the timing and exercise of those rights.

A. SECURITY INTEREST

A security interest is generally an interest in **personal property or fixtures** that secures payment or performance of an obligation. UCC § 1-201(35). The purpose of a security interest is to:

i) Make the debt *more easily collectible* if the debtor cannot or refuses to pay the obligation;

ii) Provide the secured party with *a position superior to other creditors* who might attempt to obtain the same collateral to secure or collect their debts; and

iii) Provide the secured party with *rights to obtain the collateral* if it is sold or otherwise transferred to a third party.

B. AGREEMENT

Typically, Article 9 applies to a consensual agreement that provides for a security interest. If the substance of the transaction is the creation of a security interest, then Article 9 applies regardless of the form of the transaction or the name given to it by the parties. It is, therefore, the substance of the transaction, not its form, that determines whether Article 9 is applicable. UCC § 9-109(a), cmt. 2.

An agreement is the bargain-in-fact between the parties. By contrast, a contract is the legal obligation that results from the agreement. UCC § 1-201(3), (12).

C. PARTIES

There are three types of parties with respect to a secured transaction: a secured party, an obligor, and a debtor.

1. Secured Party

A secured party is the person in whose favor a security interest is created under the security agreement. Usually, the secured party is the person who has loaned money or extended credit to the obligor. A secured party may also include a consignor; the buyer of accounts, chattel paper, payment intangibles, or promissory notes; or the holder of an agricultural lien. UCC § 9-102(a)(72).

2. Obligor

An obligor is a person who must pay (or otherwise perform) with respect to the obligation that is secured by a security interest in the collateral. UCC § 9-102(a)(59).

3. Debtor

A debtor is a person who has an interest, other than a security interest or other lien, in the collateral, such as the sole owner of the collateral. Although the debtor is usually also the obligor, the debtor need not be. UCC § 9-102(a)(28).

> **Example 1:** A loans money to B. B grants A a security interest in his car. A is a secured party. B is both an obligor and a debtor. UCC § 9-102, cmt. 2.a.
>
> **Example 2:** A loans money to B without seeking security from her. B's sister, C, cosigns the note and grants A a security interest in her car to secure the loan to B. A is a secured party. B is an obligor but not a debtor. C is both an obligor and a debtor. UCC § 9-102, cmt. 2.a.

D. COLLATERAL

Property subject to a security interest is called "collateral." The characterization of collateral as, for example, inventory or a deposit account can affect the validity of a security interest, the way in which a security interest can be perfected, and the rights of a third party in the collateral, such as a buyer of collateral. UCC § 9-102(a)(12).

1. Tangible Collateral—Goods

"Goods" encompasses anything that is "**moveable at the time that a security interest attaches**." Also included within the definition of goods are (i) fixtures, (ii) standing timber that is to be cut and removed pursuant to a contract, (iii) unborn animals, (iv) growing or unharvested grown crops, including crops produced on trees (e.g., apples), vines (e.g., grapes), or bushes (e.g., blueberries), and (v) manufactured homes. UCC § 9-102(a)(44).

a. Classification of goods

There are four classes of goods, each of which is mutually exclusive at any particular moment in time; however, the classification may change during the life of the goods.

1) Consumer goods

"Consumer goods" are those goods acquired primarily for personal, family, or household purposes. UCC § 9-102(a)(23).

2) Farm products

"Farm products" are goods that are crops or livestock and include supplies that are used or produced in farming. Excluded from farm products is standing timber for which there is not a contract to cut and remove. It is important to remember that for goods to be considered farm products, the debtor must be engaged in a farming operation. UCC § 9-102(a)(34).

3) Inventory

"Inventory" includes goods, other than farm products, that are held for sale or lease; are furnished under a service contract; or consist of raw materials, works in process, or materials used or consumed in a business. This term usually refers to goods that are consumed in a business (e.g., fuel used in operations) and includes items, even though not held for sale or lease, that are used up or consumed in a short period of time. UCC § 9-102(a)(48), inc. cmt. 4.a.

4) Equipment

"Equipment," a catchall class, consists of goods that are not consumer goods, farm products, or inventory. It usually refers to goods that are used or bought for use primarily in a business, such as employees' desks or machinery used in manufacturing. UCC § 9-102(a)(33).

b. Classification issues

1) Multiple uses by a single debtor

When the debtor uses the property for multiple purposes, the **principal use** to which the debtor puts the property determines the class of the goods. UCC § 9-102, cmt. 4.a.

2) Various uses by two or more debtors

The same property may fall into different classes with respect to different debtors. UCC § 9-102, cmt. 4.a.

3) Time for testing use

Generally, goods are classified when the security interest attaches. *See* UCC § 9-102(a)(44).

> **Example:** A retailer of pianos uses the pianos as collateral to obtain a loan. The pianos are inventory for purposes of the security interest created by the retailer. A symphony orchestra buys one of the retailer's piano to use during concerts and uses it as collateral to guarantee that it will pay the retailer for the piano. The piano is equipment for purposes of the security interest created by the orchestra.

c. Software

Software embedded in goods, such as a diagnostic computer program contained in an automobile, is treated as part of the goods in which it is embedded. Software that is not embedded in goods, such as software sold in a separate box at a retail store, is treated as a "general intangible." *See* § I.D.2.i. General intangibles, *infra*. UCC § 9-102(a)(44), (75), incl. cmts. 4.a., 25.

2. Other Collateral

There are nine other classes of personal property. The first four classes listed below are sometimes referred to as "quasi-intangible" property because a writing usually exists that defines the property right. Unlike the classification of goods, classification of these nine types of collateral does not turn on the manner in which the debtor uses the property. UCC § 9-102(a)(42).

a. Chattel paper

"Chattel paper" consists of one or more records that evidence both (i) a monetary obligation (e.g., a negotiable note) and (ii) a security interest in specific goods (e.g., a security agreement) or a lease of specific goods. UCC § 9-102(a)(11).

If the record is stored electronically, then the chattel paper is known as "electronic chattel paper." If the record is maintained on paper or another tangible medium, then the chattel paper is referred to as "tangible chattel paper." UCC § 9-102(a)(31), (78).

b. Document

A "document" refers to a document of title, which confers on the holder ownership rights in goods held by a bailee, such as a bill of lading, transport document, a dock warrant, a dock receipt, a warehouse receipt, and an order for the delivery of goods. UCC §§ 1-201(16), 9-102(a)(30).

c. Instruments

"Instruments" encompass negotiable instruments, such as promissory notes and checks, as described in Article 3, and nonnegotiable instruments that evidence a right to the payment of a monetary obligation and are transferred in the ordinary course of business by delivery, such as a certificate of deposit from a bank. When coupled with evidence of a security interest, the two combined constitute chattel paper. UCC § 9-102(a)(47), (65).

d. Investment property

"Investment property" includes both certificated and uncertificated securities, such as stock and bonds, as well as securities accounts, security entitlements, commodity accounts, and commodity contracts. UCC § 9-102(a)(49).

e. Accounts

"Accounts" include the right to payment for property sold, leased, licensed, or otherwise disposed of, or services rendered or to be rendered. Also included is a right to payment for the issuance of an insurance policy, the use of a credit or charge card, or winning a lottery. Excluded are rights to payments that are evidenced by another type of collateral, such as an instrument or chattel paper and those that arise out of a transaction that is not contained within the definition of an account. For example, a right to payment arising out of a loan transaction would, if not evidenced by an instrument or chattel paper, be a payment intangible, not an account. UCC § 9-102(a)(2).

f. Commercial tort claims

"Commercial tort claims" include tort claims possessed by an organization, or by an individual that arose in the course of the individual's business. Excluded are tort claims by an individual for personal injury or death. UCC § 9-102(a)(13).

g. Deposit account

A "deposit account" includes a savings, passbook, time, or demand account maintained with a bank. Excluded are investment property and accounts evidenced by instruments, such as certificates of deposit. UCC § 9-102(a)(29). Article 9 does not apply to a deposit account that is pledged as collateral in a consumer transaction, but such an account that is received as proceeds is subject to the rules regarding proceeds. UCC § 9-109(d)(13).

h. Letter-of-credit right

A "letter-of-credit right" is a right to payment or performance under a letter of credit, even though the beneficiary has not demanded—nor is the time ripe for — payment or performance. UCC § 9-102(a)(51).

i. General intangibles

"General intangibles" is the residual category of personal property that is not included in other types of collateral. Included among items that are general intangibles are copyrights, things in action (e.g., legal claims), payment intangibles (i.e., a general intangible under which the account debtor's principal obligation is a monetary obligation), and software-not-part-of-goods. UCC § 9-102(a)(42), (61), incl. cmt. 5d.

E. ELIGIBLE TRANSACTIONS

1. General Rule

Article 9 governs a transaction that creates, by agreement, a security interest in personal property or a fixture. In addition, a lease, consignment, agricultural lien, and even a purchase of personal property may be subject to Article 9. Also, a real-property transaction can produce an obligation, such as the promissory note secured by a mortgage, that can be the subject of an Article 9 security interest. UCC § 9-109(a)(1).

2. Leases

A true lease of goods is governed by Article 2A. Leases are covered under Article 9 only when the transaction, although in the form of a lease, is in economic reality or substance a secured transaction. It is generally determined on a case-by-case basis not by the parties' characterization of the transaction but by the economic reality of the transaction. UCC § 1-201(35).

a. Transaction creating a security interest

A transaction in the form of a lease is treated as creating a security interest if the lessee must pay consideration to the lessor for the right to possess and use the goods for the term of the lease, the payment obligation cannot be terminated by the lessee, and one of the following four conditions is also met:

i) The original term of the lease is equal to or greater than the remaining economic life of the goods;

ii) The lessee is bound to renew the lease for the remaining economic life of the goods or is bound to become owner of the goods;

iii) The lessee has an option to renew the lease for the remaining economic life of the goods for no additional consideration or nominal additional consideration upon compliance with the lease agreement; or

iv) The lessee has an option to become the owner of the goods, for no additional consideration or nominal additional consideration, upon completion of the lease agreement.

UCC § 1-203.

> **Example:** The so-called lease provides for payments of $5,000 per year for a period of five years without a right of early termination by the lessee. At the end of the five-year term, the lessee has the option to purchase the goods for the nominal price of $1. Notwithstanding the parties' characterization of the transaction, the economic reality is that it is a sale to the lessee with a security interest retained by the lessor. Thus, the transaction is governed by Article 9.

b. Protective filing

Even though a lease of goods is arguably subject to Article 2A, the lessor may nevertheless take steps to comply with Article 9's filing rules. The lessor may wish to do so when there is doubt as to whether the transaction constitutes a true lease or a sale with a retained security interest. By making such a protective filing, the lessor is not prevented from asserting that the transaction constitutes a lease, but he will be accorded perfected status in the event that a court later determines that it is not. UCC § 9-505.

3. Consignments

Consignments may fall within the scope of Article 9. If so, the consignor's security interest in the consigned goods is treated as a purchase-money security interest (PMSI) in inventory. UCC §§ 9-109(a)(4), 9-103(d). In order for a consignment to be subject to Article 9, the following requirements must be met:

i) A person (i.e., the consignor) must deliver goods to a merchant for the merchant to sell;

ii) The merchant (i.e., the consignee) must:

   a) Deal in goods of that kind,

   b) Not operate under the name of the consignor,

   c) Not be generally known by its creditors to be substantially engaged in selling the goods of others, and

   d) Not be an auctioneer;

iii) With respect to each delivery, the value of the goods delivered must be at least $1,000 at the time of the delivery; and

iv) The goods must not be consumer goods immediately before the delivery.

UCC § 9-102(19)–(21).

4. Liens

A statutory or common-law lien for services or materials (e.g., a mechanics lien) is not subject to Article 9, except for the rule regarding the priority of such a lien. *See* § IV.B.3. Statutory or Common-Law Lien Creditor, *infra*. Similarly, a landlord's lien, which arises from an interest in real estate rather than personal property, is not subject to Article 9. UCC § 9-109(d)(1), (2).

5. Agricultural Liens

Unlike other statutory and common-law liens, an agricultural lien is subject to Article 9. Included within the definition of an "agricultural lien" is an interest in farm products (e.g., crops, livestock) that secures payment or performance of an obligation for either (i) goods or services furnished with respect to the debtor's farming operation (e.g., livestock feed sold to a cattle rancher) or (ii) rent on real property leased by a debtor in connection with a farming operation. UCC §§ 9-102(a)(5), 9-109(a)(2).

6. Purchases

Generally, the sale of personal property is not subject to Article 9.

a. Sale of accounts, chattel paper, payment intangibles, promissory notes

Subject to several exceptions, the sale of accounts, chattel paper, payment intangibles, and promissory notes is subject to Article 9. UCC § 9-109(a)(3). Such transactions, however, are not subject to Article 9 if the sale is part of a sale of the business out of which they arose. In addition, the following assignments are not subject to Article 9:

i) The assignment of accounts, chattel paper, payment intangibles, or promissory notes for the purposes of collection only;

ii) The assignment of a single account, payment intangible, or promissory note in full or partial satisfaction of a preexisting indebtedness; and

iii) The assignment of a right to payment under a contract to an assignee who is also obligated to perform under the contract.

UCC § 9-109(d)(4)–(7).

b. Seller and buyer of goods

The rights of a seller pursuant to Article 2 to retain or acquire possession of goods, as well as the property interest of a buyer of goods upon the identification of such goods, are usually not treated as security interests. The seller or buyer may acquire a security interest in the goods by complying with Article 9. The retention or reservation of title by a seller of goods notwithstanding shipment or delivery to the buyer is limited in effect to a reservation of a security interest. UCC § 1-201(35).

7. Real Property Transactions

Although Article 9 is generally limited to personal-property transactions, it does apply to a security interest in a secured obligation (e.g., a promissory note), even though the obligation is itself secured by a transaction or interest to which Article 9 does not apply (e.g., a real property mortgage). UCC § 9-109(b).

II. ATTACHMENT OF SECURITY INTEREST

A. IN GENERAL

Generally, a security interest that is enforceable against the debtor with respect to the collateral is said to have "**attached**" to the collateral.

For the security interest to be enforceable against the debtor, three conditions must coexist:

i) **Value** has been given by the secured party;

ii) The **debtor has rights** in the collateral; and

iii) The debtor has authenticated a **security agreement** that describes the collateral, or the secured party has **possession** or **control** of the collateral pursuant to a security agreement.

UCC §§ 9-201, 9-203(b).

B. VALUE GIVEN

The secured party, or a person acting on behalf of the secured party, *must* give value for the security interest. Value may be given:

i) By providing **consideration** sufficient to support a simple contract;

ii) By **extending credit**, either immediately or under a binding commitment to do so (the debtor need not draw upon the credit);

iii) By, as a buyer, **accepting delivery** under a preexisting contract, thereby converting a contingent obligation into a fixed obligation; or

iv) In satisfaction of, or as security for, part or all of a preexisting claim.

UCC §§ 1-204, 9-203(b).

1. Future Advances and Other Value

In addition to value given at the time that a security agreement is entered into, the security agreement may provide that the collateral secures future value (e.g., future advances) given by the secured party. Note that with regard to perfection of a security interest, however, the financing statement is not required to refer specifically to future value. UCC § 9-204(c).

> **Example:** A debtor grants a secured party a security interest "in all inventory now owned or hereafter acquired by the debtor for a current loan of $50,000 and all future loans made by the secured party to the debtor."

2. New Value

For creating a security interest that is enforceable against the debtor, a creditor may receive a security interest in exchange for a preexisting debt. In a few instances, a creditor must give new value in order for the security interest to be perfected or have priority (*see* III.E.2.a. Temporary perfection (security interest in certificated securities, negotiable documents, or instruments), IV.C.2. Buyers in the Ordinary Course of Business (BOCB), and IV.C.4. Purchasers of Chattel Paper, all *infra*). In these circumstances, new value consists of (i) money, (ii) money's worth in property, services, or new credit, or (iii) release by a transferee of an interest in property previously transferred to the transferee. The term does not include an obligation substituted for another obligation. UCC § 9-102(a)(57).

C. THE DEBTOR'S RIGHTS IN COLLATERAL

1. Generally

For the security interest to attach to the collateral, the **debtor generally must have rights in the collateral**. The basic rule is that a security interest attaches *only* to the rights that the debtor has. A debtor's limited rights in collateral are sufficient for a security interest to attach. In a few instances, the debtor may have the power to transfer rights in the collateral to a secured party even though the debtor does not possess such rights. For example, a person with voidable title to goods may have the power to create an enforceable security interest. UCC §§ 9-203(b)(2), incl. cmt. 6; 2-403(1). Similarly, if a debtor has sold an account, the debtor still retains "rights" in the account for attachment purposes until the purchaser perfects its security interest. UCC § 9-318.

2. Consignments

Generally, if the consignor retains title to the consigned goods, the consignee does not have rights in the consigned goods. Consequently, a security interest in the consignee's inventory, for example, would not extend to the consigned goods. However, when the consignment is covered by Article 9, the consignee is treated as having the consignor's rights in the consigned goods. *See* § I.E.3. Consignments, *supra*. UCC § 9-319(a).

D. SECURITY AGREEMENT

For a security interest to attach to collateral, there must be a security agreement. In addition, the secured party must satisfy the Article 9 Statute of Frauds. This means that the security agreement must be established by the debtor's **authentication** of the agreement, or the secured party's **possession or control** of the collateral. UCC §§ 9-201(a); 9-203(b)(3), incl. cmt 3.

1. Authenticated Record

The most common means by which to evidence the debtor's assent to the security agreement is by an authenticated record. To satisfy this requirement, the security agreement must:

    i) Be in a **record**;

ii)   Contain a **description** of the collateral; and

iii)   Be **authenticated** by the debtor.

UCC §§ 9-102(a)(7), (70), (74); 9-203(b)(3).

a. Record

The agreement must be in a tangible medium (e.g., a writing on paper) or in another medium, such as electronic, that can be retrieved in a perceivable form. UCC §§ 9-102(a)(69); 9-203(b)(3).

b. Description or identification of collateral

The agreement must describe the collateral. The description of the collateral need only **reasonably identify** the collateral. It may specifically list the collateral, such as by identifying the object and its manufacturer, model and serial number, but such an exact and detailed description is not mandated. A description of the Article 9 type of collateral (e.g., "all of debtor's equipment" or "debtor's entire inventory") is usually sufficient unless the collateral is consumer goods or a commercial tort claim, but a super-generic description of collateral as "all the debtor's assets" or "all the debtor's personal property" is not sufficient. UCC § 9-108.

c. Authentication of a security agreement

A security agreement must be authenticated by the party against whom it may be enforced (i.e., the debtor). The most common method of authentication is for the debtor to sign or execute the record that evidences the security agreement. A complete signature is not necessary. The question always is whether the symbol was executed or adopted by the debtor with the present intention to adopt or accept the record. UCC §§ 9-102(a)(7); 9-203(b)(3)(A).

1) New debtor

The original authenticated security agreement between a debtor and secured party can serve as the authenticated security agreement of a person who becomes bound as a debtor to the security agreement entered into by the original debtor (i.e., a new debtor). A person becomes bound as debtor by a security agreement entered into by another person if, by operation of law other than Article 9 or by contract:

i)   The security agreement becomes effective to create a security interest in the person's property; or

ii)   The person becomes generally obligated for the obligations of the other person, including the obligation secured under the security agreement, and acquires or succeeds to all or substantially all of the assets of the other person.

The original authenticated security agreement can serve as the new debtor's authenticated security agreement with respect to existing and after-acquired property described in the original agreement. The new debtor need not execute another agreement. UCC § 9-203(d, e).

As a consequence, the secured party can file a new or amended financing statement without the need to secure the new debtor's authorization (*see* III.B.2. Debtor's Authorization, *infra*).

2. Possession of Collateral

A secured party's possession of tangible (e.g., goods) or quasi-intangible (e.g., chattel paper) collateral satisfies the Article 9 Statute of Frauds. However, the secured party's possession must be pursuant to the security agreement. UCC § 9-203(b)(3)(B), (C).

> **Example:** A lends money to B. To ensure repayment, A accepts B's stereo as collateral. A takes possession of the stereo pursuant to an oral agreement that the stereo will be returned to B when A has been repaid. The agreement and A's possession of the stereo create an enforceable security interest in A's favor.

3. Control of Collateral

Similarly, for types of collateral that typically have no physical existence (i.e., deposit accounts, electronic chattel paper, electronic documents, investment property, and letter of credit rights), a secured party's control of the collateral satisfies the evidentiary requirement that the debtor assent to the security agreement, provided the control is pursuant to the security agreement. UCC § 9-203(b)(3)(D).

> **Example:** A lends money to B. To ensure repayment, pursuant to an agreement, B pledges the money in his savings account as collateral. Instead of taking actual possession of the money, A takes control of the deposit account by getting the debtor and the bank to agree that the bank will follow A's orders without the further consent of B. Their agreement and A's control of the account create a security interest in favor of A.

E. AFTER-ACQUIRED COLLATERAL

1. General Rule

A security interest may apply not only to the collateral that the debtor owns at the time the security is granted, but also to collateral that the debtor acquires in the future. No new security agreement is necessary when the collateral is acquired later if the original security agreement provides that it applies to after-acquired collateral. If, for example, the collateral is inventory, then the description of the collateral will be something like "all inventory now owned or hereafter acquired." UCC § 9-204(a). When the parties have left out after-acquired language in situations that suggest they intended to include it (e.g., when the collateral is of a type that is self-liquidating, such as inventory or accounts), the courts are split on whether to imply it, but the majority of courts do consider it implied.

2. Exception

An after-acquired clause is not effective if the collateral is consumer goods, unless the debtor acquires them within 10 days after the secured party gives value, or a commercial tort claim. UCC § 9-204(b).

F. PROCEEDS

A security interest in collateral automatically attaches to identifiable proceeds. UCC §§ 9-203(f); 9-315(a)(2).

The term "proceeds" means:

i) Whatever is acquired upon the sale, lease license, exchange, or other disposition of collateral;

ii) Whatever is collected on, or distributed on account of, collateral;

iii) Rights arising out of collateral;

iv) To the extent of the value of collateral, claims arising out of the loss, nonconformity or interference with the use of, defects or infringement of rights in, or damage to, the collateral; and

v) To the extent of the value of collateral and to the extent payable to the debtor or the secured party, insurance payable by reason of the loss or nonconformity of, defects or infringement of rights in, or damage to, the collateral.

UCC § 9-102(a)(64).

Example 1: A secured party acquires a security interest in a debtor's inventory. The debtor sells items of inventory in exchange for checks. The secured party's security interest will attach to the checks if they are identifiable as proceeds.

Example 2: Same facts as Example 1, except now the debtor sells items of inventory and receives from buyers a promise to pay in full within 90 days. The secured party's security interest will attach to the accounts.

Example 3: Same facts as Example 1, except the inventory was damaged by a fire started by an arsonist. The secured party's security interest will attach to whatever insurance payments are due the debtor and to the debtor's commercial tort claim against the arsonist.

G. RIGHTS AND DUTIES OF THE SECURED PARTY

1. Duties Arising From the Secured Party's Possession or Control of Collateral

a. Duty of care

The secured party in possession of collateral has the **duty of reasonable care** with respect to custody and preservation of the collateral. The duty of care cannot be circumvented by an agreement between the debtor and the secured party, but the parties can determine the standards for judging such care; such standards must be reasonable. UCC §§ 9-207(a); 9-603(a).

b. Duty to keep collateral identifiable

The secured party in possession of collateral must keep the collateral identifiable but may commingle fungible collateral. UCC § 9-207(b)(3).

c. Duty to relinquish possession or control of collateral

1) Duty to relinquish possession of collateral

The secured party has a duty to relinquish possession of the collateral upon satisfaction of the secured obligation and the secured party is not committed to make advances or otherwise give value. Failure to do so constitutes conversion. UCC § 9-208.

2) Duty to relinquish control of collateral

Similarly, a secured party in control of collateral has a duty to relinquish control when there is not an outstanding secured obligation and the secured party is not committed to make advances or otherwise give value.

Generally, the secured party has 10 days from receiving an authenticated demand by the debtor to relinquish control; this time period may be varied by the parties' agreement. Upon the secured party's failure to relinquish control, the debtor has the same remedy as if the secured party failed to file a termination statement. UCC § 9-208.

2. **Rights and Risks Arising From the Secured Party's Possession or Control of Collateral**

a. **Right to charge for reasonable expenses**

The secured party in possession of collateral has the right to charge the debtor for reasonable expenses (e.g., storage, insurance, and taxes) incurred in the custody, preservation, use, or operation of the collateral; such expenses are also secured by the collateral. UCC § 9-207(b)(1).

b. **Risk of loss or damage is on the debtor**

The debtor bears the risk of accidental loss of, or damage to, the collateral; consequently, the debtor is liable to the secured party for any deficiency in effective insurance coverage. UCC § 9-207(b)(2).

c. **Right to use or operate collateral**

The secured party may use or operate collateral for the purpose of preserving the collateral or its value. In addition, use or operation with respect to collateral that is not consumer goods may be in the manner and to the extent agreed to by the debtor. UCC § 9-207(b)(4).

d. **Right to hold proceeds**

As additional security, the secured party in possession or control of collateral may hold any proceeds, except money or funds, received from the collateral. Any money or funds received must be applied to reduce the secured obligation or remitted to the debtor. UCC § 9-207(c).

3. **Assignment of Account Rights**

a. **Generally**

If the debtor assigns his right to receive payment on an account, chattel paper, or a payment intangible, then the secured party, after default or earlier if the debtor so agrees, may notify an account debtor (i.e., a person obligated on an account, chattel paper, or general intangible, but not a person obligated on a negotiable instrument) to make payment to the secured party. The notification must be authenticated by the debtor (i.e., assignor) or secured party (i.e., assignee) and must reasonably identify the rights assigned. Generally, a term in the agreement between the account debtor and the assignor that prohibits or otherwise restricts assignment is ineffective. UCC § 9-406.

b. **Effect on an account debtor**

Upon receipt of notification, the account debtor may discharge her obligation only by paying the assignee; a payment made to the assignor does not discharge the account debtor's obligation. Against the assignee, the account debtor may raise, unless waived, claims and defenses that arise from the transaction with the assignor who created the account, even those that accrue after the account debtor is notified of the assignment.

The rights of an assignee are subject to all terms of the agreement between the account debtor and the assignor and any defense or claim in recoupment arising from the transaction that gave rise to the contract. Other defenses and claims that the account debtor has against the assignor may be raised only if they have accrued prior to the account debtor's receipt of notification of the assignment. Unless the account debtor incurred the debt as a consumer, account debtor's claims and defenses may only serve to offset the amount that the account debtor owes. UCC §§ 9-404; 9-406.

H. RIGHTS OF THE DEBTOR

1. Accounting and Other Information From the Secured Party

A debtor may obtain information from a secured party about the secured obligation and the collateral in which a secured party may claim a security interest. The debtor may request an accounting from the secured party. In addition, the debtor may submit a list of collateral and a statement of the aggregate amount of unpaid secured obligations, which the secured party may approve or correct. Generally, the secured party has 14 days to respond after receiving the debtor's request. UCC § 9-210.

2. Notification of Account Debtors by the Secured Party

When there is not an outstanding secured obligation and the secured party is not committed to make advances or otherwise give value, the debtor can demand that the secured party notify account debtors (i.e., persons obligated to the debtor on an account, chattel paper, or general intangible) that they are no longer required to make payments to the secured party. The secured party must send the notification within 10 days after receiving an authenticated demand by the debtor. UCC §§ 9-102(a)(3), 9-209.

I. PURCHASE-MONEY SECURITY INTEREST (PMSI)

A PMSI is a special type of security interest that may be accorded special rules with respect to perfection and priority. A PMSI may exist only with respect to two types of collateral—goods (including fixtures) and software. UCC § 9-103.

As the name implies, a PMSI must be an attached security interest; it must meet the three requirements of value, rights, and agreement (*see* II.A. In General, *above*).

1. PMSI in Goods

A PMSI in goods exists when:

i) A secured party gave value (e.g., made a loan) to the debtor and the debtor incurred an obligation to enable the debtor to acquire rights in or use of the goods, and the value given was so used; or

ii) A secured party sold goods to the debtor, and the debtor incurs an obligation to pay the secured party all or part of the purchase price (i.e., a sale of goods on credit).

UCC § 9-103(a), (b).

Example 1: A, an automobile dealer, sells B, the debtor, an automobile and agrees to finance the automobile because B does not have the full purchase price. B, pursuant to the agreement, is to make payments on a monthly basis until the automobile has been paid in full and gives A a security interest in the automobile. A has a PMSI in the automobile.

Example 2: A, an automobile dealer, sells B, the debtor, an automobile. B does not have the full purchase price of the automobile. B goes to C, a bank, and borrows money to purchase the automobile. In exchange for the loan, B gives C a security interest in the automobile that she is purchasing from A. Pursuant to the agreement with C, B is to make payments to C until the loan for the automobile has been paid in full. C has a PMSI in the automobile.

The amount of the obligation can include expenses incurred in connection with acquiring rights in the collateral, sales taxes, duties, finance charges, interest, freight charges, administrative charges, expenses of collection and enforcement, attorney's fees, and similar obligations. UCC § 9-103, cmt. 3.

a. Consignment of goods

The security interest of a consignor in the consigned goods is a PMSI in inventory. UCC § 9-103(d).

b. Cross-collateralization of PMSIs in inventory

If inventory subject to a PMSI secures not only its own price or enabling loan but also the price or enabling loan of other purchase-money inventory, then the security interest in the inventory is a PMSI not only to the extent that the inventory secures its own price but also the price of the other inventory. UCC § 9-103(b)(2), incl. cmts. 3, 4.

Example: A seller who retains a security interest in an inventory item (Item X) to secure not only the price of X, but also all other future and existing obligations of the buyer to the seller, has a PMSI in Item X, not only with respect to the current obligation to pay for Item X, but also with respect to any existing or future obligations that arise from a PMSI in additional inventory items sold to the buyer by the seller. In other words, by cross-collateralizing PMSIs in inventory, the parties create a PMSI in each item of inventory that secures the aggregate of the PMSI obligations.

c. "Dual status" rule for non-consumer goods transaction

In a transaction other than a consumer-goods transaction, a PMSI does not lose its status as a PMSI merely because:

i) The collateral also secures an obligation that is not a purchase-money obligation (e.g., equipment that secures a bank loan to the buyer for the purchase of the equipment is subsequently used as collateral for a second bank loan to the buyer);

ii) The collateral that is not purchase-money collateral also secures the purchase-money obligation (e.g., equipment owned by the debtor prior to the time that the debtor borrows money to buy additional equipment when the previously owned equipment also serves as collateral for the purchase-money obligation); or

iii) The obligation has been renewed, refinanced, consolidated, or restructured.

Under the "dual status" rule, a security interest may be a PMSI to some extent and a non-PMSI to some extent. In such a transaction, the secured party claiming a PMSI has the burden of establishing the extent to which the security interest is a PMSI. Note that for consumer-goods transactions, the treatment of a PMSI as having a "dual status" is left to the courts. UCC § 9-103(f)–(h).

d. Application of payments

When the extent to which a security interest is a PMSI depends on the application of a payment of a particular obligation, the payment must be applied:

i) In accordance with the parties' reasonable agreement;

ii) If there is no reasonable agreement, in accordance with the manifestation of the obligor before or at the time the payment is made; or

iii) If neither (i) nor (ii) apply, then first to unsecured obligations and then to obligations secured by a PMSI in the order in which the obligations were incurred.

UCC § 9-103(e).

2. PMSI in Software

A PMSI in software exists only when the debtor acquired his interest in software in an integrated transaction in which the debtor also acquired an interest in goods (e.g., a computer), and the debtor acquired that interest in the software for the principal purpose of using the software in the goods. The security interest in the software must also secure an obligation with respect to the goods, and the secured party must hold a PMSI in the goods. UCC § 9-103(b), (c).

J. ACCESSIONS

Accessions are goods that are physically united with other goods in such a manner that the identity of the original goods is not lost, such as memory installed in a computer, or tires installed on a car. A security interest that is created in collateral that becomes an accession is not lost due to the collateral becoming an accession. Moreover, a security interest can be created in collateral that is an accession. Generally, the description of the collateral in the security agreement will determine whether a secured party acquires a security interest in the whole in the event its collateral becomes an accession. UCC §§ 9-102; 9-335(a), cmt. 5.

K. COMMINGLED GOODS

Commingled goods are goods that are physically united with other goods in such a manner that their identity is lost in a product or mass. UCC § 9-336(a).

> **Example:** Chicken eggs may be commingled goods when stored together with other chicken eggs so that the separate identity of each group cannot be ascertained. Similarly, such eggs may be commingled goods when used as an ingredient in making cakes.

There is not a security interest in specific goods that have been commingled. However, a security interest may attach to the product or mass that results when the goods are commingled, such as a security interest in inventory of a manufacturer who makes brass by combining copper and zinc. UCC § 9-336(b).

An existing security interest in collateral that subsequently becomes commingled goods is transferred to the resulting product or mass. Once the goods have been commingled, a security interest cannot be created in separate goods. UCC § 9-336(c).

III. PERFECTION OF SECURITY INTEREST

Perfection of a security interest is generally necessary for the secured party to have rights in the collateral that are superior to any rights claimed by third parties. Perfection has no relevance to the secured party's rights against the debtor. A security interest is perfected upon attachment of that interest and compliance with one of the methods of perfection. UCC § 9-308(a).

> **EXAM NOTE:** Very frequently tested is whether a security interest has attached and is perfected.

A. METHODS OF PERFECTION

Under Article 9, there are four ways by which a secured party can perfect a security interest:

i) **Filing** of a financing statement;

ii) **Possession** of the collateral;

iii) **Control** over the collateral; and

iv) **Automatic** perfection (either temporary or permanent).

> If there is another statute that governs perfection of a security interest, that statute may provide another method of perfection. For an example, see § III.F. Non-Article 9 Rules: Notation for Vehicles, *infra*.

B. FILING

A security interest in any collateral, except a deposit account, money, or letter-of-credit rights that are not a supporting obligation, may be perfected by **filing a financing statement**. Filing is the most common method of perfection. The primary objective of filing is to give interested parties notice of the existence of the security interest. UCC §§ 9-310(a); 9-312(b).

> A security interest in money may be perfected only by **possession**. A deposit account or letter-of-credit rights that are not a supporting obligation may be perfected only by **control**.

1. Financing Statement

A financing statement (sometimes referred to as a "UCC1") *must contain* the following information:

i) The **debtor's name**;

ii) The **name of the secured party** or a representative of the secured party; and

iii) The **collateral** covered by the financing statement.

This "bare bones" information is intended to provide a person, such as a potential creditor of the debtor, with enough information to make further inquiries of the debtor or secured party as to the existence and terms of a security interest. The limited-information method of recording a security interest for public access is frequently referred to as **notice filing**. UCC § 9-502(a), incl. cmt. 2.

a. Collateral related to real property

When the collateral is related to real property, the financing statement must, in addition to the information required for all financing statements, contain:

i) An indication that it covers this type of collateral;

ii) An indication that it is to be filed in the real-property records;

iii) A description of the real property to which the collateral relates; and

iv) The name of a record owner, if the debtor does not have an interest of record in the real property.

This additional information is required for (i) a fixture filing with respect to goods that are or are to become fixtures, (ii) as-extracted collateral (i.e., oil, gas or other minerals subject to a security interest that is created by a debtor having an interest in the minerals before extracted and that attaches to the minerals as extracted), and (iii) timber to be cut. UCC §§ 9-102(a)(6); 9-502(b).

b. Additional information

The financing statement should also:

i) Contain the addresses of both the debtor and the secured party; and

ii) Identify whether the debtor is an individual or organization.

UCC § 9-521(a).

Should the filing office accept for filing a financing statement that lacks such information the financing statement is nevertheless effective. UCC §§ 9-338; 9-520(a), (c).

Under the 2010 amendments to Article 9, a financing statement cannot be rejected by a filing officer for failure to include the debtor's type of organization, jurisdiction of organization, or the organization's identification number.

c. Alternatives to a financing statement

1) Security agreement as financing statement

A security agreement usually contains more information than is required of a financing statement. Consequently, a security agreement that contains the information necessary for a financing statement may be filed as a financing statement to perfect a security interest.

2) Mortgage as a financing statement

With respect to collateral related to real property, a mortgage may serve as a financing statement, provided it contains the necessary information. A mortgage is effective as of the date of its recording. UCC § 9-502(c).

d. Name of the debtor

1) Individual debtor

The 2010 amendments to Article 9 provide states with two alternatives for how an individual debtor's name must appear on a financing statement. UCC § 9-503.

a) "Only-if" rule (Alternative A)

The financing statement must reflect the name on the debtor's current (i.e., unexpired) driver's license or state-issued identification card (issued by the state in which the financing agreement will be filed). If the debtor does not have a driver's license, the filer must use either the individual name of the debtor (i.e., the debtor's current legal name) or the debtor's surname and first personal name. A majority of jurisdictions have adopted this approach.

b) "Safe harbor" rule (Alternative B)

Under the "safe harbor" rule, adopted by only a few jurisdictions, the financing statement may include the debtor's "individual name" (which the UCC does not define), the name on the debtor's driver's license, or the debtor's surname and first personal name.

2) Debtor's trade name

Identification of the debtor solely by the debtor's trade name is *insufficient*. By contrast, failure to include the debtor's trade name does not affect the effectiveness of the financing statement when the debtor's name is correctly provided. UCC § 9-503(b), (c).

3) Registered organization

When the debtor is a registered organization, the debtor's name for purposes of the financing statement must be the name shown on public organic records. A public organic record includes the articles of incorporation or equivalent formation records filed to create a business entity, the record initially filed by a business trust, legislation that creates an organization, or a government-issued charter that forms an organization. UCC §§ 9-102(a)(68), 9-503(a)(1).

4) Name change by the debtor

If the debtor changes its name and the filed financing statement consequently becomes seriously misleading (i.e., the name on the financing statement does not meet the requirement of 9-503), then the secured party has four months in which to file an amendment to the financing statement reflecting the new name. Should the secured party fail to act within this four-month window, collateral acquired by the debtor after the four-month period is not covered by the financing statement. UCC § 5-907(c).

If a new debtor becomes bound by a security agreement, and the difference between the name of the original debtor and the name of the new debtor causes the financing statement to be seriously misleading, then the secured party has a similar four-month window in which to act. UCC §§ 9-508, 9-507(c).

5) Error in the debtor's name

Because financing statements are indexed under the name of the debtor, a financing statement that fails to accurately contain the debtor's name is seriously misleading and therefore *not effective* to perfect the security interest. However, when a standard search of the filing office records under the debtor's correct name would disclose such a financing statement, the erroneous name does not make the financing statement seriously misleading. UCC § 9-506(b), (c).

6) Error in the secured party's name

An error in the name of the secured party on a financing statement is usually not seriously misleading and does not affect the perfection of the security interest because the filing system is not geared to a search based on the secured party's name. However, the secured party who files a financing statement with such an error may be subject to estoppel in favor of a holder of a conflicting claim in the collateral. UCC § 9-506, cmt. 2.

e. Description of the collateral

The financing statement must contain a description of the collateral that sufficiently indicates the collateral. This requirement can be satisfied by a description that meets the requirements for the security agreement. *See* § II.D. Security Agreement, *supra*. Alternatively, when the security interest covers all of the debtor's assets or personal property, the financing statement, unlike the security agreement, can contain a broad statement to that effect (e.g., "this financing statement covers all of the debtor's assets" or "this financing statement covers all of the debtor's personal property") without identifying each of the types of collateral covered. UCC § 9-504.

1) After-acquired property and future advances

A financing statement may be effective to cover after-acquired property if such property falls within the collateral described, whether after-acquired property is mentioned as such in the financing statement or even contemplated by the parties at the time that the financing statement was authorized. Similar treatment is accorded to future advances. UCC § 9-502, cmt. 2.

2) Proceeds

A financing statement need not make specific reference to proceeds in order for a security interest in proceeds to be perfected. UCC §§ 9-315(c); 9-502, cmt. 2.

3) Error in the description of collateral

If there is an error with respect to the collateral covered by a financing statement, then the debtor may demand that the secured party prepare a termination statement with respect to the erroneous collateral and provide the debtor with the termination statement for the debtor to file, or in the case of consumer goods, the secured party is the one who must file the termination statement. UCC § 9-513.

2. Debtor's Authorization

The debtor's signature is not required on the financing statement. The debtor must authorize the filing of a financing statement for the statement to be effective. If the debtor has authenticated the security agreement, then this authentication constitutes an authorization to file the financing statement with respect to the collateral covered by the agreement (i.e., an "*ipso facto* authorization"). Alternatively, the debtor may specifically authorize the filing of the financing statement in an authenticated record. (Note: A debtor is presumed to consent to the filing of a financing statement when the secured party seeks to perfect, by filing, a security interest in any identifiable proceeds of collateral, whether or not the security agreement expressly covers proceeds.) UCC § 9-509(a,b).

A person who files a financing statement without the debtor's authorization is liable for actual and statutory damages. UCC § 9-625(b).

3. Person Entitled to File a Financing Statement

Although the secured party or a representative of the secured party usually files the financing statement, any person may do so. The signature of the filing party is not required. UCC § 9-509(a).

4. Filing Location

a. Collateral related to real property

For collateral that is related to real property, the financing statement is generally filed in the office for recording a mortgage on the related real property ("**local filing**"). UCC § 9-501(a)(1).

b. All other collateral

For all collateral not related to real property, the financing statement is filed with the secretary of state ("**central filing**") of the state of the debtor's location. UCC § 9-501(a)(2).

1) Individual debtor

An individual is located in the state in which he maintains his principal residence. UCC § 9-307(b)(1).

2) An organization

An organization that is not a registered organization (e.g., a partnership) is located in the state in which it maintains its place of business and, if it has more than one place of business, at its chief executive office. UCC § 9-307(b)(2)(3).

3) A registered organization

A registered organization that is organized under the law of a state is located in that state (e.g., a corporation is located in the state in which it is incorporated). UCC § 9-307(e).

5. Effective Date of Filing

A financing statement is generally effective upon its delivery to the filing office and tender of the filing fee provided that it contains the basic required information. UCC § 9-516(a).

a. Effect of the filing office's refusal to accept a financing statement

The effect of the filing office's refusal to accept a financing statement for filing depends on whether the refusal is justified. UCC § 9-516(b).

1) Justified refusal

When the filing office's refusal to accept a financing statement for filing is justified, the financing statement is treated as having not been filed. Grounds upon which the filing office may justifiably refuse to accept a financing statement include the failure to tender the required fee, the failure to submit the financing statement by an authorized method or medium of communication, and the failure of the record to identify a debtor. UCC § 9-516(b).

2) Unjustified refusal

If the filing office's refusal to accept a financing statement for filing is unjustified, then the financing statement is treated as having been filed. Such a financing statement is effective except with respect to a purchaser of the collateral who gives value in reasonable reliance upon the absence of the record from the files. UCC § 9-516(a), (d).

b. Effect of the filing office's incorrect indexing of a financing statement

The effect of the filing office's incorrect indexing of a financing statement does not affect the effectiveness of the filed financing statement. UCC § 9-517, incl. cmt. 2.

> The risk of a filing-office error rests on those who search the files rather than on those who file a financing statement.

6. Length of Perfection

A financing statement is generally effective for **five years**. The financing statement is effective during this period, even though there is no obligation secured by the collateral and no commitment to make an advance, unless a termination statement has been filed. UCC § 9-515(a).

7. Continuation Statement

The effect of a financing statement may be extended by filing a continuation statement, which extends the effect of the financing statement for **another five-year period**. The continuation statement must be filed within **six months prior to the expiration** of the financing statement and requires only the authorization of the secured party, not the debtor. If a continuation statement is not filed, a financing statement ceases to be effective and any security interest or agricultural lien that was perfected by the financing statement becomes unperfected, unless the security interest is perfected otherwise. In addition, the security interest (unless otherwise perfected) is treated as never having been perfected as against a purchaser of the collateral for value. UCC §§ 9-515(c)–(e); 9-509(d).

8. Amendment of a Financing Statement

A person may amend a financing statement, such as by adding or deleting collateral covered by the statement. The amendment is generally effective as to the added item only from the date of the amendment. An amendment *does not* extend the period of effectiveness of the financing statement. UCC § 9-512.

9. Termination Statement

The effectiveness of a financing statement may be terminated by the filing of a termination statement. UCC § 9-515(d).

C. POSSESSION

A secured party may perfect a security interest in most collateral by taking possession of the collateral. As a general rule, this security interest remains perfected only while the secured party retains possession. UCC § 9-313(a).

Except for money, collateral that may be perfected by possession may also be perfected by filing. Perfection by filing does not require the secured party to be also in possession of the collateral.

Goods, instruments, negotiable documents, money, and tangible chattel paper are the only types of collateral that may be perfected by possession. A security interest in money may be perfected only by possession. A certificated security may be perfected by the secured party taking delivery of the security. UCC § 9-313(a).

D. CONTROL

A secured party may perfect a security interest in specific collateral by taking control of the collateral. The security interest remains perfected only while the secured party retains control. UCC § 9-314(a).

1. Collateral Perfected by Control

Perfection by control of the collateral may only be achieved with respect to a security interest in investment property, deposit accounts, letter-of-credit rights, electronic chattel paper, or electronic documents. Gaining control for purposes of attachment also suffices for purposes of perfection. UCC §§ 9-312(a), 9-314(a).

2. Letter-of-Credit Rights

A security interest in letter-of-credit rights, if such rights are a supporting obligation for other collateral (e.g., chattel paper) is perfected by the perfection of the security interest in the other collateral. Otherwise, perfection of a security interest in letter-of-credit rights may be perfected only by control. UCC § 9-312(b)(2).

3. Deposit Account

A security interest in a deposit account can be perfected only by control. UCC § 9-312(b)(1). A secured party has control of a deposit account if:

i) The secured party is the bank with which the deposit account is maintained;

ii) The bank, secured party, and debtor agreed in writing to follow the instructions of the secured party; or

iii) The secured party becomes the bank's customer with respect to the deposit account.

UCC § 9-104(a).

E. AUTOMATIC PERFECTION

Under some circumstances, a security interest is automatically perfected upon attachment. Such perfection may extend indefinitely or may be subject to a time limitation, in which case it is referred to as "temporary perfection." UCC § 9-309.

A security interest that is entitled to automatic perfection may, of course, be perfected through another permitted method (e.g., filing, possession, or control).

1. Indefinite Period of Perfection

a. PMSI in consumer goods

A PMSI in consumer goods is automatically perfected upon attachment. A secured party does not need to file a financing statement or have possession to have a perfected PMSI in **consumer goods**. A PMSI in other types of goods (e.g., inventory, equipment) or in automobiles *is not* automatically perfected. UCC § 9-309(1).

b. Other automatic permanent perfection

Automatic permanent perfection also occurs in other situations, the most important of which for bar exam purposes are:

i) The casual or isolated assignment of accounts or payment intangibles that does not transfer a significant part of the assignor's outstanding accounts or payment intangibles; and

ii) Sale of a payment intangible or promissory note.

UCC § 9-309.

2. Temporary Perfection

a. New value

If new value is given under an authenticated security agreement, a security interest in certificated securities, negotiable documents, or instruments is automatically perfected for 20 days from the time it attaches without filing or the taking of possession. UCC § 9-312(e).

b. Delivery of collateral to the debtor

If the secured party makes the collateral available to the debtor for the purpose of selling or exchanging the collateral, then the security interest in the collateral remains temporarily perfected for 20 days. Collateral subject to this rule includes certificated securities, negotiable documents, instruments, and goods in the possession of a bailee and for which a negotiable document has not been issued. UCC § 9-312(f), (g).

c. Interstate movement

Temporary perfection may also arise when collateral or a debtor moves from one state to another.

1) Movement of the debtor

If a debtor moves to another state, a perfected security interest remains perfected for four months after the debtor's change in location, unless perfection would have ceased earlier under the law of the debtor's former state. UCC § 9-316(a), cmt. 2. This four-month grace period also applies to collateral the debtor acquires after the debtor moves, i.e., the filer has perfection for four months in collateral acquired post-move. UCC § 9-316(h).

2) Movement of collateral

If collateral is transferred to a person located in another state who becomes a debtor (i.e., takes the collateral subject to the security interest), then a perfected security interest generally remains perfected for one year after the transfer, unless perfection would have ceased earlier under the law of the former debtor's state. UCC § 9-316(a), cmt. 2.

3) Possessory security interest—continuous perfection

A perfected possessory security interest in collateral generally remains continuously perfected, despite the movement of the collateral to another state, when the security interest is perfected under the laws of the state to which the collateral is moved. UCC § 9-316(c).

4) Effect of a lapse of perfection

If a security interest is not perfected in the second state before the expiration of the applicable temporary perfection period, then the security interest generally ceases to be perfected prospectively (i.e., upon the expiration of the temporary perfection period). With respect to a purchaser for value, such a security interest is deemed never to have been perfected. UCC § 9-316(b).

3. Proceeds

A security interest in proceeds enjoys temporary perfection and may also be entitled to indefinite automatic perfection. This perfection occurs even though the financing statement does not specifically mention proceeds. UCC § 9-315(c), (d).

a. Temporary perfection

If the security interest in the original collateral is perfected, then a security interest in proceeds is temporarily perfected for 20 days from the time it attaches. UCC § 9-315(c), (d).

b. Indefinite automatic perfection

In the following circumstances, a security interest in proceeds may continue to be perfected beyond the 20-day period:

1) Perfection pursuant to financing statement

If the original financing statement is broad enough to encompass the proceeds or the secured party takes the necessary steps to amend the financing statement to cover the proceeds within the 20-day period, the security interest in the proceeds continues to be perfected. UCC § 9-315(d)(1), incl. cmt. 5.

2) Cash proceeds

If the proceeds are identifiable cash proceeds and the security interest in the original collateral is perfected, the perfected security interest in the proceeds continues indefinitely, even though the security interest in the original collateral subsequently ceases to be perfected. The identification of cash proceeds is left to common law. UCC § 9-315(d)(2), incl. cmt. 3. Note that cash proceeds include more than just money. They also include checks, deposit accounts, and the like. UCC § 9-102(a)(9).

3) Same office

A perfected security interest in proceeds may also continue indefinitely when:

i)   A filed financing statement covers the original collateral;

ii) The proceeds are collateral in which a security interest may be perfected by filing in the office in which the financing statement has been filed; and

iii) The proceeds are not acquired with cash proceeds.

However, under this option, if the original filing ceases to be effective after the 20-day period, then the security interest in proceeds also ceases to be automatically perfected. UCC § 9-315(d)(1),(e)(1).

> Note that when the original filing ceases to be effective during the 20-day period after the security interest in the proceeds attaches, the security interest in the proceeds continues to be automatically perfected until the expiration of that period. UCC § 9-315(e)(2).

F.   NON-ARTICLE 9 RULES: NOTATION FOR VEHICLES

When property is subject to a special statute in lieu of Article 9's rules on perfection, the statute dictates the manner of perfection. The most prominent of such property subject to separate legislation is a motor vehicle that is subject to a certificate-of-title statute. For example, if the statute requires that the security interest in a vehicle be noted on the certificate of title, then a security interest in the vehicle that has been filed is not perfected. In addition, possession of the vehicle or the certification of title is not sufficient to perfect the security interest. Also, the rule granting automatic perfection to a purchase money security interest in consumer goods does not apply when the collateral is a motor vehicle. Other property, such as civil aircraft, is subject to federal statutory rules for perfection. UCC §§ 9-309(1), 311, 313(b).

G.   TIMING OF PERFECTION

A security interest is perfected upon (i) attachment of that interest and (ii) compliance with one of the methods of perfection. Although typically the security interest attaches and is then perfected, if the necessary steps for perfection are taken prior to attachment (e.g., the secured party files a financing statement that covers after-acquired property), then the security interest is perfected upon attachment.

In addition, a security interest that is perfected by one method and later perfected by another method without a lapse in perfection is continuously perfected despite the change in method. The date of perfection is the date on which the security interest first became perfected. UCC §§ 9-308(a); 9-502(d).

IV.   PRIORITIES

Article 9 sets out rules governing the priorities of conflicting interests in collateral. Unlike in bankruptcy, which provides a pro rata share to all creditors, Article 9 prioritizes the claims and pays them in order. The holder of a priority can agree to subordinate his interest to another's interest. UCC § 9-339.

EXAM NOTE: Priority problems are commonly tested and generally occur when two or more parties claim a right to the same collateral. One of the parties will always be claiming a security interest under Article 9. The determination of priority involves two steps:

i) Identify the **status of each claimant**; and

ii) Apply the **appropriate priority rule**.

A common error is the *failure to properly characterize* the status of the competing parties.

A. CLAIMANTS

Other persons with interests that may conflict with a secured party's interest traditionally fall into one of three groups:

i) Creditors;

ii) Transferees/buyers; and

iii) Other secured parties.

B. CREDITORS

1. General Creditor (Unsecured)

A general creditor is one who has a claim, including a judgment, but who has no lien or security interest with respect to the property in question (i.e., the collateral). A general creditor has no interest to assert under Article 9; this type of creditor does not have a claim to particular property owned by the debtor. A secured party *will always* prevail over a general creditor with respect to the debtor's collateral. UCC § 9-201.

2. Judicial Lien Creditor

A judicial lien creditor is a creditor who acquires a lien on the collateral by a judicial process, rather than by operation of law. A judicial lien creditor takes the property subject to a perfected security interest but generally has priority over an unperfected security interest. Even if the security interest is unperfected at the time the judicial lien comes into existence, the secured party will have priority if the only reason why it was unperfected was that the secured party had not yet given value. UCC §§ 9-102(52)(a), 9-317(a)(2).

> **Example:** On Day One, the debtor authenticates a security agreement, which describes the collateral. On Day Two, the secured party files a financing statement. On Day Three, the creditor acquires a judicial lien on the collateral. On Day Four, the secured party gives value. The secured party will have priority even though the security interest was unperfected on Day Three.

a. Exception—PMSI

If the secured party has a PMSI that is perfected before or within 20 days after the debtor receives possession of the collateral, then the security interest takes priority over the rights of a creditor that arose between the time the security interest attached and the time of filing. A secured party with a PMSI will prevail over any creditor that obtains a lien within that 20-day period. UCC § 9-317(e).

b. Advances

A security interest that secures an advance is subordinate to the rights of a person who becomes a lien creditor when the advance is made more than 45 days after the person becomes a lien creditor, unless the advance is made without knowledge of the lien or made pursuant to a commitment entered into without knowledge of the lien. Note that when the advance is made within the 45-day time period, knowledge of the lien does not prevent the holder of a security interest from having priority over the lien creditor. UCC § 9-323(a), (b).

3. Statutory or Common-Law Lien Creditor

A statutory or common-law lien creditor is a creditor who obtains a possessory lien on the property of another by operation of a statute or common-law rule. Unlike an Article 9 security interest, these are nonconsensual liens. A statutory or common-law lien has priority over a security interest, including a perfected security interest, in goods, provided:

i) The effectiveness of the lien depends on the lien holder's possession of the goods; and

ii) The lien secures payment or performance of an obligation for services or materials furnished with respect to goods by the lien holder in the ordinary course of that person's business (e.g., supplier's lien, mechanic's lien).

When the lien is statutory and the statute creating the lien expressly provides a different priority rule, such as subordination of the possessory lien to security interests, that rule governs. UCC §§ 9-317(a)(2), 9-333(b).

C. TRANSFEREES

Transferees of the collateral are persons who obtain full title to the goods as a result of a transfer of the collateral from the debtor.

> **EXAM NOTE:** A typical inquiry in a priority problem is whether the buyer takes the collateral *free from the security interest or subject to it.*

1. General Rules

a. Transferee versus secured party with a security interest

If the collateral is transferred and transferee of the collateral is not a buyer, the security interest generally continues in the collateral unless the secured party authorized the transfer free of the security interest. UCC § 9-315(a)(1).

b. Buyer versus secured party with an unperfected security interest

A buyer, other than a secured party, of collateral that is goods, tangible chattel paper, tangible documents or a security certificate takes free of an unperfected security interest in the same collateral if the buyer:

i) **Gives value**; and

ii) **Receives delivery** of the collateral;

iii) **Without knowledge** of the existing security interest.

UCC § 9-317(b).

If the collateral is intangible collateral, such as accounts, or a general intangible, such as a copyright, then there is no requirement that the buyer receive delivery of the item. UCC § 9-317(b), (d).

c. Buyer versus secured party with a perfected security interest

A buyer of collateral subject to a perfected security interest generally takes the collateral subject to that interest, unless the secured party has authorized its sale free of the security interest. UCC §§ 9-315(a); 9-317(b), (d); 9-320, cmt. 6.

2. **Buyers in the Ordinary Course of Business (BOCB)**

A buyer in the ordinary course of business (BOCB) takes free of a security interest created by the buyer's seller, even if the security interest is perfected and the buyer knows of its existence. A BOCB is a person who:

i) **Buys goods** (not including farm products);

ii) In the **ordinary course**;

iii) From a **seller** who is in the business of **selling goods of that kind**;

iv) In **good faith**; and

v) **Without knowledge** that the sale violates the rights of another in the same goods.

UCC §§ 1-201(9), 9-320. A buyer does not receive BOCB status if the merchant is a pawnbroker. UCC § 1-209, incl. cmt. 9.

> **Example:** Retailer owns a department store. Bank provides Retailer with a loan to purchase inventory, and, in exchange, Retailer gives Bank a security interest in its entire inventory. Customer purchases a television from Retailer's inventory. Customer takes free and clear of Bank's security interest in the inventory, even though it has been filed and perfected.

a. **Knowledge requirement**

The requirement that a BOCB take without knowledge means *actual knowledge* that the sale is in violation of another party's rights. Mere notice or reason to know is insufficient. UCC §§ 1-201(25), 9-320(a), incl. cmt. 3.

> **Example:** The security interest given by a bank to a used car dealer provides that the dealer must obtain the bank's permission before selling a car. A consumer buys a car from the dealer. The consumer sees a notice posted in the dealer's office that the inventory is subject to the bank's security interest. While the consumer has knowledge that the car is subject to the bank's security interest, the consumer, without more, does not have knowledge that the sale violates the security agreement. Consequently, the consumer is a BOCB who takes the car free of the bank's security interest.

b. **New value**

The buyer can purchase goods for cash, on credit, or in exchange for other goods, but does not achieve BOCB status if he acquires the goods in total or partial satisfaction of a money debt. UCC § 1-201(b)(9).

c. **Seller of goods**

This exception does not apply if the seller is a person engaged in farming operations and the buyer purchases farm products from the seller. UCC § 9-320(a).

3. **Consumer Buyer**

A consumer buyer of consumer goods takes free of a security interest, even if perfected, unless prior to the purchase, the secured party filed a financing statement covering the goods. A consumer buyer is a person who:

i) Buys consumer goods for **value**;

ii) For his own **personal, family, or household use**;

iii) From a **consumer seller**; and

iv) **Without knowledge** of the security interest.

This is often referred to as the **"garage sale" rule**, because that type of sale would qualify. UCC § 9-320(b).

a. Value

Unlike the BOCB exception, the "garage sale" exception merely requires a buyer to give value, rather than new value. Consequently, acquisition of the consumer goods in total or partial satisfaction of a money debt constitutes giving value. UCC § 9-320(b).

b. PMSI in consumer goods

A PMSI in consumer goods is automatically perfected. Filing is not required. If a PMSI in consumer goods is not filed, and the consumer buyer does not know of the PMSI, then he will take free of the security interest. If the party holding the PMSI in consumer goods does in fact file, then his security interest will be good even against a consumer buyer. UCC § 9-320.

Example: Debtor purchases a computer for his family's personal use. Debtor gives Bank a PMSI in the computer. Debtor sells the computer to Consumer Buyer. Debtor then defaults on his obligation to Bank. Bank wants to repossess the computer. Because Bank had a PMSI in the computer, Bank was not required to file in order to perfect its security interest; it was automatically perfected. If Bank did not file, then Consumer Buyer takes the computer free and clear. If Bank filed before Consumer Buyer purchased, then Bank could recover the computer from Consumer Buyer.

4. Purchasers of Chattel Paper

The sale of chattel paper can create a security interest in the purchaser. The purchaser of chattel paper has priority over the interest of a secured party who claims the chattel paper merely as proceeds of inventory subject to a security interest provided that:

i) The purchaser gives **new value** and takes possession or obtains control of the chattel paper;

ii) The purchase is made in **good faith** and in the ordinary course of the purchaser's business; and

iii) The chattel paper does not indicate that it has been **assigned** to an identified assignee other than the purchaser.

UCC § 9-330(a).

"New value" means that the purchaser must give new consideration, such as cash or credit, to the transferor. Therefore, parties who take the chattel paper as payment for a debt, or as proceeds of other collateral, are excluded.

The purchaser of chattel paper has priority over all other types of security interests in chattel paper (i.e., a security interest in chattel paper that is claimed other than merely as proceeds of inventory subject to a security interest) provided the same conditions are met except that, in lieu of the lack of an indication of assignment (*item iii above*), the purchase must be made *without knowledge* that the purchase violates the rights of the secured party. UCC § 9-330.

5. **Buyer of a Negotiable Instrument or Document**

The buyer of a negotiable instrument who qualifies as a holder in due course under Article 3, the buyer of a negotiable document of title that has been duly negotiated under Article 7, and a protected purchaser of a security under Article 8 may take free of a perfected security interest in the instrument, document of title, or security. UCC § 9-331. In addition, a purchaser of an instrument has priority over a security interest in the instrument perfected by a method other than possession if the purchaser gives value and takes possession of the instrument in good faith and without knowledge that the purchase violates the rights of the secured party. UCC § 9-330(d).

6. **Buyer Not in the Ordinary Course of Business—Future Advances**

A buyer of goods not in the ordinary course takes free of a security interest to the extent that it secures an advance made after the earlier of:

i) The time the secured party acquires knowledge of the buyer's purchase; or

ii) 45 days after purchase.

The buyer takes subject to the security interest if the advance is made pursuant to a commitment entered into without knowledge of the buyer's purchases and before the expiration of the 45-day period. UCC § 9-323(d, e).

7. **Transferee of Money or Funds**

A transferee of money usually takes the money free of a security interest. Similarly, a transferee of funds from a bank deposit account usually takes the funds free of a security interest in the deposit account. Note that a debtor is not treated as a transferee. UCC § 9-332.

A transferee is not entitled to this favorable treatment if the transferee acts in collusion with the debtor in violating the rights of the secured party. UCC § 9-332, incl. cmt. 2.

8. **Article 2 Security Interests**

When a buyer or seller has a security interest arising under Article 2, the interest has priority over a conflicting security interest created by the debtor under Article 9, as long as the buyer or seller retains possession of the goods. UCC § 9-110.

Note that an Article 2 security interest is perfected without filing. UCC § 9-110(2).

9. **"Clean" Certificate of Title**

If a certificate of title issued by one state fails to indicate that goods (e.g., an automobile) are or may be subject to a security interest perfected under the laws of a second state (i.e., a "clean" certificate of title), then the buyer of the goods can take free of the security interest, provided the buyer receives delivery of the goods after issuance of the certificate without knowledge of the prior security interest. Similarly, the holder of a conflicting security interest has priority over such an out-of-state security interest, provided the holder's interest attaches and is perfected after the issuance of the certificate and the holder does not have knowledge of the out-of-state security interest. UCC § 9-337.

D. **PRIORITIES AMONG SECURED PARTIES**

1. **General Rules**

a. **Perfected security interest versus perfected security interest**

When there are two or more perfected secured parties with rights in the same collateral, the **first to file or perfect** has priority. In other words, if both security interests are perfected, then priority dates from the **time of filing or perfection**, whichever occurs first. UCC § 9-322.

1) Lapse

When there has been filing or perfection by a secured party, a lapse (i.e., a subsequent period in which there is neither filing nor perfection by that secured party) restarts the clock for that secured party; the date of perfection for that secured party is the earlier of the date of filing or perfection that occurs after the lapse. UCC § 9-322(a)(1).

b. Perfected security interest versus unperfected security interest

If only one security interest is perfected and the other is not, then the **perfected interest takes over the unperfected one**.

c. Unperfected security interest versus unperfected security interest

If neither interest is perfected, then the "first in time, first in right" rule applies with the critical time being the time of **attachment**. UCC § 9-322(a).

1) Knowledge of other security interests

A secured party's knowledge of another security interest in the same collateral does not affect the secured party's priority. UCC § 9-322(a)(1), cmt. 4.

2. PMSI Priority Rules

Preference is generally given to a PMSI over a non-PMSI security interest.

a. PMSI in goods other than inventory or livestock

A PMSI in goods other than inventory or livestock prevails over *all other security interests in the collateral*, even if they were previously perfected, if the security interest is perfected before or within 20 days after the debtor receives possession of the collateral. UCC § 9-324.

Knowledge by the purchase-money secured party of the conflicting prior security interest does not prevent the priority of the PMSI over the earlier perfected security interest. UCC § 9-324(a), incl. cmt. 3.

b. PMSI in inventory or livestock

A PMSI in inventory or livestock prevails over all other security interests in the same collateral, even if they were previously perfected, if:

   i)   The PMSI is perfected by the time the debtor receives possession of the collateral; and

   ii) The purchase-money secured party sends an authenticated notification of the PMSI to the holder of any conflicting security interest before the debtor receives possession of the collateral. The notification must state that the purchase-money secured party has or expects to have a PMSI in the debtor's inventory or livestock and it must include a description.

UCC § 9-324(d).

Notification is required only when the previously perfected security interest has been perfected by filing. Notification is effective for a renewable period of five years for inventory and six months for livestock. UCC § 9-324(b)-(e), incl. cmt. 5.

Example: Debtor borrows money from Bank and gives Bank a security interest in all current inventory and all after-acquired inventory. Bank promptly and properly files a financing statement with regard to this security interest. One year later, Debtor purchases new inventory from Supplier, whom he has nine months to pay. Supplier takes a security interest in the new inventory obtained by Debtor.

If Supplier perfects his security interest by filing before he gives Debtor possession of the inventory and notifies Bank in an authenticated record of his security interest, then Supplier will prevail over Bank in the new inventory that Debtor purchased from Supplier.

c. PMSI versus PMSI

1) General rule

If there are two or more competing PMSIs, then **the first-to-file-or-perfect rule** generally governs priority. UCC §§ 9-324(g)(2); 9-322(a).

2) A lender with a PMSI versus a seller with a PMSI

If there are two competing PMSIs and one PMSI secures the price of the collateral for the seller of the collateral while the other PMSI secures loans enabling the purchase of the collateral, then the PMSI taken by the seller has priority over the PMSI taken by the lender. UCC § 9-324(g)(1), incl. cmt. 13.

d. Proceeds from a PMSI in goods

The priority of a PMSI in goods generally extends to the identifiable proceeds of the original collateral, but only as to proceeds in which the security interest is perfected when the debtor receives possession of the collateral or within 20 days thereafter. UCC § 9-324(a), incl. cmt. 8.

e. Proceeds from a PMSI in inventory

The priority of a PMSI in inventory extends to identifiable cash proceeds received on or before the delivery of the inventory to a buyer if:

i) The PMSI is perfected when the debtor receives possession of the inventory; and

ii) The purchase-money secured party sends an authenticated notification to the holder of the conflicting security interest, revealing the secured party's intent to acquire a PMSI in the inventory of the debtor and describing the inventory.

The priority of a PMSI in inventory generally does not extend to proceeds consisting of accounts or chattel paper. The priority can, however, extend to proceeds consisting of either chattel paper (as well as chattel paper proceeds) or instruments if the purchase-money secured party otherwise satisfies the requirements for securing a priority (e.g., takes possession of the chattel paper or instruments). UCC §§ 9-324(b); 9-330.

f. Proceeds from a PMSI in livestock

The rule for proceeds from a PMSI in inventory generally applies to proceeds from livestock in which a PMSI is held. In addition, priority extends to identifiable products in their unmanufactured states (e.g., raw milk) in which a security interest is perfected.

3. Fixtures

a. Security interest in fixtures versus real property interest

Generally, a security interest in fixtures is subordinate to a conflicting interest of an encumbrancer or owner of the related real property other than the debtor. However, a security interest in fixtures has priority over an interest in the real property with which the fixtures are associated if the security interest in fixtures is perfected by a fixture filing before the real property interest is recorded. A fixture filing is the filing of a financing statement covering goods that are or are to become fixtures. The financing statement must be filed in the office designated for the filing or recording of a mortgage on the related real property. UCC §§ 9-102(40), 9-334(c), (e)(1), 9-501.

b. Conflicts with judicial liens

A security interest in fixtures has priority over a subsequent judicial lien on the real property with which the fixtures are associated if the security interest in fixtures was perfected by any method. The method of perfection is not limited to a fixture filing; the judicial creditor who seeks a lien is not a reliance creditor who has searched the real property records. UCC § 9-334(e)(3).

c. Special rule for a PMSI in fixtures

A PMSI in fixtures has priority over a prior interest in the real property with which the fixtures are associated when:

i) The debtor has an interest of record in the real property (e.g., is an owner) or is in possession of the real property (e.g., is a lessee); and

ii) The security interest is perfected by a fixture filing before the goods become fixtures or within 20 days thereafter.

UCC § 9-334(d).

d. Construction mortgage

A construction mortgage (i.e., a mortgage that secures an obligation incurred for the construction of an improvement on land, including the cost of acquiring the land, and that indicates it is a construction mortgage in the real property records) has priority over a subsequent security interest in a fixture, *including a PMSI in a fixture*. The construction mortgage must be recorded before the goods become fixtures, and it covers only goods that become fixtures before completion of the construction. UCC § 9-334(h).

4. Proceeds

Generally, the basic rules (e.g., first-to-file-or-perfect) govern priority if there are conflicting security interests and at least one of those interests is claimed as proceeds. UCC § 9-322(a), incl. cmt. 6. Moreover, the filing or perfection date for the original collateral is treated as the filing or perfection date for the proceeds. UCC § 9-322(b)(1).

This rule controls, even when the security interest in inventory is a PMSI, because the super-priority of a PMSI in inventory does not extend to proceeds that are not cash.

Example: On Day One, SP1 perfects by filing against inventory. On Day Two, SP2 perfects by filing against accounts. On Day Three, Debtor acquires new accounts by selling inventory on credit. Both parties will have a security interest in the accounts and both are perfected. SP1 has a proceeds claim that is perfected under the same-office rule. SP2 is perfected because its security interest includes accounts and its

a. Exceptions

1) Proceeds of non-filing collateral

If the collateral is of a type for which perfection may be achieved by a method other than filing and for which secured parties who so perfect generally do not expect or need to conduct a filing search (e.g., chattel paper, deposit accounts, negotiable documents, instruments, investment properties, letter-of-credit rights), then priority in the original collateral generally continues in the proceeds, provided that:

    i) The security interest in the proceeds is **perfected**; and

    ii) The proceeds are **cash** proceeds or proceeds of the **same type as the original collateral**.

UCC § 9-322(c)(2), incl. cmt. 8.

2) Filing collateral as proceeds of non-filing collateral

If the proceeds of non-filing collateral are filing collateral (i.e., goods, accounts, commercial tort claims, general and payment intangibles, nonnegotiable documents) and the security interest in the non-filing collateral has been perfected by a method other than filing (e.g., control or possession), then priority among conflicting perfected interests in the filing collateral is determined by the **time of filing of a financing statement** that covers the collateral (i.e., the first-to-file rule). UCC § 9-322(d).

5. Future Advances

a. General rule

In determining the priority of a security interest that secures a future advance when there is a conflicting security interest in the same collateral, the first-to-file-or-perfect rule generally applies. Consequently, the time that an advance is made is usually not determinative of priority unless a financing statement was not filed with respect to the security interest and the advance, as value given, constitutes the final step for attachment and perfection of that interest. UCC § 9-323, incl. cmt. 3.

b. Exception—Time of perfection determinative

Perfection of a security interest dates from the time that an advance is made to the extent that the security interest secures an advance that:

    i) Is made while the security is only automatically or temporarily perfected; and

    ii) Is not made pursuant to a commitment entered into before or while the security interest is perfected by any other method of perfection. The advance is made "pursuant to a commitment" when the secured party is obligated to make the advance.

UCC §§ 9-102(a)(68); 9-323(a).

6. Accessions

A security interest in an accession is usually subject to general priority rules. Such a security interest, however, is subordinate to a security interest in the whole collateral that is perfected under a certificate-of-title statute. UCC § 9-335(c), (d).

> **Example:** A security interest in a car radio is subordinate to a security interest in the car perfected by notation of the security interest on the title to the car.

After default, a secured party may remove an accession from other goods if the security interest in the accession has priority over the claims of every person having an interest in the whole. A secured party that removes an accession from other goods must reimburse the holder of a security interest or the owner of the whole or other goods for physical injury to the whole or other goods, apart for the diminution in value of the whole or other goods caused by the absence of the removed accession or by any necessity for replacing it. UCC § 9-335(e), (f).

7. Investment Property, Deposit Accounts, Letter of Credit Rights

A security interest held by a secured party having control of investment property, a deposit account, or letter of credit rights has priority over a security interest held by a secured party that does not have control of the collateral. UCC §§ 9-327—329.

V. DEFAULT

A. CIRCUMSTANCES CONSTITUTING DEFAULT

"Default" is not defined by Article 9. Instead, the parties to a security agreement are free to agree to the circumstances that give rise to a default, such as the debtor's transfer of the collateral without authorization. UCC § 9-601, cmt. 3. In the absence of such an agreement, the only event of default will be the failure of the obligor to make timely payments to the secured party.

1. In General

A security agreement is a contract. Contract law therefore determines the enforceability of any terms in a security agreement.

2. Agreement Not to Assert Defenses Against an Assignee

Article 9 specifically recognizes the validity of an agreement between an account debtor and assignor that the account debtor will not assert against an assignee any claim or defense that the account debtor may have against the assignor. UCC § 9-403.

B. CONSEQUENCES OF DEFAULT

Once a default has occurred, the secured party may:

i) Seek **possession** of the collateral and, in order to satisfy the obligor's outstanding obligation, either:

    a) **Sell** the collateral; or

    b) **Retain** it in full or partial satisfaction of the obligation;

ii) Initiate a judicial action to obtain a **judgment** based on that obligation; or

iii) Subject to statutory limitations, pursue any course of action to which the debtor and obligor have agreed.

UCC § 9-601(a).

1. **Cumulative Remedies, Simultaneous Exercise**

The secured party may pursue *any or all* of these remedies and may do so simultaneously, provided the secured party acts in good faith. UCC § 9-601(c), incl. cmt. 5.

2. **Ignoring Default**

The secured party may choose to ignore a default, but such action may constitute a waiver of the secured party's rights that would otherwise arise upon the default. UCC §§ 2-209(4), (5); 9-601, cmt. 3.

3. **Security Agreement Covering Fixtures**

When a security agreement covers fixtures, a secured party may proceed as to the fixtures in accord with the rights and remedies with respect to the real property. UCC § 9-604(b), incl. cmt. 3.

When a secured party's security interest has priority over owners and individuals who encumber real property, that secured party may remove the fixture from the real property. With respect to an owner or encumbrancer who is not the debtor, the secured party is *liable for the cost of repairing any physical object damaged by the removal* but not for any reduction in the value of the real property due to the removal. UCC § 9-604.

4. **Security Interest in Accession**

After default, a secured party with a security interest in an accession that has priority over the claims of anyone having an interest in the whole may remove the accession from the other goods. UCC § 9-335.

5. **Secured Party and Account Debtors**

Upon default, a secured party may notify an account debtor (i.e., a person obligated on an account, chattel paper or general intangible, but not a person obligated on a negotiable instrument) to make payment to the secured party. In addition, the secured party may exercise any rights of the debtor with respect to the obligation of the account debtor. In a commercially reasonable manner, the secured party may collect from the account debtor, and, if the account debtor does not pay, the secured party may enforce the obligation of the account debtor. UCC § 9-607.

C. POSSESSION OF COLLATERAL

After default, a secured party is entitled to take possession of the collateral. Unless the security agreement provides otherwise, a secured party is not required to give notice of default, nor is he required to give notice of his intent to take possession of the collateral. UCC § 9-609.

1. **Limitation on Means of Possession—No Breach of the Peace**

A secured party is required to use judicial process (e.g., a replevin action) to obtain possession of the collateral unless possession can be obtained **without breach of the peace**. "Breach of the peace" is not defined by Article 9, but it is left up to court interpretation. Courts are split on whether trickery constitutes breach of the peace.

   a. **Criminal act**

   Anything that would lead to the commission of a crime typically constitutes breach of the peace. An exception generally is made for trespass with respect to the collateral itself (e.g., entering a car) or the debtor's land (e.g., seizing a car from the debtor's driveway), but it does extend to trespass of the debtor's residence or garage. UCC § 9-609(b).

b. Debtor's permission or objection

Although a secured party generally can seize collateral without breaching the peace after obtaining the debtor's permission to take the collateral, a seizure based on permission gained under color of law (e.g., participation of a police officer without judicial authorization) or through the use of, or the threat to use, force may be a breach of the peace. If the debtor physically objects to the seizure of collateral, then that seizure constitutes a breach of the peace; courts are divided over whether mere verbal objections constitute a breach of the peace.

> **Example:** B fails to make payments on the car he purchased from A. Although A cannot use any methods to threaten or force B to give up the car, A may take the car from a public street or in front of B's house without his knowledge. A may not, however, breach the peace during the repossession.

2. Rendering Equipment Unusable

As an alternative to securing possession of the collateral after a default, a secured party may render equipment unusable. This is usually followed by the disposal (e.g., sale) of the collateral on the debtor's premises. UCC § 9-609.

D. DISPOSITION OF COLLATERAL

After default, a secured party may sell, lease, license, or otherwise dispose of all or any of the collateral. Within limits, the secured party may keep the collateral (strict foreclosure) in full or partial satisfaction of the obligation. UCC §§ 9-610(a), 9-620.

1. Commercially Reasonable Standard for Disposition

All aspects of the disposition of collateral (method, manner, time, and place) must be conducted in a **commercially reasonable manner**. A disposition is commercially reasonable when conducted:

i) In the usual manner on a **recognized market**, such as a stock exchange, that has standardized price quotations for fungible goods;

ii) At the **price current** in any recognized market at the time of the disposition; or

iii) Otherwise in conformity with **reasonable commercial practices** among dealers in the type of property that was the subject of the disposition.

UCC §§ 9-610(b), (c); 9-627(b), incl. cmt. 4.

2. Price

Article 9 does not mandate a specific price that must be obtained by the secured party in disposing of the collateral. The mere fact that a higher price could have been obtained by disposing of the collateral in a different manner or at a different time does not establish that the disposition was not commercially reasonable. A low price may, however, trigger careful scrutiny by the court of the disposition and its reasonableness. UCC § 9-627(a), incl. cmts. 2, 10.

3. Time of Disposition

Likewise, Article 9 does not mandate a specific time in which a disposition must occur. Instead, circumstances may dictate that the collateral is held due to the collapse of a market for the collateral, or the collateral that is comprised of a large number of a specific items be sold over time in parcels rather than immediately in bulk in order not to depress the market. UCC § 9-610(b), cmt. 3.

4. Type of Disposition

A secured party may dispose of the collateral publicly or privately. A secured party may purchase the collateral at a public sale, but she cannot do so at a private sale unless the collateral is of a kind that is customarily sold on a recognized market (e.g., the New York Stock Exchange) or the subject of widely distributed standard price quotations. A secured party cannot purchase the collateral at a private sale when the prices are individually negotiated or when items are not fungible in a recognized market. UCC § 9-610(c), incl. cmts. 7, 9.

5. Notice of Disposition

A secured party is generally required to send an authenticated notification of disposition. The notification is required to be reasonable as to its content, the manner in which it is sent, and its timeliness. UCC § 9-611(b), incl. cmt. 2.

a. Persons entitled to notice

Notification of disposition is required to be sent to (i) the debtor, (ii) any secondary obligor, and, in the case of non-consumer goods, (iii) any other secured party or lien holder who held a security interest that was perfected by filing or pursuant to a statute, and (iv) any other party from whom the secured party has received authenticated notice of a claim or interest in the collateral. UCC § 9-611(a), (c).

b. Contents of notice

Except in a consumer goods transaction, the contents of a notification of disposition are sufficient when the notification contains:

i)   A description of the debtor and the secured party;

ii) A description of the collateral;

iii) A statement as to the method of disposition;

iv) A statement that the debtor is entitled to an accounting of the unpaid indebtedness and the charge, if any, for providing that accounting; and

v)   A statement of the time and place of a public disposition or the time after which a private disposition is to be made. UCC § 9-613.

c. Additional information for a consumer goods transaction

In addition to the above requirements for a non-consumer goods transaction, proper notice in a consumer goods transaction must also include:

i)   A description of any liability for a deficiency of the person to whom the notification is sent;

ii) The telephone number from which the redemption amount is available; and

iii) The telephone number or mailing address from which additional information concerning the disposition and secured obligation is available.

UCC § 9-614, incl. cmt. 1.

d. Timeliness of notice

In general, the test for the timeliness of a notification of a disposition is **reasonableness**. The notification should be sent sufficiently far in advance of the disposition to allow the notified party to act on the notification. UCC § 9-612(a), incl. cmt. 2.

In a transaction other than a consumer transaction, when a secured party sends a notification of disposition after default and **at least 10 days** before the earliest time for disposition set forth in the notification, the timeliness of the notice is reasonable, provided that the notice is sent in a commercially reasonable manner. UCC § 9-612(b), incl. cmt. 3.

e. Exceptions to notification

A secured party is not required to send a notice of disposition when:

i) The collateral is perishable or threatens to decline speedily in value;

ii) The collateral is of a type customarily sold on a recognized market; or

iii) The persons entitled to notification waive the right to notification.

UCC §§ 9-611(d); 624(a).

Waiver of the right to notification (item iii above) can be done only after a default has occurred. Such a waiver cannot be oral but must be manifested by an authenticated agreement. UCC § 9-624(a).

6. Application of the Proceeds From a Disposition

a. Cash proceeds

A secured party must apply, or pay over for application, cash proceeds of a disposition in the following order:

i) Reasonable expenses for collection and enforcement, including reasonable attorney's fees and other legal expenses to the extent permitted by agreement and not prohibited by law; then

ii) Satisfaction of obligations secured by the security interest or agricultural lien; then

iii) Satisfaction of any subordinate security interests, provided that the junior secured party made an authenticated demand for proceeds before distribution of the proceeds is complete; then

iv) The remainder of the proceeds to the debtor.

UCC §§ 9-608(a)(1); 9-615(a).

b. Non-cash proceeds

A secured party must apply or pay over for application non-cash proceeds of a disposition only if the failure to do so would be commercially unreasonable. If the secured party does apply or pay over for such proceeds, then he must do so in a commercially reasonable manner. UCC §§ 9-608(a)(3); 9-615(c).

c. Treatment of a surplus or deficiency

1) Surplus

If, after the required payments and applications of proceeds have been made, there is a surplus, the secured party generally must pay the surplus to the debtor. UCC §§ 9-608(a)(4); 9-615(d)(1).

2) Deficiency

If, after the required payments and applications of proceeds have been made, there is a deficiency, then the obligor generally is liable for the deficiency. UCC §§ 9-608(a)(4); 9-615(d)(2).

3) Sales of accounts, chattel paper, payment intangibles, or promissory notes

When the underlying transaction is the sale of accounts, chattel paper, payment intangibles, or promissory notes, then the debtor is not entitled to any surplus, and the obligor is not liable for any deficiency. UCC §§ 9-608(b), 9-615(e).

4) "Low price" disposition to a secured party

When a disposition of the collateral is made to a secured party, a person related to the secured party, or a secondary obligor, the secured party may lack the incentive to maximize the proceeds of the disposition. If the amount of the proceeds in such a disposition is **significantly below** the range of proceeds that a disposition to someone other than the secured party, person related to the secured party, or a secondary obligor would have brought, then the amount of the deficiency may be adjusted to reflect the higher price that would have been realized from the other person. UCC §§ 9-102(63), (64); 9-615(f), incl. cmt. 6.

5) Notice in a consumer goods transaction

In a consumer goods transaction, a secured party must send an explanatory notice to the debtor detailing the deficiency and/or surplus and the basis on which it was calculated. This explanation, which must be in writing, can be demanded by the debtor or consumer obligor, in which case the secured party has 14 days after receipt of the demand in which to send the explanation or, in the case of a deficiency, a waiver of the secured party's right to the deficiency. A secured party who fails to send such a notice may be liable for any loss caused, plus $500. UCC §§ 9-616; 9-625(e).

7. Transferee's Rights

A sale of the collateral gives the buyer at the sale all of the debtor's rights in the collateral. If the transferee/buyer acts in good faith (i.e., honesty in fact and the observance of reasonable commercial standards of fair dealing), then the disposition discharges the security interest being foreclosed and any subordinate security interests and liens, even though the secured party fails to comply with Article 9. However, the transferee takes the collateral subject to any security interests that were senior to the security interest foreclosed. UCC §§ 1-201(20), 9-617, incl. cmts. 2, 3.

8. Warranties

A disposition of collateral includes warranties of title, possession, and quiet enjoyment that generally accompany the disposition of property of the same type as the collateral. These warranties may be disclaimed or modified. UCC § 9-610(d), (e), incl. cmt. 11.

E.   ACCEPTANCE OF COLLATERAL (STRICT FORECLOSURE)

In lieu of disposing of the collateral, the secured party may usually accept the collateral in full or partial satisfaction of the obligation secured by the collateral. UCC §§ 9-620; 9-622.

1.   Full Satisfaction of an Obligation

A secured party may accept collateral in full satisfaction of an obligation secured by the collateral when:

i)   The debtor consents, after default, to the acceptance in an authenticated record; or

ii)   The debtor does not object to the secured party's proposal to accept the collateral within 20 days after the proposal is sent.

UCC § 9-620(a)–(c).

2.   Partial Satisfaction of an Obligation

A secured party may accept collateral in partial satisfaction of an obligation secured by the collateral if the debtor consents, after default, to the acceptance in an authenticated record. UCC § 9-620(a)–(c).

3.   Notification of Parties Other Than the Debtor

In addition to the debtor, a secured party wishing to accept collateral in full or partial satisfaction of the obligation must send his proposal to:

i)   Any secured party or lien holder who, 10 days before the debtor consented to the acceptance, held a security interest that was perfected by filing or by compliance with a statute, treaty or regulation; and

ii)   Any person from whom the secured party received, before the debtor consented to the acceptance, an authenticated notification of a claim of an interest in the collateral.

A secured party wishing to accept collateral in partial satisfaction must also send its proposal to any secondary obligor. An objection to the acceptance by a person to whom notification was sent is effective if it is received by the secured party within 20 days from the date that the notification was sent to that party. UCC § 9-620(a), (d), incl. cmt. 8.

4.   Special Rules for Consumer Debtors

a.   Denial of partial strict foreclose in a consumer transaction

In a consumer transaction, a secured party can accept the collateral only in full satisfaction of the obligation; an acceptance in partial satisfaction of the obligation *is not allowed*. Any attempted acceptance in partial satisfaction is void. UCC § 9-620(g), incl. cmt. 12.

b.   Denial of strict foreclosure for consumer goods—60% rule

If the goods are consumer goods in the possession of the secured party, and the debtor has paid at least 60% of the cash price in the case of a PMSI, or at least 60% of the obligation secured in a non-PMSI case, then the secured party cannot keep the goods in satisfaction of the debt; they must be sold. A debtor may waive this right to force a sale of the collateral, provided it is done after default in an authenticated agreement. UCC §§ 9-620(e), (f), incl. cmt. 12; 9-624(b).

F. REDEMPTION OF COLLATERAL

A debtor, secondary obligor, or any other secured party has the right to redeem collateral. UCC § 9-623.

1. Method of Redemption

To effect a redemption, the redeemer must fulfill all obligations secured by the collateral (e.g., payment of monetary obligations currently due, including obligations resulting from the default) and reasonable expenses, including attorney's fees, incurred by the secured party in retaking the collateral or preparing for its disposition. UCC § 9-623(b). If the security agreement contains an acceleration clause, then the redeemer must tender the entire balance of the secured obligation. UCC § 9-623, cmt. 2.

2. Time Limitation on Redemption

Redemption cannot occur if the secured party has disposed of the collateral or entered into a contract for its disposition, accepted the collateral in full or partial satisfaction of the obligation secured by the collateral, or collected on the collateral. UCC § 9-623(c).

3. Waiver of Right of Redemption

The security agreement may not contain a waiver of the right to redemption by the debtor or secondary obligor; any such attempted waiver is void. After default, a debtor or secondary obligor may waive the right of redemption in an authenticated agreement. UCC § 9-624(c).

G. REMEDIES FOR A SECURED PARTY'S FAILURE TO COMPLY

1. Basic Remedies

a. Injunctive relief

When a secured party has not proceeded in accordance with Article 9 (e.g., has failed to notify the debtor as to a disposition of the collateral), the debtor or other secured party may seek injunctive relief from a court to compel or restrain collection, enforcement, or disposition of collateral on appropriate terms and conditions. UCC § 9-625(a), incl. cmt. 2.

b. Actual damages

If a secured party fails to comply with Article 9, then the debtor or other secured party may seek damages for any loss caused by the secured party's failure. This loss may include losses resulting from the debtor's inability to obtain alternative financing or from the increased cost of obtaining such financing. UCC § 9-625(b), incl. cmt. 3.

The debtor may seek consequential damages, but she is subject to the duty to mitigate damages.

c. Minimum statutory damages for consumer goods

If the collateral is consumer goods and a secured party fails to comply with the default rules of Article 9, then a debtor or secondary obligor may recover an amount not less than the credit service charge, plus 10% of the principal amount of the obligation or the time-price differential, plus 10% of the cash price, even if the actual damages are less. UCC § 9-625(c).

d. Limitation on deficiency

1) Commercial transactions

If a secured party's collection, enforcement, disposition, or acceptance is not in accord with Article 9 and the transaction is a commercial—not a consumer—transaction, then there is a rebuttable presumption that the secured party is not entitled to collect a deficiency. The secured party can rebut this presumption in whole or in part by showing that the deficiency would have existed even had the secured party complied with Article 9. The debtor or secondary obligor may not seek damages if a deficiency is merely reduced or eliminated as a consequence of the secured party's failure to comply with Article 9. UCC §§ 9-625(d); 9-626(a)(3).

2) Consumer transactions

If the transaction is a consumer transaction and a secured party's collection, enforcement, disposition, or acceptance is not in accord with Article 9, then many courts follow the rebuttable presumption rule that is applicable to a commercial transaction. Some courts, however, apply an absolute bar rule, under which the non-complying secured party cannot recover a deficiency. UCC § 9-626(b), incl. cmt. 4.

2. Conversion Action

If a secured party improperly repossesses collateral, then the debtor may be able to pursue a conversion action under tort law, rather than under the UCC. UCC § 9-626, cmt. 2.

3. Non-liability of a Secured Party to an Unknown Debtor or Obligor

A secured party does not owe a duty to a person that the secured party does not know is a debtor or an obligor. Similarly, a secured party does not owe a duty to a debtor or an obligor of whose existence the secured party is aware, but whose identity the secured party does not know, or with whom the secured party does not know how to communicate. UCC §§ 9-604; 9-628.

Trusts

TRUSTS

Table of Contents

TRUSTS

I. INTRODUCTION TO TRUSTS

A trust is a fiduciary relationship wherein one or more trustees are called upon to manage, protect, and invest certain property and any income generated therefrom for the benefit of one or more named beneficiaries.

To create a trust, the grantor must have intended to create the trust. A trust is valid as long as it has a trustee, an ascertainable beneficiary, and assets. Trust interests are alienable, devisable, and descendible unless the terms of a trust expressly or impliedly provide otherwise.

Trusts are classified according to the method by which they are created. There are three main types of trusts: express trusts, resulting trusts, and constructive trusts.

A. OVERVIEW

1. Bifurcated Transfer

A trust involves a bifurcated transfer. The creator or settlor transfers property to a second-party trustee to be managed for the benefit of a third-party beneficiary. The trustee holds legal title, and the beneficiary holds equitable title. No consideration is required.

2. Ongoing Transfers

A trust involves an ongoing series of transfers. Trust property is divided between income and principal, and the equitable interest is divided between the beneficiary holding the possessory estate and the beneficiary holding the future interest.

3. Revocable versus Irrevocable Trusts

a. Presumption

A revocable trust can be terminated by the settlor at any time. An irrevocable trust usually cannot be terminated. Under the majority rule, a trust is presumed to be irrevocable unless it expressly states otherwise. Under the Uniform Trust Code (UTC), however, and in a minority of jurisdictions, the presumption is just the opposite—a trust is presumed revocable unless it expressly states that it is irrevocable. UTC § 602(a).

> **EXAM NOTE:** If this issue arises in an MEE question, unless the question explicitly directs you to apply either the majority or UTC rule, you should mention both presumptions in your rule statement, but apply the majority rule in your analysis.

b. Method of revocation

Absent language within the instrument prescribing the method of revocation, any action manifesting the settlor's intent to revoke will suffice. The revocation becomes effective when the action manifesting the intent occurs, rather than when the trustee or beneficiaries learn of the action.

4. Mandatory versus Discretionary Trusts

A mandatory trust requires the trustee to distribute all trust income. To protect the interests of the beneficiaries, a settlor may instead opt to create a discretionary trust, under which the trustee is given the power to distribute income at his discretion. The trustee does not abuse his discretion unless he acts dishonestly or in a way not contemplated by the trust creator.

5. Rule Against Perpetuities

Because future interests are trust components, trusts are subject to the Rule Against Perpetuities, meaning that a trust may fail if all interests there under may not vest within the applicable period of perpetuities (usually a life in being plus 21 years).

Some jurisdictions take a "wait and see" approach to the application of the rule, refraining from invalidating future interests until it is clear that they will not vest within the perpetuities period.

B. PARTIES TO A TRUST

1. Settlor

The settlor, sometimes referred to as the grantor, is the creator of the trust.

2. Trustee

The trustee holds the legal interest or title to the trust property.

a. Number of trustees

A trust may have one or more trustees.

> The same individual cannot serve as sole trustee and sole beneficiary of a trust because such an arrangement would result in a lack of enforcement power by the beneficiary against the trustee. If the trustee is the sole beneficiary, then title merges and the trust terminates.

b. Qualifications of a trustee

A named trustee must have the capacity to acquire and hold property for his own benefit and the capacity to administer the trust. Minors or insane persons will not qualify as trustees, as although they can hold property they cannot administer it. Additionally, those eligible to serve as trustees may be limited by statute.

c. Duties to perform

A trustee must be given specific duties to perform, or the trust will fail and legal and equitable title will merge in the beneficiary. The expressed intention of the settlor to create a trust along with the identification of trust property and beneficiaries is usually sufficient for the court to infer duties to be performed by the trustee.

> **Example:** A gives $1,000 to T as trustee for A's child, B, with the trust to terminate when B graduates from college. A does not outline any duties for T to perform. The court will infer the duty to accumulate income and to invest principal, to be paid to B when B graduates from college. The trust will not fail for lack of express duties.

Regarding duties of a trustee, *see* VIII. Trust Administration and the Trustee's Duties, *infra*.

d. Acceptance of trusteeship

A person designated as a trustee can accept the position:

i) By substantially complying with a method of acceptance provided for in the terms of the trust; or

ii) If the terms of the trust do not provide a method of acceptance, or the method is not made exclusive, by accepting delivery of the trust property, exercising powers as a trustee, performing duties as a trustee, or otherwise indicating acceptance of the trusteeship.

> **Example:** Settlor gives T $50,000 to invest, with income to A for life, remainder to B. T silently accepts the money. T's acceptance of the trust is presumed because he accepted the trust property.

e. Declining trusteeship

A designated trustee who does not accept the trusteeship within a reasonable time after knowing of the designation is deemed to have declined the trusteeship. A person designated as trustee may, without accepting the trusteeship, act to preserve the trust property if, within a reasonable time after acting, the person sends to a qualified beneficiary a written statement declining the trusteeship. Such person also may inspect or investigate trust property to determine potential liability under environmental or other law or for any other purpose. If a person does not accept the trusteeship, the court will appoint a successor trustee, unless the settlor expressed an intent that the trust was to continue only as long as a particular person served as trustee.

f. Failure to name a trustee

If the settlor fails to designate a trustee, then the court will appoint a trustee.

3. Beneficiary

The beneficiary holds equitable title to the property and therefore possesses the power to enforce the trust instrument. To be valid, a trust generally must name at least one beneficiary. Any individual or entity can be named as a trust beneficiary, provided the individual or entity is capable of taking and holding title to property. Such beneficiary may be unborn at the time the trust is created, provided such beneficiary will be identifiable by the time he comes into enjoyment of the trust property. Notice is not required, but acceptance by the beneficiary is required for the trust to commence for his benefit. The beneficiary, however, has the option of renouncing his rights within a reasonable time.

II. EXPRESS TRUSTS

An express trust is created as a result of the expressed intention of the owner of the property to create a trust relationship with respect to the property. There are two categories of express trusts: private express trusts and charitable trusts.

A. PRIVATE EXPRESS TRUST

A private express trust clearly states the intention of the settlor to transfer property to a trustee for the benefit of one or more ascertainable beneficiaries.

1. Elements of a Valid Private Express Trust

a. Intent

The settlor must intend to make a gift in trust. The use of common trust terms (such as "in trust" or "trustee") will create a presumption of intent to create a trust, but these words are not required. The settlor's intent may be manifested orally, in writing, or by conduct. Intent is only required to be expressed in writing when the Statute of Wills (i.e., the jurisdiction's requirements for the execution of a will) or the Statute of Frauds (UCC § 2-207) applies. To determine a settlor's intent, both in creating and administering a trust, the courts consider:

i)   The specific terms and overall tenor of the words used;

ii) The definiteness or indefiniteness of the property involved;

iii) The ease or difficulty of ascertaining possible trust purposes and terms, and the specificity or vagueness of the possible beneficiaries and their interests;

iv) The interests or motives and the nature and degree of concerns that may be reasonably supposed to have influenced the transferor;

v) The financial situation, dependencies, and expectations of the parties;

vi) The transferor's prior conduct, statements, and relationships with respect to possible trust beneficiaries;

vii) The personal and any fiduciary relationships between the transferor and the transferee;

viii) Other dispositions the transferor is making or has made of his wealth; and

ix) Whether the result of construing the disposition as involving a trust or not would be such as a person in the situation of the transferor would be likely to desire.

Restatement (Third) of Trusts § 13. The manifestation of intent must occur either prior to or simultaneously with the transfer of property. If the transfer does not take place immediately, then the intent should be manifested anew at the time of transfer. A promise to create a trust in the future is unenforceable unless the promise is supported by consideration sufficient for the formation of a contract.

> **EXAM NOTE:** The intent requirement for the creation of trusts is tested frequently. Whether a gift is given outright or in trust depends upon whether the beneficial interest vests with the **recipient** (outright gift) or a **third party** (gift in trust).

1) Ambiguous language

The intent to create a trust differs only slightly from the intent to make a gift. A determination must be made regarding whether a bifurcated transfer was intended and, if so, whether the intent was more than a mere hope or wish.

2) Precatory trusts

If a donor transfers property to a donee using language that expresses a hope or wish (rather than creating a legal obligation) that such property be used for the benefit of another, then the gift may be considered a precatory trust and not an outright gift. To be considered a precatory trust, the transfer must meet two requirements. First, it must contain specific instructions to a fiduciary. Second, it must be shown that, absent imposition of a trust, there would be an unnatural disposition of the donor's property because of familial relations or a history of support between the donor and the intended beneficiary.

3) Failed gifts

The Restatement (Third) of Trusts rejects the argument that a failed gift can be saved by a re-characterization of the donor's intent.

b. Trust property

A valid trust must contain some property that was owned by the settlor at the time the trust was created and was at that time transferred to the trust or to the trustee. Put differently, the trust must be "**funded.**" Any property interest, including real property, personal property, money, intangibles, partial interests, or future interests (whether vested or contingent) will suffice, although a mere expectancy will not. If a trust that is invalid for lack of assets is later funded, a trust arises if the settlor re-manifests the intention to create the trust. The exception is a "pour-over" gift (*see* § II.A.2.a.4). *infra*), which is valid even if made before there is identifiable trust property.

1) Trust res

The requirement of identifiable trust property, or **res**, distinguishes a trust from a debt. A trust involves the duty of one party to deal with specific property for another, whereas a debt involves the obligation of one party to pay a sum of money, from any source, to another.

> If the recipient of the funds is entitled to use them as if they are his own and to commingle them with his own monies, then the obligation to pay the funds to another is a debt, not a trust.

2) Segregation

Trust property must be identifiable and segregated. The property must be described with reasonable certainty.

c. Valid trust purpose

A trust can be created for any purpose, as long as it is not illegal, restricted by rule of law or statute, or contrary to public policy.

> Trust provisions that restrain a first marriage have generally been held to violate public policy. However, a restraint on marriage might be upheld if the trustee's motive was merely to provide support for a beneficiary while the beneficiary is single. *See* Restatement (Third) of Trusts § 29 (2003).

Situations in which one of several trust terms is violative of public policy, any alternative terms provided by the settlor will be honored, and, if there are none, the term will be stricken from the trust, but the trust will not fail altogether unless the removal of the term proves fatal.

d. Ascertainable beneficiaries

The beneficiaries of a private trust must be ascertainable (i.e., identifiable by name) so that the equitable interest can be transferred automatically by operation of law and directly benefit the person. The settlor may refer to acts of independent significance when identifying trust beneficiaries. Under the Uniform Trust Code (UTC), a trustee can select a beneficiary from an indefinite class, unless the trustee must distribute equally to all members of an indefinite class. *See* UTC § 402(c). If a beneficiary has died without the settlor's knowledge prior to the creation of the trust, then the trust will fail for lack of a beneficiary. In this case, a resulting trust in favor of the settlor or his successors is presumed.

1) Unborn children exception

Trusts for the benefit of unborn children will be upheld even though the beneficiaries are not yet ascertainable at the time the trust is created.

> **Example:** S conveys property to T "in trust for A for life, remainder to A's children." The beneficiaries are sufficiently ascertainable even if A has no children at the time of the conveyance, because the identification of A's children will be possible at the time of A's death.

2) Class-gift exception

A trust to a reasonably definite class will be enforced. Even a trust that allows the trustee to select the beneficiaries from among the members of a class is acceptable, but a trust to an entirely indefinite class will not be enforced as a private trust.

3) Charitable-trusts exception

Only private trusts must have ascertainable beneficiaries. Because, by definition, charitable trusts exist for the good of the public at large, charitable trusts must not have individual ascertainable beneficiaries.

2. Types of Express Trusts

a. *Inter vivos* trusts

Inter vivos trusts are lifetime transfers in trust. Although a simple declaration of trust will usually suffice if the settlor is also the trustee, delivery must accompany the declaration if a third-party trustee is named, whereby the settlor parts with dominion and control over the trust property.

An *inter vivos* trust can be either revocable or irrevocable. Often, *inter vivos* trusts are used to avoid the costs and delays of the probate process. Other perceived advantages of *inter vivos* trusts include lifetime asset management by a third party, privacy, and choice of law.

1) Type of property

To transfer real property to a trust, the declaration of trust must be in a writing that satisfies the Statute of Frauds. However, a writing is not required to transfer personal property to a trust, and extrinsic evidence generally is allowed to clarify ambiguities.

The trustee takes legal title upon the delivery of a deed or other document of title for real property, or upon the delivery of personal property.

2) Constructive trust

At common law, the Statute of Frauds requirement was strictly applied. The modern trend (adopted by the Restatement (Third) of Trusts, § 24) imposes a constructive trust when the required writing is lacking and orders the purported trustee to distribute the real property to the intended beneficiaries outright, rather than in trust.

3) Parol evidence rule

Generally, evidence outside of the written agreement is permitted to show the settlor's intent only if the written agreement is ambiguous on its face. A few states allow the introduction of parol evidence even if the writing is unambiguous.

4) Pour-over trust

A pour-over devise is a provision in a will that directs the distribution of property to a trust upon the happening of an event, so that the property passes according to the terms of the trust without the necessity of the will reciting the entire trust.

Example 1: T executes both a will and an *inter vivos* trust. The will provides that upon T's death, assets of the estate "pour over" into the trust.

> **Example 2:** Husband and Wife execute reciprocal wills that provide for a trust to be established under the will of the first to die, and they contain a "pour-over" devise to the trust in the will of the second to die.

a) Validity

Under the common-law doctrine of "incorporation by reference," if a will refers to an unattested document in existence at the time the will is signed, then the terms of that document could be given effect in the same manner as if it had been properly executed. Under this doctrine, for example, the terms of an amended revocable trust would not apply to the disposition of the probate estate assets because the amendment was not in existence at the time the will was executed. However, the necessity for this doctrine has been obviated under the Uniform Testamentary Additions to Trusts Act (UTATA), codified at the Uniform Probate Code (UPC) § 2-511. Under the UTATA, a will may "pour over" estate assets into a trust, even if the trust instrument was not executed in accordance with the Statute of Wills, as long as the trust is identified in the will, and its terms are set forth in a written instrument. Furthermore, if these requirements are met, the pour-over bequest is valid even if the trust is unfunded, revocable, and amendable. UPC § 2-511.

b) Revocation

If the trust is revoked, then the pour-over provision in the will must fail.

5) Totten trusts

A Totten trust is not a true trust because there is no separation of legal and equitable title. Rather, it is a designation given to a bank account in a depositor's name as "trustee" for one or more named beneficiaries. During the depositor's life, the depositor retains complete control of the account, including the ability to make deposits and withdrawals for the depositor's own benefit, and the amount in the account is subject to the claims of the depositor's creditors. During the depositor's life, the beneficiary has no rights in the account.

A Totten trust can be revoked by any lifetime act manifesting the depositor's intent to revoke, or by will. Because the amount in a Totten trust can be devised, a Totten trust is distinguishable from a joint bank account, the proceeds of which pass by law at the death of one joint tenant to the other. If the depositor does not devise the amount in a Totten trust, it passes to the named beneficiaries.

6) UTMA accounts

Every state has enacted the Uniform Transfers to Minors Act (UTMA), which provides a convenient method by which an account can be set up for a minor with a custodian who is required to manage the account until the minor reaches age 21. Such an arrangement is not a true trust because the custodian does not hold legal title to the account.

7) Life-insurance trusts

A life-insurance trust provides for the payment of the proceeds from a life insurance policy upon the death of the insured to the trust, with the terms of the trust governing the recipients of the proceeds. Therefore, a life-insurance trust is not funded at its creation. Despite this lack of significant res, a life insurance trust is a valid trust. To avoid adverse tax consequences, the trust is the owner of the insurance policy and the trust is irrevocable.

8) Living trusts

A living or revocable trust is created primarily to avoid probate of a decedent's property upon the decedent's death. A settlor transfers ownership of some or all of his assets to a revocable trust. The settlor generally names himself as the trustee of the trust and is the primary current beneficiary of the trust. Upon the settlor's death, the successor trustee named in the trust instrument is responsible for distributing the trust's assets in accord with the terms of the trust instead of a personal representative distributing the settlor's assets in accord with the terms of the settlor's will. Under a living trust, the settlor retains the flexibility of changing the successor trustee and the beneficiaries of the trust until his death. Such a trust does not protect the trust property from the settlor's creditors and does not avoid federal estate tax on the trust property.

b. Testamentary trusts

Testamentary trusts occur when the terms of the trust are contained in writing in a will or in a document incorporated by reference into a will. Testamentary trusts must comply with the applicable jurisdiction's Statute of Wills.

If a testamentary trust does not meet the requirements of the Statute of Wills, it may still be deemed a constructive trust or a resulting trust, depending on whether it is "secret" or "semi-secret."

1) "Secret" trust

A "secret" trust is not a testamentary trust. It looks like a testamentary gift, but it is created in reliance on the named beneficiary's promise to hold and administer the property for another. The intended beneficiary is permitted to present extrinsic evidence to prove the promise. If the promise is proven by clear and convincing evidence, then a constructive trust is imposed on the property for the intended beneficiary, so as to prevent the unjust enrichment of the "secret" trustee.

2) "Semi-secret" trust

A "semi-secret" trust is also not a testamentary trust. A semi-secret trust occurs when a gift is directed in a will to be held in trust, but the testator fails to name a beneficiary or specify the terms or purpose of the trust. In this situation, extrinsic evidence may not be presented, the gift fails, and a resulting trust is imposed on the property to be held in trust for the testator's heirs.

3) Modern trend

Most jurisdictions still respect the common-law distinction between "secret" and "semi-secret" trusts. However, the modern trend and that adopted by the Restatement (Third) of Trusts, § 18, calls for the imposition of a constructive trust in favor of the intended beneficiaries (if known) in both "secret" and "semi-secret" trust situations.

B. CHARITABLE TRUSTS

For a trust to be considered charitable, it must have a stated charitable purpose and it must exist for the benefit of the community at large or for a class of persons the membership in which varies. For public-policy reasons, charitable trusts are usually construed quite liberally by the courts.

1. Charitable Purpose

Purposes considered to be charitable include:

i) The relief of poverty;

ii) The advancement of education or religion;

iii) The promotion of good health;

iv) Governmental or municipal purposes; and

v) Other purposes benefiting the community at large or a particular segment of the community.

While a certain political party is not deemed to be a charitable beneficiary, those seeking to advance a political movement may be charitable beneficiaries. A determination as to whether or not a beneficiary is charitable involves an inquiry into the predominant purpose of the organization and the determination of whether or not the organization is aimed at making a profit.

The rules applying to charitable trusts are not applicable to those with both charitable and noncharitable purposes, unless two separate and distinct trust shares are capable of being administered, in which case the rules are applicable to the charitable share.

A charitable purpose can be found even if the settlor created the trust out of noncharitable motives.

a. Benevolent trusts

A merely benevolent trust is not a charitable trust unless the acts called for therein fall under the acceptable charitable purposes listed above. Most courts no longer belabor the distinction between benevolent and charitable trusts.

b. Modern trend—validate as charitable

The modern trend is to characterize a trust as charitable if possible.

2. Indefinite Beneficiaries

The community at large, or a class comprising unidentifiable members, not a named individual or a narrow group of individuals, must be the beneficiary of a charitable trust. It is possible that a very small class could still qualify as a charitable beneficiary. Further, even though the direct beneficiary may be a private individual, a charitable trust may be found when the community at large is an **indirect** beneficiary of the trust; for example, when a trust is established to put a beneficiary through law school, but it stipulates that the beneficiary must spend a certain number of years of legal practice in the service of low-income clients.

3. Rule Against Perpetuities

Charitable trusts are not subject to the Rule Against Perpetuities and may continue indefinitely. A trust can be created that calls for transfers of interest among charities, but it cannot direct the transfer of interest between a charitable beneficiary and a noncharitable beneficiary.

Example: A gift "to Sussex County Courts for as long as the premises is used as a courthouse, and if the premises shall ever cease to be so used, then to Sussex County United Way" is valid.

4. *Cy Pres* **Doctrine**

In an effort to carry out the testator's intent, under the *cy pres* doctrine, a court may modify a charitable trust to seek an alternative charitable purpose if the original charitable purpose becomes illegal, impracticable, or impossible to perform. The court must determine the settlor's primary purpose and select a new purpose "as near as possible" to the original purpose.

Because the Rule Against Perpetuities is not applicable to charitable trusts, courts are called upon to apply *cy pres* often. The settlor's intent controls, so if it appears that the settlor would not have wished that an alternative charitable purpose be selected, the trust property may instead be subject to a resulting trust for the benefit of the settlor's estate.

EXAM NOTE: If it is difficult to achieve the charitable trust purpose, apply the *cy pres* doctrine before applying a resulting trust.

---

a. Inefficiency insufficient

Cy pres is not invoked merely upon the belief that the modified scheme would be a more desirable, more effective, or more efficient use of the trust property.

b. Uniform Trust Code (UTC)

The UTC and the Restatement (Third) of Trusts both presume a general charitable purpose and authorize the application of *cy pres* even if the settlor's intent is not known.

5. Contrast: Honorary Trusts

An honorary trust is one that is not created for charitable purposes but has no private beneficiaries. The most common example is a trust for the care of a beloved pet. In the case of an honorary trust, the trustee is on her honor to administer the trust because there are no beneficiaries capable of enforcing its terms. Should the trustee fail to do so, a resulting trust may be imposed for the benefit of the settlor's estate.

A common problem that arises in the context of an honorary trust is the attempted application of the Rule Against Perpetuities. Such application is sometimes circumvented by using the trustee's life as the life in being, or by assuming that the trust will be exhausted before the perpetuities period has run.

6. Standing to Enforce

The attorney general of the state of the trust's creation and members of the community who are more directly affected than the general community usually have standing to enforce the terms of the trust and the trustee's duties. Under UTC § 405, a settlor also has standing to enforce the trust, even if she has not expressly retained an interest.

III. REMEDIAL TRUSTS

A remedial trust is an equitable remedy created by operation of law and therefore is not subject to the trust creation requirements, nor can it be challenged on Statute of Wills or Statute of Frauds grounds.

Remedial trusts are passive in that the sole duty of the trustee is to convey the trust property to the beneficiary. After this has been accomplished, the trust terminates.

A. RESULTING TRUST

When a trust fails in some way or when there is an incomplete disposition of trust property, a court may create a resulting trust requiring the holder of the property to return it to the settlor or to the settlor's estate. When a testamentary trust fails, the residuary legatee succeeds to the property interest. The purpose of a resulting trust is to achieve the settlor's likely intent in attempting to create the trust.

The primary aim of a resulting trust is the prevention of unjust enrichment. Resulting trusts may be imposed when there is:

i) A purchase-money resulting trust (i.e., title is taken in the name of one party (the holder), but some other party supplied the consideration), which creates a rebuttable presumption of unjust enrichment of the holder, unless:

   a) There is a close familial relationship between the holder of the property and the purchaser; or

   b) The purchaser manifests an intention to make a gift or loan to the holder;

ii) A failure of an express trust, either because the trust is void or unenforceable or because the beneficiary cannot be located, unless the trust provides for disposition of the trust property in cases in which the trust may fail; or

iii) There is an incomplete disposition of trust assets due to an excess corpus.

In the case of a purchase-money resulting trust, any valuable consideration other than money is sufficient so long as it is for the purchase of the property rather than for improvements, and the consideration is given at or before the time the trustee takes title. If the party claiming to be the beneficiary can prove by clear and convincing evidence that he supplied the consideration, then there is a rebuttable presumption that a resulting trust was created. However, the trustee may rebut that presumption by indicating that there was no intention to create a trust.

Modern courts will weigh the gravity of the unjust enrichment in making determinations as to whether or not to impose a resulting trust.

> **Example:** X pays the purchase price for property and causes title to the property to be taken in Y's name. Y is not a natural object of X's affection. A so-called "purchase-money resulting trust" will be created, under which the sole duty of the trustee is to return the property to the settlor or his estate.

B. CONSTRUCTIVE TRUST

Courts use constructive trusts to prevent unjust enrichment if the settlor causes: fraud, duress, undue influence, breach of duty, or detrimental reliance by a third party on a false representation.

There must have been wrongful conduct in order to impose a constructive trust. The tracing doctrine may be applied if trust property has already been sold or otherwise disposed of, allowing the beneficiary of the constructive trust to pursue the sale proceeds or other property received. In such a case, the constructive trust may be imposed either against the seller or against the buyer. However, a breach of a promise will not give rise to a constructive trust unless the promise is fraudulent, the breach is related to the devisee's or heir's promise to hold property for a third party, the breach is one in a confidential relationship, or there is a breach by the buyer to the debtor at a foreclosure sale. The burden of clear and convincing evidence is on the party seeking the constructive trust.

A constructive trust will almost always be imposed when one individual commits homicide and thereby benefits from his victim's estate.

A party with unclean hands will usually be estopped from arguing for the creation of a constructive trust.

C. GIFT-OVER CLAUSE

Some trusts include gift-over clauses, which provide for a disposition of the trust property in the event the trust purpose fails. Jurisdictions are mixed as to the treatment of such clauses, but many will honor such a clause before imposing an equitable remedy.

IV. RIGHT OF BENEFICIARIES AND CREDITORS TO DISTRIBUTION

It is the beneficiary's right to receive income or principal from the trust. Various devices have been developed to protect the trust property (and thus the beneficiary's interest) from creditors. Generally speaking, however, once trust property has been distributed to the beneficiary, any attempt to restrain the transferability of the beneficiary's interest will be invalid.

A. ALIENATION

A beneficiary's equitable interest in trust property is freely alienable unless a statute or the trust instrument limits this right. Because a transferee cannot have a greater right than what was transferred to him, any transferee from a beneficiary, including a creditor, takes an interest identical to what was held by the beneficiary.

Unless otherwise provided by statute or under the trust instrument, a beneficiary's equitable interest is also subject to involuntary alienation. A beneficiary's creditors may reach trust principal or income only when such amounts become payable to the beneficiary or are subject to her demand.

B. SUPPORT TRUST

A support trust directs the trustee to pay income or principal as necessary to support the trust beneficiary.

Creditors cannot reach the assets of a support trust, except to the extent that a provider of a necessity to the beneficiary can be paid directly by the trustee.

The Internal Revenue Code set an "ascertainable standard" limiting distributions to amounts needed for a beneficiary's "health, education, support, and maintenance." I.R.C. § 2041(b).

C. DISCRETIONARY TRUST

If the trustee is given complete discretion regarding whether or not to apply payments of income or principal to the beneficiary, then a discretionary trust exists.

If the trustee exercises his discretion to pay, then the beneficiary's creditors have the same rights as the beneficiary, unless a spendthrift restriction exists (discussed *infra* at § IV.F.). If the discretion to pay is not exercised, then the beneficiary's interest cannot be reached by his creditors.

The beneficiary of a fully discretionary trust lacks standing to challenge the actions or inactions of the trustee unless there is a clear abuse of discretion.

D. MANDATORY TRUST

A mandatory trust is the most restrictive type of trust; it is essentially the opposite of a discretionary trust. The trustee of a mandatory trust has no discretion regarding payments; instead, the trust document explains specifically and in detail how and when the trust property is to be distributed.

E. SPENDTHRIFT TRUST (RESTRAINT ON ALIENATION)

A spendthrift trust expressly restricts the beneficiary's power to voluntarily or involuntarily transfer his equitable interest. (Note that a trust restricting only involuntary transfers would be void as against public policy.) Spendthrift provisions are often inserted into trusts to protect beneficiaries from their own imprudence.

The spendthrift restriction applies only as long as the property remains in the trust, and it is inapplicable after it has been paid out to the beneficiary. An attempted transfer by the beneficiary in violation of the spendthrift restriction is effective only in that it provides authorization for the trustee to pay funds directly into the hands of the attempted transferee.

1. Exceptions

A beneficiary's creditors usually cannot reach the beneficiary's trust interest in satisfaction of their claims if the governing instrument contains a spendthrift clause prohibiting a beneficiary's creditors from attaching the beneficiary's interest. Although generally valid, most states allow certain classes of creditors to reach a beneficiary's assets, notwithstanding the spendthrift clause.

The spendthrift clause exception applies to:

i) Children and spouses entitled to support;

ii) Those providing basic necessities to the beneficiary; and

iii) Holders of federal or state tax liens.

Additionally, courts will not enforce spendthrift clauses if the settlor is also the beneficiary, because this would provide an easy way for individuals to avoid their creditors. When the settlor of a trust is also a trust beneficiary, his creditors are entitled to the maximum amount that could be distributed from the trust to the settlor, even when withdrawals are discretionary or limited by a support standard. If it is unclear whether the settlor is also the beneficiary, the courts will examine who provided the consideration for the creation of the trust.

2. Statutory Limitation

If a trust contains a spendthrift clause, then the beneficiary's interest is not reachable in bankruptcy proceedings. Further, the Employee Retirement Income Security Act (ERISA) mandates that an employee's pension benefits cannot be reached by creditors.

V. TRUST MODIFICATION

A. TERMINATION

A trust automatically terminates only when the trust purpose has been accomplished. Subject to the *Claflin* doctrine, discussed below, a trust may terminate **by consent** if the settlor is deceased or has no remaining interest in the trust, and if all of the beneficiaries and the trustee consent to the termination. The trustee by herself cannot terminate a trust. If all of the beneficiaries wish to terminate, but the trustee objects, then most courts allow the trustee to block the termination if she can show that termination would violate the settlor's intent.

1. Unfulfilled Material Purpose

Under the *Claflin* doctrine, a trustee can block a premature trust termination—even one to which all of the beneficiaries have consented—if the trust is shown to have an unfulfilled material purpose. Examples of a trust that intrinsically has an unfulfilled material purpose include discretionary trusts, support trusts, spendthrift trusts, and age-dependent trusts (those that direct the payment of principal to a beneficiary only after he attains a certain age). The most common example of a trust that has an unfulfilled material purpose is one in which the settlor provided for successive interests, in which case both the present and the future beneficiaries must agree in order for the trust to be terminated prematurely. Restatement (Third) of Trusts § 65(2).

> If a testator leaves property "to A for life, remainder to B," and B dies before A, leaving his interest to A, then A may terminate the trust because its purpose has been accomplished.

2. Revocation by Will

The traditional rule required a trust to expressly provide for its revocability by will. The UTC authorizes trust revocation by will unless the trust expressly provides for another method of revocation.

3. Revocation by Divorce

Traditionally, a spousal interest created by a trust, unlike one created by a will, was not revoked upon divorce. However, the trend now is to treat a spousal interest under a trust similarly to one under a will. *See* UPC § 2-804.

4. Equitable Deviation and Unanticipated Circumstances

A court may modify the terms of a trust if events that were unanticipated by the trustee have occurred, and the changes would further the purposes of the trust. To the extent possible, the modification must be made in accordance with the settlor's probable intention. Uniform Trust Code § 412(a).

Even if circumstances have not changed in an unanticipated manner, a court may modify the terms of a trust that relate to the management of trust property if continuation of the trust on its existing terms would be impracticable, wasteful, or would impair the trust's administration. Uniform Trust Code § 412(b).

Modification under the doctrine of equitable deviation does not require the court to seek beneficiary consent. *See* Uniform Trust Code § 411, cmt; Restatement (Third) of Trusts §§ 65, 66.

5. Court Termination of Trust

A court may prematurely terminate a trust if the trust's purpose has been achieved, or if it has become illegal, impracticable, or impossible.

B. SETTLOR'S INTENT

In most states, a settlor must expressly reserve the right to modify or terminate a trust in order to be granted such powers. In the absence of such a reservation, modification or termination can occur only with the consent of all beneficiaries and if the proposed change will not interfere with a primary purpose of the trust.

Although it is possible for a court to modify or terminate a trust over the objections of the settlor, a modification or termination is much more likely to be granted if the settlor joins in the action, because the *Claflin* material-purpose test is satisfied under such circumstances.

C. TRUSTEE'S POWER TO TERMINATE

A trustee has no power to terminate a trust unless the trust instrument contains express termination provisions.

VI. PRINCIPAL AND INCOME ALLOCATIONS

A. ALLOCATING PRINCIPAL AND INCOME

Generally, life beneficiaries are entitled to the trust income, and remaindermen are entitled to the trust principal. The beneficiary of trust principal is not entitled to trust principal until termination of all preceding estates. The remainder beneficiary has no immediate right to the possession and enjoyment of any trust property. The remainder beneficiary must await the termination of the trust to receive any trust property. All assets received by a trustee must be allocated to either income or principal. The allocation must be balanced so as to treat present and future trust beneficiaries fairly, unless a different treatment is authorized by the trust instrument.

1. Traditional Approach

The traditional approach assumed that any money generated by trust property was income and that any money generated in connection with a conveyance of trust property was principal. The traditional approach serves as the starting point for the modern approach.

2. Modern Approach

The Uniform Principal and Income Act (UPAIA), adopted in most states, focuses on total return to the trust portfolio, regardless of classifications of income or principal. Under the UPAIA, a trustee is empowered to re-characterize items and reallocate investment returns as he deems necessary to fulfill the trust purposes, as long as his allocations are reasonable and are in keeping with the trust instrument.

The trustee may not make adjustments under the UPAIA if he is also a trust beneficiary.

a. Factors to consider

The trustee must balance the following factors in determining how best to exercise such allocation:

i) The intent of the settlor and the language of the trust instrument;

ii) The nature, likely duration, and purpose of the trust;

iii) The identities and circumstances of the beneficiaries;

iv) The relative needs for regularity of income, preservation and appreciation of capital, and liquidity;

v) The net amount allocated to income under other sections of the act and the increase and decrease in the value of principal assets;

vi) The anticipated effect of economic conditions on income and principal; and

vii) The anticipated tax consequences of the adjustment.

b. Unitrust

Under a unitrust, the distinction between income and principal is not relevant because the lifetime beneficiaries are entitled to a fixed annual share of the value of the trust principal.

c. Unproductive property rule

Under the traditional approach, if a trust asset produced little or no income upon the asset's sale, then an income beneficiary was entitled to some portion of the sale proceeds under the theory that such portion represented delayed income thereon. With the emphasis having shifted to the total return from the entire portfolio and away from individual investments, this rule is now seldom applied.

d. Distributions of stock

Under UPAIA § 6(a) and most states, a distribution of stock, whether classified as a dividend or as a split, is treated as a distribution of principal. This is also true under the Revised Uniform Principal and Income Act (RUPIA). The RUPIA gives a trustee a limited power to allocate the stock dividend between income and the principal when the distributing corporation made no distributions to shareholders except in the form of dividends paid in stock.

B. ALLOCATION OF RECEIPTS

Generally, except in cases in which the application of the UPAIA is justified, allocation rules follow traditional accounting rules.

1. Amounts Received Generally

Generally, an amount received in exchange for trust property (e.g., proceeds from the sale of trust property) is allocated to **principal**. By contrast, an amount received for the use of trust property (e.g., rents received from tenants of trust property, interest received from a bank on trust funds deposited with the bank, cash dividends on stock owned by the trust) is allocated to **income**.

2. Contract Proceeds

Proceeds from life insurance policies or other contracts in which the trust or trustee is named as a beneficiary are allocated to principal unless the contract insures the trustee against loss, in which case the proceeds are allocated to income.

3. Deferred Compensation Plan Proceeds

Receipts from a deferred compensation plan (e.g., a pension plan) are considered income if characterized as such by the payor and likewise are principal if so characterized. If the payor does not characterize the payment as income or principal, then 10% of the payment is income and the rest is principal.

4. Liquidating Assets

A liquidating asset is one whose value diminishes over time because the asset is only expected to produce receipts over a limited period (e.g., patents or copyrights). Proceeds from liquidating assets are also allocated as 10% income and 90% principal.

5. Mineral Rights

Oil, gas, mineral, and water rights payments are also allocated as 10% income and 90% principal.

C. ALLOCATION OF EXPENSES

1. Expenses Charged to Income

Trust income will be charged with the following expenses:

   i) One-half of the regular compensation to the trustee and to those who provide investment, advisory, or custodial services to the trustee;

   ii) One-half of accounting costs, court costs, and the costs of other matters affecting trust interests;

   iii) Ordinary expenses in their entirety; and

   iv) Insurance premiums that cover the loss of a trust asset.

2. Expenses Charged to Principal

Trust principal will be charged with the following expenses:

   i) The remaining one-half of the regular compensation to the trustee and to those who provide services to the trustee;

   ii) The remaining one-half of accounting costs, court costs, and the costs of other matters affecting trust interests;

iii) All payments on the principal of any trust debt;

iv) All expenses of any proceeding that concerns an interest in principal;

v) Estate taxes; and

vi) All payments related to environmental matters.

VII. TRUST ADMINISTRATION AND THE TRUSTEE'S DUTIES

Before any duties are imposed, the trustee must accept the trusteeship. The trustee is then charged with safeguarding the trust property by purchasing insurance, earmarking assets, recording deeds, identifying and locating beneficiaries, and following the settlor's instructions. The trustee acts as a fiduciary, and, in most cases, his powers are not personal but rather attach to his office.

If there are two trustees, the majority of states require them to act with unanimity absent a contrary intent expressed in the trust agreement. If there are more than two trustees, however, most states require a majority only.

As a general proposition, a trustee's duties cannot be unilaterally enlarged by the settlor after the trustee has accepted his office. A well-drafted trust instrument will therefore include an **additions clause** if the settlor contemplates enlarging the trustee's responsibilities with additional trust assets. Even then, a trustee may be able to reject additions.

A. POWERS

1. Within a Trust Document

Common law grants powers to the trustee outside of those authorized within the trust document.

a. Judicial authorization

The trustee can petition the court to obtain powers not expressly authorized in the trust.

b. Modern trend

The modern trend is for the court to grant the trustee all those powers necessary to act as a reasonably prudent person in managing the trust.

2. Power to Sell or Contract

Unless otherwise provided in the trust instrument, a trustee generally has the implied power to contract, sell, lease, or transfer the trust property.

If the settlor specifies that the trustee may not sell certain property, then such property may not be sold without a valid court order permitting the sale, which order will be granted only if selling is necessary to save the trust.

3. Liability of Third Parties

A third party can potentially be held liable for his role in a breach of trust. Common law presumed that the purpose of a trust was to preserve the trust property, requiring those dealing with trustees to carefully inspect the trust property before dealing with the trustee. The modern trend presumes that the purpose of a trust is to hold and manage the trust property, and it provides greater protection to third parties.

a. Uniform Trustees' Powers Act (UTPA)

The UTPA obligates third parties to act in good faith and to give valuable consideration. Under the UTPA, third parties are protected as long as they act without actual knowledge that such action constitutes a breach of trust.

4. Other Common Trustee Powers

There are a variety of powers that the trust settlor may give to the trustee to carry out the trust's purpose.

a. Power to revoke

When the settlor names himself as trustee, the trust normally contains a power to revoke, which allows the settlor as trustee to revoke the trust in part or in its entirety.

b. Power to withdraw

Many trusts give the trustee the power to withdraw income, principal, or both from the trust to carry out the trust's purpose. The power to withdraw could also be conferred upon the settlor, which would enable the settlor to withdraw assets from the trust without revoking it.

c. Power to modify

The settlor may include the power to modify in order to give the trustee the ability to change provisions of the trust to reflect the settlor's intent.

B. DUTY OF LOYALTY AND GOOD FAITH

A trustee is bound by a broad range of fiduciary duties designed to ensure that she acts solely in the best interests of the beneficiaries when investing property and otherwise managing the trust. The trustee has a duty to administer the trust in good faith, in accordance with its terms and purposes, and in the interest of the beneficiaries. Any beneficiary has standing against the trustee if his interests are violated, and he can choose either to set aside the transaction or to ratify the transaction and recover any profits therefrom.

Even if a trustee is granted complete discretion under the trust instrument, her actions are not immune from review if it can be shown that she failed to exercise good judgment. When the trustee's decision is based exclusively on personal reasons unrelated to the settlor's goals, the trustee's decision may be overturned.

> **EXAM NOTE:** On the exam, determine whether the trustee acted reasonably (objective standard) *and* in good faith (subjective standard). Good faith alone is not enough.

1. Self-Dealing

When a trustee personally engages in a transaction involving the trust property, a conflict of interest arises between the trustee's duties to the beneficiaries and her own personal interest. The following are generally prohibited transactions with trust property:

i) Buying or selling trust assets (even at fair market value);

ii) Selling property of one trust to another trust that the trustee manages;

iii) Borrowing from or making loans to the trust;

iv) Using trust assets to secure a personal loan;

v) Engaging in prohibited transactions with friends or relatives; or

vi) Otherwise acting for personal gain through the trustee position.

> **Example:** A trustee sells stock from the trust to himself for fair market value. If the stock then goes up in value, the beneficiaries can trace and recover the stock for the benefit of the trust.

a. Irrebuttable presumption

When self-dealing is an issue, an irrebuttable presumption is created that the trustee breached the duty of loyalty.

> A trustee can employ herself as an attorney and can receive reasonable compensation, as long as the use of an attorney does not constitute a breach of trust.

b. No further inquiry

Once self-dealing is established, there need be no further inquiry into the trustee's reasonableness or good faith because self-dealing is a per se breach of the duty of loyalty.

c. Exceptions

Even when self-dealing is authorized by the settlor under the terms of the trust, by court order, or by all beneficiaries, the transaction must still be reasonable and fair for the trustee to avoid being liable for breach.

Courts tend to strictly interpret attempted exculpatory clauses relieving trustees from liability. Complete exculpatory clauses are void as contrary to public policy, and limited clauses are only honored if there is no finding of bad faith or unreasonableness.

1) Uniform Trust Act (UTA)

Under the UTA, a trustee can avoid liability if he can prove that the transaction was objectively fair and reasonable, and not affected by a conflict of interest.

2) Statutory exceptions

Many states have enacted statutes permitting a bank trust department to deposit trust assets in its own banking department, and trustees are authorized to receive reasonable compensation for their services.

2. Conflicts of Interest

If an alleged conflict of interest arises that cannot be characterized as self-dealing, then the "no further inquiry" standard is inapplicable, and the transaction is assessed under the "reasonable and in good faith" standard. The UTC provides that an investment in a corporation in which the trustee has an interest that might affect the trustee's best judgment is presumptively a breach of the duty of loyalty. The presumption of a breach can be rebutted by showing that the terms of the transaction were fair or that the transaction would have been made by an independent party. *See* Uniform Trust Code § 802(c).

> **Example:** T is the trustee for trusts A, B, and C and sells assets from trust A to trust B at fair market value. The assets increase in value after the sale. T had a conflict of interest as both the buyer and seller, but because T did not personally benefit, the presumption of self-dealing is not applicable. If T acted in good faith and did not reasonably anticipate a significant change in value, then T may not be liable for any lost profits by beneficiaries of trust A.

3. Legal Attacks on Trusts

Unless a challenge is well founded, the trustee must defend the trust against legal attacks.

4. Abuse of Discretion

Even if a trustee has complete discretion over a trust, she must still act in the best interests of the trust and its beneficiaries.

C. DUTY OF PRUDENCE

At common law, a trustee could not delegate any discretionary responsibilities because doing so would be assumed to be contrary to the settlor's intent. Under modern law, the trustee may delegate responsibilities if it would be unreasonable for the settlor to require the trustee to perform such tasks.

If a function goes to the heart of the trust or constitutes a critical function concerning the property, then the function is discretionary and is not delegable. Otherwise, the function is merely ministerial and can be delegated. These same rules apply when a trustee delegates to a co-trustee.

1. Duty to Oversee Decisions

A trustee can delegate the determination of management and investment strategies, and other duties as would be prudent under the circumstances, but must oversee the decision-making process. Otherwise, the trustee is responsible for actual losses, regardless of cause.

2. Trust Investments

At common law, trustees were limited to statutory lists of acceptable investments unless the trust instrument expressly authorized a deviation from the list. Only a few states continue to adhere to such lists.

a. Statutory legal lists

Statutory lists can be either permissive, which means the trustee may invest in securities not on the list, or mandatory, in which case the trustee must invest only in securities that are on the list. In either case, the trustee must use reasonable care, caution, and skill. Additionally, the trustee must be expressly authorized to carry on the testator's business. Generally, unsecured loans and second mortgages are improper investments. Other investments such as stocks, bonds, government securities, and mutual funds are considered proper investments.

b. Model Prudent Man Investment Act (MPMIA)

The MPMIA, first adopted in 1940, is still followed in some states and permits any investment that a prudent man would make, barring only speculative investments.

c. Uniform Prudent Investor Act (UPIA)

The UPIA, adopted by the Restatement (Third) of Trusts and the Trustee Act 2000, requires the trustee to act as a prudent investor would when investing his own property but puts less emphasis on the level of risk for each investment. The trustee must exercise reasonable care, caution, and skill when investing and managing trust assets unless the trustee has special skills or expertise, in which case he has a duty to utilize such assets.

Determinations of compliance under the UPIA are made with reference to the facts and circumstances as they existed at the time the action was made, and they do not utilize hindsight. In assessing whether a trustee has breached this duty, the UPIA requires consideration of numerous factors, including (i) the distribution requirements of the trust, (ii) general economic conditions, (iii) the role that the investment plays in relationship to the trust's overall investment portfolio, and (iv) the trust's need for liquidity, regularity of income, and preservation or appreciation of capital. UPIA § 2.

1) Duty to diversify assets

The trustee must adequately diversify the trust investments to spread the risk of loss. Under the UPIA, investing in one mutual fund may be sufficient if the fund is sufficiently diversified.

a) Individual versus corporate trustees

A presumed greater expertise creates a higher standard for professional or corporate trustees than for individual trustees.

b) Duty not absolute

A trustee is justified in not diversifying if the administrative costs of doing so (including tax consequences or changes in controlling interest of a family-run business) would outweigh the benefits.

With respect to a revocable trust, a trustee's duties are owed exclusively to the settlor. When a trust is irrevocable, acting in accordance with a settlor's directives is inadequate to absolve a trustee from liability because the trustee's obligations are owed to trust beneficiaries. However, when there are no income beneficiaries other than the settlor, the settlor may be treated as the effective owner. *See* UPIA § 3.

2) Duty to make property productive

The trustee must preserve trust property and work to make it productive by pursuing all possible claims, deriving the maximum amount of income from investments, selling assets when appropriate, securing insurance, paying ordinary and necessary expenses, and acting within a reasonable period of time in all matters.

3) Commingling trust funds

The common-law approach required each trust fund to be separated from other trust funds and from the trustee's own funds. To decrease costs and increase diversity, the modern trend is to allow some commingling of trust funds and investment in mutual funds.

If a trustee commingles trust assets with his own property and some property is lost or destroyed, however, there is a presumption that the lost or destroyed property was the trustee's and that the remaining property belongs to the trust.

Additionally, if one part of the commingled assets increases in value and another part decreases in value, there is a presumption that the assets with increased value belong to the trust and that the assets with decreased value belong to the trustee.

4) Decision making

Part of being prudent is taking care to make informed decisions regarding the investment scheme and/or delegating such decision making to an expert.

d. Modern trend—portfolio approach

The UPIA assesses a trustee's investments based on the total performance of the trust, as opposed to looking at individual investments, so that a high-risk investment that would have been considered too risky under the common law can be offset by lower-risk investments.

The law has evolved away from the common-law statutory lists and toward the prudent investor standard and the modern trend portfolio theory. Diversification has become increasingly important, as has the trustee's duty to create a paper trail supporting the reasonableness of his actions. It is recognized that in today's market, there is a strong correlation between risk and reward, and it is undesirable for trustees to be limited to low-risk investments in the current climate. However, risk tolerance varies greatly depending upon the size and the purpose of the particular trust, both of which will be taken into account in evaluating the actions of the trustee.

e. Authorized investments

Exculpatory clauses that expressly authorize all investments do not protect a trustee who acts in bad faith or recklessly, but they do give trustees more room for minor lapses in judgment.

3. Duty to Be Impartial

A trustee has a duty to balance the often-conflicting interests of the present and future beneficiaries by investing the property so that it produces a reasonable income while preserving the principal for the remaindermen.

a. Duty to sell

Regardless of what the trust document says about the trustee's ability to retain trust assets, a trustee has a duty to sell trust property within a reasonable time if a failure to diversify would be inconsistent with the modern portfolio approach.

Any delay in disposing of under-performing or over-performing property creates a duty in the trustee to reallocate sale proceeds to those beneficiaries who were adversely affected by the delay.

> **EXAM NOTE:** If a fact pattern indicates that either (i) the trust principal is appreciating but not generating a reasonable stream of income, or (ii) the trust is producing a good amount of income but the principal is depreciating, then your analysis should center on the duty of impartiality. In these situations, the trustee may be favoring one class of beneficiaries over the other.

D. INFORM AND ACCOUNT

1. Duty to Disclose

A trustee must disclose to the beneficiaries complete and accurate information about the nature and extent of the trust property, including allowing access to trust records and accounts. The trustee must also identify possible breaches of trust and promptly disclose such information to the beneficiaries.

a. Settlor's intent

The UTC requires the trustee to promptly provide a copy of the trust instrument upon request, unless otherwise provided by the settlor in the instrument.

b. Duty to notify

Unless disclosure would be severely detrimental to the beneficiaries, the trustee must notify the beneficiaries if he intends to sell a significant portion of the trust assets.

2. Duty to Account

A trustee must periodically account for actions taken on behalf of the trust so that his performance can be assessed against the terms of the trust. Trustees of testamentary trusts must account to the probate court. The UTC allows the settlor to waive the trustee's duty to report to the beneficiaries, or the beneficiaries can waive the receipt of reports.

> Waiver of the duty to report does not relieve a trustee from liability for misconduct that would have been disclosed by a report.

a. Constructive fraud

Constructive fraud occurs if an accounting includes **false factual statements** that could have been discovered to be false had the trustee properly investigated.

E. OTHER DUTIES

1. Duty to Secure Possession

The trustee must secure possession of the property within a reasonable period of time. In the case of a testamentary trust, the trustee must monitor the executor's actions to ensure that the trust receives all of that to which it is entitled.

2. Duty to Maintain

In caring for real property, the trustee must take whatever steps an ordinary owner would take, including insuring, repairing, and otherwise maintaining the property.

3. Duty to Segregate

The trustee must separate his personal property (such as money and stocks) from trust assets to ensure that they cannot be switched if one outperforms the other. An exception to this duty to segregate applies when a trustee invests in bearer bonds.

Under common law, the trustee was strictly liable for damages to the trust property even if they were not caused by a breach of the duty to segregate. The modern trend holds the trustee liable only when the breach causes the damage to the trust property.

F. POWERS OF APPOINTMENT

Usually given to a beneficiary, a power of appointment enables the holder to direct a trustee to distribute some or all of the trust property without regard to the provisions of the trust. A special power of appointment allows the donor to specify certain individuals or groups as the objects of the power, to the exclusion of others. The power can be limited as to recipient and time of exercising.

1. Interests Appointable

The donee of a power of appointment can direct the appointment of an interest of equal or lesser value to that specified in the power given to her. Thus, if a donee can appoint trust assets outright, she can also give, for example, a life estate to a permissible beneficiary.

2. Ineffective Appointments

When one with a power of appointment makes an appointment that exceeds the grant given to him, other valid appointments are not invalidated, but the property or interest that was invalidly appointed passes to the "taker in default of appointment"—that party who would have received the interest in the absence of any appointment.

VIII. TRUSTEE'S LIABILITIES

A. BENEFICIARIES' RIGHT OF ENFORCEMENT

Lost profits, lost interests, and other losses resulting from a breach of trust are the responsibility of the trustee, and beneficiaries may sue the trustee and seek damages or removal of the trustee for breach. The trustee is also not allowed to offset losses resulting from the breach against any gains from another breach. If the beneficiaries joined the breach or consented to the trustee's actions, however, equity will prevent the beneficiaries from pursuing an action against the trustee. Note, though, that a beneficiary's failure to object to the breach does not rise to the level of consent.

B. LIABILITIES FOR OTHERS' ACTS

1. Co-trustee Liability

Co-trustees are jointly liable, although the liability may be limited if only one trustee acts in bad faith or benefited personally from the breach. A co-trustee may be liable for breach for:

i) Consenting to the action constituting the breach;

ii) Negligently failing to act to prevent the breach;

iii) Concealing the breach or failing to compel redress; or

iv) Improperly delegating authority to a co-trustee.

2. Liability for Predecessor and Successor Trustees

If a trustee knew of his predecessor's breach and failed to address it or was negligent in delivering the property, then the trustee will be liable for his predecessor's breach. Successor trustees can maintain the same actions as the original trustees.

3. Trustee's Liability for Agents

A trustee is not liable for breaches committed by an agent unless the trustee:

i) Directs, permits, or acquiesces in the agent's act;

ii) Conceals the agent's act;

iii) Negligently fails to compel the agent to redress the wrong;

iv) Fails to exercise reasonable supervision over the agent;

v) Permits the agent to perform duties that the trustee was not entitled to delegate; or

vi) Fails to use reasonable care in the selection or retention of agents.

No clear-cut standard for the delegation of duties to agents exists, but it is clear that a trustee cannot delegate his duties in their entirety, but rather should limit the delegation to ministerial duties.

C. THIRD PARTIES

1. Trustee's Liability to Third Parties

Unless otherwise specified in the trust instrument or in the governing contract, a trustee is personally liable on contracts entered into and for tortious acts committed while acting as trustee. If he acted within the scope of his duties, then he is entitled to indemnification from the trust.

2. Liability of Third Parties to a Trust

When property is improperly transferred as a result of a breach of trust to a third party who is not a bona fide purchaser—one who takes for value and without notice—the beneficiary or successor trustee may have that transaction set aside. If, on the other hand, the third party is a knowing participant in the breach, then he is liable as well for any losses suffered by the trust.

Because only the trustee is allowed to bring a cause of action against the third party, the beneficiary is limited to bringing a suit in equity against the trustee to compel the trustee to sue the third party. In a situation in which (i) the trustee is a participant in the breach, (ii) the third party is liable in tort or contract and the trustee fails to pursue a cause of action, or (iii) there is no successor trustee, the beneficiary is given the option of directly suing the third party.

IX. RESIGNATION AND REMOVAL OF A TRUSTEE

A. RESIGNATION OF A TRUSTEE

A trustee may resign from the position by:

i) Providing at least 30 days' notice to the qualified beneficiaries, the settlor (if living), and any co-trustees; or

ii) Obtaining court approval.

In approving a resignation, the court may issue orders and impose conditions reasonably necessary for the protection of the trust property. In addition, any liability of a resigning trustee or of any sureties on the trustee's bond for acts or omissions of the trustee is not discharged or affected by the trustee's resignation.

B. REMOVAL OF A TRUSTEE

The court has the power to refuse to appoint or to remove a trustee if the purposes of the trust would be frustrated by the trustee's appointment or continuance in office. Absent an express provision in the trust instrument to the contrary, neither the settlor nor the trust beneficiaries are entitled to seek the removal of a trustee.

A trustee may be removed by the court under the following circumstances:

i) The trustee becomes incapable of performing his duties;

ii) The trustee materially breaches one or more of his duties;

iii) A conflict of interest arises;

iv) A serious conflict between the trustee and one or more beneficiaries, or between co-trustees, develops; or

v) The trust is persistently performing poorly as a result of the trustee's actions or inactions.

If any of the foregoing circumstances exist at the time the trustee is named and are known by the settlor, they will not necessarily suffice as grounds for removal.

A trustee who has resigned or has been removed must expeditiously deliver the trust property within the trustee's possession to the co-trustee, successor trustee, or other person entitled to the trust property. A trustee who has resigned or has been removed has the duties of trustee and the powers necessary to protect the trust property unless a co-trustee remains in the office of trustee or the court orders otherwise and until the trust property is delivered to a successor trustee or other person entitled to the trust property.

X.   FUTURE INTERESTS

A.   EQUITABLE INTERESTS

1.   Possessory Estate versus Future Interest

The party holding the possessory estate holds the present right to possess the property, whereas the future interest holders hold the present right to possess the property in the future.

2.   Common Law

At common law, if a future interest violated one of many technical drafting rules, it was typically null and void (which defeated the settlor's intent).

3.   Grantor's Future Interest

If a grantor retains a future interest, then it is a reversion, a possibility of reverter, or a right of entry.

4.   Beneficiary's Future Interest

If a beneficiary is given a future interest, then it is either a remainder or an executory interest.

B.   REVERSION

The most common future interest in the grantor is a reversion, in which the grantor has the right to possess the property after a finite estate ends. At common law, the three finite estates were the life estate, the estate for a term of years, and the fee tail.

If the grantor does not convey his entire interest but does not explicitly retain an interest, then a reversionary interest is implied.

C.   POSSIBILITY OF REVERTER

When the grantor conveys a fee simple determinable estate, he is deemed to have retained a possibility of reverter, wherein the right to possession reverts to the grantor, and the fee simple estate automatically ends, upon the happening of a specified condition or event.

D.   RIGHT OF ENTRY

When the grantor conveys a fee simple estate subject to a condition subsequent, then upon the happening of the condition subsequent, the grantor is deemed to have retained the right to enter or retake possession, but the fee simple does not end automatically.

E.   VESTED REMAINDER

A remainder is vested if the holder of the interest is ascertainable and there is no express condition precedent required before the interest becomes possessory. Under the common law, if a vested remainder is created by a trust, and the trust provides that should the beneficiary predecease the life tenant, the remainder should pass to the beneficiary's child, then the remainder divests only if the beneficiary has issue. In contrast, if the beneficiary dies without issue, the remainder does not divest, and it passes to the beneficiary's estate. Under the UPC, the result differs. Future interests under the UPC are contingent on the beneficiary surviving the distribution date. If the beneficiary does not survive the distribution date, then the interest does not vest and does not pass to either the beneficiary's issue or the beneficiary's estate.

F.   REMAINDER AS A CLASS GIFT

If the class is vested as to some but still open so that others can join it, then new members partially divest the previous members of the class in order to share the property equally.

G. EXECUTORY INTERESTS

If someone other than the grantor holds an interest that is followed by either a vested remainder subject to divestment or a fee simple subject to an executory limitation, then that person holds an executory interest.

H. PREFERENCE FOR VESTED REMAINDERS

1. Destructibility of Contingent Remainders

At common law, legal contingent remainders in real property were destroyed if they failed to vest before or at the moment the preceding estate ended. The modern trend abolishes the destructibility of contingent remainders.

2. Acceleration Into Possession

A vested remainder accelerates into possession as soon as the preceding estate ends for any reason, such as the disclaiming of the estate by its holder(s), whereas a contingent remainder does not vest until all conditions precedent have been satisfied. If the income beneficiary of a trust disclaims her interest, then the trust principal becomes immediately distributable to the presumptive remainder beneficiaries of the trust, provided no one would be harmed by making a distribution to them earlier than it would have been made had the income beneficiary not disclaimed.

a. When disclaimer is effective

Almost all states have enacted statutes that permit beneficiaries of trusts to disclaim their interest in the trust property. In most states, a disclaimer is not effective unless it is reduced to writing within nine months after the future interest would become "indefeasibly vested." For a revocable trust or a testamentary trust, the future interest in a named beneficiary becomes "indefeasbly vested" when the settlor dies. When the holder of a future interest effectively disclaims that interest, the disclaimant is deemed to have predeceased the life tenant.

1) State law

Under the laws of some states, if a life tenant disclaims a gift, the disclaimer is effective as long as it is executed within nine months of the indefeasible vesting of the interest.

2) Federal tax laws

Under federal tax laws, the disclaimer must be executed within nine months of the creation of the interest in question to avoid estate or gift taxes.

b. Generation-skipping transfer tax

An estate tax may be owed when a decedent passes property at his death. When a decedent passes property to remote descendants, a generation-skipping tax may be owed.

3. Transferability

At common law, vested remainders were transferable, and contingent remainders were not. The modern trend allows the transfer of both vested and contingent remainders.

I. CLASS GIFTS

When a future interest in a trust is in the form of a gift to a group of individuals (i.e., a class gift), the class remains open and may admit new members until (i) at least one class member is entitled to obtain possession of the gift, or (ii) the preceding interest terminates (e.g., the holder of the present life interest dies).

1. Gifts to Surviving Children

Unless the governing instrument provides otherwise, the general rule is that the gift is expressly limited to the transferor's surviving children, so that the surviving issue of a deceased child does not take.

a. Interpretation of "surviving"

When an *inter vivos* trust specifies the beneficiaries as the settlor's "surviving children," but there is an intermediary interest in another party for a term of years, the question arises whether "surviving" refers to the life of the settlor or the expiration of the other interest, should the settlor die before such expiration. Most states construe "surviving" as referring to the time of distribution, such that only those beneficiaries who survived to the end of the intermediary interest would receive. However, the minority, common-law approach is to vest the interests of the beneficiaries at the settlor's death.

Under the UPC, if a class gift is limited in favor of a class of children, then only those children alive at the time of distribution are entitled to possession of the property. However, if a child who survives the settlor but then predeceases the time of distribution has surviving issue, that issue receives the share to which the parent would have been entitled had the parent been alive at the time of distribution (i.e., a substitute gift). UPC § 2-707(b)(3).

> **EXAM NOTE:** This concept is a somewhat controversial one. If presented with a fact pattern involving a trust that creates a vested remainder in a person and then provides that the remainder should pass to that person's child if the remainderman predeceases the life tenant, the result differs depending on whether the jurisdiction follows the UPC or common-law approach. Your discussion should include this fact and explain the difference. Under common law, the remainder is divested only if the remainderman **has a child**; otherwise, the remainder is not divested and passes to the remainderman's estate. Under the UPC, however, the remainder vests only if the remainderman **survives the life tenant**. If he does not, then the remainder does not vest in him and therefore does not pass to the remainderman's estate.

2. Gifts to Issue/Descendants

The Restatement (Second) of Property presumes that the per capita distribution applies to gifts to "issue" in written instruments regardless of the state's default approach to intestate distributions to issue. The majority approach follows the default rule of the jurisdiction.

In most states, anti-lapse statutes do not apply to nonprobate gifts, and, therefore, if a gift to "issue" fails by reason of the non-survival of the issue, then children and further descendants of the deceased issue will not take under the trust. However, some states have enacted UPC § 2-707 or a similar statute, under which a **substitute gift** is created in the descendants of the deceased issue. When such statutes govern, even words of survivorship (e.g., "to those of my issue who are living") will not cut off this substitute gift.

3. Implied Gifts

When a trust that creates a class gift fails to specify the recipients of the gift in a contingency that actually occurs, e.g., the gift is made to "grantor's nieces and nephews if grantor dies without issue" and the grantor in fact dies with issue, some courts will **infer a gift** to the issue, while others will simply revert the gift to the settlor's estate.

4.   Adopted Children

In the absence of a specific provision addressing whether adoptive children are to be considered children for the purpose of taking under a written instrument, the transferor's intent controls.

At common law, adoptive children did not qualify as beneficiaries in written instruments. The modern trend is to presume that "children" includes adopted children absent a contrary intent. Under the UPC, an adopted person is included in the class gift in accordance with the UPC rules for intestate succession, which provide that an adopted person is the child of his or her adoptive parent.

> **EXAM NOTE:** If a fact pattern indicates that a child is adopted, consider it a hint that the bar examiners want to see at least one sentence discussing that the adopted child is treated as a biological child for the purpose of a trust. In many cases, the date of the adoption is also a factor, in which case a discussion about when a class closes is likely warranted.

5.   Gifts to Heirs

Qualification as an heir is determined upon the death of the transferor or at the time of distribution.

6.   Rule in Shelley's Case

At common law, the Rule in Shelley's Case prevented remainders in a grantee's heirs by merging present and future interests so that the grantee would take in fee simple absolute. Most jurisdictions have abolished the Rule in Shelley's Case, and the parties now take the present and future interests according to the language in the deed.

7.   Doctrine of Worthier Title

The Doctrine of Worthier Title is a rule of construction similar to the Rule in Shelley's Case, except that it prevents remainders in the grantor's heirs, and it still applies in some states. The presumption is of a reversion to the grantor.

Wills and Decedents' Estates

WILLS AND DECEDENTS' ESTATES

Table of Contents

WILLS AND DECEDENTS' ESTATES

I. INTESTACY

Intestacy is the default statutory distribution scheme that applies when an individual dies without having effectively disposed of all of his property through nonprobate instruments or a valid will. Intestacy statutes vary from state to state, but they generally favor the decedent's **surviving spouse** and **issue**, followed by the decedent's other relations, and they direct that property escheat to the state only if none of the statutory takers survive the decedent. The actual intent of the decedent is irrelevant with regard to any property that passes by intestacy.

The individuals who are entitled to a decedent's property if he dies intestate are the decedent's "**heirs**."

> **EXAM NOTE:** On the exam, if a will fails to dispose of all of the decedent's property, analyze the problem using the rules of intestacy for the property not included in the will.

A. GENERALLY

The primary policy involved in framing an intestacy statute is to carry out the probable intent of the average intestate decedent. The most common statutory scheme assumes that the decedent would wish for her surviving spouse to succeed to all of her property if she had no surviving issue, and otherwise to share her property with her surviving issue.

1. Uniform Probate Code

The Uniform Probate Code ("UPC") is considerably more generous to the surviving spouse than are the provisions of most state intestacy laws. Under the UPC:

i) If all of the decedent's descendants are also descendants of the surviving spouse, and the surviving spouse has no other descendants, then the surviving spouse takes the entire estate to the exclusion of the decedent's descendants.

ii) The surviving spouse takes $300,000 and 75% of the remainder of the estate if no descendant of the decedent survives the decedent, but there is a surviving parent of the decedent.

iii) The surviving spouse receives $225,000 and 50% of the remainder of the estate if all of the decedent's issue are also issue of the surviving spouse, and the surviving spouse has other issue.

iv) If the decedent has issue not related to the surviving spouse, then the surviving spouse receives $150,000 and 50% of the remainder of the estate.

v) If the decedent has a spouse but no descendants or parents, then the surviving spouse takes the entire estate.

Unif. Probate Code §§ 2-102, 2-103, 2-105.

In addition to favoring the surviving spouse, the UPC also favors the state. The decedent's property escheats to the state much sooner than under most state statutes. Unif. Probate Code § 2-102(1)(i).

2. Community Property

The general intestate distribution scheme presumes that the jurisdiction does not recognize community property. Community property considers all property acquired during a marriage as jointly owned by the parties unless it is a gift, inheritance, or devise given to only one spouse. In a community property jurisdiction, the community property of the decedent is divided equally, and 50% of the community property is given to the surviving spouse. If the decedent was intestate, then the surviving spouse generally receives the decedent's remaining 50% share of the community property. The decedent's separate property is then distributed pursuant to the general intestacy scheme.

B. SURVIVING SPOUSE

1. Marriage Requirement

To be entitled to take under an intestacy statute, the surviving spouse must have been legally married to the decedent.

a. Cohabitation insufficient

Generally, couples who live together do not qualify as spouses. A minority of jurisdictions, however, will afford couples who have registered as domestic partners or entered civil unions similar treatment to spouses for inheritance purposes.

b. Putative spouses

Even if a marriage is not valid, as long as one party believes in good faith in its validity, the spouses are termed putative and qualify as spouses for inheritance purposes.

c. Abandonment

In many states, if one spouse abandons the other for a prescribed period, then the marital relationship is terminated, and the two are no longer considered spouses.

d. Separation

Spouses who are separated, or are in the process of obtaining a divorce, remain spouses until the issuance of a final decree of dissolution of the marriage. Decrees of separation that do not terminate the status of husband and wife do not constitute a divorce. Unif. Probate Code § 2-802(a).

2. Survival Requirements

If an heir of a decedent fails to meet the survival requirement, then the heir is considered to have predeceased the decedent and does not take under the laws of intestacy.

a. Common law

The common-law requirement was that an heir must be proved to have survived the decedent by a **preponderance of the evidence**.

b. Uniform Simultaneous Death Act (USDA)

The USDA is enacted in most states to alleviate the problem of simultaneous death in determining inheritance, and it provides that when there is insufficient evidence of the order of death of two individuals, the property of each individual passes as though the other individual predeceased him. The USDA is applicable to all types of transfers of property, whether through will, joint tenancy, contract, or intestacy. However, the USDA is applied only when there is no instrument to state otherwise.

The USDA requires that an heir be proven by clear and convincing evidence to have survived the decedent by **120 hours** to take under his will or by intestacy, unless the testator has provided otherwise in his will. The 120-hour rule does not apply if its application would result in an escheat to the state.

c. UPC

The UPC has the same requirements with respect to survival as the USDA. The UPC further requires clear and convincing evidence that an **individual in gestation** at the decedent's death live for 120 hours after **birth**. Unif. Probate Code §§ 2-104; 2-108.

d. Determination of death

1) Common-law standard

In most instances, death can be determined based upon the irreversible cessation of circulatory and respiratory functions.

2) Modern standard

The modern standard redefines death as brain death. There are no established criteria for brain death, but the court will require that the determination of death under either the modern or the common-law standard adhere to the usual and customary standards of medical practice.

e. Burden of proof

Survivorship is a question of fact that must be proven by the **party whose claim depends on survivorship** (i.e., the person attempting to take under the laws of intestacy has the burden of proof). At common law, a "preponderance of the evidence" standard applied. Some jurisdictions, including the UPC and USDA, have applied the higher "clear and convincing evidence" standard as a litigation deterrent.

C. ISSUE

1. Qualifications

A decedent's issue includes all lineal descendants, including children, grandchildren, great-grandchildren, and the like, but excluding the descendants of living lineal descendants. A parent-child relationship must be established for an individual to be classified as issue of another.

a. Married parents

1) Presumption

A child of a marriage is presumed to be the natural child of the parties to the marriage.

2) Posthumously born children

A child conceived before but born after the death of his mother's husband is a posthumously born child. In most jurisdictions, a rebuttable presumption exists that the child is the natural child of the deceased husband if the child is born within 280 days of the husband's death. A posthumously born child born more than 280 days after the husband's death has the burden of proving that he is the deceased husband's natural child.

Note: The Uniform Parentage Act, Article 2, § 4, increases the number of days in which the rebuttable presumption applies to 300.

b. Adoption

References in a will to "children" are deemed to include adopted children. An adopted child is treated as a biological child for purposes of inheritance.

1) Inheritance from and through parents

Adoption curtails all inheritance rights between the natural parents and the child.

2) Inheritance from and through an adopted child

If an adopted child dies intestate, then his property is distributed among those individuals who would have been his heirs had he actually been born to his adoptive parents. Unif. Probate Code § 2-119.

3) Stepparent exception

The majority of jurisdictions, including the UPC, modify the general rule regarding adoptions when the adoption is by a stepparent. The adoption does sever the parent-child relationship with either natural parent, essentially replacing the child's family with a "fresh start." The adoption does not curtail the parent-child relationship or the inheritance rights of a natural parent who is married to the stepparent. Rather, the adoption establishes a parent-child relationship between the stepparent and child, including full inheritance rights in both directions.

However, a parent-child relationship still does exist with the other genetic parent, but only for the purpose of the right of the adoptee or a descendant of the adoptee to inherit from or through that other genetic parent. Unif. Probate Code § 2-119(b).

A minority of jurisdictions hold that the parent-child relationship with the natural parent is entirely severed. *See e.g.*, *Hall v. Vallandingham*, 540 A.2d 1162 (Md. Ct. Spec. App. 1988) (holding that an adopted child is no longer considered a child of either natural parent and loses all rights of inheritance from the natural parents).

Example: H and W are married and have a child, A. H dies, and W then marries Z, who subsequently adopts A. H's brother dies without any children of his own, without any issue, and without a surviving spouse. Can A take through his natural father, H, who would have taken part of his brother's estate, even though A has been adopted by Z? Under the **majority rule**, yes. The decedent was a descendent of the adopted child's grandparent. He is taking from his uncle. His uncle was the son of his grandparent. The adoptive parent, Z, was married to the child's other biological parent. The same result occurs if, instead of H dying, H and W had divorced, and W and Z had married, and Z adopted A. Even then, the adoption will not prevent A from inheriting from or through his natural father.

c. Equitable adoption (foster parents and stepparents)

1) In general

Foster children and stepchildren have no right to inherit from their foster parents or stepparents. However, foster parents and stepparents are treated as adoptive parents for purposes of inheritance if:

    i)   The relationship **began during the child's minority** and continued throughout her life; and

ii) It is established by **clear and convincing evidence** that the foster parent or stepparent would have adopted the child but for a legal barrier.

2) Agreement to adopt

A foster child who was never legally adopted may be treated as the child of a foster parent who dies intestate if the foster parent made an agreement with the natural parents of the child to adopt her and proceeded to treat the child as his own.

3) Limitations

Generally, under equitable adoption, a child can inherit from, but not through, the equitable adoptive parent. Additionally, the equitable adoptive parents cannot inherit from or through the child. Unlike a true adoption, the parent-child relationship and the inheritance rights between the child and the natural parents are not affected.

d. Half-bloods

At common law, relatives who shared only one common parent were not entitled to inherit from or through one another. The UPC and the majority of jurisdictions have abolished the distinction between whole- and half-blooded relatives. Unif. Probate Code § 2-107.

e. Children born out of wedlock

1) Common-law and modern trend

The common-law rule was that if a child was born out of wedlock, then she could not inherit from her natural father. The modern trend adopted by most jurisdictions is that an out-of-wedlock child cannot inherit from her natural father unless:

i) The father **subsequently married** the natural mother;

ii) The father **held the child out** as his own and either received the child into his home or provided support;

iii) **Paternity was proven** by clear and convincing evidence after the father's death; or

iv) **Paternity was adjudicated** during the lifetime of the father by a preponderance of the evidence. It has been held unconstitutional to deny inheritance rights to a nonmarital child when the father's paternity was adjudicated during his lifetime. *See Trimble v. Gordon*, 430 U.S. 762 (1977); *Reed v. Campbell*, 476 U.S. 852 (1986).

The current trend is to allow more ways for illegitimate children to prove parentage after the alleged parent is deceased.

2) Uniform Parentage Act (UPA)

The UPA requires proof of paternity before a child can inherit from or through her natural father.

a) Presumption of paternity

The child can bring an action to establish paternity for inheritance purposes at any time if a presumption of paternity exists.

b) No presumption of paternity

A child must bring an action to establish paternity for inheritance purposes within three years of reaching the age of majority when there is no presumption of paternity, or the action is barred.

c) Acknowledgment of child

A presumption of paternity arises if the father acknowledges the child as his own, either by holding the child out as his own or by stating so in writing and filing the writing with the appropriate court.

f. Posthumously conceived children

The Uniform Status of Children of Assisted Conception (USCAC) does not recognize posthumously conceived children as natural children of a parent who dies before conception. Although jurisdictions differ on whether a posthumously conceived child can receive an intestate distribution of the deceased parent's estate, the majority follows the USCAC.

2. Calculating Share

The UPC adopts the **per capita at each generation** approach, although most jurisdictions are split between the **per stirpes** and the **per capita with representation** schemes.

a. Per capita with representation

The per capita with representation approach divides the property equally among the first generation when at least one member survives the decedent, with the shares of each member of that generation who does not survive the decedent passing to the then-living issue of the nonliving member. If the nonliving member has no then-living issue, then the nonliving member does not receive a share.

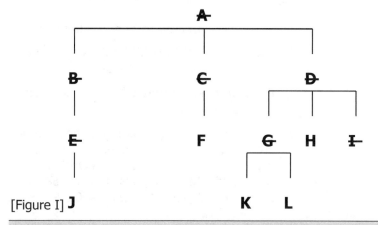

[Figure I]

Example: In Figure I. above, A dies and is predeceased by her children B, C, and D, all of whom have surviving issue. Application of a per capita by representation scheme causes A's estate to be first divided at E's generation (because there are no surviving members of B's generation) and then to be distributed among all living members and all nonliving members who are survived by issue. Because I is deceased without issue, I does not receive a share, and E, F, G, and H each take one-fourth. At J's generation, J takes E's one-fourth share in its entirety, and K and L share G's one-fourth share.

b. Per stirpes

A distribution occurs per stirpes when the issue take in equal portions the share that their deceased ancestor would have taken, if living. The estate is first divided into the total number of children of the ancestor who survive or leave issue who survive.

Example: Applying a per stirpes distribution scheme to Figure I. above, A's estate is divided equally at B's generation even though there are no survivors. J takes B's share (because E predeceased A), F takes C's share, and G and H share equally in D's share. Because G has predeceased A, K and L will equally split G's share. I, who predeceased A and left no issue, gets nothing.

c. Per capita at each generation

The per capita at each generation approach, followed by the UPC, divides the property into as many equal shares as there are members of the nearest generation of issue who survive the decedent and deceased members of that generation with issue who survive the decedent. Unif. Probate Code § 2-106(b).

EXAM NOTE: When analyzing fact patterns using the per capita at each generation approach, begin as per capita with representation, but then divide the remaining shares equally among the members of the next generation.

Example: Applying a per capita at each generation scheme to Figure I. above, A's estate is divided into four shares: one each for F and H, who survived, and one each for E and G, who left living descendants. E and G's shares are pooled and divided among J, K, and L equally. In other words, F and H each get one-fourth, and J, K, and L divide the remaining one-half equally.

d. Negative inheritance

Under common law, the only way for an individual to disinherit an heir was to execute a will disposing of all of his property, because any property not so disposed of could potentially pass to that heir through intestacy.

The UPC allows an individual to disinherit an heir by properly executing a will expressing such intent, even if not all property is disposed of within the will. The barred heir is then treated as having predeceased the decedent. Unif. Probate Code § 2-101(b).

D. ANCESTORS AND REMOTE COLLATERALS

If no surviving spouse or issue exist to succeed to the decedent's estate, then the property may be distributed to the decedent's ancestors (e.g., parents, grandparents, great-grandparents) and more remote collateral relatives (i.e., those related to the decedent through a common ancestor, such as siblings, cousins, aunts, and uncles).

1. Parentelic Approach

The parentelic approach follows collateral lines until a live taker is found, at which point the decedent's property is distributed within that taker's parentelic line. A decedent's estate would first pass to the decedent's parents and their issue (the decedent's siblings); if there are none, then to the decedent's grandparents and their issue (aunts, uncles, and cousins), and so on.

2. Degree-of-Relationship Approach

The degree-of-relationship approach results in those with closer degrees of relationship to the decedent taking to the exclusion of more remote relatives. The degree of relationship is calculated by counting the number of relatives between the living taker and the decedent using the closest common ancestor.

3. Combined Approach

The parentelic approach is used as a tiebreaker in the event that the degree-of-relationship approach results in a tie between multiple living takers sharing the same lowest degree of relationship. Those in the closer collateral line take to the exclusion of those in the more remote collateral line.

4. UPC Approach

If there is no surviving spouse or descendant, then the estate passes in the following order to the individuals designated below who survive the decedent:

    i) To the decedent's parents equally if both survive, or to the surviving parent;

    ii) If there is no surviving descendant or parent, then to the descendants of the decedent's parents;

    iii) If there is no surviving descendant, parent, or descendant of a parent, then the estate passes to the decedent's maternal and paternal grandparent, one-half to each, or to the descendants of the decedent's maternal and paternal grandparents if the grandparents are deceased;

    iv) If there is no surviving grandparent or descendant of a grandparent on either the paternal or the maternal side, then the entire estate passes to the decedent's nearest maternal and paternal relative; and

    v) If there are no surviving relatives, then the estate escheats to the state.

A parent cannot inherit through a child if her parental rights have been terminated or if the child dies before the age of 18 and there is clear and convincing evidence that the parental rights of the parent **could** have been terminated under state law. Unif. Probate Code § 2-114.

II. EXECUTION OF WILLS

A. FORMALITIES

For a will to be admissible to probate, the testator must meet the formal execution requirements of the applicable jurisdiction's statute of wills (i.e., that jurisdiction's requirements for the execution of a proper will). Although a will is usually contemplated to dispose of property, it does not necessarily have to do so. The requirements may vary depending on whether the will is in a traditional (i.e., witnessed) form or a holographic (i.e., handwritten) form. At a minimum, most jurisdictions require a signed writing that has been witnessed for traditional attested wills.

> **EXAM NOTE:** The validity of a will is the most frequently tested area of wills. Remember that a will requires a **writing** that the testator **signs** with present **testamentary intent** in the **joint presence** of two witnesses, that both witnesses **understand** the significance of the testator's act, and that the will has no legal effect until after the testator's death.

1. Writing Signed by the Testator

The entire will must be in writing and must be signed by the testator or by some other person in his presence and at his direction. A handwritten will can qualify as an attested will, so long as the other formalities are met (i.e., signature and witnesses).

Oral wills are not permitted under the UPC.

a. Location

Some states require the signature to be at the end of the will, whereas others (and the UPC) allow the signature on any part of the will. In these states, while a signature elsewhere will not invalidate the will, any language appearing after the signature will be held invalid.

b. Capacity

To create a valid will, the testator must be at least 18 years of age and of sound mind. In some states, a conservator for an individual who lacks testamentary capacity can make a will for his conservatee if a court orders him to do so. A testator meets the requirement of mental capacity if she knows (i) the nature and extent of her property, (ii) the persons who are the natural objects of the testator's bounty and have the highest moral claims to the testator's property, (iii) the disposition the testator is attempting to make, and (iv) the interrelationship of these items in connection with the testamentary plan formulated in the will.

All persons are afforded the presumption that they have mental capacity. As a result, the burden of proving that the testator lacks mental capacity rests on the contestant to the will.

c. Form of signature

The testator's complete formal name is not required, as long as the signature indicates his desire to sign (e.g., even an "X" is acceptable). If the testator signs by a mark, some jurisdictions may require that the mark be made in the presence of a witness. Additionally, in most jurisdictions and under the UPC, the will may be signed by another provided that the "conscious presence" test is satisfied (i.e., that the other person signs the testator's name, in the presence and at the express direction of the testator).

2. Witnesses

a. Signatures

The majority view is that a will must be signed in the joint presence of, and attested to by, two witnesses. There are jurisdictional differences as to the number of witnesses (e.g., some states require three). An attestation clause is not required, but it can be helpful to prove due execution of the will in cases in which the witness has no memory of signing or has a faulty memory. Also, the witnesses need not sign at the end of the will.

Will execution statutes commonly provide that another person may sign a testator's will if it is done at the testator's direction and in the testator's presence. Under the UPC, the witnesses, all of whom need not be present at the same time, must sign the will within a reasonable time after witnessing the testator sign or acknowledge the will. Unif. Probate Code § 2-502(a)(3).

Some courts have found that the testator's request that the two witnesses sign can be implied and does not have to be explicit. *See In re Estate of Graham*, 295 N.W.2d 414 (Iowa 1980).

Note that the witnesses do not necessarily have to sign in each other's presence.

b. Presence

The witnesses need not read the will, but they must be aware that the instrument is a will. In most jurisdictions, the testator must sign or acknowledge the will in the presence of the witnesses, and the witnesses must sign in the presence of the testator.

The UPC, however, does not require the witnesses to sign the will in either the presence of the testator or the presence of the other witnesses. Rather, each witness must sign only within a reasonable time of the original signature by the testator, at his direction, or while observing the testator's acknowledgment of the will. Unif. Probate Code § 2-502(a)(3).

There are two other approaches followed by some jurisdictions: the line-of-sight test and the conscious-presence test.

1) Line-of-sight test

The "line-of-sight" test, which is the traditional approach, requires the joint presence of the witnesses and the testator, who must observe or have the opportunity to observe each other sign the will. If the testator does not sign in the witnesses' presence, then that signature must be acknowledged.

For example, when a witness signs from his office, while the testator signs in his home, the attestation requirements are not satisfied because of the risk that fraud as to the authenticity of the document being signed or the identity of the witness or testator, known by voice only, could occur.

2) Conscious-presence test

The modern approach, known as the "conscious-presence" test, is broader than the line-of-sight test. The conscious-presence test requires only that the party observing the act, either testator or witness, be aware that the act is being performed.

> This method is endorsed by the UPC only for situations in which the will is signed by another person on behalf of the testator. Unif. Probate Code § 2-502(a)(2).

When a testator acknowledges her signature to witnesses over the telephone, courts have held that this does not satisfy the "conscious-presence" requirement—the witness must either observe the testator signing the will or observe the testator's acknowledgment of her will. *See In re Estate of McGurrin*, 743 P.2d 994 (Idaho Ct. App. 1987).

c. Age and competency

Witnesses must be of sufficient mental capacity and maturity to comprehend the value of the act of witnessing a will. Competency is determined as of the **time of signing**; the subsequent incompetence of a testator or witness does not invalidate a will.

d. Interest of a witness

At common law, a witness with a direct pecuniary interest under a will was not competent to witness the will. The will was invalid, unless two disinterested witnesses also witnessed the will. Many states now use a purge theory and invalidate the portion of the will providing an excess to the interested witness.

To determine the excess portion, calculate the amount the interested witness would receive if the will were invalid (i.e., under the intestacy statute or prior will) and the amount the witness stands to receive under the will. If the amount to be received under the will is greater, then the excess interest is purged. There are two exceptions: (i) the interested witness is a third witness signing along with two other disinterested witnesses, or (ii) the interested witness would have taken had the will not been probated.

The UPC, which previously followed the purge theory, has now abolished the interested witness doctrine. Unif. Probate Code § 2-505.

3. Testamentary Intent

a. Understand the nature of the act

The testator must execute the will with present testamentary intent. When the testator signs the instrument, he must understand that he is executing a will and must intend that it have testamentary effect.

b. Know and approve

Testamentary intent is a question of fact to be determined by an examination of the will and the surrounding circumstances. The words in the will are not automatically conclusive.

A will is ineffective if the testator intends it only as a joke or to accomplish some other purpose. The testator need not read the will or understand all of its technical provisions, but he must generally know and approve of its contents.

c. Integration

Through the doctrine of integration, the will consists of all pages that are present at the time of execution and that are intended to form part of the will, which can be shown either by physical connection of the pages or by the ongoing nature of the language of the will. Litigation often occurs when pages are not physically connected or there is evidence that a staple has been removed. Problems can be prevented by carefully fastening the pages before the testator signs and by having the testator sign or initial each numbered page of the will.

4. Compliance

At common law, **strict compliance** with the formal requirements of wills was required, as these were thought to serve important ritual, evidentiary, and protective functions. A minority of jurisdictions and the UPC have granted courts the power to probate a noncompliant will when there is clear and convincing evidence that the decedent intended for the document to serve as his will and has **substantially complied** with the statutory formalities. Unif. Probate Code § 2-503.

B. HOLOGRAPHIC WILLS

Holographic (i.e., handwritten) wills are recognized by the UPC and in approximately one-half of the states.

1. Signed Writing

A holographic will is one that is completely handwritten and signed by the testator. Unlike attested wills, a holographic will cannot be signed by another person on behalf of the testator. Jurisdictions differ on whether the entire will needs to be in the testator's handwriting. Some jurisdictions require a strict compliance approach under which any markings not in the testator's handwriting invalidate the will. Others, including the UPC, merely require that the material provisions of the will are written by hand. Unif. Probate Code § 2-502(b).

A holographic will **need not be witnessed**.

2. Dated

Some states require that a holographic will be dated. Other states, including those that have adopted the UPC, have no such requirement.

3. Testamentary Intent

It must be clear that the document was intended by the testator to be a will. Intent can be presumed by the use of certain language (e.g., "I bequeath") or by the testator's use of a printed form will.

The UPC expressly states that the testator's intent need not be found exclusively in the testator's handwriting, but it can be discerned from other written parts of the will or from extrinsic evidence. Unif. Probate Code § 2-502(c). A jurisdiction requiring strict compliance, however, will require that the testator's intent be discernible by the handwritten parts of the will as opposed to preprinted parts on a form will.

4. Handwritten Changes

Interlineations after the will is complete are effective in most jurisdictions that recognize holographic wills.

C. "SELF-PROVED WILL"

Under the UPC, a will that is executed with attesting witnesses may be made "self-proved" by the acknowledgment of the testator and affidavits of the witnesses before a court officer in substantial accordance with a prescribed form. The effect of executing a "self-proved will" is that it removes the necessity for testimony of the attesting witnesses in formal probate. Unif. Probate Code § 2-504. Moreover, in many jurisdictions, the witnesses' signatures on an affidavit may be counted as signatures on the will if the witnesses failed to sign the actual will.

D. NUNCUPATIVE WILLS

Nuncupative (oral) wills are generally valid only for the disposition of **personal property** in contemplation of immediate death and are invalid under the UPC and in most states. In jurisdictions where they are valid, nuncupative wills require at least two witnesses, can devise only a limited amount of personal property, and may require that the testator die within a prescribed period after making the oral will.

E. CODICILS

A codicil is a supplement to a will that alters, amends, or modifies the will, rather than replacing it. **A codicil must be executed with the same formalities as a will.**

A validly executed codicil republishes the will as of the date of the codicil and may even validate an invalid will if the codicil refers to the will with sufficient certainty to identify and incorporate it, or if the codicil is on the same paper as the invalid will. Courts look to the intent of the testator to determine whether to read the provisions of the will as having been republished as of the date of the codicil.

A holographic codicil to an attested will and an attested codicil to a holographic will are valid.

F. FOREIGN WILLS AND INTERNATIONAL WILLS

Under the Uniform International Wills Act (UIWA), a will is valid irrespective of the place where it was made, the location of the testator's assets, and his nationality, domicile, or residence, provided it complies with the act. The UIWA requires that the will be in writing, signed, and witnessed by two individuals plus a third person who is authorized to act in connection with international wills and who must prepare a certificate to attach to the will.

The testator must declare the instrument to be his will and demonstrate knowledge of its contents.

G. WILL SUBSTITUTES

A will substitute is a method of transferring a decedent's property outside of probate. Distribution of these nonprobate assets does not involve a court proceeding; it is done in accordance with the terms of a contract, trust, or deed. Will substitutes come in many forms, the most popular of which are described in this section.

1. Property Placed in a Trust

The distribution upon death of property placed in a trust by an individual during her lifetime is determined by the terms of the trust, not the terms of the individual's will or the intestate rules. The trust can be structured so that the creator (settlor) of the trust serves as the manager (trustee) of the trust and the beneficiary of the trust during the creator's lifetime, and provide for the continued management of the trust property by a trustee or its distribution upon the creator's death. Consequently, a trust can function much like a will. Nevertheless, the creation of trust is not subject to the requirements for the execution of a will, such as attesting witnesses.

a. Pour-over trust

A pour-over devise is a provision in a will that directs the distribution of property to a trust upon the happening of an event, so that the property passes according to the terms of the trust without the necessity of the will reciting the entire trust.

> **Example 1:** T executes both a will and an *inter vivos* trust. The will provides that upon T's death, assets of the estate "pour over" into the trust.
>
> **Example 2:** Husband and Wife execute reciprocal wills that provide for a trust to be established under the will of the first to die, and they contain a "pour-over" devise to the trust in the will of the second to die.

Under the common-law doctrine of "**incorporation by reference**," if a will refers to an unattested document that is *in existence at the time* the will is signed, then the terms of that document could be given effect in the same manner as if it had been properly executed. Under this doctrine, for example, the terms of an amended revocable trust would not apply to the disposition of the probate estate assets (because the amendment was not in existence at the time the will was executed). However, the necessity for this doctrine has been obviated under the Uniform Testamentary Additions to Trusts Act (UTATA), codified at the Uniform Probate Code (UPC) § 2-511. Under the UTATA, a will may "pour over" estate assets into a trust, even if the trust instrument was not executed in accordance with the Statute of Wills, as long as the trust is identified in the will, and its terms are set forth in a written instrument. Furthermore, if these requirements are met, the pour-over bequest is valid even if the trust is unfunded, revocable, and amendable. UPC § 2-511.

b. Totten trusts

A Totten trust is not a true trust because there is no separation of legal and equitable title. Rather, it is a designation given to a bank account in a depositor's name as "trustee" for a named beneficiary. During the depositor's lifetime, the depositor retains control of the passbook and the ability to make deposits and withdrawals.

A Totten trust can be revoked by any lifetime act manifesting the depositor's intent to revoke, or by will. In this way, a Totten trust is distinguishable from a joint bank account, the proceeds of which pass by law at the death of one joint tenant to the other.

2. Deed

A deed can effect a nonprobate transfer of property upon the death of the grantor if the deed is executed with the present intent of transferring a property interest to the grantee (e.g., a remainder interest). If so, then the deed need not comply with the requirements for execution of a will. However, if the grantor intends that the grantee have the property interest only upon the grantor's death (i.e., a testamentary intent), the deed is not effective to transfer the property interest unless the deed complies with requirements for the execution of a will.

Example 1: A executes a deed that transfers real property to B. The deed itself contains no conditions. A gives the deed to an independent third party, C, saying, "I want B to have this property upon my death. Please give the deed to her then." Because A gave C the deed with the intent of presently creating a remainder interest in B, the transfer is effective.

Example 2: A executes a deed that transfers real property to B. The deed itself contains no conditions. A gives the deed to an independent third party, C, saying, "I want B to have this property if she outlives me. Please give the deed to her then." Because A gave C the deed with the intent of making a testamentary transfer (i.e., requiring that B survive A in order to take the property), the transfer is ineffective unless the requirements for a testamentary transfer were satisfied.

3. Jointly Held Property with Survivorship Rights

Property that is jointly owned can pass, upon the death of a joint tenant, to the other joint tenants automatically, rather than by the terms of the deceased joint tenant's will or the intestacy rules. Many states recognize two forms of survivorship property—joint tenancy with right of survivorship and, for a married couple, tenancy by the entireties.

1. Joint bank accounts

Amounts on deposit in a bank account may be transferred at death by means of a joint or multiple-party account designation. The surviving tenant or tenants have an absolute right to the account proceeds, unless extrinsic evidence is introduced that the decedent added the tenant or tenants for convenience purposes only. For example, creating a joint account in order to give the cotenant check-writing privileges, such as can be case with the child of elderly owner of an account is considered a convenience. In such case, the cotenant is treated as agent of the original owner of the account. In that case, some courts, including those following the UPC, set aside the joint tenancy in the bank accounts. Unif. Probate Code § 6-212 cmt. Other courts still affirm the joint tenancy, relying on the parol-evidence rule to exclude evidence of the depositor's intentions. Still other courts have created a presumption that cotenants who have a present right to demand payment from a joint or multiple-party account, whether the account is in the form of a joint and survivor account or an agency account, own the account in proportion to their contributions to the account.

4. Payment made to Beneficiary on Death

A decedent may have had an agreement with a bank, employer, or some other individual or entity to distribute the property held under the contract at the decedent's death to a named beneficiary. Typically, to collect property held under a payable-on-death (POD) or transfer-on-death (TOD) agreement, the beneficiary must file a death certificate with the custodian holding the property. Examples of such agreements are a bank account with a POD designation, a security registered in beneficiary form or with a TOD designation, retirement benefits to be paid to a beneficiary, and an insurance policy on the life of the decedent.

5. Life Insurance

A beneficiary of a life insurance policy takes by virtue of the insurance contract. The proceeds are not part of the decedent's estate, unless they are payable to the decedent's estate as beneficiary.

In most states, life insurance proceeds are payable to the beneficiary named in the beneficiary-designation form filed with the insurance company, even if the insured names a different beneficiary in a later-executed will. This rule is typically justified as a matter of contract: life insurance policies generally provide that policy proceeds will be paid only to a beneficiary named on an appropriate form filed with the insurance company; other possible methods of changing a beneficiary are thus viewed as being excluded by the insurance contract. *See, generally, Cook v. Equitable Life Assurance Soc'y of the U.S.*, 428 N.E.2d 110 (Ind. 1981).

III. REVOCATION

A. ANY TIME PRIOR TO DEATH

A testator with testamentary capacity retains the ability to revoke his will at any time prior to his death, even if he has executed a valid contract not to revoke the will. In such a case, the revoked will must be denied probate, but the interested parties may bring an action for breach of contract against the estate of the decedent.

A will may be revoked wholly or partially in three ways: by **subsequent writings**, by **physical destruction of the will**, or by **operation of law**.

1. Subsequent Instrument

A testator can expressly revoke a will by a subsequent writing, a later will, or a codicil. Under the UPC, a subsequent writing expressing the intent to revoke must qualify as a valid holographic or attested will. Unif. Probate Code § 2-507(a)(1). The revocation can be express or can be implied by the terms of the subsequent instrument.

An oral revocation of a will is not valid.

a. Inconsistency

To the extent possible, the will and any codicils are read together. If there are inconsistencies, then the **later document controls** and revokes the prior inconsistencies. If a later will contains a residuary clause (e.g., "I leave all remaining assets of my estate to my brother"), then it **revokes** the first will by inconsistency. If a later will has an express revocation clause, then the first will is revoked.

> **EXAM NOTE:** On the exam, you must be able to distinguish a codicil to an existing will from a new will. If the subsequent document has a residuary clause, then it is likely a new will. If the subsequent document does not have a residuary clause but the first document does, then the subsequent document is likely a codicil.

2. Destruction With Intent to Revoke

A will may be revoked by burning any portion thereof, or by canceling, tearing, obliterating, or destroying a material portion of the will with the intent to revoke it. Both the **act** and a simultaneous **intent to revoke** must be proven to yield a valid revocation.

a. Defacement of the language required

The majority rule is that an effective canceling of a will requires defacement of the language of the will (i.e., at least some of the language must be crossed out, including the signature). The UPC, however, rejects the majority rule and requires that the destructive act merely affect some part of the will. Unif. Probate Code § 2-507(a)(2). Some states require that the method of revocation be of a type specified by statute; any other nonspecified method will be ineffective.

1) Presumption of revocation

If a will once known to exist cannot be found at the testator's death, or is found mutilated, then there is a rebuttable presumption of revocation. The presumption is inapplicable if a duplicate original is found. Extrinsic evidence is permitted to rebut the presumption.

> The attorney-client privilege does not apply to a lawyer's testimony concerning the contents of a will.

2) Only one copy destroyed

The prevailing view is that the effective revocation of the original or a duplicate original presumptively revokes all other copies of the will, but that destruction of an unexecuted copy does not.

b. Third party

A third party can revoke on behalf of the testator as long as the revocation is:

i) At the testator's **direction**; and

ii) In the testator's **conscious presence**.

If a testator calls his attorney requesting that she tear up his will, then the revocation is not valid because it was not done in the testator's conscious presence.

> An attorney can be subject to liability for failing to advise her client regarding the proper revocation or execution of his will.

3. Operation of Law

a. Divorce

In most states, divorce revokes all will provisions in favor of the former spouse, unless it can be shown that the testator intended for the will to survive. Unif. Probate Code § 2-804. In some states, however, divorce revokes a will provision for the former spouse only if the divorce is accompanied by a property settlement agreement. If a divorced couple remarries before the testator dies, then the will provisions relating to the former spouse or domestic partner are revived.

> The UPC takes a broader approach than many jurisdictions and revokes provisions containing devises to the relatives of the ex-spouse. Furthermore, the UPC also applies the revocation by operation of law doctrine to will substitutes. Unif. Probate Code § 2-804. However, due to federal express preemption, note that divorce will not automatically revoke the designation of a spouse as beneficiary of an employee benefit plan governed by the Employee Retirement Income Security Act (ERISA). 29 U.S.C. § 1144(a); *see Egelhoff v. Egelhoff*, 532 U.S. 141 (2001).

b. Separation

Separation without divorce *does not* affect the rights of the spouse or domestic partner unless a complete property settlement is in place.

4. Partial Revocation

The majority of jurisdictions and the UPC permit partial revocation to revoke a provision of a will. The majority of jurisdictions provide that if the revoked gift falls outside of the residuary, it *is not* given effect until re-execution (signed again) or republication (new document) of the will. The UPC, however, provides that partial revocation is permissible regardless of the effect, even if it increases a gift outside of the residuary clause. Unif. Probate Code § 2-507(d).

5. Alteration

A testator cannot increase a gift to a beneficiary by canceling words in his will, but he may be able to decrease the gift as long as the alteration is made to the existing language of the will rather than through the addition of new language.

6. Holographic Wills

A holographic will can be altered or revoked in whole or in part by holographic changes and without a new signature. States that allow holographic wills also allow their revocation by formal wills and vice versa. On the other hand, some state statutes require both the holographic will and any changes be signed. *See* Unif. Probate Code § 2-502 and § 2-502(b).

If a subsequent holographic will disposes of part of an estate already disposed of in a typewritten will, then the typewritten will is revoked only to the extent that it is inconsistent with the later holographic will.

B. LOST WILLS

If the decedent had possession of her original will before her death, but the will is not found among her personal effects after death, jurisdictions are split as to whether a rebuttable presumption arises that the decedent destroyed the will with the intent to revoke it.

1. Duplicates and Copies

Duplicate originals are two copies of the same will executed in the same manner, each complying with the same formalities. A duplicate original may be admitted to probate.

A copy of a will, such as a photocopy, cannot itself be admitted to probate, although it may be used as proof of testamentary intent in the case of a lost or missing will.

2. Burden on the Proponent

If a will cannot be found, then the burden is on the proponent of the existence of a will to prove the will's existence by clear and convincing evidence. An attorney's copy of an original is sufficient, whereas testimony by an interested witness is not.

3. Absence of Intent to Destroy

If there is proof that a will has been destroyed, but there is no evidence that the testator intended to revoke the will, then the will can still be probated if there is clear and convincing evidence of the lack of intent to revoke and of the contents of the will.

C. REVOCATION OF CODICILS

Revocation of a will revokes all codicils thereto, whereas revocation of a codicil does not revoke a will, but rather revives it.

Example: In 1995, the testator executes a will. One year later, he adds a codicil. In 1999, he revokes the codicil with the intention of revoking the will as well. The testator dies in 2000. The 1995 will is offered for probate, and it will be admitted because the revocation of the codicil revives the underlying will.

D. REVIVAL

1. Republication

Example: Testator executes Will 1, leaving his estate to friend A. Years later, he executes Will 2, which leaves his estate to friend B. Three years thereafter, Testator destroys Will 2 with the intention to revoke it. Testator dies one year later, survived by A, B, and Testator's child C. Who takes?

The outcome of the above scenario depends on which approach applies.

At **common law**, followed in just a few states, the revocation of a will or codicil that had revoked another will automatically revived the original will.

If the common law applies in the example above, Will 1 would be revived when Will 2 was revoked. Therefore, A would take the estate.

However, many states currently follow the **no-revival approach**. Under this approach, the second will is treated as two legal instruments, each with its own effective date. The second will functions as (1) a revoking instrument that is effective upon its execution and also (2) a dispositive instrument effective upon the testator's death. Therefore, even if the second will is revoked before the testator's death, the revocation of the first will remains in effect. If the no-revival approach applies in the example above, although the testator's assets would not be distributed until death, Will 1 was revoked immediately when Will 2 was published as if the testator physically destroyed Will 1. Because the revocation of Will 2 does not negate the revocation of Will 1, Testator's assets are distributed intestate and C takes.

The **modern approach adopted by the UPC** focuses on the testator's intent and applies a hybrid approach that depends on two considerations: (i) whether the second will is revoked by act or by another, later will; and (ii) if the second will is revoked by an act, whether the first will was wholly or partially revoked by that second will. Unif. Probate Code § 2-509.

If the second will is **revoked by another new will**, the previously revoked will (or its revoked parts if it was only partially revoked by the second will) is only revived if the terms of the new will show that the testator intended the previous will to take effect. In other words, **the court will not consider any extrinsic evidence** (e.g., oral statements by the testator) in determining whether the testator intended to revive the first will. Unif. Probate Code § 2-509(c).

If the second will is **revoked by a physical act** (i.e., burning, tearing, etc.), the burden of establishing the testator's intent depends on whether the first will was wholly or partially revoked by the second will. If the second will **wholly revoked the first will**, the court will presume that the testator did not intend to revive the first will, and the burden will be on the proponent of the first will to prove that the testator intended to revive that will. Unif. Probate Code § 2-509(a). If the second will **partially revoked the first will**, the court will presume that the testator intended to revive the revoked parts of the first will, and those portions of the first will are revived unless the challenger of the first will establishes that the testator did not intend them to be revived. Unif. Probate Code § 2-509(b). In either case, **the court is permitted to consider extrinsic evidence** (e.g., the circumstances of the revocation, testator's contemporary or subsequent statements) to determine the testator's intent. Unif. Probate Code § 2-509(a), (b).

> If the UPC approach applies in the example, the court would look at how Will 2 was revoked and whether Will 2 wholly or partially revoked Will 1. Because Will 2 wholly revoked Will 1, and because Will 2 was revoked by an act, the burden will be on A to persuade the court that Testator's intent was to revive Will 1. If A meets this burden, Will 1 will be revived and A will take the estate. If A cannot meet this burden, the court will presume that Testator did not intend to revive Will 1, and Testator's assets will be distributed intestate to C.

2. Dependent Relative Revocation (DRR)

Under certain circumstances, many jurisdictions employ the equitable doctrine of dependent relative revocation ("DRR"), which allows a court to disregard a testator's revocation that was based on a mistake of law or fact and would not have been made but for that mistake. The testator's last effective will, prior to the set-aside revocation, will once again control his estate. The doctrine of DRR can apply to partial revocations as well. Typically, courts apply this doctrine only when there is a sufficiently close identity between the bequest that was revoked and the bequest that was expressed in the invalid subsequent will.

> **Example:** T creates a second will and then writes on the first will, "I am revoking this will because I made a new will." T did not realize that the second will was not valid. The revocation of the first will is set aside, and the first will is given effect.

> **EXAM NOTE:** If you see an otherwise valid revocation based upon a mistake (whether of fact or law), begin your analysis by stating the DRR rule.

IV. WILL CONTRACTS

Will contracts include contracts to make a will, contracts to revoke a will, and contracts to die intestate, all of which are controlled by contract law.

A. WRITING REQUIREMENT

Proof of contract can be established if:

i) The will states the material provisions of the contract;

ii) The terms are contained in a written contract; or

iii) Express reference is made in the will to the contract, and extrinsic evidence proves the terms.

The UPC requires that the contract be in writing and be within the will to be enforced through probate. Unif. Probate Code § 2-514. Otherwise, the contract must be enforced through contract law.

B. CONSIDERATION

As with any other contract, consideration must be given for a will contract to be enforceable. Situations in which the beneficiary promises to care for the testator in exchange for a bequest provide sufficient consideration and make the contract enforceable.

C. ENFORCEABILITY AND REMEDY

To be enforceable in most states, a contract relative to making or not making a will must be in writing and signed by the party sought to be charged; otherwise, the plaintiff may recover only his consideration, including the fair market value of any services rendered. Whether the contract is breached will not generally be known until after the testator's death. Thus, there is no remedy for a breach while the testator is still alive.

D. RECIPROCAL PROVISIONS

1. Joint Wills

A joint will is a will signed by two or more persons that is intended to serve as the will of each. A joint will that is not reciprocal is merely the individual will of each of the persons signing the same document (and is treated as if there were several separate wills). A will that is both joint and reciprocal is executed by two or more persons, with reciprocal provisions, and shows on its face that the devises were made in consideration of the other.

2. Reciprocal Wills

Reciprocal wills are wills with identical or reciprocal provisions. Because reciprocal wills are separate, there is no contract between the parties to dispose of the property in a particular way, which means that either party can modify his will without knowledge of the other.

3. Contract Not to Revoke

In most jurisdictions, and under the UPC, the mutual execution of a joint or mutual will does not create a presumption of a contract not to revoke the will. Unif. Probate Code § 2-514. However, if a contract not to revoke is proved, and the second party attempts to make an *inter vivos* transfer not in accordance with the contract, or attempts to revoke her will after accepting the benefits under the first party's will, then a constructive trust may be imposed for the benefit of the original beneficiaries. In a joint will contract, on the death of one party, the transaction is said to become an irrevocable contract as to the survivor.

> **Example:** H and W wish to leave everything to each other with the balance to their children. H and W can either create two separate wills with reciprocal provisions (reciprocal wills), or they can create one joint will that includes reciprocal provisions stating that the property of each goes to the survivor, if any, otherwise to the children. A joint will labeled "joint and mutual," with other factors listed above, is likely to be deemed a contract not to revoke, whereas reciprocal wills are unlikely to be so deemed absent clear and convincing evidence to the contrary.

> **EXAM NOTE:** Generally, if a fact pattern includes a joint will, then the issue of a contract not to revoke is likely being tested.

V. CONSTRUCTION

A. CLASSIFICATION SYSTEM

Traditionally, a "devise" refers to a gift of real property by will, and a "bequest" or "legacy" refers to a gift of personal property by will. In most states and the UPC, "devise" is used generically to refer to any type of gift. Classifying gifts establishes the order of distribution and abatement if the estate's assets are insufficient to satisfy all of the gifts contained in the will. The judiciary often assigns classifications with reference to the intention of the testator when the will was written. The classes of gifts made under the will are distinguished by the type of item given.

1. Specific

A specific legacy, devise, or bequest is a gift of property that can be distinguished with reasonable accuracy from other property that is part of the testator's estate.

> **Example:** "My car to my dentist."

2. General

A general legacy is a gift of personal property that the testator intends to be satisfied from the general assets of his estate.

> **Example:** "$100,000 to John."

3. Demonstrative

A testator intends that a demonstrative legacy be paid from a particular source, but if that source is insufficient, then he directs that the legacy be satisfied out of the general assets of the estate.

> **Example:** "$100,000 to John from my X account, but if funds are not sufficient, then the rest paid out of general funds."

4. Residuary

A residual legacy is a legacy of the estate remaining when all claims against the estate and all specific, general, and demonstrative legacies have been satisfied.

> **Example:** "I give all the rest and residue of my property, wheresoever situated, whensoever acquired, and whether known to me or not, to John."

B. INCORPORATION BY REFERENCE

A will may incorporate by reference another writing not executed with testamentary formalities, provided the other writing:

i) **Existed** at the time the will was executed;

ii) Is **intended** to be incorporated; and

iii) Is **described in the will** with sufficient certainty so as to permit its identification.

Unif. Probate Code § 2-510. The UPC waives the requirement that the document have been in existence at the time the will was executed if the document disposes only of the testator's tangible **personal property**. The will, however, must expressly state the testator's intent. Unif. Probate Code § 2-513.

C. ACTS OF INDEPENDENT SIGNIFICANCE

1. In General

A will may provide for the designation of a beneficiary or the amount of a disposition by reference to some unattested act or event occurring before or after the execution of the will or before or after the testator's death, if the act or event has some significance apart from the will. Unif. Probate Code § 2-512 ("Events of Independent Significance"). The act may be in relation to the identification of property or of beneficiaries.

> **EXAM NOTE:** When analyzing a testator's acts on the exam, look to the timing of the event. Recall that the doctrines of republication by codicil and incorporation by reference apply only to events that occurred in the past. For example, republication by codicil looks at a will executed before the codicil, and incorporation by reference requires the document to be in existence before the execution of the will (unless the UPC exception applies). The acts of independent significance doctrine, however, is the only doctrine that applies to future acts or events.

2. Independent Legal Significance

If the testator, the beneficiary, or some third person has some control over the act or event, it may still have independent legal significance if it is unlikely that the testator or other person would perform such act solely for testamentary reasons. The execution or revocation of a will of a third person is an act of independent significance.

Example: A will might leave a certain gift to "the man who is my niece's spouse at the time of my death." The law does not presume that the niece would marry or divorce merely to complete the terms of the will.

D. LAPSE

1. Common-Law Rule

Under common law, if a beneficiary died before the testator, or before a point in time by which he was required to survive the testator under the will, then the gift failed and went to the residue unless the will provided for an alternate disposition. Absent a residuary clause, the gift passed through intestacy. A gift made by will to an individual who was deceased at the time the will was executed was treated as a lapsed gift.

2. Anti-Lapse Statute

Almost all states have enacted anti-lapse statutes providing for alternate disposition of lapsed bequests. Under the majority of the statutes, if the gift was made to a relation of the testator within a specific statutory degree, and the relation predeceased the testator but left issue, then the issue succeeds to the gift, unless the will expressly states the contrary. Most statutes require that the devisee who failed to survive was a grandparent, descendant of a grandparent, or a stepchild of the testator. Unif. Probate Code § 2-603. Most jurisdictions allow the statute to apply only to testamentary gifts. Under the UPC, however, the statute may also apply to nonprobate transfers. Unif. Probate Code §§ 2-706; 2-707.

Example: T's will provides, "I give $50,000 to my brother, B." B predeceases T. Under anti-lapse, B's issue would take the $50,000.

3. Class Gift Rule

When a gift is to an entire class and one member of the class dies, only the surviving class members take. However, if an anti-lapse statute applies (because the predeceased class member was related to the testator), then the issue of the predeceased member also will take. The majority of states and the UPC apply the anti-lapse statute first, before the determination of a class gift. Unif. Probate Code § 2-603.

The UPC extends anti-lapse to life insurance policies in which the beneficiary predeceases the policyholder. Unif. Probate Code § 2-706.

4. Residuary Rule and Future Interests

Under the UPC, if the residue is left to two or more persons and one dies, and if anti-lapse does not apply, then the remaining beneficiaries take in their proportionate shares. Unif. Probate Code § 2-604(b). This is contrary to the common-law "no residue of a residue" rule, under which the testator's heirs succeeded to any lapsed portion of a residual bequest.

Likewise, if a future interest is left to two or more persons and the gift to one of them lapses, then her share passes to the other future interest holders unless anti-lapse applies.

5. Void Gifts

Although there may appear to be no difference between a void gift and a lapsed gift, the law sometimes makes a distinction and treats them differently. A gift is void if, unbeknownst to the testator, the beneficiary is already deceased at the time the will is executed. As noted above, a lapsed gift occurs when the beneficiary predeceases the testator **after** the will has been executed. Most states allow anti-lapse statutes to apply to void gifts.

E. ABATEMENT (FIRST TO LAST)

1. Order

Gifts by will are abated (i.e., reduced) when the assets of the estate are insufficient to pay all debts and legacies. The testator may indicate his intended order of abatement, but if he fails to do so, the law prescribes an order. If not otherwise specified in the will, gifts are abated in the following order:

i) Intestate property;

ii) Residuary bequests;

iii) General bequests; and

iv) Specific bequests.

Unif. Probate Code § 3-902.

Demonstrative legacies are treated as specific legacies for abatement purposes to the extent that they can be satisfied, and otherwise as general legacies. Within each classification, abatement is pro rata.

2. Specific Bequests

A specific bequest may abate to satisfy a general legacy only if such intent was clearly indicated by the testator.

F. ADEMPTION

1. Ademption by Extinction

The doctrine of ademption applies only to specific bequests. If the subject matter of a **specific bequest** is missing or destroyed ("extinct"), then the beneficiary takes nothing, not even the insurance proceeds or the equivalent in cash. This rule does not apply when the testator was incompetent, unless the will was executed prior to the incompetency.

a. Traditional approach—"identity theory"

The intent of the testator is not relevant in most states if the bequest is extinct. If the specifically bequeathed item is not a part of the estate at the testator's death, then it is adeemed.

1) Substantial change

A substantial change in the nature of the subject matter of a bequest will operate as an ademption, but a merely nominal or formal change will not.

2) Ademption disfavored

Courts are inclined to avoid ademption by a variety of means, including the classification of a specific bequest as general or demonstrative, the classification of an *inter vivos* distribution as a mere change in form, and the creation of other exceptions to the doctrine.

b. UPC approach—"intent theory"

Under the UPC, the testator's intent at the time he disposed of the subject matter of the bequest is examined. The UPC has essentially created a "mild presumption" against ademption and has created several doctrines to avoid it. The bequest to the beneficiary is adeemed if the facts and circumstances establish that the ademption was intended. The UPC permits a beneficiary of a specific extinct gift to inherit the property acquired by the testator as **replacement property** or, if the testator is owed money relating to the extinction, the **outstanding balance**. Unif. Probate Code § 2-606(a).

If neither the replacement property nor the outstanding balance doctrine applies, then the UPC provides that a beneficiary of a specific gift is entitled to money equivalent to the value of the specific property as of the date of disposition if ademption is inconsistent with the testator's:

i)   Intent; or

ii) Plan of distribution.

Example: X's will devises 123 Main St. to his son, Y. At the time of the will's execution, X owned the property, but he later sold the property and used the proceeds to buy bonds. X still owned the bonds at this death. Under the majority rule and common law, Y would not receive the bonds at death, as the specific devise of property was adeemed. Under the UPC, Y would receive the bonds under the replacement property exception.

c. Beneficiary entitlement

If a gift is adeemed, then the beneficiary is entitled to:

i)   Whatever is left of the specifically devised property;

ii) The balance of the purchase price owing from the purchaser of the property;

iii) Any amount of condemnation award for the taking of the property, to the extent unpaid upon death; or

iv) Property acquired from the foreclosure of a security interest on a specifically devised note.

2.   Exoneration of Liens

Under the common-law doctrine of exoneration, the specific devisee of encumbered real property was entitled to have the mortgage on the property paid from the estate as a debt of the decedent, unless there was evidence of a contrary intent on the part of the testator. However, in most states, the specific devisee of encumbered property takes subject to the mortgage, notwithstanding the fact that the will contained a clause directing the executor to pay the decedent's debts. A specific devisee of encumbered property is not entitled to have the debt paid off by the residual estate unless the testator's intent to do so is clear in the will. Unif. Probate Code § 2-607. A testator can specifically require that a lien be exonerated, in which case the encumbered property will not abate to exonerate the lien unless specifically stated in the will.

Note: A general directive to pay debt is insufficient to direct the exoneration of liens.

3.   Ademption by Satisfaction

A general, specific, or demonstrative devise may be satisfied in whole or in part by an *inter vivos* transfer to the devisee after the execution of the will, if it was the testator's intent to satisfy the devise by the transfer.

a. Intent controls

The testator's intent to adeem must exist before the legacy or bequest is rendered inoperative.

b. No presumption

The UPC presumes no ademption by satisfaction, absent an express writing, and it limits the sources of evidence of the testator's intent to adeem. Unif. Probate Code § 2-609.

4. Securities

a. Pre-death changes

At common law, the treatment of a gift of securities depended on whether it was a specific or general bequest. Many states hold that a stock dividend, like a cash dividend, is a property interest distinct from stock given by a specific bequest. A bequest of stock owned by a testator when the testator's will is signed excludes subsequently acquired shares of the same stock. A bequest of a certain number of shares of a security that were owned by the testator at the time the will was executed is deemed to include any additional shares of that security or of another security acquired by reason of a stock split, reinvestment, or merger initiated by the original security. However, the beneficiary is not entitled to any pre-death cash dividends or distributions. If the bequest is a generic gift (e.g., does not specify a number of shares), then the beneficiary does not take any additional shares.

Under the UPC, which rejects the common-law approach of classifying the type of bequest, a bequest of a security that was owned at the time the will was executed will include any additional shares of that security or of another security as long as the action was initiated by the corporate entity. A stock dividend is treated like a stock split instead of a cash dividend. Unif. Probate Code § 2-605.

b. Post-death changes

The classification of a gift controls the disposition of any income earned on the gift after the testator's death. Specific bequests carry with them all post-death income, such as interest, dividends, and rent. General bequests carry with them interest earned on the amount bequeathed beginning one year after the decedent's death, at a rate set by statute. Residual bequests are not interest-bearing.

G. AMBIGUITIES AND MISTAKES

1. Plain-Meaning Rule

Courts are reluctant to disturb the plain meaning of a will regardless of mistake, although they are apt to treat certain mistakes as ambiguities.

2. Ambiguities

Traditionally, there was a distinction between patent and latent ambiguities: patent ambiguities appeared on the face of the will and were required to be resolved within the four corners of the instrument but without extrinsic evidence; latent ambiguities were not apparent from a reading of the will and were allowed to be resolved by extrinsic evidence.

Many states no longer distinguish between patent and latent ambiguities and allow both to be resolved by extrinsic evidence. If the ambiguity cannot be resolved, then the gift in question becomes part of the residue.

A few states have adopted the Restatement (Third) of Property's more liberal approach, which allows a court to reform a donative document based on clear and convincing evidence of (a) a mistake of law or fact or (b) the donor's intention.

3. Mistakes

Extrinsic evidence is admissible to show a mistake in the execution of a will, such as when the testator is **unaware** that she was signing a will. In a case of the **wrong** will being signed, courts are divided as to whether relief should be granted, although the modern trend is moving in the direction of granting relief.

No extrinsic evidence is allowed and no relief is granted if the mistake involves the reasons behind the testator making the will or a particular gift. For example, if a testator would normally make a will leaving his estate to his two children, but, under the mistaken belief that one of his children has died, he instead makes a will devising his entire estate to only the other child, the court would not allow evidence of the mistake, and only the one child would take the estate. There is an exception to this rule if the testator was fraudulently induced or the mistaken inducement appears on the face of the will.

If a will is missing provisions, then the court will not allow extrinsic evidence to show that the omission was accidental and will not grant relief. The court's rationale is that the testator presumably knew of the will's contents when he signed it.

4. Rule of Construction—Will "Speaks" at the Time of Death

Under the general rule of construction that a will "speaks" as of the time of death, a bequest of a generically described property applies to property that meets the generic description at the testator's death.

VI. POWER TO TRANSFER

A. RIGHTS OF SURVIVING SPOUSE

1. Spousal Support

The surviving spouse is entitled to the following means of support: Social Security, pension plans, homestead exemption, personal property, and family allowance.

a. Social Security

Only a spouse can receive a worker's survivor benefits from Social Security.

b. Pension plans

Pension plans governed by the ERISA are required to give spouses survivorship rights. Unlike Social Security, a surviving spouse can waive her rights in the spouse's pension plan, but such waivers are subject to strict requirements.

c. Homestead exemption

Under homestead exemption statutes, which vary by state, a certain acreage or value of real property is exempt from creditors' claims, is inalienable during the life of the owners without consent, and passes upon death by statute, not by will. The amount of the homestead exemption differs by state, but the UPC as amended in 2008 recommends a lump sum payment of $22,500, up from $15,000. Any minor child or children of the decedent are entitled to the exemption amount in the absence of a surviving spouse.

d. Personal property set-aside

Some states have a statutory list of tangible personal property or a monetary limit to which the surviving spouse or, if none, any minor child or children of the decedent are entitled.

e. Family allowance

The surviving spouse has a right to a family allowance during probate, the amount of which varies by jurisdiction. Some jurisdictions permit minor children also to receive a family allowance. Depending on the jurisdiction, the family allowance is either a set amount or one based on the marital standard of living.

2. Community Property and Quasi-Community Property

Community property consists of the earnings and certain acquisitions of both spouses during the marriage. At the death of one spouse, one-half of the community property is already owned by the other, and only the decedent's half is subject to disposition by will.

Quasi-community property is separate property that would have been community property had the parties been domiciled in a community-property state when acquired. Quasi-community property is treated like community property for distribution purposes.

3. Elective Share or Forced Share

The application of the elective share, and the property to which it applies, varies depending on the jurisdiction. In common-law states, the elective share gives the surviving spouse a fraction (often one-third) of the decedent's estate if the surviving spouse elects to take the elective share rather than any gift contained in the will. The elective share applies to all property of the decedent, regardless of when it was acquired.

The elective share does not exist in community-property states. Instead, the surviving spouse is entitled to a forced share of one-half of the community property and quasi-community property. The spouse must elect to take this share in lieu of all other interests she may have under the testator's will and must file a notice of election within a specified time period. The elective share is personal to the surviving spouse.

a. Augmented estate

The UPC subjects property acquired before marriage, as well as that acquired during marriage, to the "marital-property" portion of the augmented estate to which the surviving spouse is entitled. The UPC augmented estate is broader than the share under a community-property state, as it includes property acquired before the marriage and property gifted to the spouse during the marriage.

1) Increasing share

Under the UPC, the surviving spouse may take an elective-share amount equal to 50% of the value of the marital-property portion of the augmented estate. The marital-property portion is calculated by applying to the augmented estate a schedule of percentages that increase as the length of the marriage increases (e.g., 6% for the first year, 30% at five years). Unif. Probate Code § 2-203(a).

2) Satisfying share

The elective share is satisfied first from property already received by the surviving spouse, then from the rest of the estate. Life estates granted to the surviving spouse are considered support and do not count in the valuation. Unif. Probate Code § 2-209.

b. Right to set aside transfers

In many states, the surviving spouse can set aside *inter vivos* transfers by the decedent made during the marriage, without spousal consent, if the decedent initiated the transfer within one year of his death, retained an interest in the property transferred, or received less than adequate consideration.

c. Waiver

The right of the surviving spouse to take her elective or forced share can be **waived in writing** if the writing is signed after **fair disclosure** of its contents.

1) Scope

A spouse may waive in whole or in part, before or during the marriage, the right to receive any of the following from the estate of his spouse:

  i)   Property that would pass by intestate succession or by testamentary disposition in a will executed before the waiver;

  ii) Homestead, exempt property, or family allowances;

  iii) The right to take the share of an omitted spouse; or

  iv) The right to take against the testator's will.

2) Validity requirements

The terms of the waiver must be objectively fair and reasonable to both parties.

a) Must be in writing

The waiver must be voluntary and in writing and must be signed by the surviving spouse. It can be revoked or altered only by a subsequent writing signed by both parties, unless the waiver specifies other means of revocation.

b) Independent legal counsel

The surviving spouse must be represented by independent legal counsel at the time the waiver is signed.

c) Adequate knowledge

The surviving spouse must have had adequate knowledge of the property and financial obligations of the decedent at the time of the signing of the waiver.

4. Omitted Spouse

While a marriage after the execution of a will does not invalidate the will, a spouse who is not mentioned in a will is entitled to an intestate share of the testator's estate if the marriage began after the execution of the will, unless:

  i)   A valid **prenuptial agreement** exists,

  ii) The spouse was **given property outside of the will** in lieu of a disposition in the testator's will; or

  iii) The spouse was **specifically excluded** from the will.

Unif. Probate Code § 2-301.

a. General rule

When a spouse is omitted from a will, a rebuttable presumption is created that the omission was a mistake.

b. Traditional doctrine

The traditional view is that the presumption cannot be rebutted unless the intent to omit the spouse is apparent from the language of the will or the spouse was provided for outside of the will.

c. UPC approach

Under the UPC, an omitted spouse has the right to receive no less than her intestate share of the deceased spouse's estate from that portion of the testator's estate that is not already devised to a child or descendant of the testator if:

i)   The child is not a child of the surviving spouse; and

ii) The child was born before the testator married the surviving spouse.

The UPC expands the allowable evidence to include any other evidence that the will was made in contemplation of the testator's marriage to the surviving spouse. Unif. Probate Code § 2-301.

B.   GIFTS TO CHILDREN

1.   Advancements

The doctrine of advancements usually applies only to intestate succession. However, there is some authority for the proposition that the doctrine of advancements would apply if a will leaves property to the testator's heirs.

a. Common law

At common law, any lifetime gift to a child was presumed to be an advancement of that child's intestate share and was binding on those who would have succeeded to the child's estate had the child predeceased the decedent.

1) Burden

The child had the burden of demonstrating that the lifetime transfer was intended to be an absolute gift that was not to be counted against the child's share of the estate.

2) Hotchpot

If a gift is treated as an advancement, the donee must allow its value to be brought into the **hotchpot**. The advancement is added back into the estate, and the resulting total estate is divided by the number of children taking. The advancement is then deducted from the total share of the child to whom it was given.

> **Example:** D died intestate with a probate estate worth $150,000. D is survived by children A, B, and C, each of whom had received from D an *inter vivos* gift ($25,000 to A, $50,000 to B, and $75,000 to C). Under the advancement doctrine, the *inter vivos* gifts (totaling $150,000) are added back into the estate (for a total of $300,000) and then divided evenly among the three children (so each is entitled to $100,000) minus their individual gifts. As a result, A would take $75,000 (her $100,000 share less the $25,000 already received), B would take $50,000 (his $100,000 share less the $50,000 already

received), and C would take $25,000 (his $100,000 share less the $75,000 already received).

If a child receives an *inter vivos* share that exceeds the hotchpot share to which each child is entitled, then that child does not take but is not required to pay back into the estate.

b. Modern trend

The UPC approach, which is the modern trend, provides that a gift is an advancement only if:

i) The decedent declared in a **contemporaneous writing** (or the heir acknowledged in a writing) that the gift was an advancement; or

ii) The decedent's contemporaneous writing or the heir's written acknowledgment **otherwise indicates** that the gift was to be taken into account in computing the division and distribution of the decedent's intestate estate.

Unif. Probate Code § 2-109.

The value of an *inter vivos* gift is determined at the time the recipient takes possession or enjoys it, whichever is first. Unlike the common-law approach, the UPC applies to all heirs, not just the decedent's children.

c. Satisfaction of legacies

Lifetime gifts to beneficiaries who take under a will are examined in a similar manner and follow the same rules as advancement of intestate shares. An *inter vivos* transfer occurring between the testator and beneficiary will satisfy the gift if (i) the testator intends that the transfer satisfy a testamentary gift and (ii) there is a written acknowledgment of such satisfaction by the testator or beneficiary. Inclusively, situations in which the testator's intent is not apparent and cannot be proven will satisfy the legacy and give rise to the doctrine of ademption, if the testator makes an *inter vivos* transfer to the beneficiary of the specifically bequeathed item. *See* § V.F.3., *supra*.

2. Transfers to Minors

Because minors lack the legal capacity to hold property, the law provides various ways in which others might manage property for minors. The three property management options are: (i) guardianship, (ii) custodianship, and (iii) trusteeship. Custodianship and trusteeship are available only through the creation of a will.

a. Guardianship

A guardian has minimal power over property and must go through a difficult process to obtain the necessary court approval to act on behalf of a minor. The modern trend is to transform this function into a conservatorship, wherein the conservator acts as a trustee for the minor, with annual accounting to the court.

b. Uniform Transfers to Minors Act (UTMA)

The Uniform Transfers to Minors Act, enacted in all states, appoints a custodian to use the property of a minor at the custodian's discretion on the minor's behalf without court approval and with no accounting requirement. The custodian must turn any remaining property over to the minor upon the minor's attainment of age 21.

If the beneficiary was a minor at the time the will was executed but attains age 21 prior to the testator's death, then the property passes directly to the minor absent an instruction otherwise contained in the will.

c. Trust

The third alternative is to establish a trust for a minor, which is the most flexible of the property arrangements. A testator can tailor a trust specifically to the family circumstances and to his particular desires.

Whereas under a guardianship or conservatorship the child must receive the property at age 18 or 21, a trust can postpone possession until a time when the donor thinks the child will be competent to manage the property.

[*See the Themis Trusts outline for further discussion.*]

C. OMITTED CHILDREN

1. General Doctrine

Pretermitted heir statutes permit children of a testator under certain circumstances to claim a share of the estate even though they were omitted from the deceased testator's will. While the birth or adoption of a child after the execution of a will does not invalidate the will, such children are omitted from the will. If the testator then dies without revising the will, a presumption is created that the omission of the child was accidental.

a. Exceptions

The omitted child statute does not apply if:

    i) It appears that the omission of the child was **intentional**;

    ii) The **testator had other children** at the time the will was executed and left substantially all of his estate to the other parent of the pretermitted child; or

    iii) The testator **provided for the child outside of the will** and intended this to be in lieu of a provision in the will.

Mention of a child in only one of two instruments that are being read together or the republication of a will by codicil after the birth of a child will preclude that child from claiming as an omitted heir, although this rule is flexibly applied.

2. UPC

a. Adopted children

The UPC rule applies to children adopted or born after the execution of the will.

b. Presumption

Unlike the UPC omitted-spouse doctrine, the omitted-child doctrine does not expand the scope of evidence admissible to show the testator's intent to omit the child. However, extrinsic evidence is permitted to show the testator's lack of intent to omit the child, and ambiguities are resolved in the child's favor. The UPC does not permit the presumption to be overcome when a substantial portion of the estate is transferred to the other parent of the omitted child.

c. Omitted child's share

If the testator had no other children when the will was executed, then the child takes her intestate share. If the testator has at least one other child living at the time of the execution of the will, and the will devised property to at least one of those children, then the omitted child's share is taken from that portion of property already devised to the other child, and it must equal the share the other child receives.

While the UPC does not extend the protection of the omitted-child statute to children of whom the testator was unaware, it does extend omitted-child status to children whom the testator believed to be deceased. Unif. Probate Code § 2-302.

D. BARS TO SUCCESSION

1. Homicide

A party cannot take property from a decedent when the party was responsible for the decedent's death. This includes an intestate share, an elective share, an omitted spouse's share, exempt property, a homestead allowance, and a family allowance. Additionally, a joint tenant loses the right of survivorship benefits. The UPC and the majority of jurisdictions treat the killer as if he had predeceased the decedent. Unif. Probate Code § 2-803(b).

a. Intentional and felonious

The killing must have been intentional and felonious to bar the killer from taking. For example, involuntary manslaughter and self-defense killings do not fall within the homicide doctrine, although assisted suicide killings do. If a conviction fails, the court nonetheless may make a determination as to the lawfulness of the killing, using a preponderance of the evidence standard. Killings that were not intentional and felonious may result in the court imposing a constructive trust.

b. Killer's issue

Jurisdictions are split as to whether the killer's issue should also be barred from taking. The UPC treats the killer as if he disclaimed the property, which allows the killer's issue potentially to take under the anti-lapse, per stirpes, and per capita doctrines, if the issue qualify. Unif. Probate Code § 2-803(b).

c. Scope

Under the UPC, the homicide doctrine applies to all property, whether probate or nonprobate. Purchasers of such property for value and without notice are protected, but the killer is liable for the proceeds.

2. Disclaimer

Because acceptance of a testamentary gift is presumed, a party must actively disclaim if she wishes not to accept it. The disclaiming party is treated as if she had predeceased the decedent, and the property is distributed to the next eligible taker.

a. Requirements

Most disclaimer statutes have specific requirements that must be followed for the disclaimer to be effective. For example, an interest cannot be disclaimed once an heir or beneficiary has accepted the property or any of its benefits. Most jurisdictions require that the disclaimer be in writing, signed, and filed within nine months of the decedent's death. The nine-month period begins to run at the later of the death of the decedent or the date the interest becomes vested. However, under federal law, and for the disclaimer to be valid for tax purposes, the disclaimer must be filed nine months from the later of the decedent's date of death or the heir's or beneficiary's attainment of age 21.

When disclaiming an interest acquired through joint tenancy, the surviving joint tenant has nine months from the date of the other joint tenant's death to disclaim the interest. With future interests, while certain jurisdictions allow an heir or beneficiary up to nine months from the date the interest vests in possession to disclaim an interest, to avoid federal taxation, the interest must be disclaimed within nine months of its creation. When the future interest being disclaimed is a life estate, the testator's remaindermen are determined at the testator's death rather than the life tenant's death as would generally be the case. The remainder is accelerated because the interest passes as though the disclaimant, in this case the life tenant, predeceased the decedent.

Jurisdictions vary as to whether the disclaimer statute applies to probate property (the traditional approach) or whether it also includes nonprobate property (the modern approach) and must identify the decedent, describe the interest being disclaimed, and state the extent of the disclaimer.

b. Who may disclaim

A disclaimer can be made by a third party, such as a guardian, custodian, trustee, or personal representative, on behalf of a minor, incompetent, or decedent. A spendthrift clause in a will does not preclude a disclaimer.

3. Elder Abuse

Some states bar an individual from taking if she is guilty of elder abuse. Jurisdictions vary on the requirements, with some barring a taker when the conduct is only short of homicide and others barring a taker after a showing of abandonment. Most jurisdictions treat the abuser as if they have predeceased the decedent.

4. Aliens

A few states restrict the inheritance rights of nonresident aliens.

VII. WILL CONTESTS

A will contest is an objection raised against the validity of a will, based on the contention that the will does not reflect the actual intent of the testator. The basis of a will contest is the assertion that the testator (i) lacked testamentary capacity, (ii) was operating under an insane delusion, or (iii) was subject to undue influence or fraud.

A. PERIOD OF LIMITATIONS

Generally, a will contest must be filed within six months after the will is admitted to probate. Proper notice should also be given to all heirs and legatees under the will, as well as to creditors of the estate. Will contests must be made within the specified period after probate is opened, or the claims are barred.

B. STANDING TO CONTEST

Only directly interested parties who stand to benefit financially may contest a will, such as beneficiaries under the current or prior will. Creditors of beneficiaries, spouses of beneficiaries under prior wills, and pretermitted heirs cannot contest.

1. Decedent's Creditors

Because the decedent's creditors have the same rights regardless of whether the will is contested, general creditors cannot contest, though a judgment creditor of a beneficiary under a will may be able to contest.

2. Spouse of a Beneficiary Under a Prior Will

Neither a spouse nor any other prospective heir of a beneficiary under a prior will may contest.

3. Omitted Heir

Because the omitted heir's share is the same regardless of whether the will is contested, no omitted heir can contest a will.

C. TESTAMENTARY CAPACITY

To execute or revoke a will, the testator must be at least **18 years old** and possess a **sound mind** at the time of execution or revocation.

The testator lacks the requisite mental capacity if he, **at the time of execution**, did not have the ability to know the:

i) Nature of the act;

ii) Nature and character of his property;

iii) Natural objects of his bounty; and

iv) Plan of the attempted disposition.

The testator need only have the **ability** to know; actual knowledge is not required.

Old age alone is insufficient to constitute lack of capacity. Courts will uphold wills of elderly testators who at least grasp the big picture about their financial affairs. Adjudication of incompetence is not dispositive on the issue of testamentary capacity; the above-listed factors must also be applied. The burden of proof is on the party alleging testamentary incapacity. Only those parties that would financially benefit, if successful, have standing to contest a will.

Some states also require a deficiency in one of the following areas to prove lack of capacity: alertness and attention, information processing, thought processing, or mood modulation. Such deficiencies are also considered only if they significantly interfere with the individual's ability to understand and appreciate the consequences of his actions.

D. INSANE DELUSION

Even if a person has testamentary capacity, a defect in the testator's capacity may invalidate all or part of a will. An insane delusion is a belief for which there is no factual or reasonable basis, but to which the testator adheres despite all reason and evidence to the contrary. Courts, however, will generally not apply the doctrine to religious or spiritual beliefs.

Both undue influence and fraud require misconduct by a third party, whereas an insane delusion arises independently.

1. Rational-Person Test

The majority rule is that a belief is an insane delusion if a rational person in the testator's situation could not have reached the same conclusion.

2. "But For" Causation

Once it is determined that the testator suffered from an insane delusion, it must be shown that this was the sole cause of the testamentary disposition. The majority view requires "but for" causation, such that the testator would not have disposed of the property in the same manner but for the insane delusion.

EXAM NOTE: Remember to discuss **causation** when analyzing whether an insane delusion exists. Unless the insane delusion was the cause of the strange disposition, there is no defect in capacity.

E. UNDUE INFLUENCE

Undue influence is mental or physical coercion exerted by a third party on the testator with the intent to influence the testator such that he loses control of his own judgment. Circumstantial evidence, without any direct evidence, is insufficient to establish undue influence. Simply having an opportunity to exert influence or demonstrating the testator's susceptibility to being influenced (e.g., due to old age, poor health, or memory problems) does not establish that the testator's mind was overpowered.

Several factors are considered in determining the extent of a beneficiary's involvement in procuring the will. Among them are the beneficiary's recommendation of an attorney and providing the attorney with instructions, the beneficiary's presence during the writing and execution of the will, and the beneficiary's securing of witnesses. Once a will is determined to have been the product of undue influence, it may be invalidated in whole or in part, as long as the overall testamentary scheme is not altered thereby. Most courts will invalidate only those portions that are infected by undue influence.

1. Burden of Proof

The burden of proof rests on the contestant to show (i) the existence and exertion of influence and (ii) that the effect of the influence was to overpower the mind and will of the testator. The result must be a will that **would not have been executed but for the influence.**

2. Presumption

a. Confidential relationship

Because the defendant is in the best position to provide evidence, the majority of jurisdictions require a burden-shifting approach. If the elements of the jurisdiction's statute are satisfied, then a presumption of undue influence arises that shifts the burden to the defendant. A presumption of undue influence arises when the principal beneficiary under a will stands in a **confidential relationship** to the testator (such as the testator's attorney or physician), when he participated in executing the will, and when the gift to the beneficiary is unnatural or consists of the majority of the estate. Some jurisdictions also include whether the testator was of a weakened intellect.

No confidential relationship exists between husband and wife. To have a confidential relationship, the testator must confide, trust, or rely upon the other party as a result of his weakened or dependent state.

b. Burden of proof shifts

When a presumption of undue influence arises, the burden shifts to the beneficiary to show by a preponderance of the evidence that such influence was not exercised. Some courts have held that a higher standard applies, especially in cases involving alleged physician or attorney misconduct.

c. Treatment of a beneficiary

A beneficiary who is shown to have exerted undue influence is treated as having predeceased the testator to the extent that the gift to her exceeds her intestate share of the testator's estate.

3. Traditional Doctrine

Under the majority view, the undue influence doctrine has the following elements, all four of which must be shown:

i)   **Susceptibility** (the testator was susceptible to being influenced);

ii) **Motive** or predisposition (the influencer had reason to benefit);

iii) **Opportunity** (the influencer had the opportunity to influence); and

iv) **Causation** (the influencer caused an unnatural result).

> **EXAM NOTE:** As with insane delusions, undue influence is extremely fact-sensitive. Remember to discuss causation and the specific facts of the particular case when analyzing whether the will was a product of undue influence. Unless the undue influence is the cause of the strange disposition, there is no defect in capacity.

F. FRAUD

Fraud, like undue influence, must have been present when the will was executed. The burden of proving fraud is on the contestant.

1. Elements

The misrepresentation must be made **by the beneficiary** with both:

i) The **intent** to deceive the testator; and

ii) The **purpose** of influencing the testamentary disposition.

The result must be a will that would not have been executed but for the fraud.

2. Fraud in the Inducement

Fraud in the inducement is a knowingly false representation that causes the testator to make a different will than he would have otherwise made. A fraudulently procured inheritance or bequest is invalid *only if* the testator would not have left the inheritance or made the bequest had he known the facts.

3. Fraud in the Execution

Fraud in the execution (or "fraud in the factum") is fraud as to the very nature of the instrument or its contents.

4. Constructive Trust

A constructive trust can be imposed upon the defendant to rectify any alleged fraud or undue influence perpetrated upon the testator. A constructive trust is sometimes said to be a fraud-rectifying trust. However, a constructive trust may also be imposed when no fraud is involved but the court believes that unjust enrichment would result if the defendant retained the property.

5. Probate Must Be Contested

A person who objects to a will based on fraud or undue influence must contest its probate; the will may be partially probated if the fraud or undue influence goes only to certain provisions.

> If the fraud or undue influence prevented the execution of a will in favor of the plaintiff, then she may request the imposition of a constructive trust, although some courts impose intestate succession laws.

G. FORFEITURE CLAUSES

A no-contest clause (also called an *in terrorem* clause) is an express clause within a will designed to deter a beneficiary from suing over his share by causing him to lose his share entirely if he does so.

The majority of states and the UPC have held no-contest clauses to be unenforceable against claimants as long as the claimant had **probable cause** to contest. If the claim is spurious, then the clause is enforceable. Unif. Probate Code §§ 2-517; 3-905. A minority of states give the no-contest provision full effect, regardless of whether probable cause to challenge existed.

H. MORTMAIN ACTS AND PROVISIONS IN RESTRAINT OF MARRIAGE

1. Mortmain Acts

In some jurisdictions, the proportion of the estate that a testator who is survived by a spouse, parent, or child may leave to charity is statutorily limited. In others, a will that bequeaths property to charity may be required to have been executed more than a specified length of time before the testator's death in order to be effective. Laws containing such requirements are known as Mortmain Acts. Most states impose no such limitations on charitable bequests due to either legislative reform or judicial invalidation by reason of unconstitutionality under the Equal Protection Clause.

2. Restraints on Marriage

a. Absolute restrictions are prohibited

Provisions in a will imposing a forfeiture of a gift if the beneficiary should ever marry are invalid as against public policy. Similarly, requirements that a beneficiary may marry only with the consent of executors or trustees who would profit under the terms of the will by withholding consent have been held invalid.

b. Partial restraints are generally valid

Most provisions, however, that might initially be viewed as absolute restraints on marriage have been construed by the judiciary as mere statements of the testator's motives or attempts by the testator to provide for a person until marriage and, as such, have been upheld. Conditions in partial restraint of marriage are not against public policy if they merely impose reasonable restrictions on marriage or attempt to prevent an ill-advised marriage (e.g., to a specific individual). A provision conditioning a gift upon the beneficiary's not marrying a person outside his own religious group has been held to be valid. *In re Estate of Feinberg*, 919 N.E.2d 888 (Ill. 2009).

VIII. PROBATE AND ADMINISTRATION

A. IN GENERAL

A decedent's assets as of the date of his death are divided between probate and nonprobate property. Probate property is property that passes under intestacy or under the decedent's will. Nonprobate property passes under an instrument other than a will (e.g., joint tenancy property, life insurance, and pension plan proceeds).

Probate provides evidence of transfers of title, protects creditors by requiring payment of debts, and directs distribution of the decedent's property after creditors are paid.

> **EXAM NOTE:** When analyzing how to distribute property, first pass any **nonprobate property** to those identified in the nonprobate instrument. Any remaining property is **probate property**, and the takers of probate property depend on whether there is a valid will. If the decedent did not have a valid will (or if there is property not properly disposed of in the will), then the property is distributed **intestate**, pursuant to the jurisdiction's statute on distribution.

B. PROCEDURE

1. Jurisdiction

The administration of the decedent's probate estate is governed by statute.

a. Primary jurisdiction

The county in which the decedent was domiciled at the time of his death has jurisdiction over the decedent's personal property and over any real property within that jurisdiction.

b. Notice

Most jurisdictions require that notice be given to interested parties before the administrator is appointed.

c. Ancillary jurisdiction

Ancillary jurisdiction applies to real property located in another jurisdiction for the purpose of protecting local creditors and ensuring adherence to the jurisdiction's recording system.

d. Administration

After the court issues its "letters testamentary" or "letters of administration," the personal representative is authorized to begin performing his duties on behalf of the estate.

Bona fide purchasers from personal representatives or heirs are protected after the granting of letters of administration, even if the will presented at the time the letters were granted is subsequently invalidated.

2. UPC

Under common law, a will could be probated at any time, even decades after the testator's death. The UPC provides that probate proceedings must be brought within **three years of death**, after which there is a presumption of intestacy. The party requesting probate can choose to have it occur through either ex parte probate or notice probate. Unif. Probate Code § 3-102.

a. Ex parte probate (informal or no notice)

Ex parte probate is informal and requires no notice for the representative to petition for appointment. The original will must accompany the petition, and the executor must swear that, to the best of his knowledge, the will was validly executed.

Within 30 days of appointment, the personal representative must give notice to all interested persons, including heirs apparently disinherited by the will.

b. Notice probate (formal)

Notice probate is a formal judicial determination made after notice is given to interested parties. Any interested party can demand formal probate.

1) Reasons

A formal proceeding may be used to probate a will, to block an informal proceeding, or to secure a declaratory judgment of intestacy.

2) Final

Formal proceedings are final if not appealed.

C. CREDITOR'S CLAIMS

1. Period of Limitations

Each state has **nonclaim statutes** that bar creditors from filing claims after a specified time period has elapsed. If a claim is not made within that specified period after probate is opened, then the claims are barred.

2. Notice

The personal representative must provide notice to creditors of the estate, advising them of when and where to file claims. Failure to give the proper notice to creditors extends the time period they have to file a claim against the estate.

3. Priority of Claims

All jurisdictions have statutes that provide the order in which expenses and debts are to be paid:

i)   Administrative expenses;

ii) Last medical expenses and funeral expenses;

iii) Family allowance;

iv) Tax claims;

v)   Secured claims;

vi) Judgments against the decedent; and

vii) All other claims.

D. PERSONAL REPRESENTATIVE

A personal representative is either named in the will (executor) or appointed by the court (administrator) to oversee the winding up of a decedent's affairs. Any person with the capacity to contract may serve as a personal representative. Each state has a detailed statutory procedure for authorizing an executor or administrator to act on behalf of the estate. If an executor is not named in a will, then the court will appoint an administrator. In either case, the authority of the personal representative to act on behalf of the estate comes from the court. Generally, the personal representative must also file a bond, unless the will states otherwise.

1. Priority for Appointment

Persons who are not disqualified to serve as the personal representative should have priority for appointment in the following order:

i)   the person named in a probated will;

ii) the surviving spouse of the decedent who is a devisee of the decedent;

iii) other devisees of the decedent;

iv) the surviving spouse of the decedent;

v)   other heirs of the decedent;

vi)   45 days after the death of the decedent, any creditor.

Unif. Probate Cord § 3-203.

2.   Principal Duties

The principal duties of the personal representative are to:

i)   **Provide notice** to legatees, heirs, and claimants;

ii)   **Inventory** and collect the assets of the decedent;

iii)   **Manage** the assets during administration;

iv)   **Receive** and pay claims of creditors and tax collectors; and

v)   **Distribute** the remaining assets to those entitled thereto.

The scope of power to administer the estate varies among jurisdictions. Some jurisdictions permit unsupervised administration absent special circumstances with a final accounting to the court, while others require constant supervision and authorization.

3.   Fiduciary Duty

The personal representative of an estate is a fiduciary and owes the highest duty of loyalty and care to those whose interests he represents, which means that he cannot profit from the trust instilled in him. The personal representative is not discharged from his fiduciary duties until the court grants such discharge. Common law permits a personal representative to be held personally liable for the actions of the estate. Under the UPC, personal representatives can be sued in their representative capacity only for a breach of the fiduciary duty. Unif. Probate Code § 7-306.

4.   Closing the Estate

The personal representative is expected to complete the administration and distribute the assets promptly, including paying creditors and tax collectors. Judicial approval of the personal representative's actions is required to release the personal representative from potential liability. The personal representative may receive compensation for his services. The compensation is determined by statute based on the estate's value or by the court. However, the court may deny compensation if the personal representative has breached his fiduciary duties.

IX.   POWERS OF APPOINTMENT

A power of appointment describes the ability of the testator (donor) to select an individual (donee) who may be given the authority to dispose of certain property under the will, similar to an agent. The power is personal to the donee, meaning the donee cannot transfer the power to anyone else. The power may be (i) testamentary (i.e., exercisable only by the donee's will) or (ii) presently exercisable (i.e., the donee may exercise the power during his lifetime).

A.   TYPES

There are two general categories of powers of appointment: **general** powers of appointment and **special** powers of appointment.

1.   General Power of Appointment

A power of appointment in which there are no restrictions or conditions on the donee's exercise of the power is a general power of appointment. Thus, the donee may appoint himself, his estate, his creditors, or the creditors of his estate as a new owner. As such, if the donee exercises a general power, then the donee's creditors can reach the appointive property. The same holds true if the donee is also the donor of the power. Failure to exercise a general power of appointment causes the appointive property to revert back to the donor's estate. *See*, Unif. Probate Code § 2-608.

2. Special Power of Appointment

a. Exclusive

A special power of appointment is a more limited power than a general power of appointment in that it allows the donor to specify certain individuals or groups as the objects of the power, to the exclusion of others. This makes the power an exclusive special power of appointment. As such, the donor may decide to exclude the donee, the donee's creditors, the donee's estate, or the creditors of the donee's estate. In fact, a special power is presumed to be exclusive because it may favor some objects over others. In addition, the donor may make the donee's exercise of the power conditional on whatever factors, within legal bounds, the donor desires. Unlike with a general power, creditors are prevented from reaching the appointive property—even if the donee exercises the power—unless the transfer of property was intended to defraud the creditors.

b. Nonexclusive

A nonexclusive special power of appointment allows the donee to exercise the power to appoint among a class of individuals (e.g., grandchildren). It is nonexclusive because the donee cannot exclude a member of the class; he must appoint an equitable share to all appointees to prevent favoring one or two appointees over all others. When the donee fails to exercise the power, and when no gift in default of appointment is provided for in the will, the court will imply a gift to the objects of the special power and direct a distribution.

B. SCOPE OF AUTHORITY

1. Exercising Power

Any instrument, unless the donor directs otherwise, may be used to exercise a power of appointment. However, if the power is testamentary, then it may be exercised only by a will. Most jurisdictions hold that a residuary clause alone is insufficient to exercise any power of appointment held by the testator as donee. If there is a blanket power of appointment included within the residuary clause, then the courts will give effect to the power. A phrase such as "including any power of which I may have a power of appointment" would constitute a blanket power of appointment.

A blanket exercise clause is effective to exercise powers unless the donor of the power of appointment specifically requires the donee to refer to the instrument creating the power when exercising the power. Most states allow a donee to exercise his power of appointment to create a trust for the benefit of the object of the power rather than transferring the property outright.

2. Contracting the Power

When a donee is given a testamentary power of appointment, a contract to make an appointment is invalid because it would defeat the donor's purpose of having the donee exercise the power of appointment at the donor's death. On the other hand, if a donee is given a presently exercisable power of appointment, then a contract to appoint would be valid.

X. POWERS OF ATTORNEY

A power of attorney is an authorization to act on someone else's behalf in a legal or business matter. The person authorizing the other to act is the principal, and the one authorized to act is the agent. To be valid, a power of attorney must be in writing, signed, and dated. The principal must be mentally competent at the time she signs the document. Reasonable compensation is allowed based on the responsibilities to be performed and reimbursement of costs.

A power of attorney becomes ineffective if the grantor dies or becomes incapacitated.

A. TYPES

1. General

A general power of attorney allows an agent to handle all affairs during a period of time when the principal is unable to do so. This power of attorney is very broad and provides extensive powers to the agent, such as those related to financial matters, filing tax returns, buying and selling property, etc. Additional powers may also be granted, such as the powers to make gifts, maintain business interests, and make transfers to revocable trusts.

2. Special

A special power of attorney limits the powers to a specific function and duration, such as selling a particular piece of property when the principal is traveling or otherwise unavailable.

3. Advance Healthcare Directives

An advance healthcare directive may encompass a living will, a durable power of attorney for healthcare, or both. A living will dictates to a medical provider the healthcare that an individual wants in the event that the individual is unable to make those wants known. A healthcare power of attorney appoints an agent to make healthcare decisions on behalf of the principal if she becomes unconscious, mentally incompetent, or otherwise unable to make decisions. Unlike other powers of attorney, a healthcare power of attorney becomes **effective upon incapacitation of the principal**.

a. Execution requirements

An advance healthcare directive must be in writing, signed by the individual who is to receive the care, and either witnessed by at least two individuals or notarized. In many states, the agent or the healthcare provider cannot be a witness; in some states, a spouse, heir, or beneficiary of the individual cannot be a witness. Some states require the use of a specific form or a substantially similar form. Under the Uniform Health-Care Decisions Act (UHCDA), which has been adopted by seven states, instructions regarding future healthcare can be oral as well as written, but the appointment of a healthcare agent must be in a signed writing. UHCDA § 2.

b. Revocation

In most states, an individual may revoke an advance healthcare directive at any time. A living will may be revoked by tearing, obliterating, burning, or destroying the instrument. Revocation becomes effective when it is communicated to the testator's primary physician. Under the UHCDA, to revoke the designation of an agent, the revocation must be contained in a signed writing or be made personally to the supervising healthcare provider. UHCDA § 3. In the case of a former spouse, revocation is automatic upon annulment or dissolution of the marriage.

c. Eligible agents and surrogates

In most states, the agent must be at least 18 years old. In addition, unless he is a spouse or close relative, the agent cannot be the individual's healthcare provider or an employee of the provider. The agent may be related to the principal and may even be a devisee under the principal's will or an heir of a principal without a will.

If an agent has not been appointed or cannot serve, a surrogate may make a decision on behalf of the patient. Under family consent laws, a family member may act as a surrogate. Under the UHCDA, a hierarchy, running from the (i) patient's spouse (unless legally separated) to (ii) his adult child to (iii) his parent to (iv) his adult brother or sister, is established. If none of these relatives is reasonably available, then an adult who exhibited special care and concern for the patient and who is familiar with the patient's personal values may serve as surrogate. UHCDA § 5.

d. Authority of an agent

In most states, a healthcare power of appointment, unlike a typical power of appointment, is durable; that is, the agent's power to act on the principal's behalf is not terminated by the incapacity of the principal. Under the UHCDA, a healthcare agent's authority becomes effective only upon the incapacity of the principal and ceases to be effective upon the recovery of capacity by the principal. UHCDA § 2.

An agent must make a healthcare decision in accord with the principal's instructions or other known wishes. If such instructions do not exist, then the agent must make decisions in accordance with the agent's determination of the principal's best interest. UHCDA § 2.

B. SCOPE OF AUTHORITY

1. Durable Power of Attorney

Unless the agency states an earlier termination date, the agency continues until the death of the principal. If the power of attorney specifies that it will continue to be effective even if the grantor becomes incapacitated (but any such power ends when the grantor dies), then it is a durable power of attorney. General, special, and healthcare powers of attorney can all be made durable within the language of the document.

2. Duties

An agent has the following fiduciary duties:

i) Exercise the powers for the benefit of the principal;

ii) Separate the assets of the principal from the agent;

iii) Exercise reasonable care;

iv) Account for all transactions made on behalf of the principal; and

v) File an accounting of his administration whenever so directed by the court.

3. Liability

The typical durable healthcare power of attorney statute shields the agent from civil liability for healthcare decisions made in good faith. Agents act within the scope of the statute when they act pursuant to a properly executed durable healthcare power of attorney. In general, an agent is held responsible only for intentional misconduct, not for unknowingly doing something wrong. This type of protection is included in most power of attorney documents to help encourage people and organizations to accept the responsibility of being an agent.

4. Revocation

Powers of attorney may be revoked by the principal at any time, regardless of the principal's mental or physical condition.

Final Review Outlines

FINAL REVIEW OUTLINE: AGENCY

I. **Agency Relationship**

A. **Creation of an agency relationship**

1. **Power to bind**—may be expressed orally or in writing, implied by the principal's (P's) conduct, or misinterpreted by a third party

2. **Existence of a relationship**

- P manifests assent to an agent (A)

- A acts on P's behalf

- A's actions are subject to P's control, and

- A manifests assent or otherwise consents

B. **Principal**

1. **P's control**—P has the right to control the result or the ultimate objectives of A's work

2. **Types of Ps**

- **Individual**—a person's status as P is established by the person's intent to delegate an act and control the way in which the act is performed by another

- **Employer**—P who employs an employee to perform services and has the right to control the physical conduct of the employee's performance (P's control over day-to-day activities, supplying tools of trade, structured pay period, specialized skill level, and P directs work to completion)

- Entrepreneurs, corporations, and partnerships

C. **Agent**

1. **Consensual nature of relationship**—A must have minimal capacity, and must manifest assent and consent to act on P's behalf and to be subject to P's control

2. **Types of A's**

- **Individual**

- **Employee**—paid hourly or for long time periods, the work is integral to that of P, and the tasks are completed under P's direction

- **Independent contractor**—not subject to P's control regarding the physical conduct of A's performance

- **Gratuitous agent**—does not prevent the creation of an agency relationship, but does prevent an enforceable contract

- **Trustee**—subject to the control of the settlor or beneficiary

- **Subagent**—a person appointed by A to perform the functions that A has agreed to perform for P

D. **Formation of an agency relationship**

1. **Capacity**

- **P**—must consent to enter into the relationship and the transaction to which A purports to bind P

- **A**—just needs physical/mental capability to do whatever he has been appointed to do (minors/incompetents can be As but minors cannot form contracts, and unincorporated associations cannot be As)

2. **Consent**—both P and A must consent, but A can manifest assent by performing acts on behalf of P

3. **Consideration**—not necessary

4. **Writing**—generally not necessary

II. Liability of Principal and Agent to Third Parties

A. Contractual liability of the P

1. **Actual authority**

   - **Express actual authority**—oral or written words; clear, direct and definite language; or specific, detailed terms and instructions

     o **Intent**—P's manifestation must cause A to believe that A is doing what P wants (subjective standard) and A's belief must be reasonable (objective standard)

     o **Dissent**—P must give clear notice if P disagrees with A's actions

   - **Implied actual authority**—allows A to take whatever actions are properly necessary to achieve P's objectives, based on A's reasonable understanding of the manifestations and objectives of P

     o **Custom**—absent contrary instructions, A has implied authority to act within accepted business customs or general trade usage within an industry

     o **Acquiescence**—implied by P's acceptance of A's acts or P's failure to object to unauthorized actions of A that affirm A's belief regarding P's objectives and support A's perceived authority to act in future

     o **Delegate**—generally A is prohibited from delegating either express or implied authority to a third party without P's express authorization

2. **Apparent authority**

   - **P's behavior**—derives from the reasonable reliance of a third party on that party's perception of the level of authority granted to A by P's behavior (over a period of time)

   - Third party's reasonable belief based upon:

     o Past dealings between P and A

     o Trade customs

     o Relevant industry standards

     o P's written statements of authority

     o Transactions that do not benefit P

     o Extraordinary transactions for P

   - **A's position**—by appointing A to a specific position (e.g., VP or GM), P makes a manifestation to the public that A has the customary level of authority of that position

3. **Termination of authority**

   - **Revocation/renunciation**—effective as soon as either party gives notice to the other party (unless A's power is coupled with an interest in the subject matter of the power)

- **Agency agreement**—P and A mutually agree to terminate A's authority, or the occurrence of specified circumstances in agreement
- **Change of circumstances**—should cause A to reasonably believe that P no longer consents to A acting on P's behalf (e.g., change in law, insolvency, dramatic change in business conditions, destruction of subject matter, disaster)
- **Passage of time**—a reasonable period of time
- **P's death or suspension of powers**—not automatic; modern trend is A's actual authority terminates upon notice
- **P's loss of capacity**—modern trend is A's actual authority terminates upon notice
- **A's death or suspension of powers**—automatically terminates A's actual authority
- **Statutorily mandated termination** or **A's breach of fiduciary duty**

4. **Estoppel**—applies when a third party is justifiably induced to make a detrimental change in position because that third party believed the transaction was entered into for P and P failed to take reasonable steps and use ordinary care

5. **Ratification**—P must ratify the entire act/transaction, P must have legal capacity, ratification must be timely, and P must have knowledge of the material facts involved in the original act

B. **P's liability to third parties in tort for A's conduct**

1. **P's vicarious liability for A's torts**

- **Respondeat superior**
  - P is vicariously liable to a third party harmed by A who is an employee and who committed an act within the scope of employment
  - Scope of employment (S/E)
    - An employee is within S/E when either performing work assigned by the employer or engaging in a course of conduct subject to the employer's control
    - **Intentional torts**—may fall within S/E when conduct is within the space and time limits of employment, the employee was motivated to act for the employer's benefit, and the act was of the kind that the employee was hired to perform
    - **Work-related travel**—commuting is not within S/E but travel to perform work is within S/E
    - **Frolic and detour**
      - → Frolic—the employee's personal errand involving a significant deviation from performing work is outside S/E
      - → Detour—travel for a personal errand may be within S/E if it is merely a detour
- **A's apparent authority**—if a third party reasonably believes that A acted with actual authority and it is traceable to P's manifestation, then P is vicariously liable for A's tort (e.g., misrepresentation, defamation, conversion) even if A's conduct isn't beneficial to P

2. **P's direct liability to third parties**

- **A has actual authority or P's ratification**—P authorizes the conduct or intended its consequences, or P affirms a prior act that was done or purportedly done on P's behalf

- Negligence in selecting, supervising, or controlling A
- **Non-delegable duties**—when a responsibility is so important to the community that a person should not be permitted to transfer it to another person (e.g., inherently dangerous activities such as using explosives)

C. A's liability

1. Contract liability

- A's liability as a party to a contract
  - ○ **Disclosed P**—A doesn't become a party to the contract if he enters into it on behalf of P, and the third party has notice of both the existence and identity of P
  - ○ **Partially-disclosed P**—A becomes party to contract when the third party only has notice of P's existence (not P's identity)
  - ○ **Undisclosed P:**
    - ▪ If A binds P to the contract, and the third party has no notice of P's existence, then both P and A are parties to the contract
    - ▪ **Third-party liability to undisclosed P**—liable unless P is excluded by the contract terms or P's existence was fraudulently concealed
    - ▪ **Undisclosed P's liability to third party**—liable if the third party detrimentally changes position because of A without actual authority, and P knew of A's conduct and did not take reasonable steps to notify the third party
  - ○ **A's implied warranty of authority**—if A lacks power to bind P, then a breach has occurred
  - ○ **Fraudulent concealment**—P or A must have notice that the third party would not have dealt with P

2. Tort liability—A is liable to the third party for negligent and intentional conduct, but is not liable for P's torts

III. Rights and Duties of Parties to an Agency Relationship

A. Rights and duties of P

1. Rights of P (A can be liable in tort and contract)

- **Control of A**—right to control A's acts on P's behalf
- **A's duty of care**—A must follow P's instructions and perform duties, tasks, and transactions with reasonable care, diligence, and judgment
- **A's duty of loyalty/obedience**—A should avoid acts in A's self-interest in agency matters and refrain from secretly profiting from transactions on behalf of P
- **Notice/accounting**—P is entitled to notice of all relevant issues, and an accounting of property or funds used on behalf of P

2. Duties of P to A

- **Deal fairly and in good faith per the contract terms**—provide A with information concerning risks of physical or financial harm/loss that P knows but A does not; duty to not injure A's business reputation
- **Compensation**—if P expressly or impliedly agreed to pay A
- **Duty not to interfere**—with A's completion of agency work

- **Duty to indemnify**—against pecuniary loss suffered in connection with agency relationship and within scope of A's actual authority (but not for A's negligence or illegal or wrongful conduct)

3. **P's remedies for breach by A**—injunction, breach of contract action, tort action, rescission, restitution, accounting, termination of agency relationship, forfeiture of compensation, or disgorgement

B. Rights and duties of A

1. **Rights of A**—compensation, not have P interfere, indemnification/reimbursement, safe work environment, and contract or tort remedies

2. **Duties of A to P**

- **Duty of loyalty**—to act solely for the benefit of P (whether A is compensated or gratuitous), including not dealing with P as an adverse party without P's knowledge, not acquiring a material benefit in actions on P's behalf, not usurping business opportunities or competing with P, and not using P's confidential information

- **Performance-based duties**—contractual duties, duty of care/diligence normally exercised by A in similar circumstances, duty of obedience, duty to provide relevant information and accounting, and no commingling of accounts

FINAL REVIEW OUTLINE: CONFLICT OF LAWS

I. **Domicile**

   A. **Domicile of individuals**—individuals can only have one domicile at a time

      1. **Domicile by choice**—where the person is present with the intent to remain for an unlimited time

         • **Physical presence**—actual physical presence is required

         • **Intent**—must demonstrate intent to remain in the location (e.g., ownership of real estate, voting, payment of taxes, having a bank account, or registration of an automobile)

      2. **Domicile by operation of law**—occurs when an individual does not have legal capacity to choose a domicile

         • **Infants**—domiciled where the custodial parents are domiciled; an emancipated infant may establish her own domicile

         • **Incompetents**—a person lacking mental legal capacity to choose a domicile retains her parents' domicile; if the person chose a domicile while competent, that domicile will continue after the person becomes incompetent

   B. **Domicile of corporations**—always the state in which it is incorporated

   C. **Continuity of domicile**—presumed to continue until a new domicile is acquired; the burden of showing a change in domicile is on the party that asserts it

   D. **Change of domicile**—takes place when a person with capacity to change her domicile is **physically present** in a place and **intends** to make that place home

II. **Choice of Law (COL)**

   A. **Limitations on COL**—U.S. Constitution, state and federal statutes, and agreements of the parties can limit a court's power to apply a particular COL rule

      1. **Constitutional limitations**

         • **Due process**—under the Due Process Clause of the Fourteenth Amendment, a forum state may apply its own law to a particular case only if it has a **significant contact** or a significant aggregation of contacts with the state such that a choice of its law is neither arbitrary nor fundamentally unfair

         • **Full faith and credit**—requires a forum state to apply the law of another state when the forum state has no contacts with or interest in the controversy

            ○ Does not prevent the forum state from applying its own law when the forum has such contacts or interest in the controversy

            ○ Does not require a state to apply another state's law in violation of its own legitimate public policy

      2. **Statutory limitations**

         • **State statutes**—a state may have a statute requiring certain COL rules to be applied in a particular case

         • **Federal statutes**—certain federal statutes may preempt a state from claiming jurisdiction over certain cases (e.g., patent, antitrust, bankruptcy cases)

3. **Party-controlled COL**—courts will enforce a contractual COL provision if it is:

- A valid agreement with effective COL clause;
- Applicable to the lawsuit under the terms of the contract;
- Reasonably related to the lawsuit; and
- Not in violation of the public policy of the forum state or another interested state

B. Approaches to COL in general

1. Vested rights approach

- The law that controls is the law of the jurisdiction **where the parties' rights were vested** (i.e., where the act or relationship that gave rise to the cause of action occurred or was created)
- The forum court would first characterize the issues in the cause of action (e.g., procedure v. substance; tort, contract, property, domestic relations, etc.)

2. "Most significant relationship" approach—applies the law of the state with the most significant relationship to the issue in question

- Forum court will: (i) isolate the precise legal issue that results in a conflict between competing states; (ii) identify the policy objectives that each state's law seeks to achieve with respect to such issue; and (iii) determine each state's interest in view of its policy objectives, concluding which state has a superior connection

3. Governmental interest approach

- It is presumed that the forum state will apply its own law, but parties may request that another state's law be applied because that state has a greater interest in the outcome
- **False conflict** (i.e., the forum has no interest in the litigation)—the court applies the law of the state that does have an interest in the case
- **True conflict** (i.e., the forum and another state each have an interest in the litigation)
  - o The forum state reviews its own policies to determine which law should apply
  - o **Conflict cannot be resolved**—the law of the forum state is applied
- **Disinterested forum**
  - o *Forum non conveniens* **available**—the forum state should dismiss the case
  - o *Forum non conveniens* **not available**—the forum state may either make its own determination as to which law is better to use, or apply the law that most closely matches its own state law
  - o **No state has an interest**—the law of the forum state generally prevails

4. COL rules in federal diversity cases

- Federal district courts are generally required to apply the COL rules of the state in which it sits (only to the extent that the state's rules are valid under the Full Faith and Credit and Due Process Clauses of the U.S. Constitution)
- If a diversity case was transferred from a federal court in another state, the first state's COL rules will be applied

5. *Dépeçage*—an approach that allows the law of one state to govern one or more issues while other issues are controlled by the law of one or more other states

6. **Renvoi**

- Requires a forum court applying another state's law to apply that foreign state's COL rules

- Generally rejected today

- **Federal Tort Claims Act**—requires application of the whole law—including COL rules—of the place where the act or omission took place

C. **Rules for specific areas of substantive law**

1. **Torts**

- **Vested-rights approach**—the case is governed by the law of the place where the last event necessary to make the actor liable for the tort took place

- **Most-significant-relationship approach**

  o Policy principles are applied to determine the applicable substantive law

  o The court considers (i) the place of the injury; (ii) the place where conduct causing injury occurred; (iii) the domicile, residence, place of incorporation, or place of business of the parties; and (iv) the place where the relationship is centered

  o **Default rule**—the place of injury controls unless another state has a more significant relationship to the parties or the tort

- **Governmental-interest approach**

  o The forum state generally looks to its own law, so long as that state has a legitimate interest in applying its own law

  o Another state's law would be applied if a party requests such an application and the forum court determines that the other state's law should apply in accordance with the forum state's policies

2. **Contracts**

- **Express COL provision**—governs, unless:

  o It is contrary to public policy

  o There is no reasonable basis for the parties' choice, or

  o True consent was not given because of fraud or mistake

- **Vested-rights approach**—the applicable law depends on either where the contract was executed or where it was to be performed

  o **Place of execution**—validity, defenses to formation, interpretation

  o **Place of performance**—time and manner of performance, person obligated to perform and person entitled to performance, sufficiency of performance, excuse for nonperformance

- **Most-significant-relationship approach**

  o **Generally**—policy factors are considered, as well as:

    ▪ Location of contracting, negotiation, and performance

    ▪ Place where contract's subject matter is located, and

    ▪ Location of the parties' domiciles, residences, nationalities, places of incorporation, and places of business

- o **Default rules**—generally apply unless another state is found to have a more significant relationship with regard to the issue:
  - ▪ **Land contracts**—controlled by the law of the state of the situs of the land
  - ▪ **Personalty contracts**—controlled by the law of the state where delivery occurs
  - ▪ **Life-insurance contracts**—controlled by the law of the state of the insured's domicile
  - ▪ **Casualty insurance contracts**—controlled by the law of the state where the insured risk is located
  - ▪ **Loans**—controlled by the law of the state where repayment is required
  - ▪ **Suretyship contracts**—controlled by the law of the state governing the principal obligation
  - ▪ **Transportation contracts** (covering both persons and goods)—controlled by the law of the state of departure
- • **Governmental-interest approach**—does not change based on substantive areas of law

3. **Property**
   - • **Tangible personal property**—generally, the law of the state where it is physically located applies unless the UCC or governmental-interest approach applies
   - • **Intangible property**—generally, the law of the state in which the intangible was created or the transfer was made applies, unless the UCC or governmental-interest approach applies
   - • **Real property**—generally, the law of the state in which the real property is located applies, unless the governmental-interest approach applies
   - • **Trust property**
     - o **Transfers of trust property**—governed by the rules above based on the type of property involved
     - o **Administration of a trust**—usually governed by the law of the place where the trust is administered

4. **Inheritance**—depends upon the type of property at issue, real or personal
   - • **Personal property**—intestate and testate succession is governed by the law of the deceased's domicile at the time of death
   - • **Real property**—intestate and testate succession is governed by the law of the situs of the real property

5. **Corporations**—generally governed by the law of the state of incorporation

6. **Family law**
   - • **Marriage**—in general, valid where it took place and recognized in all other states
     - o **Exception**—a marriage that is valid in the state where it took place, but violates a prohibitory rule of the domicile of one of the parties will be void in the state where the marriage would have been prohibited if the parties immediately return to that state and become domiciled there
   - • **Divorce**—questions of law relating to the grounds for divorce are controlled by the law of the plaintiff's domicile

- **Legitimacy**—governed by the law of the domicile of the parent whose relationship to the child is in question

- **Adoption**—the forum court applies its own state law

7. **Workers' compensation**—in general, any state with a legitimate interest in an injury and its consequences may apply its workers' compensation act; the employer and employee may contractually agree to apply a particular state's law unless doing so would violate the public policy of another state with a legitimate interest

- **Recovery in more than one state**

  o When more than one state has a legitimate interest, a worker should review the workers' compensation statutes of each state before deciding where to file his claim

  o A subsequent workers' compensation award in another state is barred only if there is "unmistakable language by a state legislature or judiciary" barring such recovery; double recovery is not permitted

- **Immunity**—generally, only given to employers (not manufacturers of defective equipment)

D. **Defenses against application of foreign law**

1. **Procedural, rather than substantive**—the forum's laws of procedure, as determined by the forum state's law, always govern

2. **Laws against public policy**—if a foreign law violates the public policy of the forum state, the forum court may refuse to apply that law

3. **Penal laws**—a forum state will not enforce another state's penal laws

E. **Proof of foreign law**—generally, most states allow their courts to take judicial notice of other states' laws and federal laws and treat them as law rather than fact; federal courts must take judicial notice of the laws of all states

III. **Recognition of Foreign Judgments**

A. **Full faith and credit judgments**—if a valid judgment is rendered by a court that has jurisdiction over the parties, and the parties receive proper notice of the action and have a reasonable opportunity to be heard, the judgment will receive the same effect in other states as it receives in the state where it was rendered

1. **Judgment**—must have been brought in the proper jurisdiction; be final; and on the merits

2. **Defenses**—penal judgments, equitable defenses, inconsistent judgments; erroneous proceedings NOT a defense

B. **Federal court judgments**

1. **Federal to state**—federal courts must give full faith and credit to state court judgments

2. **State to federal**—if a federal court with diversity jurisdiction over an action issues a judgment, a state court must give such judgment the same res judicata effect that the judgment would have been given by the courts of the state where the federal court was located

C. **Recognition of judgments from foreign countries**

1. **Comity**—U.S. courts have discretion to decide whether to recognize foreign country judgments

2. **Uniform Foreign Money-Judgments Recognition Act**—covers foreign judgments that grant or deny specific lump sums of money, but excludes judgments for taxes, judgments for alimony or child support, and penal judgments

D. **Recognition of divorce judgments**—divorce decrees from other states are entitled to full faith and credit as long as the original state had jurisdiction to issue the decree and the decree is valid in the original state

1. **Bilateral divorce**—if the court has personal jurisdiction over both spouses and at least one spouse is domiciled in the state, then the divorce judgment will be valid and will be entitled to full faith and credit

2. **Ex parte divorce**—must adhere to subject-matter jurisdiction rules and personal jurisdiction must exist over one spouse; full faith and credit is not given to other marital agreements such as property rights, alimony, and child custody, but the non-domiciled spouse may agree to such judgments

3. **Child custody**—under the Uniform Child Custody Jurisdiction and Enforcement Act (UCCJEA), a court can make initial custody decisions if it is in the child's home state, and all other states must give full faith and credit to such decisions

4. **Property and alimony**

   • **Bilateral divorce**—full faith and credit is generally given to issues related to property and alimony

   • **Ex parte divorce**—the parties must settle these issues in a court with personal jurisdiction over both parties

FINAL REVIEW OUTLINE: CORPORATIONS

I. Formation

A. Pre-incorporation transactions

1. **Promoter liability**

   - **Pre-incorporation agreements**—a promoter is personally liable for knowingly acting on behalf of a corporation (C) before incorporation, and remains liable after C comes into existence unless (i) there is a subsequent **novation** releasing the promoter from liability, (ii) the third party looks only to C for performance, or (iii) the promoter had no actual knowledge that the corporation's charter has not yet been issued

   - **Fiduciary duty**—a promoter can be liable to C for violating fiduciary duties

   - **Compensation**—a promoter may seek compensation/reimbursement for related expenses, but cannot compel C to pay because the acts were not undertaken at C's direction

2. **C's liability**

   - **General rule**—C is not liable for pre-incorporation transactions, even those for the benefit of C (there is no principal-agent relationship)

   - **Adoption**—C is liable if it expressly or impliedly adopts a contract by accepting the benefits of the transaction, or gives an express acceptance of liability for the debt

B. Incorporation

1. **Articles of incorporation**

   - **Must** include the corporate name and be filed with the state

   - **May** enumerate powers that C possesses, or limit its duration; may include statement of C's legal purpose

   - **Corporate existence**—begins when the articles are filed, unless the articles establish a later date

2. **Ultra vires actions**

   - **Act**—when a C that has stated a narrow business purpose in its articles subsequently engages in activities outside that stated purpose; a third party generally cannot escape liability for a transaction that is an ultra vires corporate act

   - **Challenges to ultra vires acts** (will only be enjoined if it is equitable to do so)—a shareholder can file suit to enjoin the C's ultra vires action; C can take action against a director (D), officer (O), or employee who engaged in the action, or the state can initiate a proceeding

3. **"De jure" C**—when all statutory requirements for incorporation are satisfied, C is liable for C activities

4. **Defective incorporation**

   - **Lack of good faith**—a person who conducts business as a C without complying with the incorporation requirements is personally liable for the nonexistent C's obligations

- **Good-faith effort**—two ways to escape personal liability:
  - De facto C—the owner must make a good-faith effort to comply with the incorporation requirements and operate C without knowing the requirements were not met
  - Corporation by estoppel—a person dealing with an entity in a contractual agreement as if it were a C is estopped from denying its existence and seeking personal liability

II. Stock and Other Corporate Securities

A. Types

1. **Common stock**—a basic ownership interest that entitles the owner to vote on corporate governance matters

2. **Preferred stock**—has preference over other stock with regards to distributions

B. Issuance of stock

1. **Authorization**—by board of directors (BD) and/or shareholders (SH)

2. **Consideration**—if adequate, the stock is deemed fully paid and non-assessable

3. **Stock subscriptions**—a pre-incorporation subscription is irrevocable for six months from the date of subscription (unless all subscribers agree to a revocation)

4. **Stock rights, options, and warrants**—can also be issued by BD

5. **SH's preemptive rights**—the right of a SH to purchase newly issued shares in order to maintain the SH's proportional ownership share as provided by the articles; a waiver of preemptive rights in writing is irrevocable

6. **Securities registration**—required for public offerings of stocks; C must file a registration statement with SEC and provide the buyer with a prospectus

C. Distributions

1. BD is authorized to make distributions, usually in the form of cash dividend payments

2. **Limitations**—C cannot distribute if C is insolvent or if the distribution would make C insolvent

3. D's liability for unlawful distributions in violation of duties of care/loyalty—D is personally liable to C for the amount in excess of a lawful amount

4. **SH suit to compel distribution**—SH can sue to enforce his individual right by proving the existence of funds legally available to pay a distribution and D's bad faith for refusing to pay the distribution

D. Sale of securities

1. **Private restrictions on sale**
   - **Enforceability**—the security must be certified, the restriction must be conspicuously noted on the security certificate, and the person must have knowledge of the restriction
   - **Challenge to restrictions on transfer of stock**—the test is one of reasonableness

2. **Federal causes of action**
   - **Rule 10b-5 action**—must meet each of the following requirements:
     - The plaintiff purchased or sold the security

- o Use of interstate commerce
- o The defendant's fraudulent/deceptive conduct—untrue statements of material fact, failure to prevent misleading statements, or insider trading
- o Materiality—a reasonable investor would find the fact important in deciding whether to purchase or sell a security
- o Scienter—the defendant must make the statement intentionally or recklessly
- o The plaintiff's justifiable reliance on the defendant's fraudulent conduct
- o Harm to the plaintiff
- **Rule 16(b) action**—elements:
  - o Publicly traded Cs—must have securities traded on a national securities exchange or have assets of more than $10 million and more than 500 SHs
  - o Corporate insiders—Ds, Os, or SHs with more than 10% of stock
  - o Short-swing profits—a corporate insider both bought and sold C's stock during any six-month period
  - o SEC report of change in stock ownership

III. Governance

A. Instruments

1. **Articles of incorporation**—BD can amend the articles if no stock has been issued; if stock has been issued, then BD adopts the amendments and submits them to SHs for majority approval

2. **Bylaws**—lawful provisions for the management of C's business and the regulation of its affairs, not inconsistent with the articles

3. **Conflict between the articles and the bylaws**—the articles control

B. Organizational meeting—for appointment of Os, adoption of bylaws, and approval of contracts

IV. Shareholders

A. Meeting requirements—failure to hold meetings does not affect C's existence or invalidate C's business

1. **Annual**—primary purpose is to elect Ds

2. **Special**—may be called by BD or SHs who own at least 10% of voting shares

3. **Notice**—voting SHs must be notified of time/date/place in a timely manner no less than 10 days and no more than 60 days before the meeting; SH may waive notice either in writing or by attending the meeting

4. **Unanimous written consent**—SHs can take any action that could have been taken at a meeting by unanimous written consent

B. Voting requirements

1. **Eligibility**—generally, only record owners of voting stock are permitted to vote; an owner of voting stock at the close of business on the record date has the right to vote; C generally cannot vote its own stock

2. **Quorum requirements**—a majority of the votes entitled to be cast on a matter

3. **Cumulative voting for Ds**—SHs can cumulate votes to allow minority SHs to elect representatives to BD

4. **Proxy voting**—must be in writing and delivered to the C or its agent

5. **Voting with other SHs**

   - **Voting pool**—a binding voting agreement under which SHs retain legal ownership; does not need to be filed with the C; no time limit

   - **Voting trust**—a trust to which legal ownership of SH's stock is transferred; the trustee votes the shares and distributes the dividends in accord with trust; must be in writing, limited to 10 years, and filed with the C

   - **Management agreement**—allows SHs to alter the way the C is managed even if the agreement is inconsistent with statutory provisions

C. **Inspection of records**—a SH with a **proper purpose** (relates to SH's interest) has the right to inspect and copy corporate records upon **five days' written notice**

D. **Shareholder suits**

1. **Direct actions**—an action to enforce SH rights for breach of fiduciary duty by D or O, or an action based on grounds unrelated to SH's status

2. **Derivative actions**—SH sues on behalf of C for harm suffered by C

   - **Standing**—plaintiff must have been a SH at the time of the wrong and at the time the action is filed, must continue to be a SH during the litigation, and must fairly and adequately represent C's interests

   - Written demand upon BD must be made unless it would be futile; the futility exception is not recognized under the RMBCA; a rejection of a demand is tested against the business judgment rule

   - **Litigation expenses**—plaintiff can seek reimbursement from the C for reasonable litigation expenses

   - **Dismissal by board**—only if a majority of qualified directors decide in **good faith** after **reasonable inquiry** that the action is not in the corporation's best interest

E. **Liability**

1. **Piercing the corporate veil**

   - **Totality of circumstances**

     o Courts look to whether C is being used as a façade or alter ego for a dominant SH's personal dealings, and whether there is unity of interest and ownership between the C and its members

     o The plaintiff must prove that the incorporation was just a formality and that C neglected corporate formalities and protocols

   - **Factors considered**—undercapitalization, disregard of corporate formalities, using C's assets as SH's own assets, self-dealing with C, siphoning of C's funds, using corporate form to avoid statutory requirements, SH's domination over C, and fraudulent dealings with a corporate creditor

2. **Controlling SH's fiduciary duty to minority SHs**

   - A controlling SH is a SH (or a group of SHs acting in concert) who holds a high enough percentage of ownership in a company to enact changes at the highest level; a SH owning 50% plus one of a C's shares is automatically a controlling SH

- The duty arises if the controlling SH is selling interest to an outsider, seeking to eliminate other SHs from the C, or receiving a distribution denied to other SHs
- **Duty to disclose** information that a reasonable person would consider important in deciding how to vote on a transaction, and a **duty of fair dealing** when purchasing a minority SH's interest

V. Board of Directors

A. Composition requirements—can have as few as one; D must be a natural person and not a C; Ds are selected at the annual SH meeting

B. Term—typically one year, but may serve longer if terms are staggered; Ds can be removed by SHs with or without cause unless the articles provide otherwise; D may resign at any time with written notice to the BD, its chair, or C

C. Compensation—is permitted

D. Meeting requirements—Ds are entitled to two days' notice of the date, time, and place of **special meetings** (purpose is not required); **regular meetings** may be held without notice of the date, time, place, or purpose; BD can act by unanimous written consent without holding a meeting

E. Voting requirements

1. The assent of a **majority of Ds present** is necessary for board approval (generally)
   - To be a valid act, a quorum must have been present
   - A majority of all Ds in office constitutes a quorum

2. Agreements between Ds as to how to vote (pooling agreements) are generally **unenforceable**

3. Ds may **not** vote by proxy

F. Committees—may generally exercise whatever powers are granted to them by the BD, articles, or bylaws

G. Duties

1. **Duty of care**
   - **Prudent person**—a D has a duty to act with the care that a person in a like position would reasonably believe appropriate under similar circumstances (objective standard), and is required to use any additional knowledge and special skills he possesses when deciding how to act
   - **Reliance protection**—a D can rely on information and opinions of Os, employees, outside experts (e.g., attorneys, accountants), or committees, if D reasonably believes them to be reliable and competent
   - **Business judgment rule (BJR)**
     o Rule—a rebuttable presumption that D reasonably believed his actions were in the best interest of C; does not apply when D engages in a conflict-of-interest transaction with C
     o Overcoming the rule—it must be shown that: D did not act in good faith; D was not informed to the extent he reasonably believed was necessary; D had material interests in challenged conduct and was not objective; D failed to devote attention to C's affairs; D failed to timely investigate matters of material concern; or D received financial benefits to which he was not entitled

- o Good faith presumption—overcome in the case of fraud, dereliction of duty, condoning illegal conduct, or conflict of interest

2. **Duty of loyalty**—requires D to act in a manner that D reasonably believes is in the best interest of C

- **Self-dealing (director's conflicting interest transaction)**

    - o **Rule**—a D who engages in a conflict-of-interest transaction with his own C violates the duty of loyalty unless the transaction is protected under the safe-harbor rules; D cannot profit at C's expense

    - o **Type of transaction**—one that would normally require approval of BD and is of such financial significance to D that it would reasonably be expected to influence D's vote on the transaction (also includes dealings with persons related to D); the interest must be financial and material

    - o **Safe harbors**—disclosure of all material facts and majority approval by BD or SHs without a conflicting interest; fairness (substantive and procedural) of the transaction to C at the time of commencement

- **Usurpation of corporate opportunity**

    - o **Interest or expectancy test**—does C have an existing interest or an expectancy arising from an existing right in the opportunity

    - o **Line-of-business test**—is the opportunity within the C's current or prospective line of business, and how expansive is C's line of business

    - o **Other factors**—relationship of the third party to D and of D to C; how and when D acquired knowledge of the opportunity

- **Competition with C**—a D who engages in a business venture that competes with C has breached the duty

3. **Indemnity/insurance**

- C is **required** to indemnify D for any reasonable expense incurred in the successful defense of a proceeding against the D

- C is **prohibited** from indemnifying D against liability due to the receipt of an improper personal benefit

- C **may** indemnify in an unsuccessful defense if D acted in good faith with a reasonable belief that the conduct was in C's best interest and D did not have reasonable cause to believe the conduct was unlawful

H. **Inspection rights**—D has a right to inspect and copy C's books and records

VI. **Officers and Other Employees**

A. **Selection**—elected by the BD

B. **Authority**

1. **Actual**—as defined by the corporate bylaws or BD

2. **Implied**—to perform those tasks necessary to carry out O's duties by virtue of her status or position, so long as the matter is within the scope of ordinary business (i.e., not "extraordinary" transactions)

3. **Apparent**—if C holds O out has having the authority to bind C to third parties

C. **Duties**—same as D's duties (see above); the CEO and CFO of a publicly traded C are subject to the Sarbanes-Oxley Act, and must certify the accuracy of C's financial reports to the SEC

D. **Liability**—an O is liable to a third party if O has acted in O's personal capacity or has engaged in purposeful tortious behavior; (O is not liable merely for the performance of O's duties to C)

E. **Indemnification/insurance**—same as Ds (see above)

F. **Removal**—with or without cause at any time

G. **Other employees**—an employee can act on behalf of C to the extent of the employee's authority and is usually protected as an agent from liability for actions undertaken in accordance with that authority

VII. **Mergers and Acquisitions**

A. **Mergers**—require BD and SH approval by a majority vote at a meeting with a quorum (at least a majority of the shares entitled to vote) present for each C; required documents must be filed with the state

B. **Asset acquisition**—same as merger approval procedure except only the **transferor** C's BD and SHs are entitled to vote on the transaction; transferor C remains liable for its debts

C. **Stock acquisition**—a C can acquire stock in another C to acquire control of that C without doing a merger by exchanging its own stock for that stock or by paying cash or other property for the stock

D. **Dissenting shareholder's right of appraisal**

1. **Rule**—a SH who objects to a merger or acquisition, or whose rights are materially and adversely affected by an amendment to C's articles, may be able to force the C to buy his stock at a fair value as determined by an appraisal

2. **Qualifying SHs**—any SH entitled to vote on a merger, acquisition, or amendment of C's articles

VIII. **Termination of Corporate Status**

A. **Voluntary dissolution**

1. **Procedure after issuance of stock**—BD adopts a proposal for the dissolution of C and a majority of SHs approve

2. **Winding up**—dissolving C can continue to exist to collect assets, dispose of property not distributed to SHs, discharge liabilities, and distribute property among SHs according to their interests

B. **Involuntary dissolution**

1. Creditors can pursue involuntary dissolution only for an insolvent C

2. SHs can pursue involuntary dissolution if C's assets are being misapplied/wasted, Ds are acting illegally/oppressively/fraudulently, SHs are unable to break Ds deadlock causing irreparable injury, or if the SHs are deadlocked and fail to elect successor Ds

3. **Oppression doctrine**—doctrine of SH oppression protects minority from oppressive majority control; statutory provisions regarding involuntary dissolution are interpreted to protect the reasonable expectations of SHs

IX. **Special Types of Corporations**

A. **Closely held and close corporations**—only a few SHs; stock not publicly traded; more relaxed style of governance

B. **Foreign corporation**—incorporated in another state; must register and seek a certificate of authority from the current state

C. **Professional corporation**—the purpose is statutorily limited to the rendering of a professional service

D. **S corporation**—C avoids double taxation by passing income and expenses through to its SHs, who are then taxed directly

X. **Limited Liability Company (LLC)**—enjoys the pass-through tax advantage of a partnership and the limited liability of a corporation

A. **Creation**—created by filing articles of organization with the state, including the LLC's name, mailing address, and, if there are no members upon filing, a statement to that effect

   1. **Operating agreement**—the articles of organization only reflect an LLC's existence, but an LLC may also adopt an operating agreement to govern business; agreement can be oral, in a record, or implied by conduct; statutory default provisions apply when the operating agreement is silent; default management arrangement is member-manager

   2. **Membership**—no limit (but some states require at least two members); to become a new member requires the consent of all other LLC members (a transfer of a membership interest also requires the consent of all members)

      • **Transfer of membership**—the transferee only acquires the transferor's right to share in the LLC's profits and losses, not a right to participate in the LLC's management

      • **Termination of membership**—does not automatically trigger a dissolution of the LLC; LLC may elect to liquidate the fair value of that person's interests

      • **Allocation of profits and losses**—unless determined by an operating agreement, allocations are made according to each member's contributions to the LLC

      • **Inspection rights**—LLC members generally have inspection rights similar to SHs of Cs

B. **Management**—can be **direct** (by members) or **centralized** (by one or more managers who need not be members)

   1. **Liabilities**

      • Members are generally not liable for the LLC's obligations; managers are not personally liable for obligations incurred on behalf of the LLC

      • **Piercing the veil**—members may be liable if the veil is pierced due to undercapitalization, commingling of assets, confusion of business affairs, or deception of creditors

         ○ **Mere instrumentality test**—(i) members dominated the entity such that the LLC had no will of its own, (ii) members used that domination to commit a fraud or wrong, and (iii) the control and wrongful action proximately caused an injury

         ○ **Unity of interest and ownership test**—the LLC did not have an existence independent of the members because there was such a unity of interest and ownership between the entity and the members that the failure to pierce the veil would be unjust or inequitable

      • Creditors can obtain a charging order (judgment lien) against a member's LLC interest, requiring the LLC to pay to the judgment debtor distributions that otherwise would be paid to the member; the operating agreement cannot alter this rule to the prejudice of third parties

2. **Duties**—members owe each other and managers duties of loyalty and care

- Must account to the LLC for any benefit derived by the member related to the LLC's business, refrain from dealing with the LLC on behalf of one having an adverse interest, and refrain from competing with the LLC

- Duty of care to LLC is subject to BJR; members are not liable for simple negligence

- Fiduciary waivers are recognized in LLCs; may agree to specific activities that do not violate the duty of loyalty, as long as the agreement is not manifestly unreasonable

3. **Authority to Bind**—managers have authority to bind the LLC

4. **Dissociation**

- Member can withdraw at any time for any reason without written notice

- Withdrawal does not necessarily trigger dissolution and winding up

C. **Direct and derivative suits**

1. **Direct**—an action to enforce a member's rights as a member under the operating agreement and the state LLC statute; there must be an actual or threatened injury that is not just a result of an LLC injury

2. **Derivative**—an action by a member on behalf of the LLC to enforce the rights of the LLC; must show that a demand was made or that demand would be futile

D. **Dissolution**—an LLC may merge with another LLC or other business entity; may dissolve upon the occurrence of various events (mutual consent of members, lack of members for 90 consecutive days, court order, or events provided in the operating agreement)

1. Member may seek **involuntary dissolution** if a controlling member acts in a way that is oppressive and directly harmful to the member seeking the order; action must action violate member's reasonable expectations

2. **Winding up**—the LLC must (i) discharge the LLC's debts, obligations, or other liabilities; and (ii) settle and close the LLC's activities, and marshal and distribute the LLC's assets; may perform acts necessary or appropriate to the winding up

FINAL REVIEW OUTLINE: FAMILY LAW

I. **Getting Married**

A. **Definition**

1. **Civil contract**

- Parties must be legally capable of consent

- Marriage contract cannot be modified or terminated without state intervention

B. **Ceremonial (statutory) marriage**—the parties must obtain a license and participate in a ceremony

1. **License**

- **Requirements:**

   o Need capacity to marry—minimum age restrictions; parental consent for young

   o Waiting period between date of marriage and date of ceremony

   o Medical testing—state can mandate testing, but cannot condition a license on the results

   o Expiration date—most states impose an expiration date on a marriage license

- **When not issued**

   o One party is married to someone else

   o The parties are too closely related

   o The marriage is a "sham"

   o The parties are incapable of understanding the nature of the act

   o One or both parties is under the influence of drugs or alcohol

   o A party lacks consent due to duress or fraud

- **Same-sex marriage** is permitted in all states; all states and the federal government must recognize a same-sex marriage legally entered into in another state

2. **Solemnization** (ceremony)

- The ceremony must be performed in front of two or more witnesses

- A judge, political official, or member of the clergy must solemnize a marriage

C. **Common-law marriage**

1. **Requirements**—the parties **agree** they are married, **cohabit** as married, and **hold themselves out** to the public as married

2. **Recognition of common-law marriages**—only CO, DC, IA, KS, MT, RI, SC, TX, UT

- Under conflict-of-law principles, a marriage that is valid under the law of the place in which it was contracted is valid elsewhere unless it violates a strong public policy

3. **Legal/Mental capacity**—of age, not too closely related, understands nature of the act

4. **Intent**—must be evidenced by words in the present tense (e.g., "we are married")

D. **Heartbalm action**—a civil suit for money damages based on the damage to a jilted party's reputation; abolished in most states

II. Ending a Marriage

A. Annulment—voids a marriage and declares it as having never been valid

1. **Void marriage**—treated as if it never happened; does not need to be judicially dissolved; not legally recognized for any purpose

   - **Prior existing marriage**

     o The later marriage is void; some states allow the marriage to become valid if one party had a good-faith belief that the marriage was valid and the impediment is removed

     o Rebuttable presumption of validity of the latest marriage

   - **Incest**—a prohibition on marriage between related persons

   - **Mental incapacity**—a person who is unable to understand the nature of the marriage contract (e.g., duties and responsibilities) lacks the capacity to marry

2. **Voidable marriage**—valid until a judicial decree dissolves the marriage

   - **Grounds**—age, impotence, intoxication, fraud, duress, or lack of intent

3. **Equitable distribution of property in annulment**—a party may request an equitable distribution of property, spousal support, child support, custody, attorney's fees, and other costs related to the dissolution of the marriage

4. **Children**—children of an annulled marriage are considered marital children

5. **Defenses**

   - **Void marriage**—the only defense is to deny the existence of the impediment that makes the marriage void; removing the impediment makes the marriage voidable

   - **Voidable marriage**—equitable defenses of unclean hands, laches, and estoppel are recognized

6. **Putative marriage/spouse doctrine**—a party who participated in a ceremonial marriage and believes in good faith that the marriage is valid may use a state's divorce provisions even if the marriage is later found to be void

B. Divorce and separation

1. **Residency Requirement**—most states require at least one party to be a resident

2. **Grounds for divorce**

   - **No-fault**

     o Marriage is irretrievably broken and there is no prospect of reconciliation

     o Irreconcilable differences must exist for a specific period of time prior to the filing of the divorce action

   - **Fault**

     o Adultery—it must be shown that the spouse had the opportunity and the inclination to commit adultery; usually proven by circumstantial evidence

     o Cruelty—the plaintiff must demonstrate a course of conduct by the other party that is harmful to the plaintiff's physical or mental health and the makes continued cohabitation between the parties unsafe or improper

- o Desertion—results when one spouse voluntarily leaves the marital home with the intent to remain apart on a permanent basis; does not apply if the parties separate by mutual consent

- o Habitual drunkenness—frequent intoxication that impairs the marital relationship

- o Bigamy—when one party knowingly entered into a prior legal and existing marriage before entering into the current marriage

- o Imprisonment—of one spouse for a specified period of time

- o Institutionalization for insanity—with no reasonable prospect of discharge or rehabilitation

3. **Defenses to fault-based divorce**—must be affirmatively pleaded

- Recrimination, unclean hands, connivance, condonation, collusion, provocation, insanity, consent, justification, religion

C. Division of property

1. **Community property**—AZ, CA, ID, LA, NV, NM, TX, WA, and WI

- Most community property states require **equal division** of marital property

2. **Equitable distribution**—most states

- The objective of an equitable distribution system is a **fair distribution** of marital property, not necessarily an equal division

3. **Marital property**

- **Most states**—all property acquired during marriage

- o Some states—all property owned by either spouse ("hotchpot" approach)

- Burden of proof on party asserting property is nonmarital

- **Nonmarital property**—i.e., separate property:

- o Property acquired before the marriage

- o Property excluded by the parties' valid agreement

- o Property acquired by gift or inheritance (except for gifts between spouses)

- o Any award or settlement payment received for a cause of action or claim that accrued before the marriage, regardless of when the payment was received

- **Factors for distribution of marital property**—length of marriage; prior marriages; age, health, earnings, earning potential, liabilities, and needs of both spouses; contributions to education; income, medical needs, retirement of both spouses; homemaking and child-rearing services; value of separate property; reduction in valuation in marital property by one spouse; standard of living; economic circumstances of each spouse at time of divorce; custody of any minor children

4. **Treatment of specific types of marital property**

- **Professional licenses/degrees**—not a property interest, but can affect alimony

- **Retirement or pension benefits**—marital property if acquired during the marriage

- Personal injury claim proceeds/workers' compensation award

- o Some states—if the cause of action accrued during marriage, the proceeds or award are marital property

- Other states—allocate the proceeds or award between martial property and separate property
  - Damages for pain/suffering/disability—separate property of the injured spouse
  - Consortium losses—separate property of the non-injured spouse
  - Awards for lost wages, loss of earning capacity, and medical expenses—typically split between marital and separate property based on the portion of the award attributable from the time of the accident to the end of the marriage (marital property), and the portion attributable to loss of wages or medical expenses after the termination of the marriage (separate property)
- **Goodwill**—the reputation and clientele of a professional practice is considered marital property in some states
- **Accumulated sick and vacation days**—states split on classification, timing
- **Expectancy interest in property**—not distributable
- **Social Security benefits**—not subject to equitable distribution
- **Post-separation property**—can be marital property (most states)
- **Unexercised stock options**—marital property if acquired during marriage

5. **Tax consequences of equitable distribution**
   - Transfer of property between divorcing spouses is tax-free
   - Transferee's basis in property—same as transferor's basis

6. **Modification**—not permitted; the property division is based on the parties' assets at the time of the divorce

III. Financial Support of Spouses and Children

A. **Spousal maintenance (alimony)**—one spouse's monetary obligation to provide the other spouse with support in the form of income; it is awarded if the recipient cannot provide for his own needs

1. **Factors**—typically include financial resources, including property to be awarded in the divorce, child support, spouse's earning potential, and other spouse's ability to pay support; spouses' standard of living; time to find employment or complete any education or training necessary for a job; length of marriage; contributions to marriage (particularly those that enhanced the earning potential of the other spouse); age and physical and mental health of each spouse; marital misconduct

2. **Types of support**
   - **Lump sum**—a fixed amount; cannot be modified in the absence of fraud
   - **Permanent**—an award for the remainder of the dependent spouse's life (unless certain circumstances occur); typically awarded only when the marriage was one of long duration (15 years or more)
   - **Limited duration**—typically awarded when the marriage was of short duration, but there is still an economic need for support
   - **Rehabilitative**—to enhance and improve the earning capacity of the economically dependent spouse; limited period of time, such as until spouse receives education or employment

- **Reimbursement**—to compensate a spouse for financial sacrifices made during the marriage that resulted in a reduced standard of living to secure an enhanced standard of living in the future (rarely granted)
- **Palimony**—support provided by one unmarried cohabitant to another after the dissolution of a stable, long-term relationship (available in only a few states)

3. **Modification of support**

- The party seeking modification typically has the burden of establishing a significant change in circumstances in the needs of the dependent spouse or financial abilities of obligor that warrant the modification
- **Willful or voluntary reduction in income**—no reduction in support payments
- **Death of spouse**—terminates support
- **Remarriage**—if the receiving spouse remarries, support may be terminated
- **Cohabitation**—if the receiving spouse cohabits with someone who is not family, then spousal support may be modified if the recipient spouse's need for the support decreases as a result of the cohabitation (not automatic)
- **Retirement**—effect depends upon jurisdiction

4. **Support during marriage**—necessaries doctrine (both spouses)/family expenses law

B. **Child support**

1. **Child's right to support**

- Both parents, regardless of marital status, are legally required to support their minor children
- Visitation rights cannot be denied for nonpayment of support
- Parents can enter into private agreements regarding child support payments, but they cannot agree to any release or compromise that would negatively affect the child's welfare

2. **Nonmarital children**

- Cannot be denied child support, government benefits, or wrongful-death claims
- May inherit from their father's estate so long as paternity proved prior to the father's death
- Can become marital children when the parents marry after the child's birth, the father consents to being named on the birth certificate, the father acknowledges that he is the child's father, or a judicial decree establishes paternity

3. **Paternity**

- Evidence to establish paternity:
  o Blood tests ordered by the court
  o Prior statements regarding paternity by deceased family members
  o Medical testimony on the probability or improbability of conception
  o Defendant's acknowledgment of paternity
- **Time limit on filing of paternity petition**—unconstitutional unless there is a reasonable opportunity to pursue such an action and the limit is substantially related to the government's interest in restricting such an action

- **Marital presumption**—a child born to a married woman is the child of that woman and her husband

- **Estoppel**—a husband who is not the biological father of his wife's child may be estopped from denying his obligation to pay child support when:

    o There is a representation by the husband that he would provide for the child

    o The wife relied on his representation, and

    o The wife suffered an economic detriment as result of the reliance

4. **Personal jurisdiction over an out-of-state parent**

- A court obtains personal jurisdiction over an out-of-state parent pursuant to a long-arm provision in the Uniform Interstate Family Support Act (UIFSA)

C. **Amount of child support**—based on child-support guidelines

- Determination of parental income typically includes income from any source

1. **Methods of calculating support**

- **Income-shares model**—a child should receive the same proportion of parental income as if the parties continued to live together (most states)

- **Percentage-of-income model**—determines the minimum amount of child support by using a percentage of the supporting (i.e., noncustodial) parent's net income, determined by the number of children supported

2. **Deviations from child-support guidelines**

- Rebuttable presumption that the amount calculated pursuant to the child-support guidelines is correct

- If the court decides to deviate from the amount set forth under the guidelines, it must set forth specific findings explaining and supporting the deviation

- Once a child-support award has been paid, the obligor is not permitted to monitor how the money is expended

- The cost of providing medical insurance for the child is included in the child-support award (most states)

D. **Modification/termination of child support**

1. **Modification of support**

- **Standard**—a substantial change in circumstances regarding the child's needs or the parents' financial situation

- Most jurisdictions—no reduction for voluntary reduction in the obligor's pay

2. **Termination of support**

- Child reaches the age of majority (e.g., 18 years of age), child marries, parental rights are terminated, or the child or parent dies

- **Extensions**—child in college, disabled adult child who is unable to support himself

- A parent can be required to buy life insurance on his life for the child's benefit

- Support may be terminated if a child is emancipated before the age of majority

3. **Jurisdiction for modification of support**

- A court may not modify a child support order rendered by a court with continuing jurisdiction in another state unless the parties (including the child) no longer reside in that state or the parties expressly agree to permit another state to exercise jurisdiction

- If an aspect of a child-support obligation may not be modified under the law of the state that first imposed obligation, that aspect of the obligation may not be modified under the laws of any other state

4. **Tax consequences of child support**—not income to recipient; not deductible by payor

E. Enforcement of awards

1. **Civil contempt**—an obligor with the ability to pay may be found in civil contempt and can be sent to jail until the amount owed is fully paid

2. **Criminal contempt**—a jail sentence may be imposed upon an obligor who willingly fails to pay the amount owed

3. **Other sanctions**—interception of tax refund, report to credit bureau, suspension of driver's/occupational license, seizure of assets, garnishment of wages, ordering payment of attorney's fees

4. **Enforcement in other jurisdictions**

- Modification and enforcement of interstate child support is governed by the Uniform Interstate Family Support Act (UIFSA)

- UIFSA applies when the obligor or child resides in a jurisdiction different from the one in which the original order was issued

- Once an order is registered in another state, it is enforceable in the same manner and to the same extent as a child-support order issued by the original state

- Only the issuing state may modify the original support order; the other state's responsibility is simply to enforce the order

IV. Child Custody

A. Definition of custody

1. **Legal custody**—the right of a parent to make major decisions about the child's life (e.g., health, education, religion)

2. **Physical custody**—the right of a parent to have the child reside with the parent and the obligation to provide for routine daily care and control of the child

3. **Joint custody**

- Parents must both be willing and able to cooperate with respect to the wellbeing of the child

- **Joint legal custody**—neither parent has a superior right to make major decisions

- **Joint physical custody**—does not necessarily require 50-50 time-sharing arrangement

B. Uniform Child Custody Jurisdiction and Enforcement Act (UCCJEA)

1. **Purpose**—to prevent jurisdictional disputes with courts in other states on matters of child custody and visitation

2. **Initial custody determination (home state jurisdiction)**
   - A court has subject-matter jurisdiction to preside over custody hearings and either enter or modify custody or visitation orders if the state:
     o Is the child's home state (the state in which the child has lived with a parent or guardian for at least **six consecutive months** prior to the custody proceeding, or since birth, if the child is less than six months old), or
     o Was the child's home state in the past six months, and the child is absent from the state, but a parent (or guardian) continues to live in the state

3. **Significant-connection jurisdiction**—a court can enter or modify an order if:
   - No other state has or accepts home-state jurisdiction
   - The child and at least one parent have a significant connection with the state, and
   - There is substantial evidence in the state about the child's care, protection, training, and personal relationships

4. **Default jurisdiction**—if no state has jurisdiction through home-state or substantial-connection jurisdiction, court in state with appropriate connections to child has jurisdiction

5. **Exclusive-continuing jurisdiction**—a court that makes initial ruling has exclusive jurisdiction over matter until parties no longer reside in state, or child no longer has significant connection to state

6. **When court can decline jurisdiction**—if court has either initial or exclusive-continuing jurisdiction, it may decline to hear case if it finds forum to be inconvenient

7. **Temporary emergency jurisdiction**—child in danger, requires immediate protection
   - If there is no prior custody order, an emergency order remains in effect until a decision by the child's home state

8. **Enforcement of another state's orders**
   - **Registration of another states' order**—need not be accompanied by enforcement request
   - **Expedited enforcement of a child-custody determination**—a hearing is held on the first judicial day after service of the order (or on the first possible judicial day)
   - **Warrant for child custody**—if the child is likely to suffer serious physical injury or be removed from the state

C. **Best-interests-of-the-child standard**

1. **Standard for determining child custody**—"best interests and welfare of the child"
   - **Between parents**—the primary-caretaker during the marriage, separation, and prior to the divorce is a factor
   - **Race, religion**—cannot be used as factors in determining custody
   - **Parents' sexual conduct**—a factor only if the parent's conduct has or will have a negative effect on the child
   - **Third-party rights**
     o Parents presumptively entitled to custody of their children in cases against third parties

- o Exceptions—the legal parent is unfit or parental custody would be detrimental to the child
  - **Child's preference**—taken into account if the child is of sufficient maturity
  - **Guardian *ad litem***—a court-appointed attorney to advocate for the child's preferences and act on her behalf
  - **Siblings**—generally not separated from each other
  - **Domestic violence**—almost always a factor
    - o Some states have created rebuttable presumptions in favor of the nonabusive spouse

D. Visitation (parenting time)

1. **Noncustodial parent**—allowed reasonable visitation (or "parenting time") with a minor child
   - Denial of visitation only when it would seriously endanger a child's physical, mental, or emotional health
     - o Restrictions (e.g., supervision, denial of overnight visits) may be imposed
   - **Sexual relationship or cohabitation**—can be a basis for a restriction only if there is an adverse impact on the child
   - A parent cannot be denied visitation due to a failure to pay child support

2. **Third parties**
   - A fit parent has a fundamental right to the care, custody, and control of his children; the parent's decisions regarding third-party visitation must be given special weight
   - Visitation is sometimes granted to stepparents and same-sex nonbiological co-parents
     - o Typically limited to individuals who acted *in loco parentis* with the child prior to the divorce
   - **Grandparent visitation**—subject to the special weight given to a fit parent's decision
   - **Unwed biological father**—has a fundamental right to have contact with his child if he demonstrates a commitment to the responsibilities of parenthood

E. Enforcement

1. **Sanctions**—e.g., compensatory visitation, attorney's fees, court costs, fines, jail time
   - Tort damages awarded to parent for the period of time that the child is wrongfully out of the parent's custody

F. Modification—change-in-circumstances standard (most states)

1. **Relocation**—may be permitted if there is a legitimate and reasonable purpose for the move

G. Termination—a child-custody order terminates upon the child reaching the age of majority

1. **Death of custodial parent**—the surviving parent is usually awarded custody of the child

H. Parental consent

1. **Medical care**
   - Parental consent must be obtained regardless of the parents' marital status except in the case of an emergency

- A parent's religious beliefs can be overridden by a court to prevent serious harm to the child
   2. **Upbringing**—a parent has a right to raise her child as she sees fit, including decisions relating to the child's religious upbringing

V.   **Marital Agreements**

A.   **Types of marital agreements**

   1. **Premarital agreement**—a valid marriage is sufficient consideration
      - **Many states**—a premarital agreement must expressly state its applicability to divorce

   2. **Separation agreement**
      - Can define property division, spousal support, child support, custody, and visitation
      - Generally merged into the final judgment for divorce or else governed by contract law

   3. **Property-settlement agreement**
      - Can settle economic issues; entered into by parties before a divorce decree is issued

B.   **Validity of marital agreements**

   1. **In general**
      - A premarital agreements is enforceable if:
         o **Full disclosure** of financial status of each party at the time of execution
         o Agreement is **fair and reasonable**, and
         o Agreement is **voluntary**
      - Must be in writing and signed by the party to be charged
      - UPAA requires the party against whom enforcement is sought to prove:
         o Involuntariness; or
         o That the agreement was unconscionable when executed and she:
            ▪ Did not receive or waive fair and reasonable disclosure; and
            ▪ Did not have, or reasonably could not have had, adequate knowledge of the other's assets and obligations.

   2. **Modification of marital agreements**
      - Provision that prevents modification of property rights, including spousal support—permitted
      - Provision that prevents modification of child support—not enforceable

C.   **Agreements between unmarried cohabitants**

   1. **Cohabitation agreements**—a contract between unmarried persons is invalid if the only consideration is sexual relations; otherwise, generally enforceable

   2. **Property division between unmarried cohabitants**—equitable property distribution to avoid unjust enrichment (e.g., resulting trust, constructive trust, or quantum meruit)

VI. Relationship Between the Family and the State

A. Adoption

1. Termination of a natural parent's rights

- **Voluntary termination**—the biological parents give up their parental rights of the minor child and consent to child's adoption by the adoptive parents

  o Unwed father

    - Consent by failure to register—constitutes a waiver of the right to notice of the adoption and irrevocably implies his consent to the adoption

    - Right to object can be denied if the father does not demonstrate a commitment to the responsibilities of parenthood

  o Prospective adoptee must consent to his adoption if he is over 14 years of age

- **Involuntary termination by court**

  o Typically occurs as part of an abuse, neglect, or dependency case, or when consent to an adoption is unreasonably withheld

  o Includes abandonment or abuse of sibling, termination of parental rights over a sibling

  o Adoption and Safe Families Act—a state can move for termination of parental rights when the child has been placed outside of the home and not with a relative for 15 of the past 22 months, provided certain reunification attempts have been provided by the state

  o Some states—an adoption is permitted if a parent has abandoned the parent-child relationship

    - Objective test—parent has failed to act in a way that indicates a commitment to maintaining the parent-child relationship

    - Subjective test—parent subjectively intended to abandon the parent-child relationship

2. Legal effects of adoption

- Adoptive parents have all of the rights and responsibilities of the biological parents; adopted child has all of the rights and responsibilities of a biological child

- Most states—no visitation is permitted between the adoptee and her biological parents

B. Uniform Parentage Act (UPA)—adopted by nine states

1. Assisted reproduction

- Maternity is determined by woman who gives birth to child

- Husband of woman who is determined to be the mother of the child is the child's father

2. Gestational (surrogacy) agreement—all parties must enter voluntarily

- Intended parents agree to be parents of the resulting child

- Agreement must make provisions for proper medical care

- Agreement may not limit the right of the gestational mother to make healthcare decisions

- Consideration to the gestational mother must be reasonable

- Agreement may be terminated for cause by any of the parties, or by the court, prior to the gestational mother's pregnancy

- Agreement not approved by court is unenforceable

C. Domestic violence

1. **Perpetrator of violence**—must be in a relationship with the victim or a household or family member; generally requires a continuum of behavior, but a single episode may qualify

2. **Relief granted**—an injunctive order prohibiting defendant's further abuse of and contact with victim; can also include exclusive possession of residence, child custody, and support

3. **Process**—ex parte order with limited relief, followed by a hearing, after notice to defendant, on petition for permanent relief; violation of order can trigger criminal penalties

D. Rights and obligations of children

1. **Right to consent to medical care**

- May consent to medical treatment if over certain age

- May obtain abortion, birth control, treatment for sexually transmitted disease without parental consent

2. **Liability for torts/criminal acts**—children judged by more moderate standard

3. **Emancipation**—child has all the duties and obligations of an adult; parents have no duty to support

FINAL REVIEW OUTLINE: PARTNERSHIPS

I. Partnership Formation and Relationships

A. Formation

1. Partnership (P) requirements

- **Intent**—two or more persons or entities must intend to carry on a for-profit business as co-owners but do not need the specific intent to form a P

- **Partnership agreement (PA)**—to conduct a for-profit business as co-owners; can be implied by conduct in the absence of a written or oral agreement

- **Statute of Frauds**—a written agreement is not required for formation, but a contract that cannot be performed in one year must be in writing per the Statute of Frauds

- **Extensive activity**—a court will consider the amount of related activities directed toward achieving a business's end goal when determining whether a P exists

- **Profit sharing test:**

  o Rule—if there is profit sharing, it is presumed to be a P

  o Exceptions—sharing profits does not create a presumption of a P in six statutorily enumerated circumstances: debt payments; interest or loan charges; rent; wages; goodwill payments from the sale of a business; and annuities or other retirement or health benefits

2. Partner by estoppel

- **Case 1:** P does not exist but a person is treated as a partner of a purported P
  Case 2: P exists and a person who is not a partner of P is treated as a partner of P

- **Elements**—a person may be treated as a purported partner if:

  o There is a **representation** (oral, written, or implied by conduct) that a person is a partner in a P

  o The person **makes or consents** to the representation

  o A third party **reasonably relied** on the representation, and

  o The third party suffered **damages** as a result of that reliance

- No duty to deny the representation; merely being named by another is not enough to create liability

- It is not a defense that the purported partner was unaware that he had been held out as a partner to the specific third party if the representation was made in a public manner

- Purported partners are agents of the person making the representation

3. Nature of partnership

- **Separate legal entity**—a P may hold property and can sue and be sued

- Partners are not protected from personal liability for the P's obligations

- If there is a formal PA, it generally governs when there is a conflict between the PA and RUPA

B. Relationships of partner with P and between partners

1. **Partner as agent to P**—a partner can commit the P to binding contracts with third parties

2. **Fiduciary duties**

    - **Duty of loyalty**

        o   Rule—no competing with P business, advancing an interest adverse to the P, or usurping a P opportunity

        o   Exception—the PA can **designate** certain activities as not violating the duty (but cannot eliminate the duty altogether) and may provide a **safe harbor** allowing the other partners to authorize or ratify a transaction between a partner and the P after full disclosure of material facts

    - **Duty of care**

        o   Duty to refrain from engaging in grossly negligent or reckless conduct, intentional conduct, or a knowing violation of the law

        o   The PA may not unreasonably reduce this duty

    - **Dissociation/dissolution**—upon a partner's dissociation or the P's dissolution, the duties do not apply unless the partner is engaged in winding up the P's business

    - **Good faith and fair dealing**—The PA cannot eliminate this obligation but can prescribe reasonable standards

3. **Profits and losses**—if there is no PA or the PA is silent, each partner is entitled to an equal share of profits and losses; if the PA only specifies the division of profits, then losses are shared in same manner as profits

4. **Partner's account**—contains the partner's contributions to the P and the partner's share of the profits (less distributions, losses, and liabilities)

5. **Distributions**—a partner cannot demand a profit distribution but is entitled to have her account credited with her share of profits

6. **Partnership interest**

    - **Personal property interest**—consisting of the rights to share in the P's profits and losses and to receive distributions

    - **Transfer to third party**

        o   Rule—a partner can transfer all or part of the P interest (absent a restriction in the PA); the transferor partner retains all rights and duties of a partner (except for an interest in the distributions); transfer does not cause dissolution or dissociation

        o   Transferee rights

            ▪   Right to receive distributions, to seek judicial order for dissolution, and to an accounting upon dissolution

            ▪   No right to participate in the management or conduct of P business, access the P's records, or demand other information

7. **Property ownership**

    - **Rule**—all property acquired by the P belongs to the P and not to the individual partners; property may be acquired and titled in the name of the P or in the name of one or more partners who indicate their capacity as partners or the existence of the P

- **Intent of partners controls**—property is presumed to be P property if it was purchased with P assets or if P credit is used to get financing; but if ownership is unclear, consider other factors such as property's use, tax treatment of the property, and the source of funds to maintain or improve the property

8. **New partner**—an incoming partner must secure the consent of **all existing** partners

9. **Management rights**—each partner has equal management rights; a **majority** of partners needed to make ordinary P business decisions; the consent of **all** partners is required for matters outside the ordinary course of the P's business and for amendments to the PA

10. **Remuneration**—none, except for reasonable compensation for winding up the P's business

11. **Reimbursement and indemnification**—a P must reimburse a partner for loans made in furtherance of P business; and the P is required to indemnify partners for personal liability incurred in the ordinary course of P business

12. **Use of P property**—a partner cannot derive a personal benefit from the use or possession of P property; the partner must compensate the P for such use or possession

13. **Access to records**—a P must permit its partners and agents to access all P records

14. **Lawsuits**—a P may sue a partner for breach of the PA or for violating a duty owed to the P; a partner may sue the P or another partner to enforce the partner's rights under the PA or RUPA

15. **Dissociation**

- **Events causing dissociation:**
  - Partner's notice of withdrawal
  - Partner's expulsion due to the PA, unanimous vote of the other partners, or the partner's bankruptcy
  - Partner's death
  - Appointment of a guardian for the partner or a judicial determination of the partner's incapacity to perform his duties under the PA
  - Termination of an entity partner
- **Wrongful dissociation**—a partner is liable to the P and the other partners for damages caused by wrongful dissociation
  - P unlimited by time or undertaking—a partner's dissociation is wrongful only when it is in breach of an express provision of the PA
  - P for a definite term or undertaking—a partner's dissociation is wrongful if, before the expiration of the term or completion of the undertaking, the partner withdraws, is expelled by court order, is a debtor in bankruptcy, or is not an individual, trust, or estate and the partner willfully dissolved or terminated
- **Effect of dissociation:**
  - A dissociated partner is not permitted to participate in the management or conduct of P business
  - A partner's duty not to compete terminates upon dissociation; the partner's other duties of loyalty and care terminate with respect to post-dissociation events
  - An ongoing P must buy out the dissociated partner's P interest

- o Indemnification—the P must indemnify a dissociated partner against all P liabilities, whether incurred **before or after** the dissociation
- o Dissociated partner's liability—a dissociated partner is generally liable for P obligations incurred **before** the dissociation
- o Post-dissociation action—a dissociated partner can bind himself and the P to a transaction if the other party (i) reasonably believes the dissociated partner is a partner, (ii) does not have notice of the dissociation, and (iii) is not deemed to have knowledge of the dissociated partner's lack of authority; liability is limited to transactions within **two years** of the partner's dissociation

C. Relationships with third parties

1. Power to bind the P

- **Partner as agent of the P**—a partner can contractually bind the P when the partner acts with **actual or apparent authority**
  - o **Actual authority**—includes both express authority and implied authority
    - **Express authority**—can arise from the PA, the authorization of the partners, or a statement of authority filed with the state
    - **Implied authority**—based on a partner's reasonable belief that an action is necessary to carry out his express authority
  - o **Apparent authority**—a partner must perform the unauthorized act in the ordinary course of P business; the third party with whom the partner was dealing cannot hold the P liable if the third party knew or was notified that the partner lacked authority
  - o Transfer of titled P property—in some circumstances, a partner has authority to transfer titled P property
    - P property held in the P's name—a partner has the authority to execute an instrument of transfer in the P's name
    - P property held in a partner's name—a partner has the authority to execute an instrument of transfer in one or more partners' names
    - Recovery of P property from transferee (P property transferred without authority)—recoverable if the P interest was indicated in the transfer instrument through which the P acquired the property or if the transferee was aware that the property belonged to the P and that the partner executed the transfer without authority
  - o P's knowledge and notice—absent fraud, a partner's knowledge or notice of a fact relating to the P is generally immediately imputed to the P
  - o A person who owns all partners' interests in the P effectively has title to all of the P property and has the power to transfer title to himself
- **Statements of P authority and denial**—to clarify the existence and scope of a partner's authority, statements of P authority and denial may be filed with the state

2. Effect of a partner's tortious acts—the P is liable for a partner's tortious acts committed in the ordinary course of the P business or with P authority

3. Liability to third parties

- **P obligations**—a P is subject to suit for its obligations; partners are jointly and severally liable for all P obligations

- **Effect of judgment**—a judgment against a P is first satisfied from the P's assets, and then the partners' personal assets

- **Criminal liability**—a P can be convicted of a crime and a penalty levied on P assets

II. Partnership Changes and Termination

A. Conversion

1. **P to limited partnership (LP)**—the conversion must be approved by all of the partners of the P, and the P must file the articles of conversion with the state; former general partners remain liable for pre-conversion obligations

2. **LP to P**—the conversion must be approved by all of the general and limited partners, and the LP must cancel its LP certificate; partners remain liable as limited partners for pre-conversion LP obligations and are liable as general partners for post-conversion P obligations

3. **Effect on the P**—a conversion has no effect on the P as an entity (e.g., property owned by the P remains owned by the P; legal proceedings by or against the P continue as if the conversion had not occurred)

B. Merger

1. **Plan**—a plan of merger must set forth the names of the original and surviving entities, the type of entity the surviving entity will be, the terms and conditions of merger, the manner of converting interests and obligations of the merging entities into interests and obligations of the surviving entity, and the address of surviving entity

2. **Approval**—all partners of a general P must approve; as required by law or as specified in the PA for limited Ps

3. **Effect**—all parties other than the surviving entity cease to exist; all property and obligations of the original entities become that of the surviving entity

C. Termination of Partnership (i.e., dissolution and winding up)

1. **Events causing dissolution**

   - **P at will** (open-ended P with no fixed termination)—dissolved when a dissociating partner gives notice of withdrawal

   - **P for a term or undertaking**—dissolved when (i) the term expires or the undertaking is completed; (ii) all partners agree to dissolve the P; or (iii) a partner is dissociated due to death, bankruptcy, or other event and at least half of the remaining partners agree to dissolve the P within 90 days

   - **Any P**—dissolved upon: the occurrence of an event agreed to in the PA; an event that makes it unlawful for P business to be continued; or a judicial determination

2. **Winding up**

   - A person winding up the P business may dispose of and transfer P property and may discharge the P's liabilities; the person may distribute P assets to settle the partners' accounts

   - After dissolution, the P is bound by a partner's act that is appropriate for winding up the P as well as any act undertaken by a partner that would have bound the P before dissolution, if the other party does not have notice of the dissolution (each partner is liable to the other partners for his share of P liability)

   - Creditors have priority over partners to the P's assets

3. **Continuation of P after dissolution**—before winding up is complete, the P may resume carrying on its business as if dissolution had never occurred

III. Other Partnership Entities

A. Limited liability partnerships (LLP)—an LLP partner is not personally liable for an LLP obligation; he is only personally liable for his own personal misconduct; revocation of the state's qualification of LLP status will have same effect as cancellation

B. Limited partnerships (LP)

1. **Rule**—must be formed by at least one general partner and one limited partner; limited partner's liability for P debts is limited to her capital contribution to the P; and a limited P is not formed if a certificate of limited P is not filed

2. **Limited partner**—can only be admitted by written consent of all partners after creation; has the right to vote as permitted under the PA and the right to inspect business and financial records; can lend money and transact business like a non-partner with the LP; and is generally not personally liable for LP obligations unless the limited partner is also a general partner or participates in the control of the business

3. **General partner**
   - **Rule**—can only be admitted by written consent of all partners after creation; has the rights and powers of a partner in a P without limited partners; may contribute to LP, share in its losses and profits, and receive distributions
   - **Liability to third parties**—personally liable to third parties for obligations of the LP
   - **Termination of status**—can withdraw from the LP by giving written notice to the other partners; other events may cause a general partner's termination

4. **Contributions**—partners can contribute cash, property, or services, and are obligated to the LP with respect to any written, enforceable promise of a future contribution

5. **Profits and losses**—may be allocated on any basis if in writing; otherwise based on each partner's P contributions

6. **Distributions**—may be allocated on any basis if in writing; otherwise based on how profits/losses are shared

7. **Assignment of P interest**—a P interest in an LP is personal property that can be assigned in whole or in part; the assignee generally has rights only to receive the distribution to which the assignor partner would otherwise be entitled

8. **Termination**—occurs after dissolution and winding up
   - **P is dissolved** upon the occurrence of a specified event, written consent of all partners, withdrawal of a general partner, or a judicial determination
   - **Winding up**—general partners wind up, but if none, then limited partners may; distribution of assets first to creditors and then to partners

9. **LP derivative action**—a limited partner has the right to bring a derivative action on behalf of the LP

FINAL REVIEW OUTLINE: SECURED TRANSACTIONS

I. **In General**

    A. **Security interest (SI)**—an interest in personal property or fixtures that secures payment or performance of an obligation

    B. **Agreement**—a consensual agreement that provides for the SI; the substance of the transaction controls, not the form

    C. **Parties**

        1. **Secured party**—the person in whose favor the SI is created under the security agreement

        2. **Obligor**—the person who must pay (or otherwise perform) with respect to the obligation that is secured by the SI

        3. **Debtor**—the person who has interest, other than the SI or other lien, in the collateral, such as its sole owner (the debtor is usually also the obligor)

    D. **Collateral**—property subject to the SI

        1. **Tangible collateral**

- **Goods**—anything that is moveable at time that the SI attaches; the debtor's principal use at the time the SI attaches determines the class of the goods

  - **Consumer goods**—goods acquired primarily for personal, family, or household purposes

  - **Farm products**—goods that are crops or livestock and include supplies that are used or produced in farming

  - **Inventory**—goods, other than farm products, held for sale or lease; are furnished under a service contract; or consist of raw materials, works in process, or materials used or consumed in a business; usually refers to goods that are consumed in a business (e.g., fuel)

  - **Equipment**—catchall class; consists of goods that are not consumer goods, farm products, or inventory

- **Software**—software embedded in goods is treated as part of goods in which it is embedded; software not embedded in goods is treated as a general intangible

        2. **Other collateral**—classification is determined without reference to the debtor's use

- **Chattel paper**—one or more records that evidence both (i) a monetary obligation and (ii) a security interest in specific goods or a lease of specific goods

- **Document**—a document of title, which confers on the holder ownership rights in goods held by a bailee

- **Instruments**—encompasses both negotiable and nonnegotiable instruments

- **Investment property**—includes both certificated and uncertificated securities, as well as securities accounts

- **Accounts**—the right to payment for property sold, leased, or licensed, or services rendered

- **Commercial tort claims**—excludes tort claims by an individual for personal injury or death

- **Deposit accounts**

- **Letter-of-credit right**
- **General intangibles**—a residual category; e.g., copyrights

E. **Eligible transactions**

1. **General rule**—Art. 9 governs a transaction that creates an SI in personal property or a fixture

2. **Leases**—covered under Art. 9 when the transaction, although in the form of a lease, is in substance a secured transaction

3. **Consignments**—if subject to Art. 9, the consignor's SI in the consigned goods is treated as a PMSI in inventory

4. **Liens**—generally not generally subject to Art. 9

5. **Agricultural liens**—unlike other liens, generally subject to Art. 9

6. **Purchases**—generally, the sale of personal property is not subject to Art. 9

7. **Real property transactions**—not generally subject to Art. 9; but can apply to an SI in a secured obligation (e.g., a promissory note) even though the obligation is itself secured by a transaction or interest to which Article 9 does not apply (e.g., a real property mortgage)

II. **Attachment of SI**

A. **In general**—an SI that is enforceable against the debtor with respect to the collateral is said to have "attached" to the collateral

1. **Requirements**—(i) value given by the secured party; (ii) the debtor has rights in the collateral; and (iii) the debtor has authenticated a security agreement that describes the collateral, or the secured party has possession or control of the collateral

B. **Value given by the secured party**—can be consideration sufficient to form a contract, extending credit, accepting delivery under a preexisting contract, or in satisfaction of a preexisting claim

1. **Future advances**—may also be secured by collateral

2. **New value**—when new value is required to perfect a security interest or have priority, it can consist of:
   - Money;
   - Money's worth in property, services, or new credit; or
   - Release by a transferee of an interest in property previously transferred to the transferee.

C. **Debtor's rights in collateral**

1. **Generally**—the SI attaches only to the rights that the debtor has in the collateral

2. **Consignments**—if the consignor retains title to the consigned goods, the consignee does not have rights in them

D. **Security agreement**—the secured party must satisfy the Art. 9 Statute of Frauds (SoF)

1. **Authenticated record**—the security agreement must (i) be in a record; (ii) contain a description of the collateral; and (iii) be authenticated by the debtor
   - The description can list specific items or can identify the Art. 9 type of collateral ("all debtor's equipment) unless the collateral is consumer goods or a commercial tort claim; a super-generic description ("all debtor's assets") is not sufficient

- An original authenticated security agreement can serve as a new debtor's authenticated security agreement (i.e., the new debtor need not execute another agreement) by operation of law or by contract

2. **Possession of collateral**—can satisfy the SoF; the secured party's possession must be pursuant to the security agreement

3. **Control of collateral**—can satisfy the SoF; the secured party's control must be pursuant to the security agreement

E. **After-acquired collateral**

1. **General rule**—the SI may cover collateral owned when the security is granted and also collateral that the debtor acquires after the SI is given

2. **Exceptions**—an after-acquired clause is not effective for consumer goods, unless the debtor acquires them within 10 days after the secured party gives value, or a commercial tort claim

F. **Proceeds**—the SI attaches automatically to identifiable proceeds (i.e., whatever is acquired upon disposition of the collateral)

G. **Rights and duties of the secured party**

1. **Duties arising from the secured party's possession or control of collateral**—duty of care; duty to keep collateral identifiable; duty to relinquish possession or control of collateral

2. **Rights and risks arising from the secured party's possession or control of collateral**—right to charge for reasonable expenses; risk of loss or damage is on the debtor; right to use or operate collateral; right to hold proceeds

3. **Assignment of account rights**—if the debtor assigns his right to receive payment from the account debtor to the secured party, the secured party may notify the account debtor to pay the secured party; upon receipt of notification, the account debtor may discharge her obligation only by paying the assignee

H. **Rights of the debtor**

1. **Accounting** and other information from the secured party

2. **Notification of account debtors by secured party**—when account debtors are no longer required to make payments to the secured party

I. **Purchase-money security interest (PMSI)**

1. **PMSI in goods**—exists when:

- A secured party gave value to the debtor and the debtor used the value to incur an obligation that enabled the debtor to acquire goods; or

- A secured party sold goods to the debtor, and the debtor incurred an obligation to pay the secured party all or part of the purchase price

2. **PMSI in software**—exists only when the debtor acquired his interest in software in an integrated transaction in which the debtor also acquired an interest in goods (e.g., a computer), and the debtor acquired that interest in the software for the principal purpose of using the software in the goods

J. Accessions—goods that are physically united with other goods such that the identity of the original goods is not lost

    1. **SI created in collateral that becomes an accession**—not lost due to the collateral becoming an accession; also, an SI can be created in collateral that is an accession

K. Commingled goods—goods that are physically united with other goods such that their identity is lost in a product or mass

    1. **No SI in specific goods that have been commingled**—but an SI may attach to the product or mass that results when the goods are commingled

    2. **Existing SI in collateral that subsequently becomes commingled goods**—the SI is transferred to the resulting product or mass

III. Perfection of Security Interest—the SI is perfected upon attachment of that interest and compliance with one of the methods of perfection; perfection creates superior rights in the collateral for secured party over third parties' rights in the collateral

A. Methods of perfection—filing, possession, control, and automatic perfection

B. Filing of financing statement—gives interested parties notice of the existence of the SI; filing is a method of perfection for any SI except a deposit account, money, or letter-of-credit rights

    1. **Financing statement**—must contain (i) the debtor's name, (ii) the secured party's name, and (iii) a description of collateral; it is a notice filing

- **Alternatives**—security agreement, mortgage
- **Debtor's name**—the name on the debtor's current driver's license or state-issued identification card (most states)
  - **Debtor's trade name**—insufficient by itself; not needed if the debtor's name is correctly provided
  - **Registered organization**—the name shown on public organic records (e.g., articles of incorporation)
  - **Debtor's change of name**—the secured party has four months to amend the financing statement; if not done, collateral acquired by the debtor after the four-month period is not covered by the financing statement
  - **Error in debtor's name**—a financing statement is not effective unless a standard search under the debtor's correct name would disclose the statement
  - **Error in secured party's name**—an error in the name of the secured party generally does not affect the perfection of the SI, but could subject the secured party to estoppel in favor of another claimant
- **Description of the collateral**—unlike security agreement, the financing statement may include a super-generic description of the collateral ("all debtor's assets") if the description sufficiently indicates the collateral
  - **After-acquired property and future advances**—a financing statement may be effective to cover after-acquired property if such property falls within the collateral described, whether mentioned or even contemplated by the parties at the time the financing statement was authorized
  - **Proceeds**—an SI in proceeds is perfected even if not mentioned in the financing statement

- o **Error in description**—the secured party must prepare a termination statement with respect to the erroneous collateral

2. **Debtor's authorization**—required, but the debtor need not sign the financing statement

- "Ipso facto authorization"—the debtor's authentication of the security agreement serves as authorization to file the financing statement

- The debtor's consent to the filing is presumed when the secured party seeks to perfect an SI in any identifiable proceeds of collateral by filing

3. **Person entitled to file financing statement**—any person may do so; the signature of the filer is not required

4. **Filing location**

- **Collateral related to real property**—the office for recording a mortgage on the related real property; local filing

- **All other collateral**—the secretary of state of the state of the debtor's location; central filing

  - o Individual debtor—the state in which the debtor maintains his principal residence

  - o Nonregistered organization (partnership) debtor—the state in which it maintains its place of business and, if it has more than one place of business, at its chief executive office

  - o Registered organization (corporation)—the state in which it is organized

5. **Effective date of filing**—upon delivery to the filing office and tender of the filing fee

- **Filing office's refusal to accept**

  - o **Justified refusal** (e.g., failure to pay fee)—the financing statement is treated as having not been filed

  - o **Unjustified refusal**—the financing statement is treated as having been filed; the statement is effective except as to a purchaser of the collateral who gives value in reasonable reliance upon the absence of the record from the files

- **Filing office's incorrect indexing of a statement**—does not affect the effectiveness of a filed statement; the risk of a filing-office error rests on those who search files, not those who file the statement

6. **Length of perfection**—a financing statement is generally effective for five years

- Effective during this period, even though there is no obligation secured by the collateral and no commitment to make an advance, unless a termination statement has been filed

7. **Continuation statement**—effective to extend perfection for an additional five years; no need for the debtor's signature; if not filed, the SI is treated as never having been perfected as against a purchaser of the collateral for value

8. **Amendment of financing statement**—filed to add or delete collateral covered by the statement; effective from the date of filing; does not extend period of effectiveness of the financing statement

9. **Termination statement**—terminates effectiveness of a financing statement

C. **Possession**—an SI in goods, instruments, negotiable documents, money, tangible chattel paper, and certificated security may be perfected by possession; perfection exists only during the period of possession

D. **Control**—perfection exists only while secured party retains control

1. **Collateral perfected by control**—only an SI in investment property, deposit accounts, letter-of-credit rights, electronic chattel paper, or electronic documents

2. **Letter of credit rights**—generally, control is the only method of perfection, unless such rights are a supporting obligation for other collateral

3. **Deposit account**—control is the only method of perfection

E. **Automatic perfection**

1. **Indefinite period of perfection**

    - **PMSI in consumer goods**—automatically perfected upon attachment; a secured party does not need to file a financing statement

2. **Temporary perfection**

    - **New value**—if new value is given under an authenticated security agreement, an SI in certificated securities, negotiable documents, or instruments is automatically perfected for 20 days from attachment

    - **Delivery of collateral to debtor**—if the collateral is delivered to the debtor for the purpose of selling or exchanging it, the SI in the collateral remains temporarily perfected for 20 days

    - **Interstate movement of collateral or debtor**

        o **Movement of the debtor to another state**—four-month grace period for a perfected SI

        o **Movement of collateral to debtor in another state**—one-year grace period for a perfected SI

        o **Perfected possessory SI**—no effect on perfection when the SI is perfected under the new state's laws

        o **Effect of a lapse of perfection**—the SI generally ceases to be perfected upon the expiration of the temporary perfection period

3. **Proceeds**

    - **Temporary perfection**—if SI in original collateral perfected, SI in proceeds perfected for 20 days from attachment

    - **Indefinite automatic perfection**

        o **Pursuant to financing statement**—if the original financing statement is broad enough to cover proceeds or the secured party amends the financing statement to cover proceeds within 20 days, then the SI in proceeds continues to be perfected

        o **Cash proceeds**—if the SI in the original collateral is perfected, then the SI in the identifiable cash proceeds is perfected indefinitely

        o **Same office**—if a filed financing statement covers the original collateral and the proceeds are collateral in which an SI may be perfected by filing in the office in which the financing statement has been filed, then a perfected SI in proceeds may continue indefinitely

            ▪ Does not apply to proceeds acquired with cash proceeds
            ▪ Limitation—if the original filing ceases to be effective after the 20-day period, the SI in proceeds also ceases to be automatically perfected

F. Non-Article 9 rules: notation for vehicles—a non-Art. 9 statute controls the manner of perfection; filing is not sufficient if a statute requires a notation of the SI on the certificate of title

G. Timing of perfection—upon (i) attachment of the SI and (ii) compliance with a method of perfection; if there is a change in the method of perfection without a lapse, then the perfection dates from the date on which the SI is first perfected

IV. Priorities—Art. 9 prioritizes claims and pays them in order; the holder of a priority can agree to subordinate his interest to another's interest

A. Claimants—creditors, transferees/buyers, other secured parties

B. Creditors

1. **General creditor (unsecured)**—has a claim, including a judgment, but no lien on or SI in collateral

   - **Result:** an SI *always* prevails over a general creditor's rights in the debtor's collateral

2. **Judicial lien creditor**—acquires a lien on the collateral by a judicial process

   - **Result:** a perfected SI has priority over a judicial lien; a judicial lien has priority over an unperfected SI unless the only reason the SI was unperfected was that the secured party had not yet given value

     ○ **PMSI exception**—if a PMSI is perfected before or within 20 days after the debtor receives possession of the collateral, the PMSI has priority over a creditor's rights that arose between the time of attachment of the SI and filing

     ○ **Advances**—an SI securing an advance is subordinate to a lien creditor's rights when the advance is made more than 45 days after the person becomes a lien creditor, unless the advance or commitment is made without knowledge of the lien

3. **Statutory or common-law lien creditor**—has a possessory lien on the collateral by statute or common-law rule (i.e., a nonconsensual lien)

   - **Result:** a possessory lien has priority over any SI if the lien secures payment for goods or services furnished in the ordinary course of business (e.g., mechanic's lien) unless a statute provides different priority rule

C. Transferees—obtain full title to collateral as result of a transfer from the debtor

1. **General rules**

   - **Transferee v. secured party with an SI**—the SI generally continues in the collateral unless the secured party authorized the transfer free of the SI

   - **Buyer's rights v. unperfected SI**—the buyer takes the collateral free of the SI if the buyer (i) give value, and (ii) receives delivery, (iii) without knowledge of the SI

   - **Buyer's rights v. perfected SI**—the buyer generally takes the collateral subject to the SI

2. **Buyer in the ordinary course of business (BOCB)**—(i) buys goods (not farm products) by giving new value (cash, etc., not satisfaction of existing debt); (ii) in the ordinary course; (iii) from a seller in the business of selling goods of that kind; (iv) in good faith; and (v) without actual knowledge that the sale violates another's rights in the goods

   - **Result:** BOCB takes free of any SI in goods given by buyer's seller

3. **Consumer buyer**—(i) buys consumer goods for value; (ii) for his own personal, family, or household use; (iii) from a consumer seller; and (iv) without knowledge or record notice of the security interest

   - **Result:** a consumer buyer takes free of any SI in consumer goods unless a secured party has filed a financing statement covering the goods ("garage sale" rule)

4. **Purchasers of chattel paper**—(i) gives new value and has possession/control of collateral; (ii) purchase is made in good faith and in the ordinary course of business, and (iii) the chattel paper does not indicate an assignment to an identified assignee (for an SI claimed as proceeds of inventory), or a purchase made without knowledge that the purchase violates secured party's rights (for all other SIs)

   - **Result:** a purchaser of chattel paper has priority over an SI in the chattel paper

5. **Buyer of negotiable instrument or document**—the buyer takes free of any SI

6. **Buyer not in the ordinary course of business** (future advances)

   - The buyer generally takes free of any SI that secures an advance made after the earlier of (i) the time the secured party acquires knowledge of purchase or (ii) 45 days after purchase

   - The buyer takes subject to the SI if the advance is made pursuant to a commitment entered into without knowledge of the buyer's purchases and before the expiration of the 45-day period

7. **Transferee of money or funds**—generally takes free of an SI in money or funds; a debtor is not treated as a transferee

8. **Article 2 security interest**—an Art. 2 SI of a buyer or seller with possession of the goods has priority over an Art. 9 SI

9. **"Clean" certificate of title**—a buyer without knowledge of a prior SI not noted on the title takes the goods free of that SI

D. **Priorities among secured parties**

1. **General rules**

   - **Perfected SI v. perfected SI**—the first to file or perfect has priority; a lapse in filing or perfection restarts the clock

   - **Perfected SI v. unperfected SI**—a perfected SI has priority over an unperfected SI

   - **Unperfected SI v. unperfected SI**—the first to attach has priority ("first in time, first in right" rule)

2. **PMSI priority rules**

   - **PMSI v. non-PMSI**—generally, a PMSI has priority

   - **PMSI in goods other than inventory or livestock v. any SI**—a PMSI has priority if perfected before or within 20 days after the debtor receives possession of collateral

   - **PMSI in inventory or livestock v. any SI**—a PMSI has priority if perfected by the time the debtor receives possession of the collateral, and the purchase-money secured party sends an authenticated notice of the PMSI to the holder of any conflicting SI before the debtor receives possession of the collateral (notification is required only when the SI was perfected by filing)

   - **Perfected PMSI v. perfected PMSI**—the first to file or perfect has priority

     ○ **Exception**—a seller with a PMSI has priority over a lender with a PMSI

- **Proceeds from PMSI in goods**—priority of a PMSI in goods generally extends to the proceeds of the original collateral, if the SI is perfected when the debtor receives possession of collateral or within 20 days thereafter

  3. **Fixtures**

     - **SI in fixtures versus real property interest**—an SI in fixtures has priority over an interest in the real property with which the fixtures are associated if the SI in fixtures is perfected by a fixture filing before the real property interest is recorded

     - **Perfected SI in fixtures versus subsequent judicial lien**—a perfected SI in fixtures has priority

     - **PMSI in fixtures v. prior real property interest**—a PMSI in fixtures has priority if it is perfected by a fixture filing before the goods become fixtures or within 20 days thereafter

     - **SI in fixtures v. prior construction mortgage**—a prior construction mortgage has priority if recorded before the goods become fixtures

  4. **Proceeds**

     - **General rule**—"first to file or perfect" rule applies; the filing or perfection date for the original collateral is the filing or perfection date for the proceeds

       o **Proceeds of non-filing collateral**—the priority of the original collateral generally continues in the proceeds if the SI in the proceeds is perfected and the proceeds are cash proceeds or proceeds of same type as the original collateral

  5. **Future advances**

     - **General rule**—"first to file or perfect" rule generally applies; the time that an advance is made usually does not determine priority

  6. **Accessions**—general priority rules govern; after default, a secured party may have the right to remove the accession

  7. **Investment property, deposit accounts**—an SI held by a secured party with control over the collateral has priority over a secured party without control over the collateral

V. **Default**—undefined by Art. 9; left up to the parties

   A. **Circumstances constituting default**

      1. **In general**—a security agreement is a contract; contract law determines the enforceability of any terms in a security agreement

      2. **Agreement not to assert defenses against an assignee**—permitted by Art. 9

   B. **Consequences of default**—the secured party may (i) seek possession of the collateral and sell it or retain it, or (ii) sue for a judgment based on the obligation

      1. **Cumulative remedies, simultaneous exercise**

      2. **Ignoring default**—may be treated as waiver of the secured party's rights

      3. **SI in fixtures**—the secured party may remove the fixture from the real property if the SI has priority; the secured party is liable for repair costs

      4. **SI in accession**—the secured party may remove the accession from other property if the accession SI has priority

      5. **Secured party and account debtors**—upon default, the secured party may notify an account debtor to pay the secured party

C. **Possession of collateral**—a secured party is not required to give notice of default, nor of an intent to take possession of the collateral

1. **Limitation on means of possession**—no breach of the peace

2. **Rendering equipment unusable**—permitted

D. **Disposition of collateral**

1. **Standard for disposition**—all aspects of the disposition must be commercially reasonable (method, manner, time, and place)

2. **Price**—no specific price must be obtained; the mere fact that a higher price could have been obtained does not establish unreasonableness

3. **Time of disposition**—no specific time is required; immediate disposition is not always required

4. **Type of disposition**—disposition may be by either public or private sale, but the secured party cannot purchase the collateral at a private sale

5. **Notice of disposition**—the secured party is generally required to send an authenticated notification of disposition

   - **To**—(i) debtor, (ii) any secondary obligor, (iii) any other secured party or lien holder who has an SI perfected by filing, and (iv) any party who has notified the secured party of a claim or interest in the collateral

   - **When**—at least 10 days before disposition

   - **Exceptions to notification**—(i) the collateral is perishable or threatens to decline speedily in value; (ii) the collateral is of a type customarily sold on a recognized market; (iii) the person has waived his right in an authenticated writing

6. **Application of proceeds from disposition**

   - **Cash proceeds**—first to reasonable disposition expenses, then to satisfy the secured obligation, then to satisfy subordinate SIs (if the secured party made an authenticated demand before distribution is complete), and any remainder to the debtor

   - **Non-cash proceeds**—applied or paid over for application only if the failure to do so would be commercially unreasonable

   - **Treatment of a surplus or deficiency**—generally, the debtor is entitled to any surplus and is liable for any deficiency

     o Not the case for sale of accounts, chattel paper, payment intangibles, or promissory notes

   - **"Low price" disposition to secured party**—the amount of the deficiency may be adjusted to reflect the higher price that would have been realized from another person

   - **Notice in consumer goods transaction**—the secured party must send written notice as to any deficiency or surplus to the debtor upon demand

7. **Transferee's rights**—the sale of the collateral gives the buyer at the sale all of the debtor's rights in the collateral; the collateral remains subject to any senior SI

8. **Warranties**—the disposition of the collateral includes the warranties of title, possession, and quiet enjoyment; the warranties may be disclaimed or modified

E. **Acceptance of collateral (strict foreclosure)**

1. **Full satisfaction of obligation**—(i) the debtor consents, after default, to acceptance in an authenticated record; or (ii) the debtor does not object to the secured party's proposal to accept the collateral within 20 days after the proposal is sent

2. **Partial satisfaction of obligation**—the debtor consents, after default, to acceptance in an authenticated record

3. **Notification of parties other than the debtor**—the secured party must notify any other secured party or lien holder of record, or person who timely notified the secured party of a claim of an interest in the collateral

4. **Special rules for consumer debtors**

   - **Partial satisfaction**—acceptance of the collateral in partial satisfaction of the obligation is not permitted in a consumer transaction; the secured party can only accept the collateral in full satisfaction of the obligation

   - **Strict foreclosure**—if the consumer goods are in possession of the secured party, no strict foreclosure is permitted if the debtor has paid at least 60% of the cash price in the case of PMSI, or 60% of the obligation in the case of non-PMSI; the goods must be sold, not kept in satisfaction

     o Waiver permitted, but only after default and in an authenticated agreement

F. **Redemption of collateral**

1. **Method of redemption**—the redeemer must fulfill all obligations secured by the collateral and reasonable expenses incurred by the secured party in retaking the collateral or preparing for its disposition; an acceleration clause can require the redeemer to tender the entire balance of the secured obligation

2. **Time limit on redemption**—redemption is not permitted after disposition or foreclosure

3. **Waiver of right of redemption**—only permitted after default and by an authenticated agreement

G. **Remedies for a secured party's failure to comply**

1. **Basic remedies**

   - **Injunctive relief**—sought by debtor from a court to compel or restrain the secured party

   - **Actual damages**—any losses suffered by the debtor due to the secured party's failure to comply with Art. 9

   - **Consumer goods: minimum statutory damages**—a debtor or secondary obligor may recover an amount not less than the credit service charge, plus 10% of the principal amount of the obligation or time-price differential, plus 10% of the cash price, even if actual damages are less

   - **Limitation on deficiency** for failure to comply with Art. 9

     o **Commercial transactions**—there is a rebuttable presumption that the secured party is not entitled to collect a deficiency; rebutted by showing that the deficiency would have nevertheless existed; no damages if the deficiency is only reduced or eliminated as a consequence of the secured party's failure to comply with Art. 9

     o **Consumer transactions**—many courts apply the same rule as for commercial transactions, but some courts bar deficiency

2. **Conversion action**—by the debtor against the secured party for the improper possession of the collateral

3. **Non-liability of secured party to unknown debtor or obligator**

FINAL REVIEW OUTLINE: TRUSTS

I. **Trust Requirements**

   A. **Grantor/settlor**—the creator of a trust

   B. **Intent** to create a trust

   C. **Trustee**—holds legal interest or title to the trust property; a court will appoint a trustee if the settlor fails to designate one or more

   D. **Ascertainable beneficiary**—holds equitable title to the trust property; a beneficiary must impliedly or expressly accept his interest

   E. **Trust assets**

II. **Express Trusts**

   A. **Private express trust**—clearly states the intention of the settlor to transfer property to a trustee for the benefit of one or more ascertainable beneficiaries

      1. **Elements**

         • **Intent**

            o **Rule**—the settlor may manifest the intent to make a gift orally, in writing, or by conduct; manifestation of intent must occur prior to or simultaneously with the transfer of property (use of common trust terms will create a presumption of intent)

            o **Precatory trust** (expresses a hope or wish that the property transferred be used for the benefit of another rather than creating a legal obligation)—must contain specific instructions to a fiduciary, and must be shown that absent imposition of a trust, there would be an unnatural disposition of the donor's property because of familial relations or history of support between donor and intended beneficiary

         • **Trust property**

            o A trust must be funded with identifiable trust property (res), but if a trust that is invalid for lack of assets is later funded, a trust arises if the settlor re-manifests the intent to create a trust

            o Trust property must be identifiable and segregated, and it must be described with reasonable certainty

         • **Valid trust purpose**—a trust can be created for any purpose as long as it is not illegal or contrary to public policy; if one of several trust terms violates public policy, alternative terms will be honored, or, if none, the term will be stricken; but the trust will not fail unless removal of the term is fatal

         • **Ascertainable beneficiaries**

            o **Rule**—beneficiaries must be identifiable by name so that the equitable interest can be transferred automatically by operation of law and directly benefit the person; the settlor may refer to acts of independent significance to identify the beneficiaries

            o **Exceptions**—trusts for the benefit of unborn children or to a reasonably definite class will be upheld, and charitable trusts (trusts that exist for the good of the public at large) do not need individual ascertainable beneficiaries

2. **Types**
  - **Inter vivos**
    - ○ **Rule**
      - ▪ **Delivery**—must accompany the declaration of trust if a third-party trustee is named, whereby the settlor parts with dominion and control over the trust property
      - ▪ **Writing**—required only for real property; a court will impose a constructive trust when a writing is lacking
      - ▪ **Parol evidence**—evidence outside of the written agreement is permitted to show the settlor's intent only if the written agreement is ambiguous on its face
    - ○ **Pour-over trust**—a provision in a will that directs the distribution of property to a trust upon the happening of an event, even if the trust instrument was not executed in accordance with the Statute of Wills, as long as the trust is identified in the will and its terms are set forth in a written instrument
    - ○ **Totten trust**—a designation given to a bank account in a depositor's name as trustee for a named beneficiary (no separation of legal and equitable title); can be revoked by any lifetime act manifesting the depositor's intent to revoke, or by will
    - ○ **Life-insurance trust**—proceeds go to trust upon insured's death; trust is owner of policy and trust is irrevocable
    - ○ **Living trust**—typically settlor names himself trustee until death; settlor can change successor trustee and beneficiaries until death; trust property not protected from creditors or federal estate taxation
  - **Testamentary**
    - ○ **Definition**—occurs when the terms of the trust are contained in writing in a will or in a document incorporated by reference into a will
    - ○ **"Secret" trust**—looks like a testamentary gift, but is created in reliance on the named beneficiary's promise to hold and administer the property for another (a constructive trust is imposed on the property for the intended beneficiary)
    - ○ **"Semi-secret" trust**—occurs when a gift is directed in a will to be held in trust, but the testator fails to name a beneficiary or specify the terms or purpose of the trust (a resulting trust is imposed on the property to be held for the testator's heirs)
    - ○ **Modern trend**—impose a constructive trust in favor of the intended beneficiaries (if known) in both secret and semi-secret trusts

B. **Charitable trusts**

1. **Purpose**—relief of poverty, advancement of education or religion, good health, governmental purposes, and other purposes benefiting the community at large

2. **Indefinite beneficiaries**—the beneficiaries must be the community at large (directly or indirectly)

3. **Rule against perpetuities**—exempt; may continue indefinitely

4. *Cy pres* **doctrine**—a court may modify a charitable trust to seek an alternative charitable purpose if the original one becomes illegal, impracticable, or impossible to perform

5. **Honorary trusts**—have no private beneficiaries (usually for a pet)

III. **Remedial Trusts** (equitable remedy not subject to trust requirements)

A. **Resulting trust**

1. **Purpose**—when a trust fails, a court will create a resulting trust requiring the holder of the property to return it to the settlor or his estate to prevent unjust enrichment

2. **When imposed**—purchase-money resulting trust, failure of express trust, or incomplete disposition of trust assets due to excess corpus

B. **Constructive trust**—used to prevent unjust enrichment if the settlor causes fraud, duress, undue influence, breach of duty, or detrimental reliance by a third party on a false representation

C. **Gift-over clause**—provides for the disposition of trust property if trust purpose fails

IV. **Beneficiary/Creditor Rights to Distribution**

A. **Alienation**—a beneficiary's equitable interest in trust property is freely alienable unless a statute or trust instrument limits this right

B. **Support trust**—directs the trustee to pay income or principal as necessary to support the trust beneficiary; creditors cannot reach these assets unless providing a necessity to the beneficiary (trustee can pay directly)

C. **Discretionary trust**—the trustee is given complete discretion regarding whether or not to apply payments of income or principal to the beneficiary; creditors have the same rights as a beneficiary if the trustee exercises discretion to pay

D. **Mandatory trust**—the trustee has no discretion; the trust document explains in detail how and when trust property is to be distributed

E. **Spendthrift trust**—expressly restricts the beneficiary's power to voluntarily or involuntarily transfer his equitable interest; creditors usually cannot reach the trust interest if the governing instrument contains a spendthrift clause (unless for child or spousal support, basic necessities providers, and tax lien holders)

V. **Trust Modification**

A. **Termination**

1. **Rule**—a trust terminates automatically only when the trust purpose has been accomplished; a trust may terminate by consent if the settlor is deceased or has no remaining interest, and all the beneficiaries and the trustee consent; or by a court if the purpose has been achieved or becomes illegal, impracticable, or impossible

   - A revocable trust can be terminated by the settlor at any time, and an irrevocable trust usually cannot be terminated

   - **Majority rule**—a trust is presumed to be **irrevocable** unless it expressly states otherwise

   - **UTC rule**—a trust is presumed to be **revocable** unless it expressly states otherwise

2. **Unfulfilled material purpose**—a trustee can block a premature trust termination if the trust is shown to have an unfulfilled material purpose (e.g., discretionary trusts, support trusts, spendthrift trusts, and age-dependent trusts)

3. **Revocation**—must be expressly provided for by will or divorce

4. **Doctrine of equitable deviation**—court may modify terms of a trust without seeking beneficiary consent (i) due to unanticipated circumstances if the changes would further the

purposes of the trust; or (ii) the terms relate to management of trust property and existing terms would be impracticable or wasteful or impair the trust's administration

B. Settlor's intent—the settlor must expressly reserve the right to modify or terminate a trust in order to be granted such powers; otherwise modification or termination can occur only with the consent of all beneficiaries and if the proposed change will not interfere with a primary purpose of the trust

C. Trustee's power to terminate—none, unless the trust contains express termination provisions

VI. Principal and Income Allocations—life beneficiaries entitle to trust income and remaindermen entitled to trust principal

A. Allocating principal/income—allocation must be balanced so as to treat present and future trust beneficiaries fairly unless otherwise authorized

- UPAIA—trustee can re-categorize and reallocate as necessary to fulfill trust purpose

- Stock distribution—treated as the distribution of principal whether classified as a dividend or a split

B. Allocation of receipts—generally amount received in exchange for trust property is allocated to principal; amount received for use of trust property is income

C. Allocation of expenses—one-half of the trustee's compensation and one-half of accounting and other costs is charged to income; the remaining one-half of those expenses is charged to principal

VII. Trust Administration and Trustee's Duties

A. Powers

1. **Rule**—the trustee has the powers necessary to act as a reasonably prudent person in managing the trust (e.g., revoke, withdraw, or modify), including the implied power to contract, sell, lease, or transfer the trust property

2. **Third parties**—must act in good faith and give valuable consideration; they are not liable if they act without actual knowledge that such action constitutes a breach of trust

B. Duty of loyalty and good faith

1. **Rule**—duty to administer the trust in good faith (subjective standard) and to act reasonably (objective standard) when investing property and otherwise managing the trust solely in the best interests of the beneficiaries

2. **Self-dealing**

- **Rule**—when the trustee personally engages in a transaction involving trust property, a conflict of interest arises between the trustee's duties to the beneficiaries and her own personal interest

- **Prohibited transactions**—buying or selling trust assets, selling property between trusts that the trustee manages, borrowing from or making loans to the trust, using trust assets to secure a personal loan, engaging in prohibited transactions with friends or relatives, or otherwise acting for personal gain through the trustee position

- **Irrebuttable presumption**—that the trustee breached the duty of loyalty when self-dealing is an issue; no further inquiry into the trustee's reasonableness or good faith is required because self-dealing is a per se breach

- **Exceptions**—even when self-dealing is authorized (by the settlor, court order, or all beneficiaries), the transaction must still be reasonable and fair to avoid liability for breach

3. **Conflicts of interest**—assessed under the "reasonable and in good faith" standard if an alleged conflict of interest cannot be characterized as self-dealing

C. **Duty of prudence**

1. **Rule**—the trustee may delegate responsibilities if it would be unreasonable for the settlor to require the trustee to perform such tasks; however, a critical function concerning the property is discretionary and not delegable

2. **Duty to oversee decisions**—the trustee can delegate the determination of management and investment strategies but must oversee the decision-making process

3. **Trust investments**

- **Prudent investor rule**—requires the trustee to act as a prudent investor would act when investing his own property (putting less emphasis on risk level); the trustee must exercise reasonable care, caution, and skill when investing and managing trust assets

- Factors considered in determining compliance include:

    o Trust's distribution requirements

    o General economic conditions

    o Investment in relation to the trust's overall investment portfolio

    o Trust's need for liquidity, income regularity, and preservation or appreciation of capital

- **Duty to diversify**—the trustee must adequately diversify the trust investments in order to spread the risk of loss under a total performance portfolio approach, but not if administrative costs would outweigh the benefits

- **Duty to make property productive**—by pursuing all possible claims, deriving the maximum amount of income from investments, selling assets when appropriate, securing insurance, paying expenses, and acting within a reasonable period of time in all matters

- **Duty to be impartial**—the trustee must balance the interests of the present and future beneficiaries by investing property so that it produces a reasonable income while preserving the principal for the remaindermen, and sell trust property within a reasonable time if a failure to diversify would be inconsistent with the total performance portfolio approach

D. **Inform and account**

1. **Duty to disclose**—complete and accurate information about the nature and extent of the trust property, including allowing access to trust records and accounts, if the trustee intends to sell a significant portion of the trust assets

2. **Duty to account**—must periodically account for actions taken on behalf of the trust so that the trustee's performance can be assessed against the terms of the trust

E. **Other duties**—to secure possession of property within a reasonable time; to maintain real property; to segregate personal property from trust assets (the trustee is only liable when a breach of duty to segregate causes damage to trust property)

F. **Powers of appointment**—usually given to the beneficiary; enables the holder to direct a trustee to distribute some or all of the trust property without regard to the provisions of the trust

VIII. Trustee's Liabilities

A. **Beneficiaries' right of enforcement**—lost profits, interests, and other losses resulting from a breach of trust are the trustee's responsibility; beneficiaries may sue the trustee and seek damages or removal of the trustee for breach

B. **Liabilities for others' acts**—co-trustees are jointly liable; the trustee is liable for a predecessor's breach if he failed to address it or was negligent in delivering property; generally, the trustee is liable for an agent's breach if the trustee directs or conceals the agent's act or fails to exercise reasonable supervision over the agent

C. **Third parties**

1. The trustee is personally liable on contracts entered into and for tortious acts committed while acting as trustee; can seek indemnity from the trust if the trustee was acting within the scope of the trustee's duties

2. When property is improperly transferred as a result of a breach of trust to a third party who is not a bona fide purchaser, a beneficiary or successor trustee may have the transaction set aside

IX. Resignation and Removal of Trustee

A. **Resignation**—30 days' notice to qualified beneficiaries, living settlor, and co-trustees, or by court approval

B. **Removal**—by court due to trustee being incapable of performing or materially breaching duty, conflict of interest, conflict between trustee and a beneficiary, poor trust performance

X. Future Interests

A. **General rule**—a grantor retains a reversion, possibility of reverter, or right of entry; the beneficiary is given a remainder or an executory interest

B. **Class gifts**—the share of a deceased class member is paid to that class member's surviving issue; for a gift to surviving children, the general rule is that the surviving issue of a deceased child do not take unless the governing instrument provides otherwise

FINAL REVIEW OUTLINE: WILLS AND DECEDENTS' ESTATES

I. **Intestacy**

  A. **Generally**

    1. **Uniform Probate Code (UPC)**

- Surviving spouse (SS) takes the **entire estate**
  - All of decedent's descendants are also descendants of SS, and SS has no other descendants, or
  - Decedent (D) has SS, but no descendants or parents
- SS takes **$300,000 and 75%** of the remainder of the estate
  - No descendant of D survives D, but D has a surviving parent
- SS takes **$225,000 and 50%** of the remainder of the estate
  - All of D's issue are also issue of SS, and SS has other issue
- SS takes **$150,000 and 50%** of the remainder of the estate
  - D has issue not related to SS

    2. **Community property (CP)**—all property acquired during the marriage is jointly owned by both spouses unless it is gift, inheritance, or devise given to only one spouse

- CP is divided equally—SS owns 50% of CP outright
- If D dies intestate, then D's 50% of CP is given to SS and D's separate property (SP) is then distributed pursuant to the general intestacy scheme

  B. **Surviving spouse**

    1. **Marriage requirement**—SS must have been legally married to D

- **Putative spouses**—qualify if the spouse believes in good faith in the validity of an invalid marriage
- **Separation**—spouses are still married until the issuance of a final dissolution decree

    2. **Survival requirement**—SS (or other heir) must survive D to inherit (or take under a will)

- **Common law**—must have survived D for any length of time
- **Uniform Simultaneous Death Act** (USDA)
  - 120-hour rule—must have survived D by 120 hours
  - Insufficient evidence of order of death—the property of each individual passes as though the other individual predeceased him
- **Determination of death**
  - Common law—irreversible cessation of circulatory and respiratory functions
  - Modern standard—brain death (for which there are no established criteria)
- **Burden of proof**—on the party whose claim depends on survivorship
  - Common law—preponderance of the evidence
  - USDA—clear and convincing evidence

C. **Issue**—all lineal descendants, including children, grandchildren, great-grandchildren, etc.

1. **Parent-child relationship**

- **Married parents**

  o Child of a marriage—presumption: the child is the natural child of the parties to the marriage

  o Posthumously-born children—rebuttable presumption: the child is the child of the deceased husband if the child is born within 280 days of his death

- **Adopted child**

  o Reference in a will to "child" includes an adopted child

  o Treated like a biological child for inheritance purposes

  o No inheritance rights between the genetic parents and the adopted child

  o Stepparent exception—an adoption by a stepparent establishes a parent-child relationship between the stepparent and the child (with full inheritance rights) but does not curtail the parent-child relationship of the genetic parent who is married to the stepparent nor the right of the adoptee (or a descendant of the adoptee) to inherit from or through the other genetic parent

- **Foster parents and stepparents**

  o Generally, no inheritance rights between a child and a foster parent or stepparent

  o Equitable adoption

    ▪ A relationship started during the child's minority and established by clear and convincing evidence that a legal barrier prevented adoption, or

    ▪ A foster parent agreed with the genetic parents to adopt the child and the foster parent treated the child as his own

  o Effects

    ▪ The child can only inherit from (not through) the equitable adoptive parent

    ▪ Equitable parents cannot inherit through or from the child

    ▪ Inheritance rights between the child and the genetic parents is unaffected

- **Half-bloods**—treated the same as whole-bloods

- **Children born out of wedlock**

  o **Modern trend**—cannot inherit from the natural father unless:

    ▪ The father subsequently married the natural mother;

    ▪ The father held the child out as his own and lived with the child or provided support;

    ▪ Paternity is proven by clear and convincing evidence after the father's death; or

    ▪ Paternity is adjudicated during the father's lifetime by a preponderance of the evidence

  o **Uniform Parentage Act (UPA)**—requires proof of paternity for a child to inherit

    ▪ When a father holds a child out as his own—presumption of paternity; the child can bring an action to establish paternity at any time

- Otherwise—no presumption of paternity; the child must bring an action within three years of reaching the age of majority

- **Posthumously-conceived child**—not recognized as a child of the deceased parent

2. **Calculating share**

- **Per capita with representation**

    o Property is divided equally among the first generation with at least one living member

    o The share of a non-living member of that generation passes to the living issue of that member

    o Non-living member with no living issue—no property is allocated to the non-living member

- **Per stirpes**

    o Issue equally share the portion that the deceased ancestor would have taken if living

    o The estate is first divided into the total number of children of the ancestor who survive or leave issue who survive

- **Per capita at each generation**

    o Property is divided into as many equal shares as there are living members of the nearest generation of issue and deceased members of that generation with living issue

- **Negative inheritance**—to disinherit an heir through properly executed will

D. **Ancestors and remote collaterals**—when there is no SS or descendant

1. **Parentelic approach**—follows collateral lines until a live taker is found; D's property is distributed within that taker's parentelic line

2. **Degree-of-relationship approach**—calculated by counting the number of relatives between the living taker and D using the closest common ancestor

3. **Combined approach**—those in a closer collateral line take to the exclusion of those in a more remote collateral line

4. **UPC approach**

- D's parents equally if both survive or all to the surviving parent if only one survives

- Then to descendants of D's parents

- Then to D's living maternal/paternal grandparents

- Then to descendants of D's deceased grandparents

- Then to D's nearest maternal/paternal relative

- Finally D's estate escheats to state

II. **Execution of Wills**

A. **Formalities**

1. **Valid will requirements**

- Writing signed by the testator (T)

- Two or more witnesses
- T has present testamentary intent

2. **Writing signed by T**

- Entire will must be in writing (can be handwritten, if the signature and witness requirements are met)
- Signed by T
  - Location of signature
    - Some states—at end, otherwise the will is invalid
    - Other states (UPC)—anywhere on the will, but the portion of the will after the signature is invalid
  - Form of signature—T's formal name is not required if the name used indicates T's intent
  - Signature on T's behalf—permitted by a person in T's presence and at T's direction
- T's Capacity
  - T must be at least 18 years old and of sound mind
  - T meets mental capacity if she knows (capacity is presumed unless challenged):
    - Nature and extent of her property
    - Persons who are the natural objects of T's bounty
    - Disposition she is trying to make, and
    - Testamentary plan

3. **Witnesses (W)**

- **Number**—at least two; some states require three
- **Signatures**
  - Signed by T (or by a person on T's behalf) in the joint presence of two Ws
    - UPC—T may acknowledge his signature to Ws; Ws need not be present at the same time
  - Signed by two Ws
    - No need for an attestation clause
    - Ws need not sign at the end of the will
    - Ws must sign in the presence of T
    - UPC—W may sign within a reasonable time after witnessing T sign or acknowledge the will
  - Presence
    - Line-of-sight (traditional) test—T and Ws see (or have the opportunity to see) each other sign the will
    - Conscious-presence (modern) test—T and W must be aware through any sense that each is signing the will
- **Knowledge of instrument**
  - Ws must be aware that the instrument is a will, but need not know its contents

- **Age and competency**—W has sufficient mental capacity/maturity to comprehend the value of the act of witnessing; determined at the time of signing

- **Interested W doctrine**—W who receives a gift under will

  - Common law—an interested W is not competent as a W; the will is invalid unless there are at least two disinterested Ws

  - Purge theory—a gift to W is denied to the extent of the amount in excess of W's intestate rights

  - UPC—interested W doctrine is abolished

4. **Testamentary intent**

   - T must execute a will with present testamentary intent, must understand that he is executing a will, and intend that it have testamentary effect

   - T must generally know and approve of the will's contents, but need not understand all provisions

5. **Integration**—a will consists of all pages present at the execution and intended to be a part of the will

6. **Compliance with statutory requirements**

   - **Common law**—strict compliance

   - **UPC**—substantial compliance if there is clear and convincing evidence of T's intent

B. **Holographic wills**—a will in T's handwriting

   1. **Handwritten document**

      - **Some states**—entire will must be in T's handwriting

      - **Other states (UPC)**—only the material provisions must be in T's handwriting (e.g., a filled-in printed form)

   2. **Must be signed by T**—proxy not permitted

   3. **Witnesses**—not required

   4. **Date**—required by some states

   5. **Testamentary intent**

      - **Some states**—established by reference to printed parts of the will or extrinsic evidence

   6. **Handwritten changes after will completed**—effective

C. **"Self-proved" will**—a will acknowledged by T and affirmed by Ws before a court official

   - **Effect**—removes the need for testimony of the attesting Ws at a formal probate proceeding

D. **Nuncupative (oral) wills**

   1. **Most states (UPC)**—not permitted

   2. **Some states**—permitted, but valid for disposition of limited personal property made in contemplation of immediate death

E. **Codicils**—changes or additions to a will

   1. **Execution**—the same formalities as for a will must be observed

2. **Effect**—republishes the will as of the date the codicil was executed

- May validate an invalid will

F. **Will substitutes**—methods for transferring property outside of probate

1. **Revocable trusts**

2. **Pour-over wills**—a devise of T's property to a trust created during T's life

3. **Bank accounts and securities registered in beneficiary form**

4. **Payable-on-death clause in contract**

5. **Life insurance**—policy proceeds are not part of D's estate unless payable to the estate as beneficiary

6. **Deeds**—unconditionally delivered to the grantee during D's lifetime or delivered to an escrow agent during D's lifetime with instructions to turn over to grantee upon D's death

7. **Totten trusts**—a type of revocable trust set up with a bank (similar to a payable-on-death account)

III. **Revocation of Will**

A. **Any time prior to T's death**

1. **Subsequent instrument**—an oral revocation of a will is not valid

- Revocation can be express or implied by the terms of a subsequent instrument

- **Inconsistency**—the later document controls and revokes prior inconsistencies

2. **Destruction with intent to revoke**

- **Destruction**—burning, canceling, tearing, obliterating, or destroying a material portion of the will

  o Most states—requires defacement of some language of the will

  o Some states (UPC)—the destructive act need only affect some part of will

- **Rebuttable presumption of revocation**—when a will once known to exist cannot be found

  o Inapplicable if a duplicate original is found

- **Destruction of executed will**—presumptively revokes all other duplicate originals

- Third party can revoke for T if done at T's direction and in T's conscious presence

3. **Operation of law**

- Divorce

  o Most states (UPC)—revokes will provisions for the former spouse unless contrary to T's intent

  o Some states—revokes will provisions for the former spouse if there is a property settlement agreement

4. **Partial revocation**—permitted, but if a revoked gift falls outside of residuary, revocation is not given effect until re-execution or republication of will

5. **Alteration**—T cannot increase a gift by canceling words in the will, but can decrease a gift as long as the alteration is made to the existing language rather than through the addition of new language to the will

B. **Lost wills**

   1. **Duplicates/copies**—a duplicate original is permitted, but not a photocopy

   2. **Burden on proponent**—proof by clear and convincing evidence

C. **Revocation of codicils**—revives the will (contrast: the revocation of a will revokes all codicils to the will)

D. **Revival**

   1. **Republication**

      • **Implied**

         o **Common law**—automatic revival of the original will upon revocation of a subsequent will; followed in just a few states

         o **UPC**—look for testator's intent, based on (i) whether the second will is revoked by act or by a later will; and (ii) if the second will is revoked by an act, whether the first will was wholly or partially revoked by that second will

            ▪ Second will revoked by **another new will**—the previously revoked will is only revived if the terms of the new will show that T intended the previous will to take effect; no extrinsic evidence

            ▪ Second will revoked by **physical act**—extrinsic evidence permitted

               → Whole revocation—presumption that T did not intend to revive the first will; burden on the proponent of the first will

               → Partial revocation—presumption that T intended to revive the revoked parts of the previous will; burden on the challenger of the first will

      • **Express**—T acknowledges the original will with testamentary formalities

   2. **Dependent Relative Revocation (DRR)**—T's revocation of the will is disregarded if it was based on a mistake of law or fact and would not have been done but for that mistake

IV. **Will Contracts**

A. **Writing requirement**—the will states the contract's material provisions; the terms are contained in a written contract; or the will expressly references a contract and extrinsic evidence proves its terms

B. **Consideration requirement**—e.g., B promises to care for T in exchange for a bequest

C. **Enforceability**—only if signed by the party sought to be charged; no remedy for breach while T is still alive

D. **Reciprocal provisions**

   1. **Joint wills**—a single instrument that serves as the will of more than one person

      • Does not by itself create a presumption of a contract not to revoke

   2. **Reciprocal wills**—identical or reciprocal provisions in separate wills

      • Does not by itself create a presumption of a contract not to revoke

   3. **Contract not to revoke**

      • If evidence establishes (e.g., the wills state that devises were made in consideration of reciprocal devises), the contract becomes irrevocable upon death of first party; a constructive trust is imposed on property transferred by the second party in violation of the contract

V. **Construction of Will**

A. **Classification system of gifts**

1. **Specific**—property distinguished with reasonable accuracy from T's other property

2. **General**—property to be satisfied from general estate assets

3. **Demonstrative**—property to come from a particular source

4. **Residuary**—property remaining after all specific, general, and demonstrative gifts are made

B. **Incorporation by reference**—another writing not executed with testamentary formalities may dictate the distribution of T's property if it:

- Existed at time of execution of the will,

- Is intended to be incorporated, and

- Is described in the will with sufficient certainty to permit identification

C. **Acts of independent significance**—designation of a beneficiary or disposition by reference to some unattested act or event occurring before or after the execution of the will or T's death if the act or event has some significance apart from the will

D. **Lapse**—if the beneficiary dies before T, the gift lapses and passes to the residuary beneficiary, or if none, via intestacy

1. **Anti-lapse statute**—if the beneficiary was T's relative and left issue, then the issue succeeds to the beneficiary's gift

- Applies to class gifts

- **UPC**—also apply to non-probate transfers

2. **Residuary lapse**

- **Common law**—a lapsed residuary interest passes by intestacy ("no residue of a residue")

- **UPC**—a lapsed residuary interests passes to the remaining residuary beneficiaries

3. **Void gifts**—gift to a beneficiary, who unbeknownst to T, is already deceased when the will was executed

- Anti-lapse statute also applies to void gifts

E. **Abatement** (first to last)—reduction/elimination of gifts when assets insufficient

1. **Order**—gifts abate in the following order:

- First, intestate property

- Then, residuary bequests

- Then, general bequests

- Then, specific bequests

- **Note:** a demonstrative gift is treated as a specific bequest; if it cannot, then it is treated as a general bequest

F. Ademption—the denial of a gift to a beneficiary because the property is no longer in T's estate

1. **Ademption by extinction**—applies only to specific bequests
   - **Traditional approach**—"identity theory"
   - **UPC approach**—"intent theory" (mild presumption against ademption)

2. **Exoneration of liens**
   - **Common law**—a beneficiary of encumbered real property can have the lien paid off
   - **Most states (UPC)**—a beneficiary of encumbered real property is not entitled to have the lien paid off

3. **Ademption by satisfaction**—a gift may be satisfied by inter vivos transfer of property after the execution of the will if that is T's intent
   - **UPC**—presumes no ademption by satisfaction absent an express writing

G. Ambiguities and mistakes

1. **Plain meaning rule**—reluctance to disturb the plain meaning of a will regardless of mistake

2. **Ambiguities**—can be resolved by extrinsic evidence

3. **Mistakes**—extrinsic evidence is admissible to show that there was a mistake in the will's execution

4. **Rule of construction**—the will "speaks" at the time of T's death

VI. Power to Transfer

A. Rights of surviving spouse

1. **Elective share or forced share**
   - **Common law state**—SS can elect to take a share of T's augmented estate rather than the gifts left to SS in the will
     - o The right may be waived by a signed writing after fair disclosure before or during the marriage
   - **Community property state**—SS is entitled to one-half of community and quasi-community property (forced share)
     - o SS must elect to take the forced share in lieu of any interest under T's will

2. **Omitted spouse**—a spouse who married T after T's will was executed and who is not a beneficiary in the will
   - Rebuttable presumption that the omission was by mistake; the omitted spouse is entitled to the intestate share
     - o Traditional doctrine—the presumption is rebutted if T's intent to omit the spouse is apparent from the language of the will or if the spouse was provided for outside of the will
     - o UPC—a valid prenuptial agreement also rebuts the presumption

B. **Gifts to children**

1. **Advancements of inheritance** (corresponds to ademption by satisfaction for gift by will)

   - **Common law**—a lifetime gift is presumed to be an advancement of the child's intestate share; the child has the burden to prove otherwise

   - **Modern trend (UPC)**—the gift is an advancement if D declared in a contemporaneous writing that the gift was an advancement, or the heir acknowledges that the gift was an advancement in writing

2. **Controlled transfers to minors**—guardianship, conservatorship, transfer pursuant to the Uniform Transfers to Minors Act, trust

C. **Omitted child**—a child born after T's will is executed

1. **Rebuttable presumption**—that the omission was by mistake

   - The presumption is rebutted by (i) intentional omission; (ii) T had other children when will executed, left estate to other parent of omitted child; (iii) T otherwise provided for the child

2. **Omitted child's share**

   - **T's only child**—intestate share

   - **Other children**—omitted child shares equally in property devised to the other children

D. **Bars to succession**

1. **Homicide**—the killer of D cannot take under D's will or through intestacy

   - Killer is treated as if he predeceased D

2. **Disclaimer**—permitted but must be affirmatively done because acceptance of the gift is presumed

   - The disclaiming party is treated as if she predeceased D

VII. **Will Contests**

A. **Standing to contest**—only directly interested parties who stand to benefit financially may contest a will; not T's general creditors nor the spouse or prospective heir of a beneficiary under a prior will

B. **Lack of testamentary capacity**—T lacks capacity if, at the time of the will's execution, T did not have the ability to know the nature of act, the nature and character of his property, the natural objects of his bounty, and the attempted disposition plan

C. **Insane delusion**—a belief for which there is no factual or reasonable basis, but to which T adheres despite all reason and evidence to the contrary

1. **Rational person test**—a rational person in T's situation could not have reached the same belief

2. **"But for" causation**—the delusion was the sole cause of the testamentary disposition

D. **Undue influence**—mental or physical coercion exerted by a third party on T with the intent to influence T such that he loses control of his own judgment and executes an unnatural will

1. **Confidential relationship**—T, as a result of his weakened or dependent state, confided, trusted, or relied upon the other party

   - No confidential relationship between husband and wife

- Burden of proof is on the beneficiary to show by a preponderance of the evidence that there was no undue influence
- The beneficiary is treated as though he predeceased T to the extent the gift exceeds the beneficiary's intestate share

E. **Fraud**—a misrepresentation made by the beneficiary when the will was executed with the intent to deceive T and with the purpose of influencing the disposition, resulting in a will that would not have been executed but for the fraud

F. **Forfeiture clause**—designed to deter a beneficiary from suing over his share by causing him to lose his share entirely if he does so

   1. **Most states (UPC)**—a forfeiture clause is unenforceable against a beneficiary who has probable cause to contest

VIII. Probate and Administration—probate property is property that passes under T's will or by intestacy

A. **Procedure**

   1. **Jurisdiction**—the place where D is domiciled at the time of death has jurisdiction over D's personal property and any real property located there

   2. **Notice**—given to interested parties

   3. **Timing**

      - **Common law**—a will could be probated at any time
      - **UPC**—probate proceedings must be brought within three years of death

B. **Creditor's claims**

   1. **Period of limitations**—a claim must be made within a specified period after probate is opened

   2. **Notice**—the personal representative must provide notice to creditors

   3. **Priority of claims**—administrative expenses, last medical expenses and funeral expenses, family allowance, tax claims, secured claims, judgments against D, all other claims

C. **Personal representative**—executor (named in will), administrator (appointed by court)

   1. **Priority for appointment**—the person named in the will; the surviving spouse who is a devisee; other devisees; the surviving spouse; other heirs; any creditor (45 days after death)

   2. **Principal duties:**

      - Provide notice to legatees, heirs, and claimants
      - Inventory, collect, and manage D's assets
      - Receive and pay claims of creditors and tax collectors
      - Distribute remaining assets

   3. **Fiduciary duty**—owes the highest duty of loyalty and care to those represented

      - **Common law**—can be personally liable for the actions of the estate
      - **UPC**—can only be sued in a representative capacity for breach of fiduciary duty

IX. **Powers of Appointment** (the power to decide to whom property is given)

A. **Types**

1. **General power of appointment**—no restrictions or conditions on the exercise of the power

2. **Special power of appointment**—places limitations on the holder's exercise of the power

B. **Scope of authority**

1. **Exercising power**

- Any instrument, unless the donor directs otherwise, may be used to exercise the power

- Testamentary power of appoint can only be exercised via will

    o Mere residuary clause in a will is not sufficient to exercise a power, but use of the phrase "including any power of appointment I may possess" is generally effective

2. **Contracting the power**—the holder can do so if presently exercisable power

X. **Powers of Attorney**

A. **Types**

1. **General**—the agent can handle all affairs when the principal is unable to do so

2. **Special**—the agent's powers are limited to a specific function and/or duration

B. **Scope of authority**

1. **Durable power of attorney**—agency continues until the death of principal, even if the principal becomes incapacitated

2. **Fiduciary duties**

3. **Liability**—the agent is only responsible for intentional misconduct

4. **Revocation**—the powers can be revoked by the principal at any time